Brief Contents

D0080271

i

Stepping Stones

A Guided Approach to Writing Sentences and Paragraphs

Stepping Stones

SECOND EDITION

A Guided Approach to Writing Sentences and Paragraphs

Chris Juzwiak

Glendale Community College

Bedford/St. Martin's

Boston ◆ New York

For Bedford/St. Martin's

Executive Editor for Developmental Studies: Alexis Walker
Senior Developmental Editor: Joelle Hann
Senior Production Editor: Ryan Sullivan
Senior Production Supervisor: Nancy Myers
Senior Marketing Manager: Christina Shea
Editorial Assistant: Emily Wunderlich
Copy Editor: Steven Patterson
Indexer: Melanie Belkin
Photo Researcher: Connie Gardner
Permissions Manager: Kalina K. Ingham
Art Director: Lucy Krikorian
Text Design: Claire Seng-Niemoeller
Cover Design: Marine Bouvier Miller
Cover Art: Sara Hillman
Composition: Cenveo Publisher Services
Printing and Binding: RR Donnelley and Sons

President: Joan E. Feinberg
Editorial Director: Denise B. Wydra
Editor in Chief: Karen S. Henry
Director of Development: Erica T. Appel
Director of Marketing: Karen R. Soeltz
Director of Production: Susan W. Brown
Associate Director, Editorial Production: Elise S. Kaiser
Managing Editor: Shuli Traub

Library of Congress Control Number: 2011943130

Manufactured in the United States of America.

6   5   4   3   2   1

f   e   d   c   b   a

For information, write: Bedford/St. Martin's, 75 Arlington Street, Boston, MA 02116
(617-399-4000)

ISBN: 978-0-312-67599-8 (Student edition)
ISBN: 978-0-312-57652-3 (Instructor's annotated edition)

Acknowledgments

Preface for Instructors

If your teaching experiences are like mine, many of the students entering your classroom have encountered repeated difficulty in the past. As children or young adults, they may have had negative experiences learning writing and grammar, considering these pursuits boring or confusing. They may even enter your course expecting to fail. Their prospects for success are not improved by textbooks that assume that students can make great strides in their writing skills based on minimal examples and activities. For example, how many students can truly learn to generate good ideas based on a few examples of clustering, listing, and freewriting and a few activities? And will they really be able to organize their ideas effectively based on only one or two examples of outlining? Often, when students are asked to make big leaps from their current skill levels to the skill levels required for college success, they become frustrated—and many of them give up.

Stepping Stones addresses these challenges head-on. The book is based on the premise that if students are taken through a thorough and seamless sequence of engaging instruction and activities, they will master writing and grammar skills with enthusiasm. More advanced students will proceed quickly through the activities, gaining confidence, while less skilled students will get all the "stepping stones" they need to reach mastery. All along, students learn by doing practices that grow incrementally more challenging as they move through each chapter. Building skills and confidence gradually means that no student gets left behind.

ON THE FIRST EDITION

Over my years of teaching, I became dissatisfied with the available textbooks, finding that they either presented material in a manner that did not interest students or oversimplified instruction, making it difficult for students to truly learn writing and grammar concepts and transfer them to their own writing. Therefore, I spent nights and weekends writing my own writing and grammar materials, developing carefully sequenced instruction and exercises. The response from my students was immediate and enthusiastic. When I sought to avoid boredom and confusion with clear, inventive, and fun materials, I saw a transformation in students' attitude and behavior: They became readily self-motivated, demanding more high-quality, high-interest learning activities and tools.

Starting in 2004, I directed a three-year Carnegie Foundation SPECC grant (Strengthening Pre-Collegiate Education in Community Colleges) in which my colleagues and I were able to test more thoroughly the materials that I developed and to study students' writing and learning processes. We spent hundreds of hours observing students as they wrote and completed exercises, and even more time watching videotape of students working at computers, noting how they started and stopped compositions; cut, added, and moved text; and generally worked through their individual composing processes. We also interviewed students about their writing processes and responses to various learning materials. The students in the study responded enthusiastically, and their skills improved markedly. Through this research, my colleagues and I became convinced that developmental learners flourish when their critical thinking and imagination are challenged with fresh, precisely honed sequences of instruction and activities. The positive responses to the materials that I developed prompted me to write the first edition of *Stepping Stones*.

ON THE SECOND EDITION

The second edition of *Stepping Stones* has also benefited enormously from my ongoing pedagogical research, conversations with colleagues from across the nation, and—most important—from three years of using the first edition in my classroom. I used the text in several classes each semester with a vigilant eye to refining the content, looking for cues from my students on how well the instructional sequences in the book were working. The pedagogical premise and promise of *Stepping Stones*—that students won't have to make unreasonable "cognitive leaps" within the instructional sequences—guided my revision. I am confident that both you and your students will benefit from the more finely honed content of this new edition.

Beyond the classroom, my revision strategies were informed by new pedagogical research, funded by grants from the California Basic Skills Initiative (CBSI) and the Hewlett Foundation. At my campus, twelve developmental composition instructors and a host of student co-inquirers participated in IMPACT (Incremental, Motivational Pedagogy & Assessment Cycles Training), a program developed with funds from CBSI. We confirmed that developmental students thrive on clear, carefully structured *learning sequences* that move smoothly from basic to advanced levels, providing ample activities. (We like to call it "drill and *thrill*" to correct the misconception that sustained practice must be boring.) Our instructional innovations have realized a solid 15 percent increase in student success in our college's basic writing program. The second edition of *Stepping Stones* incorporates many of the best features of this progressive pedagogy, such as training in "organizational cognition" (critical thinking about outlines) and a "build it / fix it" approach to sentence construction and grammaticality.

Finally, during a year's sabbatical, I was able to attend conferences and visit campuses in seven states, discussing basic skills pedagogy with scores of talented, dedicated faculty, some of whom had worked with *Stepping Stones* and others of whom were simply eager to hear about new instructional approaches. Countless refinements in the book resulted from these dialogues. In fact, of all the influences that shaped my revision of *Stepping Stones*, the contributions of fellow faculty were the richest and most crucial.

FEATURES

Writing Coverage Helps Students Generate and Organize Ideas with Confidence

Recognizing that two of the most serious challenges that developmental writers face are, first, coming up with solid ideas and, second, organizing those ideas, I wanted *Stepping Stones* to give more help with these tasks than any other text of its kind.

Students first learn how to evaluate topics for personal relevance and then learn *the inner dynamics* of clustering, listing, questioning, and freewriting. Through a sequential, color-coded demonstration of the "layering" process that occurs during brainstorming, students become more invested in these **idea-generating techniques**.

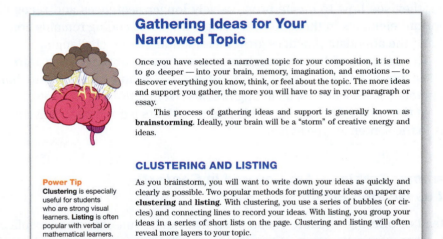

Gathering Ideas for Your Narrowed Topic

Once you have selected a narrowed topic for your composition, it is time to go deeper — into your brain, memory, imagination, and emotions — to discover everything you know, think, or feel about the topic. The more ideas and support you gather, the more you will have to say in your paragraph or essay.

This process of gathering ideas and support is generally known as **brainstorming**. Ideally, your brain will be a "storm" of creative energy and ideas.

CLUSTERING AND LISTING

Power Tip
Clustering is especially useful for students who are strong visual learners. **Listing** is often popular with verbal or mathematical learners.

As you brainstorm, you will want to write down your ideas as quickly and clearly as possible. Two popular methods for putting your ideas on paper are **clustering** and **listing**. With clustering, you use a series of bubbles (or circles) and connecting lines to record your ideas. With listing, you group your ideas in a series of short lists on the page. Clustering and listing will often reveal more layers to your topic.

Next, two dedicated chapters give students **unusually thorough guidance in organizing and outlining their ideas**. For example, in preparation for in-depth instruction in outlining, students first practice ordering single-word items, then phrases, and then sentences.

A separate chapter provides fun and innovative activities to help students develop **vivid details** to bring their ideas to life. The chapter focuses on generating concrete details, action details, quoted details, sensory details, emotive details, comparative details, and more.

By connecting writing concepts from chapter to chapter, the book makes sure that there are no gaps in instruction that will confuse students or slow them down.

An Innovative Color-Coding System Guides Students to Master Sentence Patterns

This system combines visual explanations, consistent labels, extensive and carefully sequenced practices, and inventive activities. In the first grammar chapter, students learn about the **building blocks of sentences** and their

KEY TO BUILDING BLOCKS

FOUNDATION WORDS

NOUNS

VERBS

DESCRIPTIVE WORDS

ADJECTIVES

ADVERBS

CONNECTING WORDS

PREPOSITIONS

CONJUNCTIONS

functions. These building blocks are color-coded within examples throughout the grammar chapters, showing how these words work together and imprinting the patterns of effective sentences (noun + verb; noun + verb + comma + conjunction + noun + verb; etc.).

With each successive chapter, students see how to use these building blocks to construct progressively longer and more complicated sentences.

For example, in Chapter 10, "The Simple Sentence," students first get a visual overview of the sentence patterns they will be asked to create.

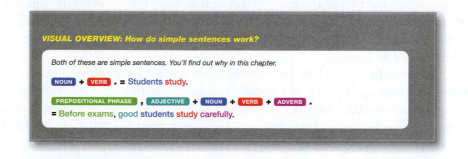

Then, they see how to create progressively longer sentences and recognize important elements in them. At every stage, the color coding remains consistent and the abundant practices grow incrementally more challenging.

The process of building each sentence type is broken down into the smallest possible steps—with plenty of examples and practice—to build competency in all learners, including ESL and Generation 1.5 students.

At the end of most grammar chapters, students learn how to solve problems in the sentence type at hand.

Grammar Problems Are Covered in Context— Not as Isolated Errors

Instead of offering separate chapters on fragments, run-ons, comma splices, and other common errors, *Stepping Stones* addresses these problems in the context of the sentence patterns in which they are most common. This approach focuses students on their abilities as problem-solvers rather than on their identities as writers with problems. It also builds students' awareness of situations in which errors are most likely to occur, making them better editors of their own writing. When students connect their grammar skills and their writing skills, they then move from understanding the basics to writing effectively at the college level.

A Precise and Colorful Design Appeals to Visual Learners

Stepping Stones uses color and visuals to make information clearer and more appealing to visual learners and to students who in the past may have been discouraged in reading and writing (see example at the top of the next page). Aside from color-coding the building blocks of sentences, *Stepping Stones* uses color to identify main ideas, support, and other key writing concepts to underscore the structure of effective writing.

Additionally, color photographs and illustrations engage students and clarify important concepts.

Moving from Outline to Paragraph: An Opening Example

Take a look at how one student went from an outline to a successful paragraph:

Mrs. Nevis, my eleventh-grade geography teacher, was the worst teacher I've ever had. To begin with, she always picked on students and seemed to enjoy it. For example, my friend Jerry had a hard time memorizing the names of countries, so she called him a "brainless wonder." Also, she laughed at students when they made a mistake or answered incorrectly. I could never pronounce the word "Antarctic," so she always made me say it just so she could laugh at me. Her favorite way to pick on students, however, was to make us stay after school for no reason at all. Once, when I sneezed three times in a row, she assigned me one hour of detention. Next, she had very poor teaching skills. For instance, she could never explain a problem or an idea clearly. One time, when we asked her the difference between a glacier and an ice floe, she got so confused that she told us to look it up on the Internet. When she graded our essays, she never gave us useful comments. She once gave me a grade of "C" on a paper, and her only comment was "Try harder." Finally, she had distracting personal habits. She actually liked to eat food during class and even talked with her mouth full! Also, her clothes looked like she had slept in them or cleaned out her garage in them. If there were an award for worst teacher in history, Mrs. Nevis would get my vote.

MAIN IDEA
Mrs. Nevis was my worst teacher.

TRANSITIONAL EXPRESSION
To begin with,

SUPPORT POINT 1
she picked on students.
– used rude nicknames
– laughed at us
– made us stay after school

TRANSITIONAL EXPRESSION
Next,

SUPPORT POINT 2
she had poor teaching skills.
– did not explain ideas clearly
– put no comments on essays

TRANSITIONAL EXPRESSION
Finally,

SUPPORT POINT 3
she had distracting personal habits.
– ate food while teaching
– wore dirty, wrinkled clothes

NEW TO THIS EDITION

The second edition of *Stepping Stones* has been streamlined to keep students focused on what's most important. Chapters that guide students through every step of building sentences, recognizing common writing problems, and developing paragraphs have been concentrated to provide exactly the information that basic writers need and no more.

More opportunities for self-assessment and review help students at all levels. New pre-tests—called "What Do You Know?"—in every chapter allow students to identify areas that need work, while newly interactive reviews at the end ("Bringing It All Together") help them review their learning and retention.

A new reference section offers additional at-a-glance help. Located at the back of the book, this material includes **Quick Guides** that allow students to quickly review fundamental concepts such as fragments and run-ons. Also included is an index of helpful lists, charts, and visuals; a list of correction symbols; and a color-coded list of sentence parts and patterns.

QUICK GUIDE TO Run-Ons and Comma Splices

Four Groups of Words Cause Run-Ons (RO) and Comma Splices (CS):

I, you, she/he, it, they, we (page 286)
Class was cancelled we left. (RO)
Class was cancelled, we left. (CS)

this, that, these, those (page 288)
My friend lied that upset me. (RO)
My friend lied, that upset me. (CS)

then, next, also, plus, for example, for instance (page 290)
We ordered then we ate. (RO)
We ordered, then we ate. (CS)

therefore, as a result, consequently, however, furthermore, in addition, instead, nevertheless (page 292)
Jim studied therefore, he passed. (RO)
Jim studied, therefore, he passed. (CS)

Fix It!
Add a period OR a semicolon OR a comma with a joining word (and, or, but, so, nor, for, yet).

Run-On or Comma Splice → Fix It
Class was cancelled we left.   Class was cancelled. We left.
Class was cancelled, we left.   Class was cancelled; we left.
                                  Class was cancelled, so we left.

For more on run-ons and comma splices, see Chapter 11, pages 283–300.

R-4

Hundreds of new exercises in the book—and online—provide abundant options for skill practice. Students can chart their progress using the new **"Challenge Meter"** that shows the difficulty level of each exercise, from "warmup" at the beginning of the chapter to "mastery" at the end. More quizzes on the companion Web site provide additional practice with a gradebook that lets instructors track student progress.

KEY TO CHALLENGE METER

| WARMUP |
| EASY |
| MODERATE |
| ADVANCED |
| MASTERY |

Identify the difficulty level of each activity using the key above.

WARMUP

ACTIVITY 1

Create ten simple sentences, matching subjects and verbs from the columns below. Begin by creating five sentences from the two columns on the left. Then, create five more sentences from the two columns on the right. Remember to start each sentence with a capital letter and end it with a period. The first sentence has been written for you.

Subject	Verb	Subject	Verb
cells	heals	smoke	procrastinate
we	sings	Elvis	hurts
Beyoncé	infect	reading	rises
love	divide	jealousy	lives
viruses	collaborate	I	enlightens

Cells divide.

Grammar instruction follows a "Build It / Fix It" model. So that students can first easily understand sentence patterns, and then work through common errors in those patterns, grammar chapters have been separated into "building" sections that cover the essentials of the given skill, and "fixing" sections that explain what mistakes to watch for in the sentence pattern. These are highlighted in the text as "Build It" and "Fix It."

A new section called "Expanding Your Writing" encapsulates more advanced writing skills. Chapters on developing details, using patterns of development, and moving from paragraphs to essays are now included in a discrete section so that instructors can choose material that is appropriate for all of their students, including those working at a faster pace.

A thematic reader offers engaging new readings and apparatus selected to appeal to basic writers. Almost all readings—and several themes—in the mini-reader are new, drawn from contemporary authors such as Yiyun Li, Gary Soto, and Amy Tan. Inspiring topics that students will want to respond to include Work and Career, Prejudice and Forgiveness, and Addiction and Risks. The apparatus offers prompts for peer discussion, paragraph writing, and discussion of the rhetorical modes, and it has been streamlined for clarity and interest.

More support for instructors. New "Time-to-Teach" advice, available in the complimentary Instructor's Annotated Edition, offers a built-in lesson plan at the beginning of each chapter. New author videos on the companion Web site offer ideas for teaching in the developmental classroom, including how to access students' "intellectual humanity" and successfully sequence exercises for maximum skill retention.

Time-to-Teach
Suggested lesson plan. To shorten, skip lesson 2.

1. **Assign:** Complex Sentences, 303–8. Activities 1–4.
   Teach: Review. Conditions and Outcomes, 310–311. Activities 5–7.

2. **Assign:** Correct Punctuation, 313. Activities 8, 9.
   Teach: Sentence Variety, 315–17. Activities 10, 11.

3. **Assign:** Activity 12.
   Teach: Review. Fix It: Problems in Complex Sentences, 320–24. Activities 13–15.

4. **Assign:** Activity 16.
   Teach: Review.

Note: In response to instructors' requests, *answers to odd-numbered exercises* have been removed from the back of the print editions of *Stepping Stones*. Instead, we have made answers to all exercises available to instructors on the free companion Web site (as well as an odd-numbered set), in formats that allow for easy printing or posting for students' use, as instructors see fit.

YOU GET MORE CHOICES WITH *STEPPING STONES*, SECOND EDITION

Stepping Stones doesn't stop with a book. Online and in print, you'll find free and affordable premium resources to help students get even more out of the book and your course. You'll also find convenient instructor resources, such as a downloadable instructor's manual, additional exercises, and PowerPoint slides. For information on ordering and to get ISBNs for packaging these resources with your students' books, see page xv. You can also contact your Bedford/St. Martin's sales representative, e-mail sales support (**sales_support@bfwpub .com**), or visit **bedfordstmartins.com/steppingstones/catalog**.

The free site for *Stepping Stones* at bedfordstmartins.com/stepping stones offers an abundance of resources for instructors and students, including downloadable diagnostic and mastery tests, access to hundreds of book-specific exercises on *Exercise Central*, PowerPoint slides for in-class review, and access to useful forms for brainstorming, outlining, and peer review. Also available are more models of student writing, tutorials on avoiding plagiarism and doing research, and more.

Exercise Central 3.0 **at bedfordstmartins.com/exercisecentral** is the largest database of editing exercises on the Internet—and it's completely **free**. This comprehensive resource contains more than 9,000 exercises that offer immediate feedback; the program also recommends personalized study plans and provides tutorials for common problems. Best of all, students' work reports to a gradebook, allowing instructors to track students' progress quickly and easily.

Get More Resources with an Access Package

WritingClass, Bedford/St. Martin's customizable course space, offers exercises, diagnostics, writing and commenting tools, step-by-step multimedia lessons, and LearningCurve, an interactive learning tool that adapts to students' skill levels and helps them build proficiency in grammar. Take a tour at **yourwritingclass .com**. For information on how to package *WritingClass* with your book, see page xv. ISBN: 978-0-312-57385-0

Re:Writing Plus, **now with *VideoCentral*,** gathers all of our premium digital content for the writing class into one online collection. This impressive resource includes innovative and interactive help with writing a paragraph; tutorials and practices that show how writing works in students' real-world experience; *VideoCentral: English*, with more than 140 brief videos for the writing classroom; the first-ever peer review game, *Peer Factor*; *i-cite: visualizing sources*; plus hundreds of models of writing and hundreds of readings. *Re:Writing Plus* can be purchased separately or packaged with *Stepping Stones* at a significant discount. ISBN: 978-0-312-48849-9

Exercise Central to Go: Writing and Grammar Practices for Basic Writers **CD-ROM** provides hundreds of practice items to help students build their writing and editing skills. No Internet connection is necessary. **Free** when packaged with the print text. ISBN: 978-0-312-44652-9

The Bedford/St. Martin's ESL Workbook, **Second Edition,** includes a broad range of exercises covering grammatical issues for multilingual students of varying language skills and backgrounds. Answers are at the back. **Free** when packaged with the print text. ISBN: 978-0-312-54034-0

The *Make-a-Paragraph Kit* is a fun, interactive CD-ROM that teaches students about paragraph development. It also contains exercises to help students build their own paragraphs, audiovisual tutorials on four of the most common errors for basic writers, and the content from *Exercise Central to Go: Writing and Grammar Practices for Basic Writers.* **Free** when packaged with the print text. ISBN: 978-0-312-45332-9

The Bedford/St. Martin's Planner includes everything that students need to plan and use their time effectively, with advice on preparing schedules and to-do lists plus blank schedules and calendars (monthly and weekly). The planner fits easily into a backpack or purse, so students can take it anywhere. **Free** when packaged with the print text. ISBN: 978-0-312-57447-5

E-book Options

Bedford/St. Martin's e-books let students do more and pay less. For about half the price of a print book, the e-book for *Stepping Stones* offers the complete text of the print book combined with convenient digital tools such as highlighting, note-taking, and research. Both online and downloadable options are available in popular e-book formats for computers, tablets, and e-readers. For details, visit **bedfordstmartins.com/ebooks**.

Instructor Resources

You have a lot to do in your course. Bedford/St. Martin's wants to make it easy for you to find the support you need.

The Instructor's Annotated Edition of *Stepping Stones* contains answers to all practice exercises, in addition to numerous teaching ideas, reminders, and cross-references useful to teachers at all levels of experience. ISBN: 978-0-312-57652-3

Bedford Coursepacks allow you to plug *Stepping Stones* content into your own course management system. For details, visit **bedfordstmartins.com/coursepacks**.

Resources for Teaching Stepping Stones, **Second Edition,** offers advice for teaching developmental writing from five expert instructors, including lead author Chris Juzwiak. Contributors cover such practical topics as different teaching approaches, working with ESL and Generation 1.5 students, and supporting students with disabilities. Available as a print booklet or as a downloadable PDF from the book's companion Web site. ISBN: 978-0-312-57676-9

Diagnostic Tests and Exercises for Stepping Stones, **Second Edition,** provides diagnostic pre- and post-tests and additional exercises to build students' writing and grammar skills. Answers are provided at the back. Available as a print booklet or as a downloadable PDF from the book's companion Web site. ISBN: 978-0-312-57650-9

Presentation Slides (in PowerPoint) for *Stepping Stones* cover 16 major topic areas—such as commonly confused words and dangling modifiers—and are designed to help spark class discussion. Formatted as multiple-choice questions, followed by answers, this resource is available for free on the instructor's side of the companion Web site at **bedfordstmartins .com/steppingstones**.

Testing Tool Kit: Writing and Grammar Test Bank **CD-ROM** allows instructors to create secure, customized tests and quizzes from a pool of nearly 2,000 questions covering 47 topics. It also includes 10 prebuilt diagnostic tests. ISBN: 978-0-312-43032-0

Teaching Developmental Writing: Background Readings, **Third Edition,** edited by Susan Naomi Bernstein, former cochair of the Conference on Basic Writing, offers essays on topics of interest to basic writing instructors, along with editorial apparatus pointing out practical applications for the classroom. ISBN: 978-0-312-43283-6

ORDERING INFORMATION

Use these ISBNs when ordering the following supplements packaged with your students' copy of *Stepping Stones,* Second Edition:

WritingClass:
ISBN: 978-1-4576-1423-1

Re:Writing Plus:
ISBN: 978-1-4576-1422-4

The Bedford/St. Martin's ESL Workbook, **Second Edition**:
ISBN: 978-1-4576-1417-0

Exercise Central to Go **CD-ROM**:
ISBN: 978-1-4576-1418-7

Make-a-Paragraph Kit **CD-ROM**:
ISBN: 978-1-4576-1421-7

The Bedford/St. Martin's Planner:
ISBN: 978-1-4576-1416-3

ACKNOWLEDGMENTS

Stepping Stones would not have been possible without the diligence, insights, and plain hard work of a large number of instructors, students, and other contributors.

Reviewers

Throughout the development of the first edition, a dedicated group of instructors reviewed every page of the manuscript, offering helpful comments and fresh ideas to make the book more useful to students and other teachers. A few of these instructors are expert in teaching ESL and Generation 1.5 students, and their comments helped us address the needs of those students throughout the text. I am indebted to the following insightful instructors: Barbara Craig, Del Mar College; Kristen di Gennaro, Pace University; Matthew Fox, Monroe Community College; Sally Gearhart, Santa Rosa Junior College; Susan Brown Rodriguez, Hillsborough Community College; and Valerie Russell, Valencia Community College. Many other instructors reviewed the first edition at different points or offered comments through focus groups or workshops, and I'd like to extend a warm thank you to them as well: Shannon Bailey, Austin Community College; Kay Blue, Owens Community College; Rhonda Carroll, Pulaski Technical College; Frank Cronin, Austin Community College; Gigi Derballa, Asheville-Buncombe Technical Community College; Connie Gulick, Central New Mexico University; Lisa Hatfield, Portland State University; Paula Ingram, Pensacola Junior College; Karen Lemke, Adams State College; Lourdes Lopez-Merino, Palm Beach Community College; Craig Machado, Norwalk Community College; Patricia McGraw, Cape Cod Community College; Caryn Newburger, Austin Community College; Viethang Pham, Cerritos College; Francie Quaas-Berryman, Cerritos College; Karen Roth, University of Texas, San Antonio; Jennifer Rusnak, Florida Community College at Jacksonville; Kimberly Samaniego, California State Long Beach; Jack Swanson, Cerritos College; Melissa Thomas, University of Texas, San Antonio; Monette Tiernan, Glendale Community College; Julie Tilton, San Bernardino Valley College; Christine Tutlewski, University of Wisconsin–Parkside; Rhonda Wallace, Cuyahoga Community College; Shelley Walters, Temple College; Ronald Weisberger, Bristol Community College; Elizabeth Whitehead, Bristol Community College; Julie Yankanich, Camden County College; and Betsy Zuegg, Quinsigamond Community College.

For the second edition, I am indebted to those reviewers who gave us feedback on how they used—or would use—the book, as well as to another extremely helpful editorial board who helped shape this revision. Members of the editorial board for the second edition, comprising instructors across the country, included Stephanie Brown, Los Angeles Harbor College; Francine Jamin, Montgomery College–Takoma Park/Silver Spring Campus; Irma Luna, San Antonio College; Marie McGrath, Golden West College; Maria Nissi, Flathead Valley Community College; Francie Quaas-Berryman, Cerritos College; Greg Rathert, Anoka-Ramsey Community College; and Gordon Richiusa, Saddleback College. I'd like to extend a big thank you to everyone.

I am also grateful to the following reviewers: Tamara Danley, Northeastern State University; Kristen di Gennaro, Pace University; Cheryl J. Fish, Borough of Manhattan Community College; Nancy Forrest, Alamance Community College; Sally Gearhart, Santa Rosa Junior College; Kendra Haggard, Northeastern State University; Mary Anne Keefer, Lord Fairfax Community College; Julie M. Kissel, Washtenaw Community College; Jennifer McCann, Bay de Noc Community College; Anna Lee McKennon, Mt. San Antonio College; Virginia Nugent, Miami Dade College; Jessica Rabin, Anne Arundel Community College; Marie Reeves, Cincinnati Christian University; Kathy Roark-Diehl, NMSU–Alamogordo; Nancy

Spradlin, Cerritos College; Patsy Sutton, University of Central Missouri; Karen Taylor, Belmont Technical College; Dorothy T. Terry, Tougaloo College; and Melissa Vargas, Treasure Valley Community College.

Students

Several student writers contributed paragraphs and essays to this book and its supplements. I am grateful for their dedication and for their willingness to share their work. These students include Angela Adkins, Jennifer Baffa, Samantha Castaneda, Francisco Fragoso, Arlene Galvez, Leanna R. Gonzales, May Hampton, Susan Janoubi, Sarah Littmann, Cleva Nelson, Anallely Orozco, Adam F. Perez, Brian Rickenbrode, Maurice Rivera, Ekaterina Savchenkova, and Angela Vargas.

Other Contributors

I am also grateful to a number of other people whose hard work made this book possible. Julie Nichols of Northwest Florida State College carefully and energetically crafted exercises for both the book and its supplements, while Denise Ezell, assistant professor at Glendale Community College, crafted hundreds of invaluable new exercises for the book's companion Web site. Connie Gardner researched images and also cleared art permissions, while Eve Lehmann cleared text permissions under the guidance of Linda Winters. Brian DeTagyos created colorful illustrations to aid students' understanding of writing and grammar points.

For their insightful contributions to *Resources for Teaching Stepping Stones*, I would like to thank Matthew Fox of Monroe Community College, Sally Gearhart of Santa Rosa Junior College, Erin M. O'Brien of University of Massachusetts Boston, and Susan Brown Rodriguez of Hillsborough Community College.

At Glendale Community College, several colleagues inspired me to think outside the pedagogical box. For their guidance, I am grateful to Hasmik Barsamian, Denise Ezell, Linda Griffith, Elena Grigori, Lara Kartalian, Darren Leaver, Mark Maier, Sarah McLemore, Alice Mecom, Brett Miketta, Nancy Nevins, Ellen Oppenberg, Chris Pasles, Hollie Stewart, and Monette Teirnan.

Bedford/St. Martin's and Beyond

At Bedford/St. Martin's, a large number of people were part of bringing *Stepping Stones* into being. Early on, Stacy Luce, my Bedford/St. Martin's sales representative, and Rachel Falk, former marketing manager for developmental English, helped to connect me and Bedford/St. Martin's. As the book headed toward signing, David Mogolov, now Market Development Manager for New Media, helped me to shape my ideas and offered many valuable suggestions based on his own market experience and extensive reviews. Executive Editor Alexis Walker and former Executive Editor Carrie Brandon continued to share market knowledge and other insights, and have helped to shape a strong message for the book.

Throughout the book's development, President Joan E. Feinberg, Editorial Director Denise B. Wydra, and Editor in Chief Karen S. Henry have generously contributed many wise ideas and thoughtful suggestions for *Stepping Stones* based on years of experience listening to, and responding to the needs of, writing instructors. Throughout the development process, editorial assistants Andrew Flynn and Emily Wunderlich assisted with countless tasks large and small, from helping to find engaging readings to running numerous review programs and managing a multitude of administrative details. Later in the process, Alicia Young stepped in to help with the ancillaries. Director of Development Erica T. Appel oversaw the book's entire development, offering invaluable guidance on the daily tasks involved in getting a big job done.

Making *Stepping Stones* colorful and engaging while ensuring its ease of use was a design challenge ably met by Art Director Anna Palchik and designer Claire Seng-Niemoeller. Their creativity, energy, and problem-solving skills resulted in a design as attractive as it is practical. Additionally, Elise Kaiser and Shuli Traub oversaw many details regarding the production of the book. Senior Production Editor Ryan Sullivan skillfully guided the book through the production process, offering many practical suggestions and helping to solve a range of problems with patience, intelligence, and good humor. Ryan brought on Steven M. Patterson as the copyeditor and Jennifer Greenstein, Diana George, Lori Lewis, and Dorothy Hoffman as proofreaders, all of whom deserve praise for their thoroughness and careful eye for details.

Also contributing to the look of the book was Marine Bouvier Miller, who designed the appealing cover for this edition. Several talented people helped to shape and produce the Web site and electronic ancillaries for *Stepping Stones*, namely, Marissa Zanetti, Rebecca Merrill, and Lindsey Jones, guided by the expertise of Harriet Wald, and the entire New Media team.

In marketing, sincere thanks go to Karen R. Soeltz, Jane Helms, and Senior Marketing Manager Christina Shea for their creative ideas in getting out the word on *Stepping Stones* and coordinating a number of sales efforts to help the book reach its audience.

My enduring gratitude goes to Beth Castrodale, the first editor of this book, who, with her insightful criticism, intellectual rigor, and collaborative generosity, helped bring my ideas and experience into book form. Senior Editor Joelle Hann brought formidable rigor and vision to the book's second edition. I learned so much from her example of uncompromising excellence, equanimity, and intellectual stamina.

I also want to thank my family members and friends, whose unflagging enthusiasm and patience were as crucial to this work as any other component: Doug Mann, Lael Mann, Estella Martinez, Ruth Owens, Sandra and Ernie Gomez, Catherine Leh, James Geyer, Shelley Aronoff, Michael Ritterbrown, Christine Menardus, George Gharibian, Ildy Lee, and Marilyn Selznick. Your support made all the hard work worthwhile.

Chris Juzwiak

Contents

PART TWO   **Expanding Your Writing**   137

7   Developing Details   139

8   Patterns of Development   171

13   More Complex Sentences   328

14   Sentences with Modifiers   356

15   Using Verbs Correctly   381

16   Using Pronouns Correctly   416

PART FOUR   A Writer's Reader   439

17   School and Learning   441

18   Prejudice and Forgiveness   449

19   Parents and Parenting   454

20   Work and Career   461

21   People and Pets   467

22   Deprivation and Privilege   473

Readings by Patterns of Development

This table of contents organizes the readings in Part Four of *Stepping Stones* ("A Writer's Reader," page 439) according to the patterns of development they use. (Within each category, readings are listed in order of appearance. Each reading may appear in more than one category.) For more information on the patterns of development, see Chapter 8.

Introduction for Students

Can a single class make a difference in your life? We definitely believe it can. If you commit to regularly attending and participating in this class, and to doing all of the assigned work, your writing will certainly improve. And better writing skills increase your likelihood of achieving success not just in this class but in all of your college courses and in the workplace, where clear, correct communication is essential.

Stepping Stones will help you get the most out of your class by giving you plenty of examples, activities, and other support to improve your writing and grammar skills. To help you work through the book on your own, we have

- kept the explanations clear and direct so that you can get to work on the activities as quickly as possible
- arranged the activities from easy to difficult so that you can build mastery gradually and confidently
- made the activities creative and fun to challenge your thinking and spark your imagination

The following sections explain how to get the most out of *Stepping Stones*.

FINDING WHAT YOU NEED IN *STEPPING STONES*

Here, we review several important features that can help you find just what you need in this text.

Index. In any book, the index (an alphabetical list of topics covered, with page numbers) is often the quickest way to find a topic of interest. For the index in *Stepping Stones*, turn to page 517 at the back of the book. Say you are looking for all of the relevant information on topic sentences. You would turn to *T* in the index and then scan down until you find "topic sentences." Next to this entry, you will find all the pages on which this subject is discussed.

Detailed list of contents. This resource, on pages xix–xxviii, lists all the chapters in the book and tells you what topics are covered in each one. Page numbers are provided for each chapter and its subtopics so you can find information. Your instructor may refer you to certain chapters and chapter subsections, so be sure that you are comfortable with using the table of contents.

Additionally, each chapter begins with a brief list of contents to give you a preview of the topics covered.

Readings by "patterns of development." This list, on pages xxix–xxx, organizes the readings in Part Four according to the various patterns of development discussed in Chapter 8, providing page numbers. You can turn to this list whenever you want to see additional models of different types of writing (description, exemplification, narration, and so on).

Page headers. As you page through the book, you will find headings at the very top of the left- and right-hand pages. Take a look:

22   Chapter 2 • Developing a Topic

Narrowing a Topic   **23**

The left header shows the number and the title of the chapter that you are in. The right header shows the major section that you are in.

Reference Material

This section, located at the back of the book, helps you keep track of important topics in your writing class.

Quick Guides. These pages offer quick summaries of major grammatical issues such as fragments, run-ons, and noun-verb agreement.

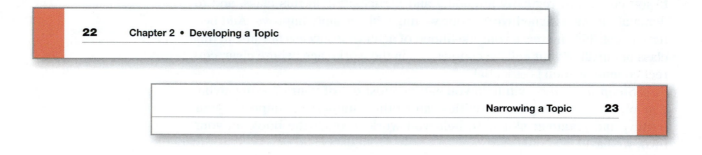

List of helpful lists, charts, and visuals. This resource, at the back of the book, directs you to important writing and grammar aids that you might want to turn to regularly.

List of correction symbols. When your instructor marks writing or grammar issues in your papers, he or she might use various correction symbols. These symbols and their meanings are presented at the back of the book to help you translate your instructor's markings.

USING SPECIAL FEATURES TO IMPROVE YOUR WRITING

Stepping Stones has a number of special features to help make you a better writer. Let's look at a few of them.

"What Do You Know?" pre-tests. Each chapter begins with a self-test that helps you identify what you already know—and what still needs work. These questions get you thinking about the topic before you work with it in greater detail.

Abundant activities. The following experience might be familiar to you: You are given instruction in something several times, but it doesn't "sink in" until you actually perform the task yourself. *Stepping Stones* is based on the "learning by doing" philosophy, giving you lots of activities that help writing and grammar lessons stick in your mind.

Again, assignments grow more and more challenging as you progress through chapters. You may find that you go through earlier practices quickly but need more time to complete later ones. This is natural and expected. You may want to attempt more challenging exercises more than one time.

For even more practice, and to get a lesson plan, visit the free Web site that accompanies this book: **bedfordstmartins .com/steppingstones**.

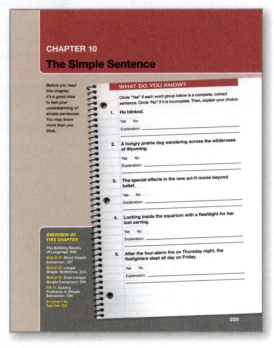

Use the challenge meter. Every exercise in the grammar chapters is rated according to a challenge meter. Increasing "bars" show the difficulty level. In general, exercises begin easy and become more challenging. When you reach the end of the chapter, you are working at a more advanced level. Watch the orange bars increase as you master each skill.

KEY TO CHALLENGE METER	
WARMUP	
EASY	
MODERATE	
ADVANCED	
MASTERY	

Identify the difficulty level of each activity using the key above.

ACTIVITY 1

WARMUP

Create ten simple sentences, matching subjects and verbs from the columns below. Begin by creating five sentences from the two columns on the left. Then, create five more sentences from the two columns on the right. Remember to start each sentence with a capital letter and end it with a period. The first sentence has been written for you.

Subject	Verb	Subject	Verb
cells	heals	smoke	procrastinate
we	sings	Elvis	hurts
Beyoncé	infect	reading	rises
love	divide	jealousy	lives
viruses	collaborate	I	enlightens

Cells divide.

Color-coding of sentence parts and patterns in the grammar chapters. Chapter 10, "The Simple Sentence," describes the various "building blocks" of language that we use to create sentences. So that you can see how these building blocks work together, they are color-coded within examples throughout the grammar chapters (see top of next page).

At the beginning of each grammar chapter, you get a preview of how the building blocks are used to create the sentence type discussed in the chapter:

VISUAL OVERVIEW: How do simple sentences work?

Both of these are simple sentences. You'll find out why in this chapter.

NOUN + VERB . = Students study.

PREPOSITIONAL PHRASE , ADJECTIVE + NOUN + VERB + ADVERB .
= Before exams, good students study carefully.

Helpful tips in the margins.   These tips provide extra advice, explain writing and grammar terms, and refer you to additional exercises on *Stepping Stones'* companion Web site.

Power Tip
You may use very short sentences in your college writing, but do not overuse them. Too many might suggest that your thinking and writing are simplistic. Effective writers save very short sentences for special emphasis.

For more practice with building simple sentences, visit **bedfordstmartins .com/steppingstones.**

Terminology Tip
In English grammar, the verb that follows a helping verb is often called the *main verb*. Often, the main verb is an action verb.

BRINGING IT ALL TOGETHER:
The Simple Sentence

In this chapter, you have learned about the building blocks of language, the simple sentence, and fragments. Confirm your knowledge by filling in the blank spaces in the following sentences. If you need help, review the pages listed after each sentence.

✓ _____ and _____ are known as foundation words because they are the foundation of all verbal communication. (page 226)

✓ A noun is a word that identifies a person, place, or thing. There are three types of nouns—_____, _____, and _____—and a noun substitute: _____.
(page 228)

✓ There are three types of verbs. An _____ verb expresses an action and is easy to identify. A _____ verb must be connected to more information, usually a descriptive word. A _____ verb must be connected to another verb. (page 231)

✓ _____ and _____ are descriptive words.

"Bringing It All Together" chapter reviews.   These post-tests at the end of each chapter summarize important information and allow you to review what you've learned. Fill in the blanks in each sentence and revisit any skill that needs more practice.

A thematic reader.   This resource, in Part Four ("A Writer's Reader"), offers not only good models of professional writing but also a source of ideas for your own writing. Each reading is accompanied by writing assignments and by questions that help you study and understand strategies used by experienced writers.

GETTING EXTRA HELP

Stepping Stones comes with a free and easy-to-use companion Web site: **bedfordstmartins.com/steppingstones**. This site offers hundreds of additional practices, annotated examples of student writing, and other resources to help you improve your writing and grammar skills. Registration is easy; just follow the "Sign me up" link.

Aside from offering exercises written specifically for *Stepping Stones*, the Web site provides access to thousands more practices on *Exercise Central* as well as model documents, advice on avoiding plagiarism, and more.

Stepping Stones

A Guided Approach to Writing
Sentences and Paragraphs

PART ONE
The Academic Paragraph

CHAPTER 1

Seeing the Big Picture: Paragraphs, Purpose, and Audience

Before you read this chapter, it's a good idea to test your understanding of paragraphs, purpose, and audience. You may know more than you think.

For each question, select all the answers that apply.

WHAT DO YOU KNOW?

1. **Short paragraphs in newspapers, magazines, and Web sites allow you to read quickly. These are "popular" paragraphs. On the other hand, "academic" paragraphs are much longer. The purpose of academic paragraphs is:**

    ___ to pack a lot of information in the space provided.
    ___ to show that the writer is an intellectual.
    ___ to encourage the reader to slow down and think carefully.

2. **Every time you write, you write *for someone*. In academic writing, the person for whom you are writing is called:**

    ___ the editor.
    ___ the author.
    ___ the audience.
    ___ the writer.

3. **If you are writing an e-mail to your boss explaining why you deserve a raise, what type of audience are you addressing?**

    ___ personal
    ___ professional
    ___ academic

4. **Every time you write, you write for a *reason* or *purpose*. What are some of the common purposes for writing in college?**

    ___ to inform
    ___ to educate
    ___ to inspire
    ___ to persuade

5. **If you are writing a composition for a college class, which of the following describes the type of language you will need to use?**

    ___ Correct grammar is appreciated.
    ___ Correct grammar is optional.
    ___ Correct grammar is required.

Understanding Paragraphs

Let's begin with an obvious question: What is a paragraph? Many people will be able to provide only a general or unclear definition. Related questions include:

- What should an ideal paragraph look like?
- How long should it be?
- Are there rules for constructing a paragraph?
- Why do so many paragraphs look so different from one another?

Knowing the answers to these questions will give you a more confident vision for your writing projects.

ACADEMIC AND POPULAR PARAGRAPHS

scholarly journal: a publication — similar to a magazine, but often without advertising — in which scholars, professors, and specialists publish their research and their ideas

In your reading experiences, you may have noticed that paragraphs come in a variety of shapes and sizes.

Some paragraphs are quite long, with many sentences. In general, they have a main idea and plenty of supporting examples and details. For convenience, we will call these **academic** paragraphs. They are commonly found in textbooks, college essays, and scholarly journals. Academic paragraphs encourage readers to slow down and reflect on the ideas being discussed.

Other paragraphs are quite short, with only a few sentences. These paragraphs may or may not contain a main idea, and they may or may not have supporting examples and details. We will call these **popular** paragraphs. They are commonly found in newspapers, magazines, Web sites, and personal communication, such as e-mails. Popular paragraphs allow readers to move quickly, grabbing key pieces of information as they go.

The following writing samples illustrate the difference between popular and academic paragraphs. Although the articles are about the same length, the one on the left contains only three (academic) paragraphs, while the one on the right contains fourteen (popular) paragraphs. Take a look, and then complete the activities that follow.

Low-income students who graduate from high school with at least minimal qualifications for four-year institutions enroll at half the rate of their high-income peers. Only 78 percent of students from low-income families who rank as top achievers on tests of college readiness actually attend college. In contrast, nearly the same share of students from high-income families who rank at the bottom of such tests do so. The conventional view is that students from low-income families don't enroll or complete college because they are not academically qualified. But the New Century evidence paints a different and more hopeful picture. Despite the considerable obstacles they encounter as they grow up, many high school students from

Secondhand smoke kills more than 600,000 people worldwide every year, according to a new study.

In the first look at the global impact of secondhand smoking, researchers analyzed data from 2004 for 192 countries. They found 40 percent of children and more than 30 percent of nonsmoking men and women regularly breathe in secondhand smoke.

Scientists then estimated that passive smoking causes about 379,000 deaths from heart disease, 165,000 deaths from lower respiratory disease, 36,900 deaths from asthma, and 21,400 deaths from lung cancer a year.

Altogether, those account for about 1 percent of the world's deaths. The study was paid for by

low-income, disadvantaged households are qualified but are choosing not to attend college or to attend colleges that are less selective than their qualifications justify.

What can be done to help such students get the ticket to college? Clearly, more generous financial aid is part of the answer. The financial barriers to college enrollment among students from low-income families are great—and growing. Since the early 1970s, the value of federal aid packages for low-income students has fallen precipitously as a percentage of college costs. In the same period, college costs as a portion of family income have remained unchanged for the top 40 percent of the family income distribution while increasing substantially for low-income families. Without a big increase in federal and state support for means-tested student aid programs, a growing number of qualified students from low-income households will find the door to higher education and upward mobility closed for them and their children.

The nation's colleges and universities should also do more to help children from low-income families. They should mount more aggressive efforts to identify and recruit students from low-income families with strong academic potential early in their high-school careers, providing them with better information about the course requirements and procedures for college admission. Colleges should also expand their financial aid programs for low-income students. Currently, more four-year colleges offer financial aid to athletes and students with "special nonacademic talents" than to disadvantaged students. Finally, more colleges should follow the lead of the Universities of California, Florida, and Washington and design admissions programs that evaluate the academic accomplishments of applicants in light of such obstacles as family income, parental education, and social environment. Doesn't an SAT total score of 1200 combined with an A average mean something different for an applicant raised in a low-income household and educated in a run-down public school than for an applicant from a high-income home who was educated in an outstanding private school?

Laura D'Andrea Tyson
"Needed: Affirmative Action for the Poor"

the Swedish National Board of Health and Welfare and Bloomberg Philanthropies. It was published Friday in the British medical journal *Lancet*.

"This helps us understand the real toll of tobacco," said Armando Peruga, a program manager at the World Health Organization's Tobacco-Free Initiative who led the study. He said the approximately 603,000 deaths from secondhand smoking should be added to the 5.1 million deaths that smoking itself causes every year.

Peruga said WHO was particularly concerned about the 165,000 children who die of smoke-related respiratory infections, mostly in Southeast Asia and Africa.

"The mix of infectious diseases and secondhand smoke is a deadly combination," Peruga said. Children whose parents smoke have a higher risk of sudden infant death syndrome, ear infections, pneumonia, bronchitis, and asthma. Their lungs may also grow more slowly than kids whose parents don't smoke.

Peruga and colleagues found the highest numbers of people exposed to secondhand smoke are in Europe and Asia. The lowest rates of exposure were in the Americas, the Eastern Mediterranean, and Africa.

Secondhand smoke had its biggest impact on women, killing about 281,000. In many parts of the world, women are at least 50 percent more likely to be exposed to secondhand smoke than men.

While many Western countries have introduced smoking bans in public places, experts said it would be difficult to legislate further.

"I don't think it is likely we will see strong regulations reaching into homes," said Heather Wipfli of the Institute for Global Health at the University of Southern California in Los Angeles, who was not connected to the study. She said more public smoking bans and education might persuade people to quit smoking at home.

In the U.K., the British Lung Foundation is petitioning the government to outlaw smoking in cars.

Helena Shovelton, the foundation's chief executive, said smoking parents frequently underestimate the danger their habit is doing to their children.

"It's almost as if people are in denial," she said. "They absolutely would not do something dangerous like leaving their child in the middle of the road, but somehow, smoking in front of them is fine."

Maria Cheng, Associated Press
"More Than 600,000 Killed by Secondhand Smoke"

ACTIVITY 1

In each writing sample on pages 4–5, count the underline{number of sentences} in each paragraph. Then, read one or more paragraphs to get an idea what kind of information the author includes. Finally, in the space provided, write your own definition or description of a popular or academic paragraph.

1. "Needed: Affirmative Action for the Poor," by Laura D'Andrea Tyson

    Paragraph 1: _____

    Paragraph 2: _____

    Paragraph 3: _____

    An *academic* paragraph is _____

    _____

    _____

2. "More Than 600,000 Killed by Secondhand Smoke," by Maria Cheng

    Paragraph 1: _____

    Paragraph 2: _____

    Paragraph 3: _____

    Paragraph 4: _____

    Paragraph 5: _____

    A *popular* paragraph is _____

    _____

    _____

    _____

ACTIVITY 2: Teamwork

For each of the following writing samples, identify whether the author is using popular or academic paragraphs. Then, in the space provided, explain why the paragraphs are popular or academic.

EXAMPLE:

Tolls on state turnpikes will be raised by as much as fifty cents by early 2012 if a state legislative committee's plan is approved.

"We can't maintain our roadways at the current level of funding," said state senator Rick Bartley, chair of the State Transportation Committee and a chief architect of the plan. "Unless we raise tolls — or take funds from other projects — desperately needed road and bridge repairs will not be possible."

In response, Rita Mendos, Ways and Means Committee chair, commented, "That's a lot of nonsense. We shouldn't be looking at fifty-cent toll hikes until we have exhausted all other possibilities."

Type of paragraphs: _____popular_____

Explanation: The paragraphs have only one to three sentences. The author wants the readers to move quickly, grabbing key pieces of information as they go.

1.   A Middleton teen is in critical condition after crashing her sport utility vehicle into the Myers Road overpass on Route 87 Tuesday evening, state police reported.

    Seventeen-year-old Lexie Peters, a senior at Catholic Memorial High School, was taken to Mercy Hospital in Rogersville after the crash. Witnesses reported that her vehicle, which was traveling south on Route 87 at around 11 p.m., swerved a few times before the crash. No other vehicles were involved.

    Police are investigating the cause of the accident.

Type of paragraphs: _____

Explanation: _____

_____

_____

2.   Binge drinking, consuming a large volume of alcohol in a brief period, is a common and serious problem at many colleges (Comer, 2007). Disturbing findings from several studies have led some experts to call binge drinking "the No. 1 public health hazard" for full-time college students (Wechsler et al., 1995). Researchers have found that 43.4 percent of college students binge drink at least once annually, with around 50 percent of students engaging in this behavior six or more times a month (Sharma, 2005; Wechsler et al., 2004, 2000, 1997, 1994). Disturbingly, alcohol is a factor in nearly 40 percent of academic problems and in 28 percent of all drop-out cases (Anderson, 1994). Additionally, binge drinking has been linked to car accidents, bodily injury, date rape and other aggressive behavior, and psychological problems (Wechsler & Wuethrich, 2002). As a result, the problem affects not only the drinker but also his or her friends and acquaintances, and even strangers. Even students who are well-behaved and nonaggressive when sober can act out in disturbing, even violent, ways when they have had too much to drink. In the mid-1990s, a survey of U.S. college students found that those most likely to binge drink tended to center their social lives on parties, to engage in other high-risk behaviors, and to live in fraternity or sorority houses (Wechsler et al., 1995). Many universities are targeting these at-risk populations by offering counseling and alternatives to drinking-centered social activities, among other responses. Additionally, some universities are declaring certain dorms "substance-free."

CONTINUED >

Type of paragraph: _____

Explanation: _____

_____

_____

3.   Hip-hop music speaks to me like no other music. First of all, I just love the sound of it. Great rappers like Mos Def and Nelly have an energetic vocal style that gets me to my feet, and they get a solid rhythm down even if there's no drumming or other music in the background. When there is music, whether from instruments or sampling, the sound can be even richer. Drum tracks, guitar riffs, and even horns add to the energy and style. Second, I love the poetry and storytelling of hip-hop music. The poetry comes partly from rhyming, but it's more than that; the words of these artists (like Kanye West talking about giving "salty looks") can create vivid pictures in the listeners' minds. Also, whether they are singing about their own lives or things that are going on in the streets or in the larger world, talented rappers know how to "tell it like it is"; they tell stories that their listeners can relate to. Finally, I love the tradition of inventiveness in hip-hop music. For example, artists sample tracks of other musicians to create new songs. Also, hip-hop has inspired invention in the worlds of fashion and dance. Artists are always coming up with new clothing styles and dance moves that fans want to imitate. For all these reasons, I love hip-hop, and it will always keep me moving and thinking.

Type of paragraph: _____

Explanation: _____

_____

_____

4.   Detective Banes could tell by the way Phillips walked into the interrogation room that he had something to hide. Phillips shuffled in, pale and slouched, and he was wearing sunglasses, of all things, on this dark and rainy day.

"Take those off," Banes said, pointing to the glasses, "and sit down."

Phillips hesitated, then removed his glasses, revealing bloodshot eyes. Without the glasses he looked more like the kid he was than the murderer he might be. Phillips sat down and leaned so far back in the chair his head rested on the back.

"Let's talk about what you were doing on the night of the thirteenth," Banes began.

"That's easy," Phillips laughed. "I had Chinese takeout and went to bed at ten."

"All right," Banes replied, smiling in spite of himself. "But let's talk about what happened between the fortune cookie and lights out."

Type of paragraphs: _____

Explanation: _____

_____

_____

5.   I am pleased to report on the excellent performance of shipping manager Dave Nuñez for the year ending December 31, 2011. Dave is hard-working, highly competent, and admired by his employees.

Dave is one of our most skilled workers. In 2011, he took steps to improve his performance even more, including attending educational seminars and the special managers' course. Also, he created and implemented our new shipping efficiency program this year, and this program has increased the productivity of our shipping operation by 25 percent since it began in March.

Additionally, Dave's shipping crew is the most efficient in the company's history, and this year he introduced a bonus program to reward top employees in the shipping department. This incentive program has increased productivity even further. Dave's employees appreciate his efforts and take pride in their work.

Type of paragraphs: _____

Explanation: _____

_____

_____

Understanding Your Purpose

Now, let us turn to the issue of *why* you write. Every time you write, you write for a reason, or **purpose**. To illustrate this simple point, complete the following activity.

ACTIVITY 3: Teamwork

Discuss with your classmates the reason, or purpose, for each of the following writing projects. Then, fill in the blank below with the author's likely purpose.

EXAMPLE: a customer's complaint about poor service

Her purpose: to have the store improve its customer service _____

CONTINUED >

1. a supervisor's one-year review of your job performance

   Her purpose: _____

   _____

2. an e-mail in which you give a friend directions to your apartment

   Your purpose: _____

   _____

3. a movie critic's review of a new action film

   His purpose: _____

   _____

4. a scary new novel from Stephen King

   His purpose: _____

   _____

5. a medical researcher's article about the discovery of a new AIDS drug

   His purpose: _____

   _____

WRITE TO INFORM, ENTERTAIN, OR PERSUADE

As a college writer, you should have a clear sense of purpose for each composition that you write. Knowing your purpose will help you make effective choices about the information you include and how to present this information.

In the broadest sense, the purpose of all writing is to communicate information and ideas. However, there are three key purposes for much of the writing that you will do in this class and in college. These purposes are: to inform, to entertain, and to persuade.

To Inform

For many of your college writing assignments, you will be asked to provide information on specific issues or topics. In order to increase your reader's knowledge and understanding of the issue or topic, you should provide clear and accurate information. For the following topics, your purpose would be to inform the reader:

- Discuss how to study effectively for a test in college.
- Identify the causes of the Boston Tea Party.

- Explain how to prepare for a job interview.
- Write a detailed description of the *Mona Lisa.*

Mona Lisa: A famous portrait done by the Italian painter Leonardo da Vinci in the sixteenth century

To Entertain

When you write to entertain, you go beyond mere facts and information. Instead, you want to stimulate your reader's imagination and emotions. In order to do this successfully, make your ideas as creative and vivid as possible. For the following topics, your purpose would be to entertain the reader. (*Note:* Entertainment includes ideas that are humorous, dramatic, tragic, or inspirational.)

- Discuss the human suffering in the battle of Gettysburg.
- Describe what it feels like to fall in love.
- Write a portrait of an "evil" or "heroic" person you know.
- Tell the story of the proudest moment of your life.

To Persuade

For other college writing assignments, you will be asked to challenge (and hopefully change) your reader's opinion on specific issues or topics. In order to do this successfully, you will have to show clear thinking and provide good evidence for your position. For the following topics, your purpose would be to persuade the reader:

- Convince your college to reduce tuition fees.
- Argue *for* or *against* steroid use in professional sports.
- Persuade one of your professors to give less homework.
- Argue whether animal shelters should euthanize stray dogs and cats.

Here is a chart that will help you recognize and understand some key purposes for your writing:

PURPOSE	DESIRED EFFECT	REQUIREMENTS	RELATED TERMS
To inform	Increase your reader's knowledge and understanding.	Provide clear and accurate information.	to educate to enlighten
To entertain	Captivate your reader's imagination and emotions.	Use creative and vivid ideas.	to amuse to captivate to inspire
To persuade	Change your reader's mind about something.	Show clear thinking and provide evidence for your position.	to influence to convince to motivate

Power Tip
Some writing assignments may have multiple purposes. However, you should identify which of these purposes is your *primary purpose*. Keep that in mind as you develop your ideas.

ACTIVITY 4

For each of the following writing assignments, decide whether the purpose is to inform, to entertain, or to persuade. Then, in the spaces provided, write down the purpose, the desired effect, and the requirements for the writing.

EXAMPLE: Write a humorous blog on the different types of baseball fans.

Purpose: to entertain

Desired effect: captivate your reader's imagination and emotions

Requirements: use creative and vivid ideas

1. As a nursing student, write a report describing your patient's condition.

   Purpose: _____

   Desired effect: _____

   Requirements: _____

2. Write a letter to your younger brother or sister, encouraging him or her to enroll in college.

   Purpose: _____

   Desired effect: _____

   Requirements: _____

   _____

3. Write about a struggle that you and your family went through and survived.

   Purpose: _____

   Desired effect: _____

   Requirements: _____

4. Write a letter to your credit card company, asking them to excuse a penalty for a late payment.

   Purpose: _____

   Desired effect: _____

   Requirements: _____

   _____

5. For your world history class, write a paper explaining the causes of the fall of the Roman Empire.

   Purpose: _____

   Desired effect: _____

   Requirements: _____

ACTIVITY 5: Teamwork

Read each of the following passages. Discuss the purpose of each one with your classmates, and then write the purpose in the space provided. Also, write a brief explanation of why you think the passage is written with that purpose in mind, giving examples from the passage.

EXAMPLE:

My daughter, who just got engaged, asked me what it means to have a good marriage. I had to think about her question, but then I came up with an answer that satisfies me, and I hope it satisfied her. To me, a good marriage is being with someone you look forward to seeing at the end of the day, even after years of togetherness. The two of you will have your disagreements, but you will always come back to wanting to share the stories, fun times, and difficulties of your lives. A good marriage is one in which you find balance, not only in responsibilities but also between together time and alone time; you give each other space and room to grow. Perhaps most important, a good marriage is one in which each person truly respects the other, for when respect isn't there, nothing positive can happen. Last, but certainly not least, a good marriage requires laughter. I'm not kidding when I tell people that I married my husband because he makes me laugh more than anyone else. Then, I realized that he was smart and good-looking, too!

Purpose: _The purpose of this paragraph is to inform._

Explanation: _The author provides clear and accurate information to explain what makes a good marriage. One good example of this is "a good marriage is one in which you find balance, not only in responsibilities but also between together time and alone time."_

1. Spending days at my grandparents' farm in the country taught me to appreciate where food comes from. Every morning, my grandfather would wake me up in the dark, around 4 A.M., to go out to the barn and milk the cows. I would be sleepy but excited. We'd open the creaky wooden door, and I'd smell cows and hay. At first, Grandpa just had me watch him while he set up the stool next to the cow and placed the bucket under the udder. Then I got to help him milk. One of the cows, Broodie, mooed and licked my face. Her tongue was like a giant sponge. After that, Grandpa and I walked to the chicken coop where we'd reach under the chickens to get the fresh eggs. Some of the chickens squawked at us and beat their wings. The eggs were still warm and Grandpa let me hold a couple as we finished our morning chores. Back at the house, Grandma made a huge breakfast for us, using the eggs and milk that we had collected. The food was made more delicious because we were hungry from our chores. I felt proud of our work.

CONTINUED >

Purpose: _____

Explanation: _____

_____

_____

2.   Students at my college should avoid eating at campus food facilities because of unsanitary conditions. In a two-week investigation of our campus restaurants, my friends and I discovered a lack of reasonable cleanliness. In fact, some of the practices were so disgusting that we vowed to take our cause to the college's administration. At the first restaurant (Burgs), we discovered some employees who did not wash their hands after handling raw meat, and others who served food after it had been dropped on the floor. At the second restaurant (the cafeteria), old grease was dripping from the stove fans, and food scraps had been swept into the corners but not removed. At the third restaurant (Salad-n-Slice), we accompanied a city health inspector, who found rodent droppings in a food storage area and behind the stove. He also noticed that vegetables were being cut on a surface that had recently held raw beef. From these examples, it is clear that the college administration should act soon and decisively to improve sanitation in these facilities. Otherwise, students might be missing more class due to illness such as food poisoning.

Purpose: _____

Explanation: _____

_____

_____

_____

3.   It's not necessarily true that the longer you study, the greater your chances of scoring well on a test. Time alone won't guarantee your success. You must study *effectively*, making the best use of your time. First, before an exam, consult with your instructor. Instead of asking, "What's on the test?" you can request guidelines about what topics will be covered and how you can best prepare. This information will provide a purpose for your study. Next, find a place to study where you will remain awake and undistracted: a desk in a library is better than a bed near a television. Then, with your purpose in mind, reread your lecture notes, textbook sections, and other materials. Underline key information and mark points that you do not understand. When you have finished this review, go back to these points and try to answer them. Use any chapter summaries or review materials that are available. Finally, if the instructor has provided sample test questions — or if review questions are available in the textbook — try to answer them. They will help you do a final check of your readiness for the exam.

Purpose: _____

Explanation: _____

_____

_____

_____

Understanding Your Audience

Whenever you write, you always write for *someone*. If you are writing in a diary or journal, you will probably be writing for yourself. However, with most writing projects, you will be writing for *someone else* — your **audience**, or readers.

As a college writer, you should be aware of three general types of audience: personal, professional, and academic.

In your personal writing, you communicate with family, friends, and acquaintances. These people can be considered your **personal audience**. Today, much of our personal writing is done electronically through e-mail, text messaging, and social networking sites.

Professional writing is used for business, journalism, and most forms of public communication. When you write for a **professional audience** (employers, employees, customers, clients, newspaper readers, and so on), your goal is to communicate public — not personal or private — information.

Finally, when you write assignments for your college classes, you will be writing for an **academic audience**. In this situation, your main academic audience will be your instructors or professors. The larger academic audience also includes students, faculty, scholars, and researchers. Your goal is to provide ideas and information that readers can trust. Academic writing includes college essays, textbooks, and scholarly journals and books.

ACTIVITY 6

For each of the following pieces of writing, decide who the specific audience is. Then, write the type of audience (personal, professional, or academic) in the space provided.

EXAMPLE: An in-class essay exam for your literature class.

Type of audience: _____*academic*_____

1. A first-year evaluation of your performance as a dental assistant.

Type of audience: _____

2. A letter to your bank requesting further information on the rejection of your loan application.

Type of audience: _____

CONTINUED >

3. A report for your psychology class on the services offered by the college's Mental Health Center.

   Type of audience: _____

4. A letter to your cousin serving in the U.S. Army in Afghanistan.

   Type of audience: _____

5. A chapter in your world history book on the Trojan War.

   Type of audience: _____

Knowing the audience for your writing can help you make important decisions about how to communicate effectively. Specifically, you should:

1. Use <u>language</u> that is appropriate for your audience.
2. Provide <u>information</u> that is appropriate for your audience.

USE LANGUAGE THAT IS APPROPRIATE FOR YOUR AUDIENCE

slang: informal language often used between friends or within other social groups. *Dis* for *disrespect* is an example of slang.

If you are writing an e-mail or text message to a friend, you can use abbreviations (like *CU* for *see you* or *UR* for *you are*) that make your writing fast and fun. You will probably use some slang, and you may break grammar rules. On the other hand, if you are writing a letter to your manager at work, you will want to avoid abbreviations, slang, and any profanity that could offend or confuse your manager. Although you will want your writing to be clear and easy to understand, your grammar will probably be "relaxed" — correct enough for clear communication but not perfect.

Finally, if you are writing an essay on cloning for your biology class, your instructor will expect you to use more formal language and grammar. Also, you may need to use some technical language related to the topic of cloning. Because your audience (the instructor) will be knowledgeable about the topic, such language will be acceptable, even expected. You will also need to follow grammar rules carefully and to write complete, correct sentences.

The following chart summarizes the expectations of a few common audiences for whom you will write.

Different Audience Expectations for Writing

AUDIENCE TYPE	EXAMPLES	GRAMMAR	VOCABULARY
Personal	family, friends, Facebook users, etc.	Correct grammar is optional.	Informal English: slang and abbreviations are accepted
Professional	boss, credit card company, newspaper readers, etc.	Correct grammar is appreciated or expected.	Standard English
Academic	instructors, professors, other students, scholars, etc.	Correct grammar is required.	Standard English, sometimes with technical or specialized vocabulary

ACTIVITY 7: Teamwork

With your classmates, discuss what type of language would be appropriate for each of the following pieces of writing. Then, describe the language, referring to the three features shown in the previous chart.

EXAMPLE: a memo to employees about changes to health benefits

Appropriate language: _Standard English and correct grammar_

1. a paper on exploration of the American West for a history class

   Appropriate language: _____

   _____

2. a letter to the principal of your child's elementary school

   Appropriate language: _____

   _____

3. an online party invitation (to friends)

   Appropriate language: _____

   _____

4. an in-class essay exam for your literature class

   Appropriate language: _____

   _____

5. an e-mail to your supervisor asking for a meeting about a project you are working on

   Appropriate language: _____

   _____

INCLUDE INFORMATION THAT IS APPROPRIATE FOR YOUR AUDIENCE

If your audience has little knowledge about your topic, you will need to include the most **basic** information possible. For example, if you are giving car maintenance advice to someone who knows little about cars, you will need to provide very basic advice, such as the need to change the oil regularly.

If your audience has a lot of knowledge or experience, you may skip very basic information and move directly to more **advanced** information. A car expert would already know about the need for regular oil changes but might want to hear about the latest technology for increasing engine efficiency.

If your audience is somewhere in between, you will need to provide an **intermediate** level of information — not too simple, and not too advanced. If the information you provide is too simple for your audience, you may lose their interest; if the information is too advanced for your audience, they may not understand your writing.

Power Tip

For some writing assignments, you may be required to cover a *range* of information, from basic to advanced. For example, even though your college instructors will usually know a lot about the topics they assign, they might want you to include some basic information so that they know you understand the topic fully. Whenever you are in doubt about the type of information that is appropriate for a writing assignment, ask your instructor.

To decide what kind of information is appropriate for your audience, always answer this question: *How much experience or knowledge does my audience have regarding the topic?*

Whether the information you provide is basic, intermediate, or advanced, be sure that it is as precise and accurate as possible.

ACTIVITY 8

Write down the type of information (basic, intermediate, or advanced) that would be appropriate for the following audiences.

EXAMPLE: a description of the making of stained-glass windows for second graders

Appropriate information: *basic*

1. an essay on jazz for your modern dance instructor

   Appropriate information: _____

   _____

2. a paragraph on campfire safety for first-year Girl Scouts

   Appropriate information: _____

3. a description of how wine is made for a group of wine drinkers

   Appropriate information: _____

4. an explanation of how to use PowerPoint for your mother or father

   Appropriate information: _____

5. a list of safety reminders for hikers climbing Mount Everest for the second time

   Appropriate information: _____

BRINGING IT ALL TOGETHER:
Seeing the Big Picture

In this chapter, you have learned about paragraphs, purposes, and audiences for your writing. Confirm your knowledge by filling in the blank spaces in the following sentences. If you need help, review the pages listed after each sentence.

✔ There are two general types of paragraphs. Longer paragraphs that encourage readers to slow down and reflect deeply are called _____ paragraphs. Shorter paragraphs that allow readers to move quickly, grabbing key pieces of information as they go, are called _____ paragraphs. (page 4)

✔ There are three general purposes for most of the writing that you do. If your goal is to increase your reader's knowledge and understanding, the purpose is to _____. If your goal is to captivate your reader's imagination and emotions, the purpose is to _____. Finally, if your goal is to change your reader's mind about something, the purpose is to _____. (pages 10–11)

✔ There are three general types of audience to keep in mind when you write. These audiences are _____, _____, and _____. (page 15)

✔ When you write a college assignment, you must use _____ grammar and _____ English. In addition, some _____ vocabulary may be required. (page 16)

✔ When you write a college assignment, be careful to include information that is appropriate for your audience. Depending on what your instructor requires, this information may be _____, _____, or _____ (or a combination of these). (page 17)

CHAPTER 2

Developing a Topic

Before you read this chapter, it's a good idea to test your understanding of developing a topic for college writing. You may know more than you think.

For each question, select all the answers that apply.

WHAT DO YOU KNOW?

1. **Which of the following topics is the narrowest in scope?**

   ___ *Write about a big mistake that you regret making.*

   ___ *Write about common mistakes made by new college students.*

   ___ *Write about the ways in which human beings learn from their mistakes.*

2. **Here is a sample writing topic: *Write about money*. What type of topic is this?**

   ___ a broad topic

   ___ a limited topic

   ___ a narrow topic

3. **The process for gathering more ideas for your topic is called:**

   ___ outlining.

   ___ brainstorming.

   ___ proofreading.

   ___ editing.

4. **There are four popular writing methods for getting your ideas down on paper. Which of the following is NOT one of these methods?**

   ___ clustering

   ___ revising

   ___ listing

   ___ freewriting

5. **When you choose a writing topic, you can ask a number of questions to help you decide what to write about. Which of the following questions will NOT help you make good choices?**

   ___ Do I know a lot about the topic?

   ___ Am I interested in sharing my ideas about this topic?

   ___ Which topic will be the easiest?

   ___ What would I like to learn about this topic?

Understanding Broad, Limited, and Narrow Topics

In Chapter 1 you learned about the features of different types of paragraphs, purposes, and audiences. As you now know, in college you will typically write academic paragraphs in response to specific assignments.

Some assignment topics are very broad or general, giving students a lot of choice in what to write about. Other topics are more carefully defined, giving students a limited choice in what to write about. In other cases, a topic may be very narrow, giving students very little choice in what to write about.

As a college student, you should be able to recognize the type of topic you have been assigned. To work effectively with a topic, you should know how much choice you have and how much further narrowing, if any, you will have to do.

Now, let's look at some sample writing assignments for a cultural geography class. The instructor might make the writing assignment broad, limited, or narrow:

BROAD   Discuss modern China.

For this assignment, you would have a great deal of choice in what to write about. For example, you could write about Chinese politics, economy, education, art, or other aspects of contemporary China. Now, let's look at a more limited topic:

LIMITED   Discuss China's population problems.

For this assignment, you would have a limited choice in what to write about because the instructor has narrowed the topic to "population problems." Now, let's look at an even more limited topic:

NARROW   Discuss the success of China's one-child policy.

For this assignment, you have very little choice in what to write about because the instructor has narrowed the topic from "population problems" to a specific policy: China's one-child policy. The professor has even noted that you must focus on the success of this policy.

ACTIVITY 1: Teamwork

Examine each of the following groups of topics. Then, decide which topic offers the most choice in what to write about, which one offers a limited choice, and which one offers little choice. Label each topic broad, limited, or narrow.

EXAMPLE: Discuss your favorite professional soccer player. _____ narrow _____

Discuss professional soccer. _____ broad _____

Discuss last year's World Cup. _____ limited _____

CONTINUED >

1. Discuss college education. _____

   Discuss an enjoyable aspect of your college experience. _____

   Discuss the benefits of going to college. _____

2. Discuss your favorite *Harry Potter* book or movie. _____

   Discuss whether *Harry Potter* is children's literature. _____

   Discuss the popularity of *Harry Potter*. _____

3. Discuss a favorite feature of Facebook. _____

   Discuss social networking on the Internet. _____

   Discuss the differences between Facebook and Twitter. _____

4. Discuss the symptoms of depression. _____

   Discuss a time when you felt depressed. _____

   Discuss psychological disorders. _____

5. Discuss the importance of grades in college. _____

   Discuss your GPA (Grade Point Average). _____

   Discuss whether your teachers grade too hard. _____

Narrowing a Topic

If you are assigned a broad or limited topic, you will need to narrow it to a more specific topic. The scope of your topic should fit the required length of the composition. Your instructor will usually require a certain length for your writing assignment. Here are some common lengths for college writing assignments (typed and double-spaced):

- an academic paragraph (one page or less)
- a short essay (one to three pages)
- a standard essay (three to five pages)
- a long essay or research paper (more than five pages)

Suppose that you have been assigned the following topic:

BROAD TOPIC   Discuss your college experiences.

Clearly, this topic is too broad for a paragraph or a short essay. There are so many experiences that you could discuss — and so many examples to provide — that you would never complete the assignment successfully in the space of a paragraph or a short essay. Here is how the topic could be narrowed for a standard essay.

> **LIMITED TOPIC**   I will discuss my <u>struggles</u> in college.

In a standard essay (three to five pages), you could effectively describe a number of struggles that you've had in college, such as keeping up with homework, communicating with instructors, selecting classes, and paying for tuition and books. You would have plenty of room to provide specific examples and details to illustrate each of these struggles. For a paragraph or short essay, you would need to narrow the topic more tightly.

> **NARROWED TOPIC**   I will discuss <u>a difficult class</u> I've had.

In the space of a short essay or paragraph, you would be able to provide a few good examples to illustrate the difficulties that you have had in just one class.

ACTIVITY 2

Change each of the following broad topics to a limited topic. Then, change the limited topic to a narrow topic.

EXAMPLE: **Broad:** Discuss something that you are good at or something that you know a lot about.

> **Limited:** I am good at sports.
>
> **Narrow:** As a running back, I have contributed to the success of my college football team.

1. **Broad:** Discuss something that you are good at or something that you know a lot about. (*Hint:* For the limited topic, identify your ability or knowledge. For the narrow topic, identify a situation in which you have used that ability or knowledge.)

   Limited: _____

   Narrow: _____

   _____

2. **Broad:** Discuss a decision that you made that was good or bad for you. (*Hint:* For the limited topic, identify the decision. For the narrow topic, state why it was good or bad for you.)

   Limited: _____

   Narrow: _____

   _____

CONTINUED >

3. **Broad:** Discuss a person who has played an important role in your life. (*Hint:* For the limited topic, identify the person. For the narrow topic, identify the important role that the person played in your life.)

   Limited: _____

   Narrow: _____

   _____

4. **Broad:** Discuss a powerful memory from your childhood. (*Hint:* For the limited topic, identify the memory. For the narrow topic, state why the memory is so powerful.)

   Limited: _____

   Narrow: _____

   _____

5. **Broad:** Discuss something important that you feel is missing from your life. (*Hint:* For the limited topic, identify the thing that is missing from your life. For the narrow topic, state why this thing is important to you.)

   Limited: _____

   Narrow: _____

   _____

Selecting a Topic That Works for You

When you have a choice of topics, be sure to consider which topic will work best for you. In other words, decide which topic will *motivate* you to write and give you the *best results*. Here is a list of criteria that you can use to evaluate topics:

- Does the topic appeal to you immediately? Does it seem interesting, exciting, or fun? (A topic that grabs your interest will motivate you.)

- What can you learn from this topic about yourself or the world you live in? Would you like to explore this topic and learn more? (Intellectual curiosity — the desire to learn more — will also motivate you.)

- Do you know a lot about this topic? Do you have a lot to say about it? (Having a lot to say about a topic will motivate you.)

- Is this a topic that you would like to discuss with other people? Would you like to show your finished composition to others? (The desire to share your ideas with other people will motivate you.)

ACTIVITY 3

For this activity, write your narrowed topics from Activity 2 in the line that says "Narrowed Topic." Score each topic according to the four criteria listed, using the following key: **3** = definitely   **2** = somewhat   **1** = not really. Finally, add the four scores together for the total score.

1. Narrowed Topic _____

   The topic seems exciting or fun.   3 2 1

   I would like to learn something from this topic.   3 2 1

   I know a lot about this topic.   3 2 1

   I would like to share my ideas about this topic with others.   3 2 1

   Total score: _____

2. Narrowed Topic _____

   The topic seems exciting or fun.   3 2 1

   I would like to learn something from this topic.   3 2 1

   I know a lot about this topic.   3 2 1

   I would like to share my ideas about this topic with others.   3 2 1

   Total score: _____

3. Narrowed Topic _____

   The topic seems exciting or fun.   3 2 1

   I would like to learn something from this topic.   3 2 1

   I know a lot about this topic.   3 2 1

   I would like to share my ideas about this topic with others.   3 2 1

   Total score: _____

4. Narrowed Topic _____

   The topic seems exciting or fun.   3 2 1

   I would like to learn something from this topic.   3 2 1

   I know a lot about this topic.   3 2 1

   I would like to share my ideas about this topic with others.   3 2 1

   Total score: _____

5. Narrowed Topic _____

   The topic seems exciting or fun.   3 2 1

   I would like to learn something from this topic.   3 2 1

   I know a lot about this topic.   3 2 1

   I would like to share my ideas about this topic with others.   3 2 1

   Total score: _____

ACTIVITY 4: Teamwork

With a few of your classmates, identify which of your topics in Activity 3 scored the highest, and explain why you believe these topics would (or would not) motivate you to write and help you get the best results in your composition.

Gathering Ideas for Your Narrowed Topic

Once you have selected a narrowed topic for your composition, it is time to go deeper — into your brain, memory, imagination, and emotions — to discover everything you know, think, or feel about the topic. The more ideas and support you gather, the more you will have to say in your paragraph or essay.

This process of gathering ideas and support is generally known as **brainstorming**. Ideally, your brain will be a "storm" of creative energy and ideas.

CLUSTERING AND LISTING

Power Tip
Clustering is especially useful for students who are strong visual learners. **Listing** is often popular with verbal or mathematical learners.

As you brainstorm, you will want to write down your ideas as quickly and clearly as possible. Two popular methods for putting your ideas on paper are **clustering** and **listing**. With clustering, you use a series of bubbles (or circles) and connecting lines to record your ideas. With listing, you group your ideas in a series of short lists on the page. Clustering and listing will often reveal more layers to your topic.

Start by writing down your **narrowed topic** at the top of the page (for listing) or in a bubble in the center of the page (for clustering). Several obvious or **big ideas** related to your topic will usually pop into your head right away. Then, as you focus on each of these big ideas individually, some **related examples** should come to mind to support those ideas. Finally, if you focus on each of these examples one at a time, you may recall **specific details** to illustrate and support the examples.

The graphic below provides a guide to the brainstorming process. The color codes demonstrate the layers of your topic that get revealed in the process.

NARROWED TOPIC

BIG IDEAS

RELATED EXAMPLES

SPECIFIC DETAILS

Clustering

Clustering involves using a series of bubbles (circles) and connecting lines to record your thoughts. Clustering is especially helpful for students who have trouble organizing their ideas; the bubbles and lines help group related items together.

Here is an example of clustering using the color coding above. Notice that the narrowed topic, *Problems at my workplace*, is placed in a bubble in the center of the page, and the big ideas are connected to it. You will get more practice with clustering in Chapter 3. For now, take a look.

Next, focus on one big idea at a time and provide related examples for each:

Finally, focus on one example at a time, adding specific details to illustrate each example. When you reach this final level of support, remember to look back at your topic to stay focused.

ACTIVITY 5

Answer the following questions about the cluster immediately preceding this activity.

1. What are the three related examples of an unsafe environment?
   _____

2. What are causes of hazards in the stockroom? _____
   _____

3. What specific details are related to the floors? _____
   _____

4. How many specific details about the stairs are named? _____

ACTIVITY 6

Complete the cluster below. Follow these steps:

1. Write the name of your favorite college course in the center bubble.

2. Fill in the *green* bubbles with big ideas about why this is your favorite course.

3. Fill in the *purple* bubbles with examples to support your big ideas.

NOTE: You may leave some bubbles empty or add extra bubbles if necessary.

My favorite course:

ACTIVITY 7: Teamwork

With classmates, compare what you wrote in the bubbles for Activity 6. See if your classmates found good examples that you might be able to use in your cluster as well. Then, discuss whether you could add some yellow bubbles (specific details) to some of the purple bubbles.

Listing

Some students do not like using bubbles and lines to record and connect their ideas. Instead, they prefer to list ideas on paper or a computer screen. If you use this method, it is helpful to think of your list as *a series of short lists*. This will help you group related ideas together.

Here is an example of listing using color coding. Notice that the narrowed topic, *Problems at my workplace*, is placed at the top of the page, and the big ideas are listed below, with space between each one.

From this point, you can build your list by working on one big idea at a time. For each big idea, give yourself at least five minutes to list related examples and specific details.

Problems at My Workplace

Unsafe environment

hazardous stockroom — boxes on floor are a tripping risk, poor lighting

dangerous floors — slippery, messes not cleaned up

unsafe stairs — railings missing, loose treads

Bad communication

ACTIVITY 8

Use the listing technique to brainstorm ideas for one of the following topics.

- **Topic 1:** a perfect vacation
- **Topic 2:** responsibilities that you had as a child
- **Topic 3:** the most important person in your life right now
- **Topic 4:** stress factors in your life
- **Topic 5:** ways to relax

Clustering and listing are not always as neat as the previous examples suggest (see the examples on pp. 31–32). Because you will be writing quickly, expect to have to squeeze in ideas and bubbles where you don't have enough space. Also, don't expect your cluster or list to be perfectly organized.

When you use clustering or listing, keep the following points in mind:

- Although these methods can help you keep related ideas grouped together, **do not worry about organizing your thoughts** at this point.
- Ideas are likely to pop into your head rapidly and randomly. Just **let your thoughts flow**, write them down, and keep moving.
- **Do not worry if you repeat some ideas.** Repetition during brainstorming can help you identify ideas that are especially important for your topic.
- Try to fill up your page with thoughts, and **do not stop working** too soon. It is often during the last minutes of your brainstorming that you discover your most powerful ideas.

Now, take a look at some examples of clustering and listing from real students:

Clustering

Canal on the corner

old street w/ cracks

unclean street

background

blood stain on road

People talking in low voices

Crowd at edges of scene—looks like a reporter is taking notes

scattered newspapers

sirens

Human sufferings— A Tragedy

her mouth is a little open

he's wearing a blue jacket and white shirt that are stained with his blood

hand out, showing wedding ring

woman the girl who passed out

the dead man

his head turned to left

he doesn't have his shoes, but his socks are still on

he's lying down in the street, spread out

An older woman caught the woman who passed out

her right slipper is off her foot

She's leaning into the other woman's knee

he has thick black hair, not too short or too long

he's getting pale

his body is partly covered by newspapers from his chest to his feet

She's Asian

She's wearing a white shirt w/ polka dots and black slacks

her body looks limp

Listing

Rock climbing photo 6

Drive

test of manhood   weather change

Strenuous vacation   dark, winds, drizzling

China, Australia, Brazil

group of close friends   could not believe

falling down   midlife crisis

250-to-300-foot walk   they would look down

money at stake   lucky hat

extreme sports   he was respected and

Fathers all age ages   he was the one that was

at-home dads   scared to do things

Emotions   Senses

scared   * Smell = mist fresh air

fired up   ** sig sights = th friend the other end

CONTINUED >

nauseous   * Sound = deer, wind, animals,
~~evil~~   music, MP3
focus   * Taste = the last meal, vomit
sweating   touch = rope, ruff shirt wet, sweat
live or dead   6th sense = visualize himself
upset, how did I get into this?   somewhere else

lesson
no limits
challenge
better confidence
inspirational

From Activity 3, select one of your narrowed topics, perhaps one that received a high score in your own evaluation. On a blank sheet of paper, brainstorm on your topic using either clustering or listing.

QUESTIONING

Another brainstorming method is **questioning**. With this method, you use the five Ws of critical thinking: *Who? Where? When? What? Why?* These questions can help you get below the surface of your topic and look at it from different viewpoints.

- **Who** are the important people involved in my topic?
- **Where** did the events connected to my topic take place?
- **When** did the experiences in my topic occur?
- **What** important things happened in relation to my topic?
- **Why** did these things happen, and **why** did people act the way they did?

ACTIVITY 10: Teamwork

With classmates, form *W* questions for the following topics. (It is not necessary to answer the questions.) If one *W* does not fit a topic, just write "does not fit" in the space provided.

EXAMPLE: Discuss a powerful dream you've had.

Who? _were the people in my dream_

Where? _did the events in my dream take place_

When? _did the events in my dream happen_

What? _happened in my dream_

Why? _did these things happen_

1. Discuss a powerful memory from your childhood.

   Who? _____

   Where? _____

   When? _____

   What? _____

   Why? _____

2. Write about your "fantasy" job: the job you would have if anything were possible.

   Who? _____

   Where? _____

   When? _____

   What? _____

   Why? _____

Like clustering and listing, questioning can reveal layers of ideas in your topic. Here is an example. Notice that the *W* words serve as the big ideas:

NARROWED TOPIC   Problems at my workplace

1. BIG IDEA   *Who?*

   RELATED EXAMPLE   Maggie, shift leader

   SPECIFIC DETAILS   Lies, plays favorites

   RELATED EXAMPLE   Dan and Becky, co-workers

   SPECIFIC DETAILS   Arrive late and leave early, lazy, call in sick

   RELATED EXAMPLE   Tom, manager

   SPECIFIC DETAILS   Bad communication, won't listen

2. BIG IDEA   *Where?*

   RELATED EXAMPLE   In the stockroom and break room

   SPECIFIC DETAILS   Employees leave messes, smoke, gossip, hide out

RELATED EXAMPLE	On the sales floor
SPECIFIC DETAILS	Employees don't work together, not enough help, shift leader won't pitch in

3. | BIG IDEA | ***When?*** |
|---|---|
| RELATED EXAMPLE | During evening shifts |
| SPECIFIC DETAILS | Tom goes home, Maggie is in charge, only two salespeople |
| RELATED EXAMPLE | Started two months ago |
| SPECIFIC DETAILS | Since Maggie became shift leader |

4. | BIG IDEA | ***What?*** |
|---|---|
| RELATED EXAMPLE | Bad leadership |
| SPECIFIC DETAILS | Shift leaders play favorites, manager is bad communicator |
| RELATED EXAMPLE | Not enough help |
| SPECIFIC DETAILS | Only four workers on weekends, only one cashier, too many workers call in sick |

5. | BIG IDEA | ***Why?*** |
|---|---|
| RELATED EXAMPLE | The manager is not accountable |
| SPECIFIC DETAILS | He has no supervisor, he never admits he is wrong |
| RELATED EXAMPLE | Owners don't care |
| SPECIFIC DETAILS | They live in another state, they own other businesses |
| RELATED EXAMPLE | Employees don't care |
| SPECIFIC DETAILS | Only a part-time job, they are young and immature |

If you use this method for brainstorming, keep the following points in mind:

- You may use the five *W*s in any order you like, but try to **start with one that is easy for you**. Many students find it easy to begin with *who*, *where*, or *when*.

- **Sometimes, two *W*s will produce similar answers or ideas.** This is fine. Repetition can be useful because it can help you identify ideas that might be especially important for your topic.

- **Not all the questions work for every topic.** Generally, you should be able to use three or four of the *W*s for a given topic. If one *W* does not make sense for your topic, move on to the next *W*.

- **The five *W*s should jump-start your brainstorming**, but they should not restrict the free movement of your thinking. Once your brain warms up, you may decide to start clustering or listing instead.

ACTIVITY 11

Select one of your narrowed topics from Activity 3. (If your instructor agrees, you may continue working with the same narrowed topic that you used for Activity 9.) On a blank sheet of paper, go deeper into your narrowed topic using the **questioning** method illustrated on pages 33–34.

FREEWRITING

Another method of generating ideas is called **freewriting**. With freewriting, you simply write down your thoughts as you would in a diary or personal journal without worrying about grammar, spelling, or punctuation. Write down whatever comes to mind, even if it seems silly or disconnected at first. This process gives your mind time to warm up and may help you uncover more ideas than you thought you had on a topic.

Here is an example of freewriting on the narrowed topic, *Problems at my workplace.*

I can't believe how much I hate my job! On Saturday I came home from work dead tired, it was soooooooooo busy and we only had four workers on the sales floor. Of course, Maggie won't lift a finger to serve a customer because she has to "supervise" (which basically means talking on the phone to her boyfriend). At one point I slipped on some spilled liquid on the floor and twisted my ankle. And where were my wonderful co-workers? Off smoking in the stockroom which is not allowed anyway and it wasn't their break time. And Tom makes me so mad — he won't listen to anything I have to say, he never admits that he's wrong and his parents think that he's perfect. I am surprised that this business stays open but the owners (Tom's parents of course!) use it as a tax shelter or something funny like that. The whole thing is a big mess and I don't know if I can survive another weekend. . . . HELP!

tax shelter: a financial setup that reduces or eliminates taxes

The next step in freewriting is to read what you have written and circle two or three big ideas that you would like to explore further. Remember to select ideas that are closely connected to your topic (in this case, *Problems at my workplace*). Here is what this student circled in her original freewriting:

I can't believe how much I hate my job! On Saturday I came home from work dead tired, it was soooooooooo busy and we only had four workers on the sales floor. Of course, (Maggie won't lift a finger) to serve a customer because she has to "supervise" (which basically means talking on the phone to her boyfriend). At one point I slipped on some spilled liquid on the floor and twisted my ankle. And (where were my loyal co-workers?) Off smoking in the stockroom which is not allowed anyway and it wasn't their break time. (And Tom makes me so mad —) he won't listen to anything I have to say, he never admits that he's wrong and his parents think that he's perfect. I am surprised that this business stays open but the owners (Tom's parents of course!) use it as a tax shelter or something funny like that. The whole thing is a big mess and I don't know if I can survive another weekend. . . . HELP!

This student's next step is to select one of these ideas and freewrite about it for five minutes. Once again, the idea is to *just keep writing* until the time is up, even if the ideas go off the topic somewhat. Here is what the student wrote:

Maggie is such a pain! When Tom made her a shift leader she got a BIG ATTITUDE she also flirts with Tom and gets away with murder. Like I said, she spends more time on the phone with her boyfriend than she does helping us or assisting customers. She also lets Dan and Becky take longer breaks and come in late just because they are friends of hers. Of course, when I complained about this she told me to mind my own business which is sooooooooo unprofessional—not like she cares anyway. This is just a part-time job for her and she is only 18 years old. A shift leader is hardly president of the united states, but the power goes to her head. She never ASKS me to do anything she ORDERS me. She needs a reality check. . . .

Next, read what you have written and circle one or two of the most powerful ideas. Then, select one idea from *either* your first or second freewriting and freewrite about that idea for five minutes.

Continue this process of freewriting, reading, circling, and freewriting again until you have explored all your ideas about the topic or until you run out of time.

ACTIVITY 12

Using freewriting, discuss *someone you admire*. Follow these steps:

1. Freewrite for ten minutes on the topic.

2. Read what you wrote and circle two or three big ideas that you would like to develop.

3. Select ONE of those ideas and freewrite on it for five minutes.

4. Read what you wrote and circle one or two big ideas that you would like to develop.

5. Select ONE idea from *either* your first or second freewriting. Then, freewrite on this idea for five minutes.

6. If you wish, continue this exercise until you have fully explored your ideas on the topic.

If you use this method to brainstorm your topic, keep the following points in mind:

- **Freewriting generally requires more time** than the other methods, so it may not be ideal for timed writing assignments in class. Make sure you practice one of the other methods as a backup for timed writing assignments.

- **Freewriting does not count as a draft of your composition.** After you complete your freewriting activity, you will still need to write an outline for your composition and *then* write your first draft.
- **You might start with freewriting to warm up your brain,** then switch to clustering or listing when the ideas start to come faster.

ACTIVITY 13

Select one of your narrowed topics from Activity 3. (Do not select a topic that you have already used in a previous exercise.) On a blank sheet of paper, generate more ideas for your narrowed topic using the **freewriting** method illustrated above.

BRINGING IT ALL TOGETHER:
Developing a Topic

In this chapter, you have learned about developing college writing topics — how to recognize them, narrow them, and select ones that will work well for you. Confirm your knowledge by filling in the blank spaces in the following sentences. If you need help, review the pages listed after each sentence.

✔ Topics that give students a lot of choice in what to write about are called _____ topics. Topics that give students very little choice in what to write about are called _____ topics. Topics that give students a moderate amount of choice — not a lot or a little — are called _____ topics. (page 21)

✔ When narrowing a topic for a writing assignment, you should consider the required length of the assignment. Four common length requirements for college writing are: 1) _____, 2) _____ _____, 3) _____, and 4) _____ _____. (page 22)

✔ When selecting a writing topic, you should select one that will motivate you to write and help you get the best results. To determine which topic will work well for you, you can ask four questions. These questions are: 1) _____, 2) _____ _____, 3) _____, and 4) _____ _____ (page 24)

CONTINUED >

✔ When gathering more ideas for a narrowed topic, you can use any of four methods for getting your ideas down on paper. These methods are: 1) _____, 2) _____, 3) _____, and 4) _____. (pages 26, 32, and 35)

✔ Brainstorming often reveals more layers to your topic. These layers are: 1) _____, 2) _____, 3) _____, and 4) _____. (page 26)

✔ When going deeper into a narrowed topic, you may repeat ideas from time to time. Repetition during brainstorming is not bad. Instead, it can help you _____. (page 30)

✔ During brainstorming, your most powerful ideas may come forth in _____. For this reason, it is important to take your time and be patient with the brainstorming process. (page 30)

✔ If you use freewriting as your preferred brainstorming method, it is important to remember that your freewriting is NOT a _____ for your essay. (page 37)

CHAPTER 3

Organizing Your Ideas

Before you read this chapter, it's a good idea to test your understanding of strategies for organizing your ideas. You may know more than you think.

For each question, select all the answers that apply.

WHAT DO YOU KNOW?

1. **Which of the following words expresses a *big idea*?**
   (*Hint:* The other words are *related examples*.)

   ___ ostrich
   ___ pigeon
   ___ birds
   ___ canary

2. **When you are arranging a list of items, which ones will generally come first?**

   ___ big ideas
   ___ related examples

3. **Which one of the following strategies requires you to recognize an item that does *not* fit with other items in a group?**

   ___ grouping
   ___ eliminating
   ___ ordering

4. **Which of the following sentences are *related examples*?**
   (*Hint:* The other item is a big idea.)

   ___ My counselor gave me a checklist of required courses.
   ___ My counselor recommended several excellent instructors.
   ___ My counselor helped me prepare for academic success.
   ___ My counselor showed me how to organize my schedule.

5. **Which of the following items does not fit with the group below?**

   ___ applying for financial aid
   ___ meeting with an academic counselor
   ___ buying a bus pass
   ___ purchasing textbooks

Organizing Basics

In Chapter 2, you learned how to brainstorm for a topic. Now, you'll learn how to organize ideas in preparation for developing an effective outline. Organizing involves several strategies, the most common of which are

- **ordering:** arranging your ideas in a logical way
- **grouping:** putting related ideas together
- **eliminating:** removing ideas that are not related to your topic

Often, doing these activities is like solving a puzzle, and it can be a lot of fun. The more you practice them, the more your organizing skills will improve.

ORDERING

The first skill to practice is **ordering**. To order your ideas effectively, you will need to be able to recognize the difference between **big ideas** and **related examples**. Big ideas usually come first, and they are followed by related examples. Look at the following list:

jobs
clerk
engineer
cook

The word *jobs* expresses a big idea because there are many types of jobs. The words *clerk, engineer,* and *cook* are examples of jobs.

Ordering Single-Word Items

As shown in the previous example, a *single word* can express either a big idea or a related example. Now, take a look at the following lists and decide which one is ordered correctly:

carrots	**vegetables**
broccoli	tomatoes
vegetables	carrots
tomatoes	broccoli

The second list is correct: The word *vegetables* expresses a big idea because there are many types of vegetables. The words *broccoli, tomatoes,* and *carrots* are examples of vegetables.

ACTIVITY 1

Rewrite each of the following lists, putting the *big idea* first. If a list is correct as is, write "OK" on the first line.

EXAMPLE: peanuts   *nuts*

cashews   *peanuts*

nuts   *cashews*

almonds   *almonds*

1. hamster _____

cat _____

pet _____

dog _____

2. shirt _____

clothes _____

socks _____

tie _____

3. rain _____

snow _____

weather _____

thunder _____

4. wires _____

electrical _____

plug _____

fuse _____

5. transportation _____

bicycle _____

helicopter _____

automobile _____

6. church _____

apartment _____

house _____

building _____

Power Tip
While working through the activities in this chapter, use a dictionary to look up the meaning of any words you do not recognize. Doing so will help you complete the activities successfully and build your vocabulary at the same time.

If you used clustering—putting related ideas in bubbles—to generate ideas, you will need to order your ideas in the same way. The following activity will give you practice with moving items from clusters to lists. (For more on clustering, see Chapter 2.)

ACTIVITY 2

Study the clusters below, and then draw lines from the *big idea* to the related examples. Next, move the items to a list, putting the big idea first.

EXAMPLE:

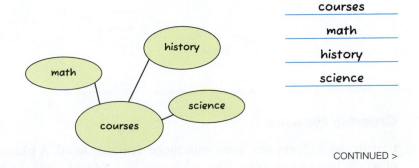

_____ *courses*

_____ *math*

_____ *history*

_____ *science*

CONTINUED >

1.

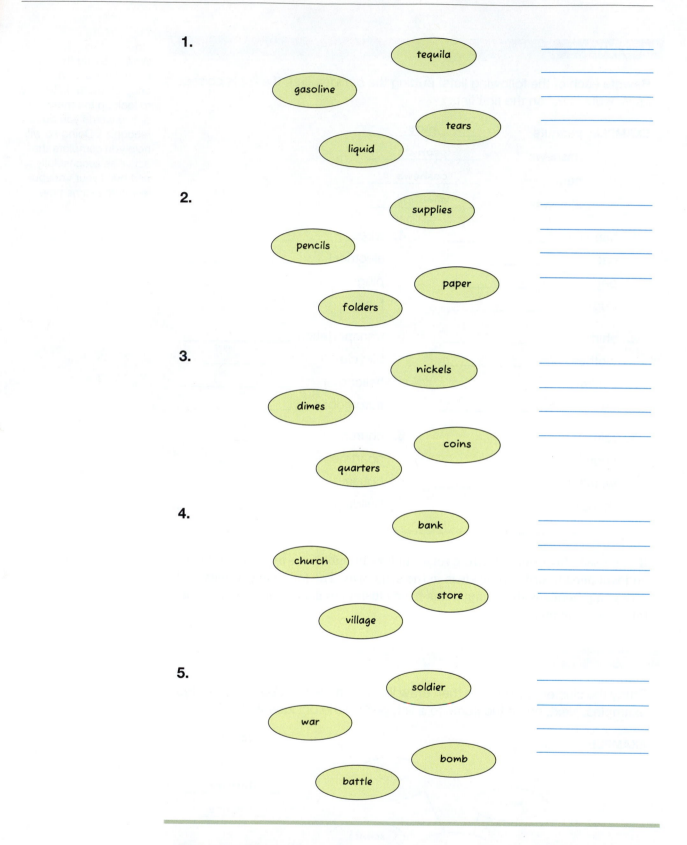

tequila

gasoline

tears

liquid

_____
_____
_____
_____

2.

supplies

pencils

paper

folders

_____
_____
_____
_____

3.

nickels

dimes

coins

quarters

_____
_____
_____
_____

4.

bank

church

store

village

_____
_____
_____
_____

5.

soldier

war

bomb

battle

_____
_____
_____
_____

Ordering Phrases

Usually, we express our ideas with more than one word. A **phrase** is a group of words that can express either a *big idea* or a *related example*. For example, the phrase *healthy food* expresses a big idea because there are many types of healthy food. The phrases *organic fruits and vegetables, whole-grain breads and cereals,* and *low-fat milk and cheese* are each an example of healthy food.

ACTIVITY 3

Rewrite each of the following lists, putting the *big idea* first. If a list is correct as is, write "OK" on the first line.

EXAMPLE: look in the want ads

write a résumé

look for a job

prepare for interviews

____look for a job____

___look in the want ads___

_____write a résumé_____

___prepare for interviews___

1. ice cream sundae _____

   cherry snow cone _____

   cold desserts _____

   frozen banana _____

2. build a sand castle _____

   lie in the sun _____

   put on lotion _____

   day at the beach _____

3. dust furniture _____

   vacuum carpets _____

   wash the floor _____

   household chores _____

4. my dream wedding _____

   three-layer cake _____

   lots of friends and family _____

   great music _____

5. learning procedures _____

   meeting co-workers _____

   starting a new job _____

   filling out forms _____

6. reread chapters _____

   review material with
   classmates _____

   review notes _____

   study for a test _____

ACTIVITY 4

In clustering, we often write *phrases* in cluster bubbles. In the following exercise, study the clusters, and then draw lines from the *big idea* phrases to the related examples. Next, move the phrases from the bubbles to a list, putting the big idea first.

EXAMPLE:

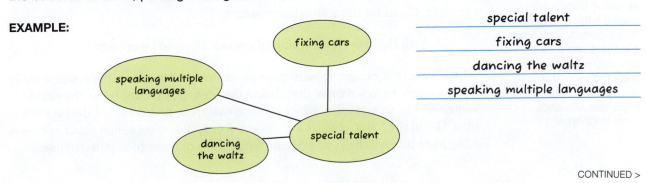

_____special talent_____

_____fixing cars_____

____dancing the waltz____

__speaking multiple languages__

CONTINUED >

1.

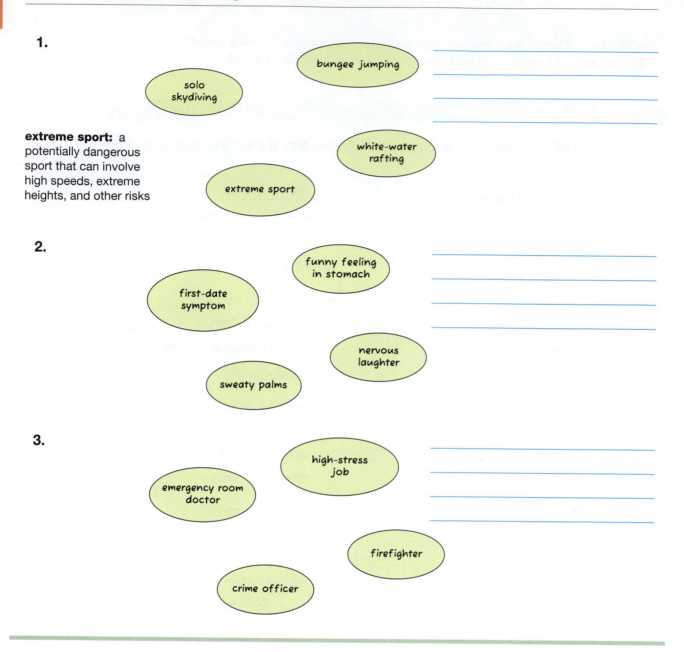

extreme sport: a potentially dangerous sport that can involve high speeds, extreme heights, and other risks

solo skydiving

bungee jumping

white-water rafting

extreme sport

2.

funny feeling in stomach

first-date symptom

nervous laughter

sweaty palms

3.

high-stress job

emergency room doctor

firefighter

crime officer

Ordering Sentences

Sometimes, when we brainstorm, we use a **complete sentence** to express our ideas. A complete sentence can express either a *big idea* or a *related example*. Consider the following sentence:

Making Halloween costumes allows children to be creative.

When we use a complete sentence to express a big idea, there will usually be *two or more key words* that define the idea. For example, in the previous sentence, the words *making, costumes, children,* and *creative* define the big idea. Get in the habit of marking the key words in any sentence that expresses a big idea; this will help you decide what types of examples you can use.

Now, here are some related examples of how *making costumes* allows *children* to be *creative*:

> Children can be any character they want to be.
> They can use any materials they want to: scrap paper, glue, paint.
> They can enter imaginary worlds while wearing their costumes.

Each sentence expresses an example of creativity related to making costumes. Notice also that each sentence contains *two or more key words* that define the example (such as *be any character they want to be . . . use any materials they want to . . . enter imaginary worlds*). So, whether a sentence expresses a big idea or a related example, there will always be two or more key words that define the meaning of the sentence.

ACTIVITY 5: Teamwork

Working with one or two classmates, identify and underline the *key words* that define the *big idea* in each sentence. Each sentence will have at least two key words.

EXAMPLE: It's possible to have a <u>fun</u> yet <u>inexpensive</u> <u>vacation</u>.

1. College can be a rewarding experience.
2. Camping has become an expensive form of recreation.
3. Good communication skills can be learned.
4. Learning geometry requires a lot of memorization.
5. Artificial sweeteners often have a bitter taste.

ACTIVITY 6

Rewrite each of the following sets of sentences, putting the *big idea* first. The *related examples* can be in any order. Begin with your favorite example and end with your least favorite; or, begin with your least favorite example and end with your favorite.

EXAMPLE: It can save money.

It can help you eat nutritiously.

Cooking is a good skill to have.

It's satisfying for yourself and others.

Cooking is a good skill to have.

It can help you eat nutritiously.

It can save money.

It's satisfying for yourself and others.

Power Tip

If you have trouble identifying the big idea, remember to mark the *key words* in each sentence. See page 44 for more on key words.

CONTINUED >

1. I was afraid my parachute would not open.

   Stepping out of the plane took my breath away.

   Skydiving was a frightening experience.

   Free-falling made my heart stop.

2. The pay and benefits were poor.

   My old job was not a good one.

   My hours changed every week.

   I wasn't learning many new skills.

3. College offers social and work connections.

   Education improves one's self-esteem.

   Degree holders earn better salaries.

   Getting a college degree is beneficial.

4. College students run up credit card debt paying for books and fees.

   College students experience financial difficulties due to the high cost of education.

   College students often borrow money from friends and family.

   College students get big government loans that are hard to pay back.

5. Responsible dating requires both partners to share expenses.

   Responsible dating requires honest communication.

   Responsible dating offers a more mature approach to dating.

   Responsible dating takes into consideration both persons' tastes and interests.

GROUPING

The second skill that is useful for organizing your ideas is **grouping**. To group ideas effectively, you will need to be able to recognize items that are *related to one another.* Often, when we brainstorm, our ideas come to us in random order. When we organize these ideas, we need to sort through them and put them in distinct groups.

Grouping Single-Word Items

Let's begin with lists of single-word items that need to be put in separate groups. Let's see how one group of items could be sorted into two groups.

Items to be grouped: piano / rock / jazz / drums / hip-hop / guitar

Group 1: musical instruments
    piano
    drums
    guitar

Group 2: types of music
    rock
    jazz
    hip-hop

Notice that as you group items, you begin to develop a sense of the *big idea* that connects the items to one another. For example, the big idea that connects the items in group 1 is *musical instruments*; the big idea that connects the items in group 2 is *types of music.*

ACTIVITY 7

Rearrange each of the following sets of items into separate groups, following these steps:

- At first, leave the first lines after "Big Idea" blank.
- Fill in the other lines with the items that should go in each group, making sure to keep related items together.
- Think of a big idea that connects the items in each group and write it on the first line, following the example above.

1. wine / cola / tea / beer / champagne / coffee

Group 1:

Big Idea: _____

Examples: _____

_____

_____

Group 2:

Big Idea: _____

Examples: _____

_____

_____

CONTINUED >

2. pen / notebook / diary / highlighter / crayon / calendar

Group 1:   **Group 2:**

Big Idea: _____   **Big Idea:** _____

Examples: _____   **Examples:** _____

_____   _____

_____   _____

3. brunette / redhead / eyebrows / mustache / blonde / sideburns

Group 1:   **Group 2:**

Big Idea: _____   **Big Idea:** _____

Examples: _____   **Examples:** _____

_____   _____

_____   _____

4. accountant / landscaper / banker / ranger / secretary / lifeguard

Group 1:   **Group 2:**

Big Idea: _____   **Big Idea:** _____

Examples: _____   **Examples:** _____

_____   _____

_____   _____

5. rabbit / snake / chipmunk / lizard / frog / squirrel

Group 1:   **Group 2:**

Big Idea: _____   **Big Idea:** _____

Examples: _____   **Examples:** _____

_____   _____

_____   _____

ACTIVITY 8: Teamwork

Exchange your answers to Activity 7 with a classmate. Did you sort any of the items differently? How do your big ideas for each group compare? Can you find any ways to refine or improve your big ideas?

Grouping Phrases

As you learned in Chapter 2, clustering is a method that helps us group related ideas. The bubbles and lines are a visual reminder to keep related ideas in separate groups or *clusters*. Often, clusters express ideas in *phrases.* Here is an example of a small clustering that keeps related phrases in separate groups:

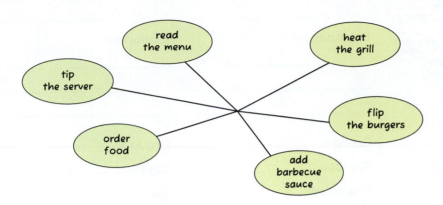

Group 1: eating in a restaurant
read the menu
order food
tip the server

Group 2: grilling burgers
heat the grill
flip the burgers
add barbecue sauce

Lists can also be used to group phrases, as shown in the example below the cluster. Notice that a *big idea* connects the items in each group.

Keep in mind that clusters are rarely this simple and neat. As we move from a cluster to a list (and to an outline), we have to be on the lookout for items that are incorrectly grouped together.

ACTIVITY 9

Move the items from each of the following clusters into separate groups, *being careful of items that are clustered incorrectly.* Follow these steps:

- At first, leave the line after "Group 1" and "Group 2" blank.
- Fill in the other lines with the items that should go in each group, making sure to keep related items together.
- Think of a *big idea* that connects the items in each group and write it on the first line.

EXAMPLE:

scraping plates

heating stove

washing dishes

clearing table

setting table

cooking meal

Group 1:

Big Idea: before-dinner tasks

Examples:

setting table

heating stove

cooking meal

Group 2:

Big Idea: after-dinner tasks

Examples:

clearing table

scraping plates

washing dishes

CONTINUED >

1.

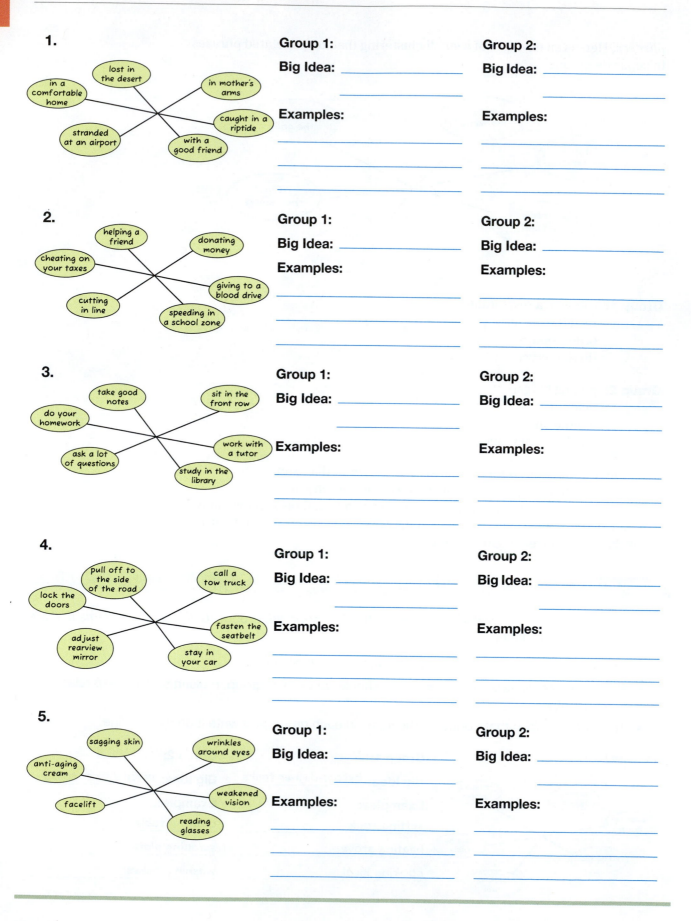

Group 1:

Big Idea: _____

_____

Examples:

_____

_____

_____

_____

Group 2:

Big Idea: _____

_____

Examples:

_____

_____

_____

_____

2.

Group 1:

Big Idea: _____

Examples:

_____

_____

_____

Group 2:

Big Idea: _____

Examples:

_____

_____

_____

3.

Group 1:

Big Idea: _____

_____

Examples:

_____

_____

_____

_____

Group 2:

Big Idea: _____

_____

Examples:

_____

_____

_____

_____

4.

Group 1:

Big Idea: _____

_____

Examples:

_____

_____

_____

Group 2:

Big Idea: _____

_____

Examples:

_____

_____

_____

5.

Group 1:

Big Idea: _____

_____

Examples:

_____

_____

_____

Group 2:

Big Idea: _____

_____

Examples:

_____

_____

_____

ACTIVITY 10: Teamwork

Exchange your answers to Activity 9 with a classmate. Did you sort any of the items differently? How do your big ideas for each group compare? Can you find any ways to refine or improve your big ideas?

Grouping Sentences

Like words and phrases, sentences can also be grouped together by topic. To come up with a *big idea* to connect sentence groups, it's a good idea to circle the key words in the sentences and ask yourself how these words are related. (For more on key words, see page 44.)

ACTIVITY 11: Teamwork

Move the sentences from each of the following lists into separate groups, following these steps:

- At first, leave the lines after "Big Idea" blank.
- Fill in the other lines with the sentences that should go in each group, making sure to keep related sentences together.
- Think of a *big idea* that connects the items in each group and write it on the first line, using a complete sentence. (To get this idea, you might want to circle key words in the sentences and ask yourself how these words are related.)

EXAMPLE: Roberta planted flowers in front of the house.

Del cleaned out the gutters.

Manuel painted the living room.

Tamsin cut the grass and swept the porch.

Pat polished the floors until they sparkled.

Doug dusted and cleaned the bathrooms.

Group 1:

Big Idea: Everyone helped with outside chores to make the house look great.

Examples:

Roberta planted flowers in front of the house.

Del cleaned out the gutters.

Tamsin cut the grass and swept the porch.

Group 2:

Big Idea: Everyone helped with inside chores to make the house look great.

Examples:

Manuel painted the living room.

Pat polished the floors until they sparkled.

Doug dusted and cleaned the bathrooms.

1. Medical professionals often work long hours with few breaks.

   Nurses, medical assistants, and other health professionals are in high demand.

   Medical work can be physically and emotionally tiring.

CONTINUED >

Health professionals get the satisfaction of helping others.

Health workers are under pressure to care for many patients.

Starting salaries for nurses can approach $40,000.

Group 1:   **Group 2:**

Big Idea: _____   **Big Idea:** _____

_____   _____

Examples: **Examples:**

_____   _____

_____   _____

_____   _____

_____   _____

_____   _____

_____   _____

2. Many parents allow their children to eat sweetened cereals.

Schools often serve items like french fries and corn dogs for lunch.

More daycare centers are serving fresh fruit for snacks.

Saturday morning commercials advertise mostly junk foods.

Media campaigns are promoting healthy food choices.

The local high school has removed the soda vending machines.

Group 1:   **Group 2:**

Big Idea: _____   **Big Idea:** _____

_____   _____

_____   _____

Examples: **Examples:**

_____   _____

_____   _____

_____   _____

_____   _____

_____   _____

_____   _____

3. Rachel sits slumped in class.

When meeting strangers, Sarah looks them directly in the eye.

Juan usually crosses his arms when he talks to others.

Michael leans forward toward the person who is talking.

At school, Jessica sits up straight and tall at her desk.

Robert lowers his eyes when girls approach him.

Group 1:   **Group 2:**

Big Idea: _____   **Big Idea:** _____

_____   _____

Examples: **Examples:**

_____   _____

_____   _____

_____   _____

_____   _____

_____   _____

_____

ELIMINATING

One of the most important skills you will need for organizing your ideas is **eliminating**. When we brainstorm, we write down all the ideas that come to mind, without judging their individual value. However, as you move from brainstorming to outlining, you will need to select your best ideas (those that are most appropriate for the topic) and eliminate those that are weak (ideas that do not fit the topic especially well). Generally, you will want to look for groups of related items that clearly support the topic and eliminate isolated items that do not fit. With practice, your ability to recognize and eliminate these items will improve.

Eliminating Single-Word Items

Again, let's start with single-word items. You can see that most of the following words are related; however, one of the words is not. Can you find the unrelated item?

> forgiveness
> understanding
> impatience
> humor

Forgiveness, understanding, and humor are all *positive* qualities, ones that most of us would like a friend or partner to have. Impatience, a *negative* quality, doesn't fit, so we could eliminate it.

ACTIVITY 12

For each group of words below, do the following:

- Cross out the item that does not fit.
- For the remaining items, think of a *big idea* that connects them and write it on the first line of the new list.
- Add the remaining items to the list, using an order of your choice.

EXAMPLE: Big Idea: _____categories of movies_____

comedy _____comedy_____

action _____action_____

horror _____horror_____

~~theaters~~

1. Big Idea: _____

tornado _____

hurricane _____

flood _____

damage

2. Big Idea: _____

diamond _____

necklace _____

earring _____

bracelet

3. Big Idea: _____

teaching _____

firefighting _____

farming _____

danger

4. Big Idea: _____

organs _____

mind _____

muscles _____

bones

5. Big Idea: _____

treadmill _____

weights _____

aerobics _____

bicycle

6. Big Idea: _____

picture _____

print _____

painting _____

frame

ACTIVITY 13: Teamwork

Exchange your answers to Activity 12 with a classmate. Did your choices about what items to eliminate vary in any cases? If so, see if you can determine which answer is correct and why. Can you find any ways to refine or improve your big ideas?

Eliminating Phrases

Just as you need to eliminate words from your brainstorming that do not fit your topic, you must eliminate unrelated phrases. The following activity will give you practice with this skill.

ACTIVITY 14

For each cluster, do the following:

- Cross out the item that does not fit.
- For the remaining items, think of a *big idea* that connects them and write it on the first line.
- Add the remaining items to the list, using an order of your choice.

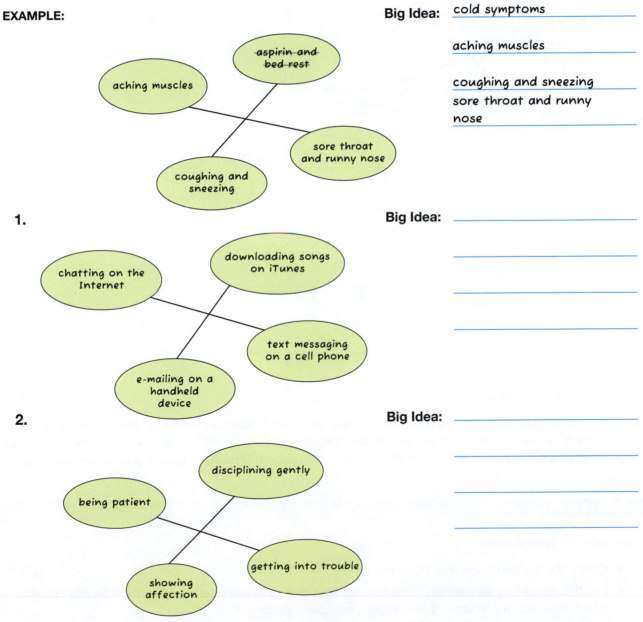

EXAMPLE:

aspirin and bed rest

aching muscles

sore throat and runny nose

coughing and sneezing

Big Idea: cold symptoms

aching muscles

coughing and sneezing
sore throat and runny nose

1.

chatting on the Internet

downloading songs on iTunes

text messaging on a cell phone

e-mailing on a handheld device

Big Idea: _____

_____

_____

_____

2.

being patient

disciplining gently

getting into trouble

showing affection

Big Idea: _____

_____

_____

_____

CONTINUED >

3.

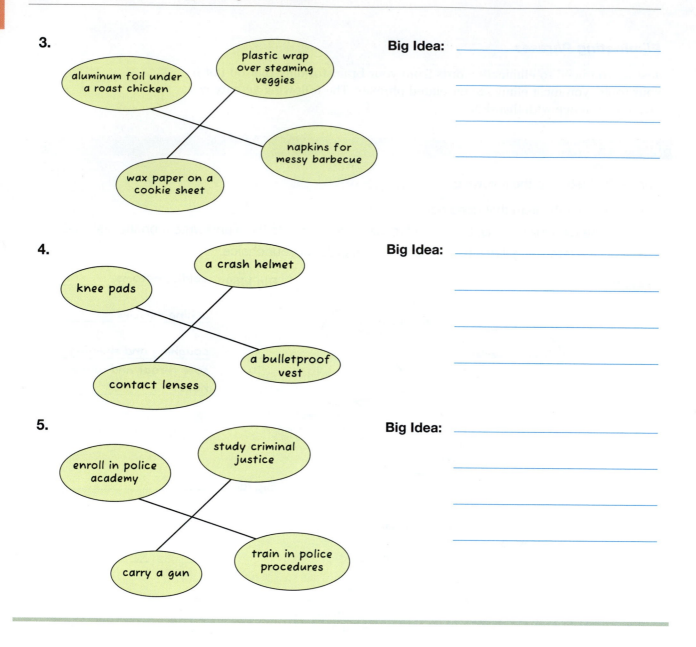

Big Idea: _____

_____

_____

_____

4.

Big Idea: _____

_____

_____

_____

5.

Big Idea: _____

_____

_____

_____

Eliminating Sentences

Like words and phrases that do not fit your topic, irrelevant sentences should also be eliminated. To come up with a *big idea* to connect the remaining sentences, it's a good practice to circle the key words in the sentences and ask yourself how these words are related. (For more on key words, see page 44.)

ACTIVITY 15

For each list, do the following:

- Cross out the sentence that does not fit.
- For the remaining sentences, think of a *big idea* that connects them and write it on the first line of the new list. Try to state this idea as a complete sentence.
- Add the remaining sentences to the list, using an order of your choice.

EXAMPLE: Kids of every age need support.

~~Grandparents may babysit.~~

Teens test parents' limits.

Babies are totally dependent.

Big Idea: Parenting can be
challenging.

Babies are totally dependent.

Teens test parents' limits.

Kids of every age need support.

1. My mom hasn't had the flu in
two years.

I drink gallons of water and
sweat out the virus.

My dad takes large doses
of vitamin C.

My sister goes straight to bed
and rests.

Big Idea: _____

_____

_____

_____

_____

2. Ask for a lower credit-card
interest rate.

Shop only during sales.

Put all debt on the lowest-interest
credit card.

Make more than the minimum
payment each month.

Big Idea: _____

_____

_____

_____

_____

_____

interest: a charge for
borrowing money that is
typically a percentage of
the amount borrowed

3. Oil from roads contaminates
water supplies.

Emissions from cars and factories
trap heat and harm air quality.

Garbage landfills leak harmful
chemicals.

Recycling has only limited benefits.

Big Idea: _____

_____

_____

_____

_____

4. Open-air stadiums give concerts
a free, natural feeling.

The lighting at a concert
can set a certain mood.

The ticket price of a concert
is important.

A good sound system involves
listeners in the music.

Big Idea: _____

_____

_____

_____

_____

CONTINUED >

5. Make a list of your accomplishments at work.

Big Idea: _____

_____

Know what raise is reasonable based on your accomplishments.

_____

_____

File your federal tax return on time.

_____

Set up a meeting to speak to your employer.

_____

_____

_____

COMBINING STRATEGIES

In most writing situations, you will need to use all the organizing strategies (ordering, grouping, and eliminating) at the same time. In the following activities, you will be required to

1. **group** related items into separate groups
2. **order** the items in each group by putting the big idea first and the related examples in an order of your choice
3. **eliminate** any items that do not fit in either group

ACTIVITY 16

For each list that follows, you will be given *one* of the big ideas. For each list, do the following:

- Determine the other big idea.
- For each group, write the big idea on the first line.
- Add the examples under the appropriate big idea, eliminating any items that do not fit.

EXAMPLE: Web sites / camping / cruise / maps / resort / travel agent / vacations / binoculars

Group 1:

Big Idea: vacations

Examples: resort

cruise

camping

Group 2:

Big Idea: tools for planning

Examples: travel agent

Web sites

maps

Eliminate one item: binoculars

1. toothpaste / deodorant / razor / grooming tool / teeth / toothbrush / shampoo / comb

    Group 1:   **Group 2:**

    Big Idea: _grooming tool_   **Big Idea:** _____

    Examples: _____   **Examples:** _____

              _____   _____

              _____   _____

    Eliminate one item: _____

2. lunch / restaurant / appetizer / dessert / breakfast / dinner / courses / main course

    Group 1:   **Group 2:**

    Big Idea: _courses_   **Big Idea:** _____

    Examples: _____   **Examples:** _____

              _____   _____

              _____   _____

    Eliminate one item: _____

3. rent / salary / income / gift certificate / food / lottery winnings / bank / utilities

    Group 1:   **Group 2:**

    Big Idea: _income_   **Big Idea:** _____

    Examples: _____   **Examples:** _____

              _____   _____

              _____   _____

    Eliminate one item: _____

4. blood pressure / heart attack / ambulance / stroke / pulse / medical technician / seizure / breathing rate / vital signs (signs of life) / body temperature / concussion

    Group 1:   **Group 2:**

    Big Idea: _vital signs (signs of life)_   **Big Idea:** _____

    Examples: _____   **Examples:** _____

              _____   _____

              _____   _____

    Eliminate two items: _____

CONTINUED >

5. infancy / friendship / childhood / parent / life stages / family history / lover / adulthood / friend / adolescence / spouse

Group 1:

Big Idea: _life stages_

Examples: _____

_____

_____

_____

Group 2:

Big Idea: _____

Examples: _____

_____

_____

_____

Eliminate two items: _____

ACTIVITY 17: Teamwork

Each of the following items consists of two joined clusters. In each cluster, the *big idea* appears in a central (green) bubble. Work with one or two classmates to do the following:

- For each group, write the big idea on the first line.
- Add the related examples under each big idea, eliminating any items that do not fit.
- Watch out for items that are clustered incorrectly.

EXAMPLE:

Group 1:

Big Idea: _officers_

Examples: _colonel_

lieutenant

captain

major

Group 2:

Big Idea: _actions_

Examples: _observe enemy_

advance

fire

retreat

Eliminate one item: _tank_

1.

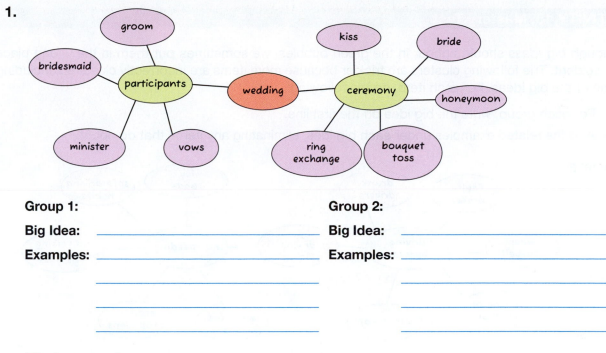

Group 1:

Big Idea: _____

Examples: _____

_____

_____

_____

Group 2:

Big Idea: _____

Examples: _____

_____

_____

_____

Eliminate one item: _____

2.

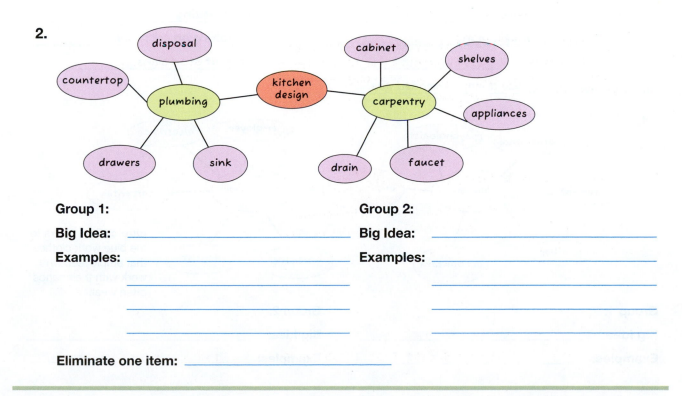

Group 1:

Big Idea: _____

Examples: _____

_____

_____

_____

Group 2:

Big Idea: _____

Examples: _____

_____

_____

_____

Eliminate one item: _____

ACTIVITY 18: Mastery Test

Although *big ideas* should appear in the green bubbles, we sometimes put them in the wrong place by accident. The following clusters are trickier because more items are incorrectly clustered, including some of the big ideas. For each item, do the following:

- For each group, write the big idea on the first line.
- Add the related examples under each big idea, eliminating any items that do not fit.

EXAMPLE:

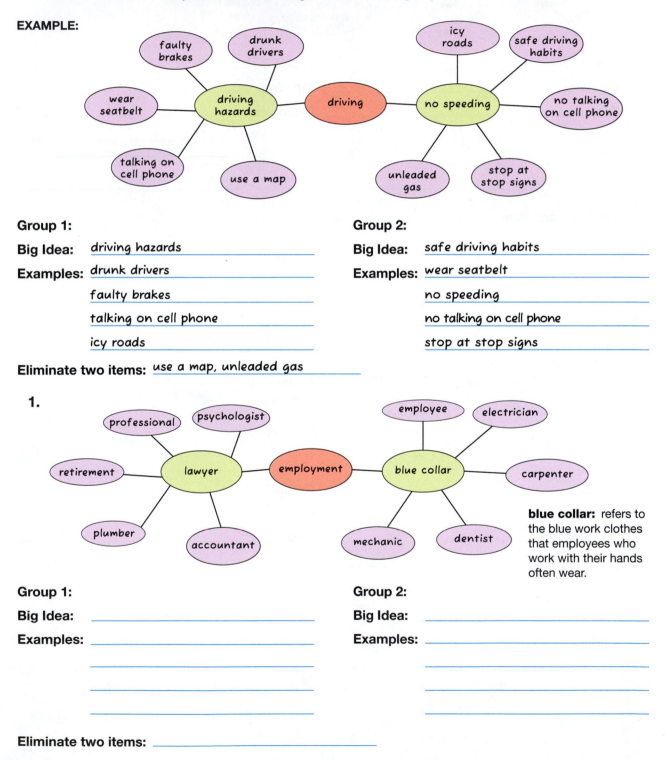

Group 1:

Big Idea: driving hazards

Examples: drunk drivers

faulty brakes

talking on cell phone

icy roads

Eliminate two items: use a map, unleaded gas

Group 2:

Big Idea: safe driving habits

Examples: wear seatbelt

no speeding

no talking on cell phone

stop at stop signs

1.

blue collar: refers to the blue work clothes that employees who work with their hands often wear.

Group 1:

Big Idea: _____

Examples: _____

_____

_____

_____

Group 2:

Big Idea: _____

Examples: _____

_____

_____

_____

Eliminate two items: _____

2.

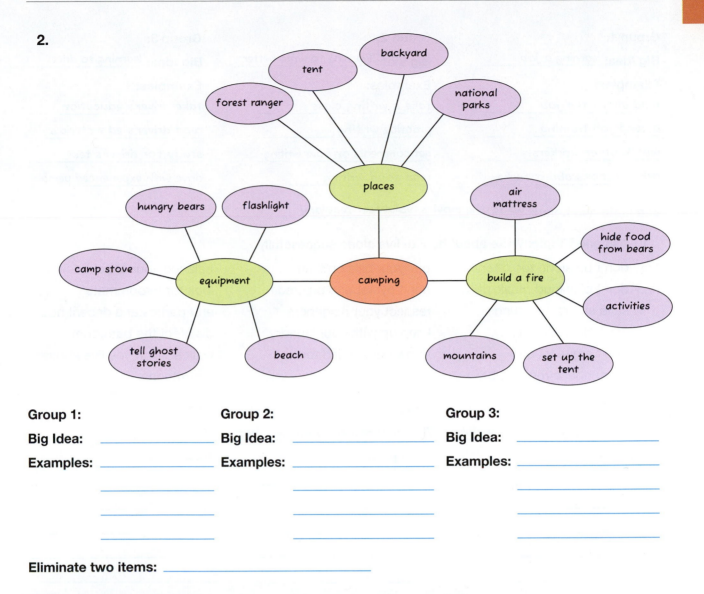

Group 1:

Big Idea: _____

Examples: _____
_____
_____
_____

Group 2:

Big Idea: _____

Examples: _____
_____
_____
_____

Group 3:

Big Idea: _____

Examples: _____
_____
_____
_____

Eliminate two items: _____

ACTIVITY 19: Mastery Test

In this activity, you will need to form three ordered lists from three scrambled lists. Each list should begin with a *big idea*. You will be given *two* of the big ideas. For each set of lists, do the following:

- Determine the third big idea.
- For each group, write the big idea on the first line.
- Add the related examples under each big idea, eliminating any items that do not fit.

EXAMPLE: **Assigned Topic: Discuss how you learn important skills.**

go to the movies	study for driver's test	drive with experienced person
attend job training	practice writing	read about the job
take driver's education	learning a job	learning to write better
read good writing	watch other workers	get comments on your writing
ask questions about tasks	take a writing class	
read driver's ed materials	volunteer regularly	

CONTINUED >

Group 1:

Big Idea: learning a job

Examples:

read about the job

attend job training

watch other workers

ask questions about tasks

Group 2:

Big Idea: learning to write better

Examples:

take a writing class

practice writing

get comments on your writing

read good writing

Group 3:

Big Idea: learning to drive

Examples:

take driver's education

read driver's ed materials

study for driver's test

drive with experienced person

Eliminate two items: go to the movies, volunteer regularly

1. **Assigned Topic: Write about how to live alone successfully.**

don't be alone too often	pay your bills on time	balance your checkbook
don't play loud music	don't overspend on credit	look for a roommate
save emergency funds	respect your neighbors	end parties at a decent hour
wash dishes regularly	keep up with your laundry	disinfect the bathroom
don't argue loudly	throw out spoiled food	walk softly if you live above
clean house responsibly		someone

Group 1:

Big Idea: clean house responsibly

Examples:

_____

_____

_____

_____

_____

Group 2:

Big Idea: respect your neighbors

Examples:

_____

_____

_____

_____

_____

Group 3:

Big Idea: _____

Examples:

_____

_____

_____

_____

_____

Eliminate two items: _____

2. **Assigned Topic: Discuss the benefits of managing your life online.**

e-mail friends	improve your virus protection	find your grades
visit celebrity Web sites	find movie schedules	get free Web access
download songs	research your papers	join live chat rooms
socializing online	exchange personal photos	play video games
e-mail your teachers	register for classes	
try Internet dating	finding entertainment options online	

Group 1:

Big Idea: socializing online

Examples:

_____

_____

Group 2:

Big Idea: finding entertainment options online

Examples:

_____

_____

Group 3:

Big Idea: _____

_____

Examples:

_____

_____

_____

_____   _____   _____

_____   _____   _____

Eliminate two items: _____

ACTIVITY 20

Go back to one of the clusters or lists that you generated for Chapter 2 and do the following:

- Make sure that the ideas are *grouped* in a way that makes sense. (You can write your changes on the cluster or list, or transfer your work to a fresh piece of paper.)
- Make sure that there is a *big idea* that connects the items in each group.
- Make sure that the ideas are *ordered* in a way that makes sense, especially if you are working with a list.
- *Eliminate* any items that do not fit your topic.

BRINGING IT ALL TOGETHER:
Organizing Your Ideas

In this chapter, you have studied several strategies for organizing your ideas. Confirm your knowledge by filling in the blank spaces in the following sentences. If you need help, review the pages listed after each sentence.

✔ Organizing your ideas involves three strategies. These strategies are _____, _____, and _____. (page 40)

✔ The strategy that requires you to distinguish big ideas from related examples is _____. When arranging a list of items, the _____ usually comes first. (page 40)

✔ The strategy that requires you to identify related items is called _____. Once you have identified related items, you sometimes have to develop a _____ to show how these items are related. (page 47)

✔ The strategy that requires you to identify items that do not fit is called _____. In brainstorming, you may write down quite a few items that will not fit when you move to your outline; therefore, these items should be _____. (page 53)

CHAPTER 4
Outlining Your Paragraph

Before you read this chapter, it's a good idea to test your understanding of outlining paragraphs. You may know more than you think.

For each question, select all the answers that apply.

WHAT DO YOU KNOW?

1. **Which one of the following best expresses the function of an outline?**
   ___ to indent and space sentences
   ___ to order, group, and eliminate ideas
   ___ to edit and proofread text

2. **When finalizing your *main idea* for a paragraph, what strategy is helpful?**
   ___ using colorful details
   ___ expressing your idea as a complete sentence
   ___ adding a transitional expression

3. **Including transitional expressions in your outline can help with which of the following?**
   ___ finalizing your main idea
   ___ moving from one support point to another in your drafts
   ___ making the outline look bigger
   ___ remembering to include the expressions in your final paragraph

4. **Which of the following items are key features of an outline?**
   ___ main idea
   ___ support points
   ___ related examples
   ___ freewriting

5. **Which of the following items is considered a problem in an outline?**
   ___ an item (idea, example, or detail) that does not fit
   ___ an item that repeats another item
   ___ an item that is missing
   ___ an item that is unclear

Outlining Basics

In the previous chapter, you learned how to organize your ideas. In this chapter, you will learn about outlining, an important process for planning paragraphs and other writing assignments. All outlines have the same basic functions, which are already familiar to you from Chapter 3:

- They **order** ideas, starting with big ideas (which become *support points*) and moving to related examples and specific details.
- They **group** items that are related to one another.
- They **eliminate** any items that do not fit together.

Take a look at the following outline, in which key features are noted. (It is based on a cluster from Chapter 2; see page 27.)

ASSIGNED TOPIC   *Write about your workplace*

MAIN IDEA

Three serious problems make my workplace an unpleasant environment.

The **main idea** responds to your assigned topic. It connects all the support points and examples that follow.

SUPPORT POINT 1

The leadership is poor.
- shift leader plays favorites
- manager is a bad communicator
- ~~I should be a manager~~
- shift leader and manager don't help with customers

SUPPORT POINT 2

The staffing is inadequate.
- only four workers on weekends
- only one cashier
- too many workers call in sick

The **support points** are based on the *big ideas* from clusters or lists, and they back up the main idea.

SUPPORT POINT 3

There are serious personality problems.
- manager is insensitive
- older and younger employees argue
- guys harass the girls
- ~~they should hire better people~~

Related examples are grouped under each support point.

Unrelated ideas are eliminated.

ACTIVITY 1

For the following activity, refer to Chapter 3, Activity 19, question 2 (Managing Your Life Online, pages 64–65). Move the items from question 2 in Activity 19 to the outline form that follows. Use the outline above as a model. To get you started, the main idea has been filled in for you. You will need to:

- turn each *big idea* from Activity 19 into a *support point*. (The first support point has been provided for you.)
- write each support point as a complete sentence.
- write three related examples below each support point. These examples can be left as short phrases.

CONTINUED >

MAIN IDEA	Going online can be beneficial. (BECAUSE...)

SUPPORT POINT 1	It can help you with school.	**SUPPORT POINT 3**	

SUPPORT POINT 2

A note about outline formats: In your college career, you will use many different outline formats. In this book, we show a simple format, with a main idea followed by support points (usually three) and blanks for related examples. Once you understand this, you will be able to transition to other outline formats with greater confidence.

Sometimes, you may have only two support points. At other times, you may have more than three support points. In these cases, ask your instructor for suggestions. Often, you may be allowed to leave the third point blank, or, if you have extra support points, you may be able to write them on the back of the outline.

UNDERSTANDING KEY FEATURES OF OUTLINES

The following sections give more details on the three key features of outlines: the main idea, the support points, and the related examples.

Feature 1: The Main Idea

In college, each paragraph that you write must contain a *main idea* that responds directly to an assigned topic. Consider the following assignment:

> Discuss the career you would choose if anything were possible.

In writing a main idea for this topic, you should do all of the following:

- Identify a career of your choice.
- Use *key words* from the assigned topic (*career, if anything were possible*).
- Express your idea as *a complete sentence*.

Here are three students' main ideas that respond to this assigned topic:

If anything were possible, I would be a pilot for my career.
I would like to be an elementary school teacher if any career were possible.
The career I would pick if anything were possible is president of the United States.

Notice that each main idea identifies a specific career. Also, each one uses key words from the assigned topic (*if anything were possible, career*). Finally, each main idea is expressed as a complete sentence.

Power Tip
You may think that making outlines is a waste of time, but organizing your ideas before you write can actually save time, especially if you are writing under a deadline.

ACTIVITY 2

For each of the following assigned topics and main ideas, do the following:

- In the main idea, underline any words repeated from the assigned topic.
- In the main idea, circle the key phrase that responds to the assigned topic.
- To ensure that the main idea is expressed as a complete sentence, put a check mark over the capital letter at the beginning of the sentence and over the period at the end of the sentence.

EXAMPLE:

Assigned Topic: Identify an activity at which you would like to excel.

Main Idea: ✓I would like to excel at ⟨repairing bicycles⟩.✓

1. **Assigned Topic:** Discuss how you manage your money.

   Main Idea: _____

   _____

2. **Assigned Topic:** Discuss what qualities make you a good or bad friend.

   Main Idea: _____

3. **Assigned Topic:** Describe something that scares you.

   Main Idea: _____

4. **Assigned Topic:** Explain how successful you are at time management.

   Main Idea: _____

   _____

5. **Assigned Topic:** Discuss your attitude toward cheating in school.

   Main Idea: _____

Power Tip

Whenever you have trouble coming up with a main idea, look back at ideas that you've brainstormed in response to an assigned topic. You might circle words in your brainstorming that directly respond to the assigned topic. Then, use these words in your main idea. In Chapter 6, you will learn how to turn main ideas into a *topic sentence*, an important feature of effective paragraphs.

Feature 2: The Support Points

In an outline, you'll need to include *support points* that back up your main idea. Often, these are drawn from the *big ideas* in your clusters and lists. Make sure to state the support points as complete sentences.

Compare the following (partial) outline with the cluster on page 70. Notice that the first support point is based on the big idea "bad leadership" in the cluster.

Here is the start of an outline that turns the big ideas into support points:

MAIN IDEA Three serious problems make my workplace an unpleasant environment.

SUPPORT POINT 1 The leadership is poor.
- shift leader plays favorites
- manager is a bad communicator
- shift leader and manager don't help with customers

Often, adding the word *because* to the end of your main idea will help you develop support points that make sense. For example, suppose your main idea is

Good communication between parents and teenagers is important (*because* . . .)

Now, you will have to complete this thought with a support point that makes sense. Here are several examples of how you might complete this idea:

It builds trust.
It avoids misunderstandings.
It shows care and concern.

Notice that each support point is expressed as *a complete sentence* and connects clearly with the main idea. You should always verify that each support point makes sense by reading it in conjunction with the main idea. For example:

Good communication between parents and teenagers is important *because* it builds trust.

This idea makes clear sense. However, suppose you tried to express your support point as a single word (like *trust*) or as a short phrase (like *builds trust*). When you connect a single word or short phrase to your main idea, it will not make sense:

Good communication between parents and teenagers is important *because* trust.

Good communication between parents and teenagers is important *because* builds trust.

ACTIVITY 3

Using the items from this cluster, fill in the outline form that follows. Remember to write the main idea and the support points as *complete sentences*.

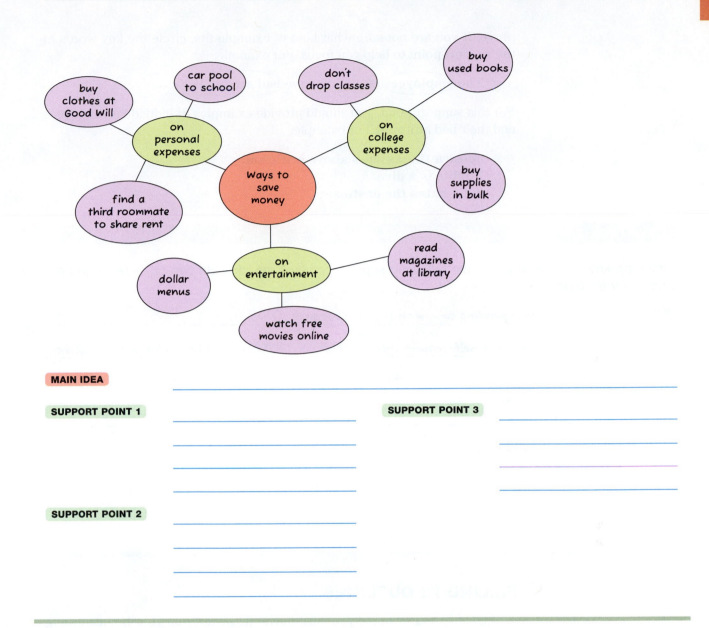

MAIN IDEA _____

SUPPORT POINT 1 _____ **SUPPORT POINT 3** _____

_____ _____

_____ _____

_____

SUPPORT POINT 2 _____

_____

_____

_____

Feature 3: The Related Examples

For each support point in your outline, you will need to provide _related examples_ to illustrate your point. For example, if you say,

The stockroom at my workplace is unsafe.

your readers will expect you to name some _related examples_ of how the stockroom is unsafe. For example:

slippery floors
boxes falling from shelves
old electrical wiring

In an outline, your examples may be expressed as _short phrases_ or even as _single words_. Be sure that your examples fit with the point you are trying to

For more practice with outlining, visit **bedfordstmartins.com/ steppingstones.**

prove. If you are not sure what kind of example fits, circle the key words in the support point to help you focus. For example:

The (employees) at my job have (bad attitudes.)

For this support point, you should provide examples of individual employees and their bad attitudes. For example:

> **Jessica thinks she's above criticism.**
> **Robbie is a diva.**
> **Jake hates the customers.**

ACTIVITY 4

Circle the key word or words in the following support points. Then, provide two or three *related examples* for each point.

MAIN IDEA   I like spending time with friends (because...)

SUPPORT POINT 1   I can be myself around them.   **SUPPORT POINT 3**   We have a lot of fun together.

_____   _____

_____   _____

_____   _____

SUPPORT POINT 2   They help me in different ways.

_____

_____

_____

FILLING IN OUTLINES

Again, to write an outline, you must move the items from your brainstorming to an outline form. As shown on page 67, outlining requires the same strategies that you practiced in the previous chapter: ordering, grouping, and eliminating. Moving items from your list or cluster requires patience and careful thinking.

ACTIVITY 5

For each of the topics in this activity, you are presented with scrambled ideas in both list and cluster form. For each assigned topic, do the following:

- Print a blank outline form from this book's Web site, at **bedfordstmartins.com/steppingstones** (see Useful Forms), or create your own. If listing is your preferred brainstorming method, refer to the list; if clustering is your preferred brainstorming method, refer to the cluster.

- Move the items from the list or cluster to the outline form. Start by filling in the *main idea* and the *support points,* putting the support points in an order that makes sense to you. Both the main idea and support points should be stated as complete sentences, and the main idea should include some key words from the assigned topic.

- Go back and fill in the related examples for each support point, eliminating items that do not fit.

Assigned Topic 1: Discuss your favorite restaurant.

Burt's BBQ Shack

there's an old tractor inside	football championship celebrations
I love the fun decorations	you sit at old picnic tables
BBQ is my favorite food	my sixteenth birthday party
some of my best memories are at Burt's	my family goes on New Year's Day
it's open seven nights a week	Burt's been in business for 15 years
the shredded beef sandwich is piled high	the coleslaw is better than my mom's
the pork ribs are meaty and sweet	sawdust on the floor
all the food is outstanding	the prices are very reasonable

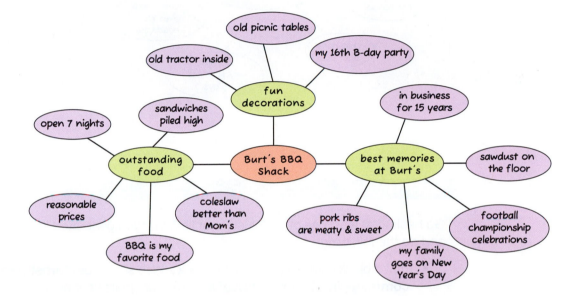

Assigned Topic 2: Discuss whether or not music has an important role in your life.

Music — not important to me

audio books in my car	prefer listening to other things
country music irritates me	studying for school
rap music makes me angry	heavy metal gives me a headache
bad reactions to music	one day I may like music
jazz and hip-hop	iPod and iTunes
my girlfriend loves music	news radio
live basketball broadcasts	classical music relaxes some people
distracts me from important activities	staying focused at work
learning my football plays	2Pac and Mos Def
downloading songs	Internet options

CONTINUED >

Go back to at least one of the clusters or lists that you generated in Chapter 2 and do the following:

- Print a blank outline form from this book's Web site, at **bedfordstmartins .com/steppingstones** (see Useful Forms), or create your own.

- Move the items from the list or cluster to the outline form. Start by filling in the *main idea* and the *support points*, putting the support points in an order that makes sense to you. Both the main idea and support points should be stated as complete sentences.

- Go back and fill in the related examples for each support point, eliminating items that do not fit.

The next page contains scrambled information for two outlines. For each one, do the following:

- Identify the main idea and write it in the outline as a complete sentence.

- Identify the support points and write them in an order that makes sense to you, using complete sentences.

- Fill in the three related examples for each support point.

Assigned Topic 1: Discuss something you don't like doing.

cleanings hurt my gums	MAIN IDEA	_____
I paid over $100 for a filling	SUPPORT POINT 1	_____
he always finds more cavities		_____
he says I'm grinding my teeth down		_____
Novocaine injections sting		_____
he said I may be developing gum disease	SUPPORT POINT 2	_____
treatments are expensive		_____
the dentist always gives me bad news		_____
a crown or bridge would bankrupt me		_____
drilling leaves my jaw sore	SUPPORT POINT 3	_____
I don't like going to the dentist		_____
check-ups cost $85		_____
treatments are always painful		_____

Assigned Topic 2: Discuss the best or worst teacher you ever had.

he came to my family's celebrations	MAIN IDEA	_____
he had a fun class Web site	SUPPORT POINT 1	_____
helped us get involved in extracurricular activities		_____
he had a good sense of humor		_____
he brought in interesting guest speakers		_____
started every class with a joke	SUPPORT POINT 2	_____
he related to us outside the classroom		_____
we played learning games in teams		_____
listened to our personal problems		_____
he could laugh at himself when he made a mistake	SUPPORT POINT 3	_____
he used creative teaching methods		_____
Coach Hendricks was my best teacher		_____
he appreciated the students' humor		_____

USING TRANSITIONAL EXPRESSIONS IN OUTLINES

Moving from one support point to another requires a **transitional word or phrase**. These transitional cues help your reader follow the development of your thoughts.

Before you write a paragraph, remember this simple but tremendously important step: *On your outline, write transitional words or phrases for each of your support points.* If the transitional expressions are not on your outline, you may forget to include them in your paragraph, making it difficult for your reader to understand the flow of your ideas.

The following example shows how you can add transitions to each part of an outline for a paragraph.

Major Transitional Expressions

↓

Group 1
First,
In the first place,
For starters,
To begin with,

Group 2
Second,
In the second place,
More important,
In addition,
Next,

Group 3
Third,
Finally,
Most important,
Last,

MAIN IDEA

To begin with,

SUPPORT POINT 1

Second,

SUPPORT POINT 2

Finally,

SUPPORT POINT 3

ACTIVITY 8

Go back to at least two of the earlier outlining activities (1, 3, 4, 5, or 7) and fill in transitional words or phrases in them. Then, for the remainder of this chapter, add transitional expressions to each outline that you work on.

SOLVING PROBLEMS IN OUTLINES

After completing your outline—and before you begin writing your paragraph—it is a good idea to double-check the outline to make sure that it is free of the common problems discussed in the following sections.

A Missing Item

When filling in an outline based on brainstormed ideas, you may find that you are *missing support points or examples*. Therefore, outlining is a great way to identify weaknesses in your ideas even before the paragraph-drafting stage. The result will be a much stronger, fully developed paragraph. Let's look at the following cluster:

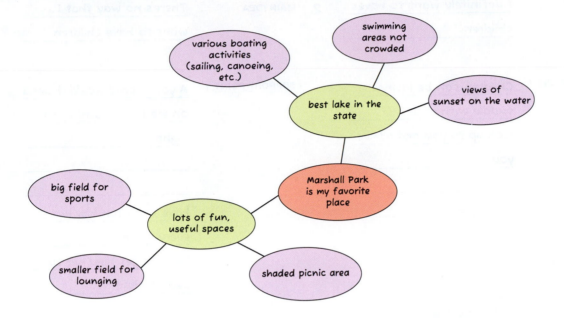

Now, let's see how a student might build an outline based on this cluster, assuming that her instructor requires three support points and three examples for each support point.

MAIN IDEA Marshall Park is my favorite place.

SUPPORT POINT 1 It has the best lake in the state.
  – various boating activities
  – swimming areas not crowded
  – views of sunset on the water

SUPPORT POINT 2 It has lots of fun, useful spaces.
  – big field for sports
  – smaller field for lounging
  – shaded picnic areas

As you can see, the writer is missing a third support point with examples. Therefore, she would need to add another support point (such as *It has a huge botanical garden with many varieties of flowers*) and related examples. In some cases, you might have enough examples but be missing a support point. In other cases, you might have a support point but not enough examples.

ACTIVITY 9

Add the missing support points and examples to the following outlines. You will have to make up the missing information, but make sure that the support points are appropriate for the examples and vice versa.

1. **MAIN IDEA**   I definitely want to have children.

SUPPORT POINT 1   Children can be loving.
cuddle with you
look up to you and admire you
_____
_____

SUPPORT POINT 2   _____
_____
make you laugh
fun to play with
never boring

SUPPORT POINT 3   Children can give you a sense of pride.
great to see them growing up smart and strong
nice to see them doing well in school
_____
_____

2. **MAIN IDEA**   There's no way that I want to have children.

SUPPORT POINT 1   A young child would depend on me from morning to night.
_____
have to watch his/her every move
have to get him/her to bed at night

SUPPORT POINT 2   I would never be as free as before.
wouldn't be able to see friends that often
wouldn't be able to relax
_____
_____

SUPPORT POINT 3   _____
_____
clothes and shoes cost a lot
expensive grocery bills
_____
_____

3. **MAIN IDEA** I would never get a tattoo.

SUPPORT POINT 1 _____

_____

parents would be angry
minister would be offended

_____

SUPPORT POINT 2 I am afraid of the pain.

_____

_____

healing process can hurt
infection could cause pain

SUPPORT POINT 3 _____

_____

artist might mess it up
might not like the design
after a year or two
might look bad as my skin
ages

4. **MAIN IDEA** I would get another tattoo.

SUPPORT POINT 1 Tattoos represent who I am.

zodiac symbol for my
birth month
anchor for marines

_____

SUPPORT POINT 2 _____

_____

girlfriend has a swan on
her back
father has marines symbol

_____

SUPPORT POINT 3 _____

_____

body is pierced in six
different places
hair is dyed purple and
spiked
I wear a spiked collar

An Item That Does Not Fit

One problem that can occur with your outline is including *an item that does not fit*. An item does not fit when it is not clearly connected to a main idea or support point. Take a look at this outline, in which just the first support point has been developed with examples. Can you see a problem with one of the examples?

MAIN IDEA I have excellent people skills.

SUPPORT POINT 1 My friends often turn to me for advice.
- My friend Malika asks my opinion on relationship problems.
- My friend Tari asks me for job advice.
- My best friend, Emile, has the most problems of all.

For more practice with outlining, visit **bedfordstmartins.com/steppingstones.**

SUPPORT POINT 2   I am good at resolving conflicts in my personal life and at work.

SUPPORT POINT 3   I work well with others.

You might have noticed that the third example (*My best friend, Emile, has the most problems of all*) doesn't fit with the main idea (*I have excellent people skills*) or with the support point it's under (*My friends often turn to me for advice*). A better example would show how the writer's friend Emile turns to him for advice. For instance, a good example might be *My best friend, Emile, asks me for parenting advice.*

When you have finished an outline, first read each support point together with the main idea to make sure the point fits the main idea. Then, check the related examples under each support point to make sure they belong. If they do not, change them so that they fit better.

ACTIVITY 10: Teamwork

In the following outlines, cross out any item that does not fit. Then, use your imagination and write in a new item that does fit.

1. MAIN IDEA   The Olive Grove is my favorite restaurant.

SUPPORT POINT 1   It has a romantic atmosphere.

soft music

candles on the table

intimate tables for two

SUPPORT POINT 2   The food is delicious.

chewy, cheesy pizza

cheap prices

best New York cheesecake

SUPPORT POINT 3   Everyone has a favorite restaurant.

parking valets are fast

waitresses are attentive and helpful

managers yell at the staff

2. MAIN IDEA   Music is important in my life.

SUPPORT POINT 1   It helps me work better.

cleaning the house

stocking the shelves at my job

wearing earplugs

SUPPORT POINT 2   It calms me down.

I'm nervous a lot

after a fight with my parents

when I'm stuck in traffic

SUPPORT POINT 3   It motivates me.

helps me get up in the morning

motivates my girlfriend

gets me going at the gym

3. **MAIN IDEA** Physical exercise is not an important part of my life.

   SUPPORT POINT 1 I grew up in a home where exercise was not important.

   parents never exercised

   I stayed inside, watching TV or playing video games

   my dad likes professional football

   SUPPORT POINT 2 I am just too lazy to exercise.

   none of my friends exercise

   I'd rather take a nap than exercise

   my muscles refuse to work

   SUPPORT POINT 3 I am too busy doing other things.

   studying

   a lot of friends

   working a part-time job

4. **MAIN IDEA** There are good reasons why I don't own a car.

   SUPPORT POINT 1 I like using public transportation.

   it's less expensive

   meet new people

   I can study on the bus

   SUPPORT POINT 2 Owning a car is too expensive.

   a motorcycle is cheaper

   insurance

   mechanical repairs

   SUPPORT POINT 3 I have a bad driving record.

   one DUI

   don't trust police

   two speeding tickets

An Item That Repeats Another Item

Another problem that can occur with outlines is *an item that repeats another item*. Sometimes, we express the same idea more than once, but we do not recognize this repetition because we have changed the words. Take a look at this example:

MAIN IDEA I like buying secondhand clothing.

SUPPORT POINT 1 It is less expensive than new clothing.

SUPPORT POINT 2 It doesn't cost as much as new clothes.

SUPPORT POINT 3 It is cheaper than new clothing.

Even though each support point uses different words, each one repeats the same idea (about used clothing being less expensive than new clothing). However, repetitions are not always this easy to spot, so you have to be very careful about the ideas and words that you use. Now, here is an example of three *distinct* support points:

MAIN IDEA	I like buying secondhand clothing.
SUPPORT POINT 1	It is less expensive than new clothing.
SUPPORT POINT 2	Many items are in "like new" condition.
SUPPORT POINT 3	Some older clothes are better made than new items.

ACTIVITY 11

In the following outlines, cross out any item that repeats another item. Then, use your imagination and write in a new item that is *distinct* from the others.

1. **MAIN IDEA** My dream career is nursing.

   SUPPORT POINT 1 Nurses help other people.

   give patients dignity and hope

   provide a high standard of medical care

   treat patients with tenderness and concern

   SUPPORT POINT 2 Nurses have good compensation and good job security.

   nurses are always in high demand

   salaries are very competitive

   nurses are always able to find work

   SUPPORT POINT 3 Nurses are admired.

   shown as competent and helpful in TV dramas

   seen as role models

   media show positive images of nurses

2. **MAIN IDEA** Mario's Gym is the best place to work out.

   SUPPORT POINT 1 The equipment is high-quality.

   state-of-the-art workout machines

   good equipment

   brand-new free weights

   SUPPORT POINT 2 The location is convenient.

   near my home, school, and work

   close to a highway exit

   close to me

   SUPPORT POINT 3 It's a good deal.

   regular monthly fee is $30

   you get a discount if a friend signs up

   fees rarely go up

3. MAIN IDEA — My mother is the person I admire most.

SUPPORT POINT 1 — She raised a family without help from others.

my father disappeared

never accepted welfare or food stamps

she was a single parent

SUPPORT POINT 2 — She got a college education while raising us.

went to school in the evenings

studied late at night instead of sleeping

graduated with a 3.8 grade point average

SUPPORT POINT 3 — She takes care of her health and appearance.

never overeats

stays physically active

watches her weight

4. MAIN IDEA — In two semesters of college, I have improved my study habits.

SUPPORT POINT 1 — I am more active in class.

take careful lecture notes

ask the professor questions

share my ideas in discussion groups

SUPPORT POINT 2 — I make studying a priority in my schedule.

I study during the week and on weekends

three hours every weekday evening

Sunday is an all-day homework day

SUPPORT POINT 3 — I go to my professors when I need help.

for reading a draft of my paper

when I don't understand the material

if I am confused about the lesson

An Item That Is Unclear

The last major problem that can occur in outlines is the use of *an item that is unclear*. Often, items are unclear because they express an idea that is not specific enough. Be especially careful about single-word items in your outline; it is common for single-word items to be general too.

An unclear item in your outline can lead to a serious breakdown of organization in your paragraph. Always try to correct any unclear items *before* you attempt to write your paragraph. In the examples below, compare the unclear words (in bold) with the specific examples in the revision. Can you see the difference?

UNCLEAR — The first-aid training was **good**. I learned a lot of **cool stuff**.

SPECIFIC — The first-aid training was practical and complete. I learned how to clean and dress a wound, administer CPR, treat a patient for shock, and summon emergency assistance.

> **UNCLEAR**   Tyndall College should do more for struggling students.
>
> Tyndall College should **help** struggling students.
>
> **SPECIFIC**   Tyndall College should provide more tutors for struggling students.

For unclear (imprecise) words to look out for, see Chapter 7, pages 140–41.

ACTIVITY 12: Teamwork

In the following outlines, cross out and replace any unclear items. You can work with another student or on your own.

1. **MAIN IDEA**   Volunteering benefits both the volunteers and their communities.

SUPPORT POINT 1   Volunteering helps people in need.

fund-raising helps serve disaster victims

donating food benefits the hungry

building a playground is nice

SUPPORT POINT 2   Volunteer work teaches volunteers new skills.

how to work with others

how to manage money

how to do it

SUPPORT POINT 3   Volunteer work makes volunteers feel connected to their communities.

meet their neighbors during projects

a sense of satisfaction

get to know local government officials

2. **MAIN IDEA**   Three key qualities are essential in a president of the United States.

SUPPORT POINT 1   A president should be honest.

not lie to American citizens or other members of government

not ignore the law to carry out policies

be good

SUPPORT POINT 2   A president should work tirelessly to help Americans.

pursue affordable health care

be there for the military

provide greater funding for schools and teachers

SUPPORT POINT 3   A president should do good stuff in international relations.

meet regularly with world leaders to avoid conflicts

promote nuclear disarmament

provide humanitarian aid to poor nations

3. `MAIN IDEA`   I definitely want to have children.

`SUPPORT POINT 1`   Children keep you young.

playing games

reading children's stories

active

`SUPPORT POINT 2`   Children can make you proud.

doing well in school

being polite and respectful to others

being children

`SUPPORT POINT 3`   Children make you happy when you're older.

give you grandchildren

won't let you down

visit on holidays

4. `MAIN IDEA`   I am a loyal fan of fast food.

`SUPPORT POINT 1`   It is cheap.

dollar menus

don't pay much

don't have to leave a tip

`SUPPORT POINT 2`   It is convenient.

fast food is no hassle

a fast-food restaurant on every block

many have drive-through

`SUPPORT POINT 3`   It tastes good.

lots of salt and grease

delicious dipping sauces

flavorful

Combined Problems

Often, an outline will have more than one problem. The following activity will give you practice in identifying and fixing multiple problems in an outline.

ACTIVITY 13: Mastery Test or Teamwork

In each outline below, do the following:

- Label any item that 1) does not fit, 2) repeats another item, or 3) is unclear.
- Note where items are missing. (Assume that each main idea should have three support points and each support point should have three examples.)

1. **MAIN IDEA**   Rita Cervino is the best manager I have worked with.

   SUPPORT POINT 1   She is competent and experienced.

   She has been a manager for ten years.

   She studied business management in college.

   She knows what she is doing.

   SUPPORT POINT 2   She listens to her employees.

   She holds weekly meetings to hear employee concerns.

   When a worker raises a concern, she addresses it.

   Stuff she does lets you know she hears you.

   SUPPORT POINT 3   She works as hard as her employees do.

   If her workers stay late for a deadline, she does too.

   She is fair in distributing work.

   No employee works harder than she does.

2. **MAIN IDEA**   To prevent the spread of germs, follow this procedure for hand washing.

   SUPPORT POINT 1   Use soap and water properly.

   Wet your hands with warm water.

   Use a generous amount of soap.

   Apply the soap.

   SUPPORT POINT 2   Do it right.

   Rub your hands together until suds form.

   Wash all parts of your hands, including under the nails.

   Don't rush.

   SUPPORT POINT 3   Rinse properly.

   Many people rinse too quickly.

   Hold your hands under warm water.

   Rub them together for at least ten seconds.

BRINGING IT ALL TOGETHER:
Outlining Your Paragraph

In this chapter, you have learned about the basic features of an academic outline and how to avoid common errors in your outlines. Confirm your knowledge by filling in the blank spaces in the following sentences. If you need help, review the pages listed after each sentence.

✔ All outlines have three basic functions. Their functions are to _____ ideas, _____ them, and _____ any ideas that do not fit. (page 67)

✔ The main features of an outline for an academic paragraph are: 1) _____, 2) _____, and 3) _____. Also, it is good to write _____ directly on your outline so that you do not forget them in your paragraph. (pages 68, 69, 71, and 76)

✔ There are four common errors that occur in outlines. These errors are: 1) _____, 2) _____, 3) _____ _____, and 4) _____. (pages 77, 79, 81, and 83)

✔ An item on your outline may be unclear if it is not _____ enough. You should be especially careful about _____ items, as it is common for them to be unclear. (page 83)

CHAPTER 5

Composing the Paragraph

Before you read this chapter, it's a good idea to test your understanding about how to compose an academic paragraph. You may know more than you think.

For each question, select all the answers that apply.

WHAT DO YOU KNOW?

1. **The topic sentence for an academic paragraph should accomplish two things. What are they?**

   ___ ask a general question

   ___ respond clearly to the assigned topic

   ___ state the name of the assignment

   ___ express your original point about the assigned topic

2. **What must you be careful to *avoid* when you move from your outline to your paragraph?**

   ___ changing key words

   ___ adding all your support points

   ___ leaving out transitional expressions

   ___ adding unrelated information

3. **What will happen if you write your topic sentence as a fragment?**

   ___ You will make a major grammatical error.

   ___ Your topic sentence will sound incomplete.

   ___ Your original point may not be clear.

   ___ Nothing will happen.

4. **How do you develop strong examples for your paragraph?**

   ___ Make sure the examples fit with your main idea.

   ___ Repeat the same examples a few times.

   ___ Use extra words to fill space.

   ___ Express each example in at least one separate, complete sentence.

5. **What should a concluding sentence do?**

   ___ Use as many transitional expressions as possible.

   ___ Introduce a new idea.

   ___ Restate the main idea of your paragraph in a fresh way.

   ___ Make the paragraph look longer.

Moving from Outline to Paragraph: An Opening Example

Take a look at how one student went from an outline to a successful paragraph:

> Mrs. Nevis, my eleventh-grade geography teacher, was the worst teacher I've ever had. To begin with, she always picked on students and seemed to enjoy it. For example, my friend Jerry had a hard time memorizing the names of countries, so she called him a "brainless wonder." Also, she laughed at students when they made a mistake or answered incorrectly. I could never pronounce the word "Antarctic," so she always made me say it just so she could laugh at me. Her favorite way to pick on students, however, was to make us stay after school for no reason at all. Once, when I sneezed three times in a row, she assigned me one hour of detention. Next, she had very poor teaching skills. For instance, she could never explain a problem or an idea clearly. One time, when we asked her the difference between a glacier and an ice floe, she got so confused that she told us to look it up on the Internet. When she graded our essays, she never gave us useful comments. She once gave me a grade of "C" on a paper, and her only comment was "Try harder." Finally, she had distracting personal habits. She actually liked to eat food during class and even talked with her mouth full! Also, her clothes looked like she had slept in them or cleaned out her garage in them. If there were an award for worst teacher in history, Mrs. Nevis would get my vote.

We will now look at how each part of a paragraph is developed.

MAIN IDEA
Mrs. Nevis was my worst teacher.

TRANSITIONAL EXPRESSION
To begin with,

SUPPORT POINT 1
she picked on students.
- used rude nicknames
- laughed at us
- made us stay after school

TRANSITIONAL EXPRESSION
Next,

SUPPORT POINT 2
she had poor teaching skills.
- did not explain ideas clearly
- put no comments on essays

TRANSITIONAL EXPRESSION
Finally,

SUPPORT POINT 3
she had distracting personal habits.
- ate food while teaching
- wore dirty, wrinkled clothes

Writing an Effective Topic Sentence

The **topic sentence** expresses the main idea of a paragraph, and it often appears first in the paragraph. To write a topic sentence, transfer the main idea from your outline, making sure that it is written as a complete sentence. (For more on complete sentences, see Chapter 10, page 221.) Once you have done this, check that the topic sentence does two things: 1) responds clearly to the assigned topic and 2) expresses your original point or opinion about the topic.

In many cases, you might also add other words to make the topic sentence more personal and original. However, the words you add should not change the meaning of the main idea. Here is an example:

ASSIGNED TOPIC   *Write about your best or worst teacher.*

MAIN IDEA   Mrs. Nevis was my worst teacher.

TOPIC SENTENCE   Mrs. Nevis, my eleventh-grade geography teacher, was the worst teacher I've ever had.

Power Tip
A subject is the *main actor* in a sentence, or *who* or *what* the sentence is about. A verb expresses an *action* or a *state of being*. A sentence needs both a subject and a verb to create a complete thought.

In each of the following topic sentences, the assigned topic has been underlined once, and the original point or opinion has been underlined twice. In each case, notice that the new words added to the topic sentence do not change the meaning of the main idea.

ASSIGNED TOPIC	*Write about your favorite restaurant.*
MAIN IDEA	Tango is my favorite restaurant.
TOPIC SENTENCE	Since I went to <u>Tango</u> for my sixteenth birthday, it has been <u>my favorite restaurant</u>.

ASSIGNED TOPIC	*Write about music in your life.*
MAIN IDEA	Music helps me survive.
TOPIC SENTENCE	<u>Music</u> has always <u>helped me survive</u> difficult times <u>in my life</u>.

ASSIGNED TOPIC	*Write about one thing that you couldn't live without.*
MAIN IDEA	One thing I couldn't live without is my car.
TOPIC SENTENCE	<u>My 1996 Honda Civic</u> is one thing that I <u>couldn't live without</u>.

ACTIVITY 1

In each of the following topic sentences, underline the assigned topic once. Then underline the student's original point or opinion about the topic twice.

EXAMPLE:

ASSIGNED TOPIC   *Write about your friends.*

MAIN IDEA   My best friends are more important to me than my family.

TOPIC SENTENCE   Since I moved away from home two years ago, <u>my best friends</u> <u>have become more important to me than my family</u>.

1. **ASSIGNED TOPIC**   *Write about a hobby you enjoy.*

   MAIN IDEA   My favorite hobby is customizing motorcycles.

   TOPIC SENTENCE   My favorite hobby is customizing motorcycles.

2. **ASSIGNED TOPIC**   *Write about social networking.*

   MAIN IDEA   Social networking helped me reconnect with old friends.

   TOPIC SENTENCE   Thanks to social networking, I have reconnected with friends from my past.

3. **ASSIGNED TOPIC**   *Write about a powerful memory.*

   MAIN IDEA   The first time I saw the ocean is a powerful memory.

   TOPIC SENTENCE   Certain memories have a powerful impact on me, like the first time I saw the Pacific Ocean.

4. ASSIGNED TOPIC   *Write about an experience that taught you something important.*

MAIN IDEA   I learned important things about children when I worked at a nursery school.

TOPIC SENTENCE   While working at a nursery school for six months, I learned important things about children's behavior.

5. ASSIGNED TOPIC   *Write about how a parent or relative influenced your behavior.*

MAIN IDEA   My Aunt Isabelle taught me to respect women.

TOPIC SENTENCE   I am grateful to my Aunt Isabelle, who was a single mother, for teaching me to respect women.

ACTIVITY 2

Choose one of your completed outlines from Chapter 4. On a separate sheet of paper (or on a computer), write the topic sentence for this outline.

Avoiding Problems in Topic Sentences

The most important function of a topic sentence is to state your main idea *clearly*. In order to do this, you will need to avoid four common errors:

1. accidentally changing the meaning of your main idea
2. asking a question
3. making an announcement
4. writing a sentence fragment

ACCIDENTALLY CHANGING THE MEANING OF YOUR MAIN IDEA

When you move from outline to paragraph and turn your main idea into a topic sentence, you might change the word order or add new words to make your idea more personal or original. That's okay. However, *be careful not to change the meaning of your main idea accidentally*. Students sometimes do this by:

- leaving out key words
- changing key words, or
- adding new information that is not clearly connected to the topic.

In each of the following topic sentences, the student's main idea is not clear because key words have been left out or changed, or new information has been added.

ASSIGNED TOPIC   *Discuss your favorite restaurant.*

MAIN IDEA   Tango is my favorite restaurant.

For more help with topic sentences, go to **bedfordstmartins.com/ steppingstones**, and click on Six Ways to Form a Topic Sentence.

TOPIC SENTENCE	I have liked Tango since my sixteenth birthday when I first ate there.
PROBLEM	In the topic sentence, the student has left out the key words, *favorite restaurant*. This changes the meaning of the main idea.
ASSIGNED TOPIC	*Discuss the role of music in your life.*
MAIN IDEA	Music helps me survive.
TOPIC SENTENCE	Music helps many people survive.
PROBLEM	In the topic sentence, the student has changed the key word *me* to *many people*. This changes the meaning of the main idea.
ASSIGNED TOPIC	*Discuss something you could not live without.*
MAIN IDEA	One thing I couldn't live without is my car.
TOPIC SENTENCE	My car causes me a lot of problems, but I couldn't live without it.
PROBLEM	In the topic sentence, the student has added the new information *causes me a lot of problems*. This changes the meaning of the main idea.

ACTIVITY 3

For each of the following items, decide if the topic sentence changes the meaning of the main idea. If it does, write one of the following phrases in the blank space: *key words left out, key words changed,* or *new information added.*

If the topic sentence does NOT change the meaning of the main idea, write *OK.*

EXAMPLE:

ASSIGNED TOPIC   *Discuss why you enrolled in college.*

MAIN IDEA   I decided to enroll in college because I wanted a better life for myself and my daughter.

TOPIC SENTENCE   I decided to enroll in college, and this has changed my life forever.

key words left out

1. **ASSIGNED TOPIC**   *Discuss a challenging experience you've had.*

   MAIN IDEA   Being a single mom is the most challenging experience of my life.

   TOPIC SENTENCE   Being a single mom is the most challenging experience of my life and it has taken a toll on my health.

2. **ASSIGNED TOPIC**   *Discuss a costly mistake you have made.*

   MAIN IDEA   Waiting two years to visit my college's financial aid office was a costly mistake.

   TOPIC SENTENCE   Waiting two years to visit the financial aid office was a stupid thing to do.

3. **ASSIGNED TOPIC**   *Discuss a celebrity whose behavior has disappointed you.*

   MAIN IDEA   For me, Tiger Woods will always be a fallen hero.

   TOPIC SENTENCE   For me, Tiger Woods will always be a hero.

4. **ASSIGNED TOPIC**   *Discuss your choice of a major in college.*

   MAIN IDEA   Foreign Languages was my major in college, but I changed it because there are few job opportunities.

   TOPIC SENTENCE   There are few job opportunities in Foreign Languages.

5. **ASSIGNED TOPIC**   *Write about what it's like to attend college for the first time or to return to college.*

   MAIN IDEA   Returning to college after serving in the Iraq war has changed my attitude about academic success.

   TOPIC SENTENCE   Returning to college after serving in the Iraq war has changed my attitude about relationships, money, and academic success.

ASKING A QUESTION IN YOUR TOPIC SENTENCE

If you write your topic sentence as a question, your original point or opinion about the topic may not be clear. This is the case in the following sample topic sentences. Take a look:

   MAIN IDEA   Tango is my favorite restaurant.

   TOPIC SENTENCE   What is my favorite restaurant?

   PROBLEM   This question does not express an original point or opinion about the topic. It merely asks a question.

   REVISED TOPIC SENTENCE   Although my city has many great restaurants, Tango is my favorite.

Here is another example:

MAIN IDEA	Music helps me survive.
TOPIC SENTENCE	Does music help me survive?
PROBLEM	This question does not express an original point or opinion about the topic. It merely asks a question.
REVISED TOPIC SENTENCE	During the most difficult times in my life, music has helped me survive.

ACTIVITY 4: Teamwork

Rewrite each question as a topic sentence that clearly states an original point or opinion about the topic. The first part of the sentence has been done for you.

EXAMPLE: Should girls ask guys out on dates?

Girls should ask guys out on dates to show that girls have equal power.

1. How can you impress your instructor?

You can impress your instructor by

2. When should you consider dropping a class?

You should consider dropping a class when

3. What would happen if I won the lottery?

If I won the lottery, I would

4. How can I improve my relationship with my parents?

To improve my relationship with my parents, I can

5. Where is a good place to study?

A good place to study is

MAKING AN ANNOUNCEMENT IN YOUR TOPIC SENTENCE

If you write a topic sentence as though you are making a general announcement, you are likely to leave out your original point or opinion about the topic. This is the case in the following topic sentences. Take a look:

Topic sentences that make general announcements

In this essay, I will discuss my favorite restaurant.
The topic of my paragraph is music.
I am going to write about my car.

| **PROBLEM** | In each topic sentence, the student forgets to express an original point about the topic. Instead, the sentences make general announcements. |

REVISED TOPIC SENTENCES

Since I first ate at Tango, it has been my favorite restaurant.

Music has changed my life in several ways, all of them good.

My car is important to my career, my family life, and my well-being.

ACTIVITY 5: Teamwork

Rewrite each general announcement as a topic sentence that clearly states an original point about the topic.

EXAMPLE: In this paragraph, I will discuss the benefits of sleeping well.

Sleeping well helps me function more effectively during the day.

1. I would like to talk about my boyfriend's smoking habit.

_____

2. My topic today is falling in love.

_____

3. I have been asked to write about communication in my family.

_____

4. In this essay, I am going to discuss my greatest fear.

_____

5. The main idea for my paragraph is airport security.

_____

WRITING THE TOPIC SENTENCE AS A FRAGMENT

In order to be grammatically correct, a topic sentence needs to have both a subject and a verb, and it must express a complete thought. If any of these elements is missing, your topic sentence will be a **fragment**. (For more information on fragments, see Chapter 10, pages 246–53.) If you write a fragment for your topic sentence, you may also unintentionally leave out your original point about the topic. Consider these examples:

Topic sentences as fragments

My favorite restaurant.

The importance of music in my life.

Living without my car.

PROBLEM   Each topic sentence is missing either a main verb or a main subject, which makes the sentence a fragment. This is a serious grammatical error. The student's specific point about the topic is also missing in each sentence.

Power Tip

Notice that when the topic sentence is written as a fragment, it sounds more like a *title* than an opening sentence with a complete thought.

For more practice with fragments, go to **bedfordstmartins.com/ steppingstones**.

ACTIVITY 6: Teamwork

Rewrite each fragment as a topic sentence that clearly states a specific idea about the topic in a complete, correct sentence.

EXAMPLE: My first semester in college.

During my first semester in college, I made a few serious mistakes.

1. Taking my lunch to school.

   _____

2. Lazy study habits.

   _____

3. Looking for a job.

   _____

4. Winter, my favorite season.

   _____

5. Tips for online dating.

   _____

ACTIVITY 7

Return to the topic sentence that you wrote in Activity 2 on page 91 and check that it is free of errors.

Writing the First Support Point

After you have written an error-free topic sentence, it is time to develop your first support point. Follow these steps:

- Copy the transitional expression that introduces your first support point from your outline. If your outline doesn't include a transitional expression, add one. Put a comma after this expression. (For more on transitional expressions, see Chapter 4, page 76, and page 98 of this chapter.)
- Follow the transitional expression with the first support point from your outline, making sure that it is a complete sentence with a subject and a verb. Take a look:

MAIN IDEA Mrs. Nevis was my worst teacher. **TRANSITIONAL EXPRESSION** To begin with, **SUPPORT POINT 1** she picked on students.	Mrs. Nevis, my eleventh-grade geography teacher, was the worst teacher I've ever had. To begin with, she picked on students frequently and unfairly.

As with the topic sentence, you may change the word order or add words, but be careful not to change the meaning of the support point. Follow the same guidelines that you learned for the topic sentence:

- Do not leave out any important key words from the support point.
- Do not change any essential key words from the support point. (However, you may use words with similar meanings in some cases.)
- Do not add inappropriate new information to the support point. (However, as in the previous example, you may add descriptive language and other information that won't change the essential meaning of the support point.)

ACTIVITY 8: Teamwork

Following are main ideas from different outlines, followed by the first support point and three versions of a sentence based on this support point. Working with two or three classmates, do the following for each sentence:

- If a sentence changes—or confuses—the meaning of the support point, underline the parts of the sentence that cause the problem.
- Explain how the sentence changes or confuses the meaning of the support point.
- If a sentence does not significantly change the meaning of the support point, write "OK" next to it.

EXAMPLE: **Main idea:** Babbo's Pizza is my favorite restaurant.

Support point: To begin with, the service is excellent.

Sentence: To begin with, <u>the staff makes you feel welcome</u>.
A welcoming staff is only one part of good service.

Sentence: To begin with, I can count on professional service.
OK

Sentence: To begin with, <u>the whole experience is excellent</u>.
The "whole experience" is broader than just the service.

1. **Main idea:** My cousin's community service was a life-changing experience.

    Support point: In the first place, he learned that other people's problems are worse than his own.

    Sentence: In the first place, he learned that everyone has problems.

    _____

    _____

    Sentence: In the first place, he learned that his own problems are not so bad.

    _____

    _____

CONTINUED >

Sentence: In the first place, he realized that his own problems are not as bad as other people's problems. _____

2. **Main idea:** My habit of waiting until the last minute creates problems in my life.

   Support point: First, I never get projects done on time.

   Sentence: First, I never turn papers in on time. _____

   Sentence: First, I never get projects done on time, and I'm always late for work. _____

   Sentence: First, I'm always late turning in projects. _____

When you first learn to write support points, you will need to avoid three main problems:

1. forgetting transitional expressions
2. writing support points as fragments
3. accidentally combining the support point with the first example

These problems usually occur when you are working quickly and not following your outline carefully. Remember, the outline is your navigation system: you should refer to it closely throughout the writing process. If you ignore any important information in your outline, you may get lost while writing the paragraph or cause your reader to become lost.

REMEMBER TRANSITIONAL EXPRESSIONS

As you learned in Chapter 4, transitional expressions are essential for good academic writing; they help the reader follow your ideas, especially in a long paragraph. If you forget transitional expressions, your reader may have difficulty following your thoughts. If you are worried about this, *use a highlighter* to mark transitional expressions on your outline.

Here is a chart of major transitional expressions that help introduce support points:

SUPPORT POINT 1	SUPPORT POINT 2	SUPPORT POINT 3
First,	Second,	Third,
In the first place,	In the second place,	Last,
For starters,	More important,	Most important,
To begin with,	To follow,	Finally,
One reason is . . .	Another reason is . . .	A final reason is . . .

For more on transitional expressions, see Chapter 4, page 76, and page 105 of this chapter.

ACTIVITY 9: Teamwork

Take out your outline and highlight the transitions in it. If it is missing transitions, add them now. Then, exchange your outline with a peer and mark possible transitions in each other's work. If it is helpful, refer back to Chapter 4—and the chart on page 98.

DO NOT WRITE SUPPORT POINTS AS FRAGMENTS

When students begin a sentence with a transitional expression, they sometimes forget to include both a subject and a verb in the sentence. (Again, the subject is the *main actor* in a sentence; it is *who* or *what* the sentence is about. A verb expresses an *action* or a *state of being.*) Consider the following examples:

MAIN IDEA Tango is my favorite restaurant. **TRANSITIONAL EXPRESSION** To begin with, **SUPPORT POINT 1** the food is delicious.	Although I have eaten at many good restaurants, Tango stands out as my favorite. To begin with, delicious food.
MAIN IDEA Music is important in my life. **TRANSITIONAL EXPRESSION** First, **SUPPORT POINT 1** it helps me relax.	Even though I don't get to listen to music as often as I would like, it is important in my life because it helps me relax, work, and party. First, helping me relax.
MAIN IDEA I could not live without my car. **TRANSITIONAL EXPRESSION** In the first place, **SUPPORT POINT 1** I need it for work.	I could not live without my car because I need it for work, to help my family, and to escape. In the first place, for work.

Now, let's look at these three support sentences from the previous examples:

To begin with, delicious food.
First, helping me relax.
In the first place, for work.

When you begin a sentence with a transitional expression, remember that what *follows the comma* must be a complete sentence with a subject and a verb. Do not let the presence of the transitional expression cause you to write a fragment. Now, let's revise the examples to make them complete, correct sentences:

SUBJECT **VERB**

To begin with, the food is delicious.

SUBJECT **VERB**

First, music helps me relax.

SUBJECT **VERB**

In the first place, I need my car for work.

If it is helpful, cover up the transitional expression with a finger and look at the word group that follows. If the word group is a fragment, revise it. (For more on avoiding fragments, see Chapters 10 and 12.)

AVOID COMBINING THE SUPPORT POINT WITH THE FIRST EXAMPLE

When you move from the outline to the paragraph, you might accidentally combine two items that should be expressed in separate sentences. This can cause confusion for your reader. When you write a support point, be sure not to mention the first example in the same sentence. Take a look at the following examples of this error:

MAIN IDEA
 	
Tango is my favorite restaurant.
 	
TRANSITIONAL EXPRESSION
 	
To begin with,
 	
SUPPORT POINT 1
 	
the food is delicious.
 	
  – spicy appetizers
  – tender, juicy beef
  – decadent desserts
	Although I have eaten at many good restaurants, Tango stands out as my favorite. To begin with, the spicy appetizers are delicious.

Here, the writer has combined the first support point (*the food is delicious*) with the first related example (*spicy appetizers*). This error will cause significant confusion for readers because they will assume that the point here is about the appetizers instead of the food in general.

MAIN IDEA
 	
Music is important in my life.
 	
TRANSITIONAL EXPRESSION
 	
First,
 	
SUPPORT POINT 1
 	
it helps me relax.
 	
   – before a big test
   – getting to sleep
   – after a fight with my girlfriend
	Even though I don't get to listen to music as often as I would like, it is important in my life because it helps me relax, work, and party. First, music helps me relax before a big test.

Here, the writer has combined the first support point (*music helps me relax*) with the first related example (*before a big test*). Readers will assume that the point here is all about using music to relax before a test instead of using music to relax in a variety of ways.

ACTIVITY 10: Teamwork

With two or three classmates, read each main idea, its first support point, and the examples for the support point. Then, read the sentences that come after them and do the following:

- If the first related example has been combined with the support point, underline the words in the sentence that show the presence of the first related example. Then, write "Combined" next to the sentence.
- If the sentence is fine as is, write "OK" next to it.

EXAMPLE: Main idea: Kaleidoscopes are my passion.

    Support point: First, I love the images.

        — the bright colors

        — the fluid movement

        — the endless arrangements

    Sentence: First, I get excited by the beautiful images.   OK

    Sentence: First, the images delight my imagination.   OK

    Sentence: First, I love the images <u>with their rainbow colors</u>.

    Combined

1. **Main idea:** The police in my community work hard to have good communication with the residents.

   Support point: In the first place, they ride bikes so they can stop and chat with people.

           — people who have questions

           — children

           — business owners

CONTINUED >

Sentence: In the first place, they ride bikes so they can stop and answer people's questions. _____

Sentence: In the first place, they ride bikes because it's easier to slow down and talk to people. _____

Sentence: In the first place, they ride bikes because it's easier to provide information to people who need it. _____

2. **Main idea:** As long as I am in college, living at home with my parents makes good sense.

   Support point: To begin with, I don't have to struggle financially.

   — paying rent

   — paying for food

   — paying for books and tuition

   Sentence: To begin with, as long as I am living at home with my parents, I won't have financial struggles, like paying my own rent. _____

   Sentence: To begin with, I don't have to pay for my own apartment and struggle with money. _____

   Sentence: Living at home with my parents means that I am more financially secure. _____

ACTIVITY 11

Return to the draft of your paragraph that you began in Activity 2 and write your first support point. Place it immediately following the topic sentence. Remember to use a transitional expression and write your support point as a complete sentence (not a fragment).

Writing the Related Examples

After writing the first support point, it is time to develop your related examples. Follow these guidelines:

- Discuss the examples *one at a time.*
- Write at least one complete sentence for each example.
- Add some specific details to each example.
- Use *minor* transitional expressions to move from example to example.

DISCUSS THE EXAMPLES ONE AT A TIME

As you learned in Chapter 1, academic paragraphs typically contain more than five sentences, and sometimes they have as many as ten or fifteen sentences. To achieve this level of development in your paragraph, you will need to discuss the examples one at a time, writing at least one complete sentence for each example. If you rush and combine all your examples into only one or two sentences, you will not meet the minimum requirement for the paragraph. More important, your paragraph may appear poorly developed and superficial.

Below, the examples have been squeezed into one sentence:

Power Tip
Be aware that some graders of standardized tests and exit tests will actually assign a lower score to even well-written paragraphs if they are very brief.

MAIN IDEA Music is important in my life. **TRANSITIONAL EXPRESSION** First, **SUPPORT POINT 1** it helps me relax. – before a big test – getting to sleep – after a fight with my girlfriend	Even though I don't get to listen to music as often as I would like, it is important in my life because it helps me relax, work, and party. First, nothing calms me down and relaxes me like music. For instance, it settles my nerves when I have a big test coming up, when I can't get to sleep, and after I've had an argument with my girlfriend. I argue with my girlfriend a lot.

In this example, the writer has merged all the examples into one sentence. As a result, the paragraph feels rushed, and the last sentence (*I argue with my girlfriend a lot.*) seems like a weak afterthought instead of a careful development of the examples. Students who find themselves in this situation often feel stuck and do not know how to move ahead. To avoid this problem, discuss the examples one at a time, giving each its own sentence.

Now, let's see a revision of the previous paragraph, with each example discussed in a separate, complete sentence:

MAIN IDEA Music is important in my life. **TRANSITIONAL EXPRESSION** First, **SUPPORT POINT 1** it helps me relax. – before a big test – getting to sleep – after a fight with my girlfriend	Even though I don't get to listen to music as often as I would like, it is important in my life because it helps me relax, work, and party. First, nothing calms me down and relaxes me like music. For instance, I tend to get nervous before a big test, so I listen to soft music on my iPod to calm down. If I have trouble getting to sleep, gentle classical music works better for me than a sleeping pill. Also, fighting with my girlfriend is a high-anxiety event for me; fortunately, I can relax and remember how much I love her by listening to our favorite singer, Norah Jones.

Here, the student has written one complete, thoughtful sentence for each related example. Not only does this method allow him to illustrate each example more effectively, it also ensures that he will have a fully developed paragraph. Of course, it is also perfectly acceptable to write *more than one* sentence for each related example.

ADD SOME SPECIFIC DETAILS TO THE EXAMPLES

In your outline, you generally write related examples as short phrases. However, as you present examples in your paragraph, try to develop them with specific details that *bring the examples to life* and *give them personality.*

Here, the writer has *not* added specific details to the examples:

MAIN IDEA
 	
 I could not live without my car.
 	
 TRANSITIONAL EXPRESSION
 	
 In the first place,
 	
 SUPPORT POINT 1
 	
 I need it for work.
 	
    – to make deliveries
    – to drive clients
    – for business travel
	I could not live without my car because I need it for work, to help my family, and to escape. In the first place, my car is essential for my job. For example, I use it to make deliveries. Sometimes, I drive clients in my car. I also use it for business travel.

Here, the writer has discussed the related examples one at a time and written a separate, complete sentence for each example. However, the writer has not added any specific details to bring the examples to life. As a result, the examples seem bland and unconvincing. It feels like the writer doesn't really care about the ideas in the paragraph.

Now, consider this example in which the writer has added specific details to the related examples:

MAIN IDEA
 	
 I could not live without my car.
 	
 TRANSITIONAL EXPRESSION
 	
 In the first place,
 	
 SUPPORT POINT 1
 	
 I need it for work.
 	
    – to make deliveries
    – to drive clients
    – for business travel
	I could not live without my car because I need it for work, to help my family, and to escape. In the first place, my car is essential for my job. Because I work for an interior designer, I am on the road five days a week delivering fabric and wallpaper samples, catalogs, and small decorative pieces, such as lamps and vases. Often, my boss wants clients to visit showrooms

Power Tip
You do not necessarily have to develop details for *every* example, especially if you are writing under time pressure. However, it's always a good idea to look back at all of your examples and ask which ones could be made more vivid through added details.

and design centers and depends on me to take them in my car. Also, at least once a month, I am expected to attend a regional design conference. Without my car, all of these tasks would be impossible.

Here, we get a vivid and convincing picture of why the writer needs a car for his job. The specific details bring the examples to life and give the writing personality. In Chapter 7, you will learn some fun and effective strategies for developing details in your writing.

USE MINOR TRANSITIONAL EXPRESSIONS TO MOVE FROM EXAMPLE TO EXAMPLE

In addition to the major transitional expressions that you use to introduce your support points, you will need a variety of *minor* transitional expressions to help you move smoothly from example to example. Remember, writing a paragraph is a process of constant movement or *transition* from one idea to another. Without transitional expressions, some of your ideas may seem "stuck together" rather than well developed.

Here is a chart of useful minor transitional expressions:

MINOR TRANSITIONAL EXPRESSIONS	
For example,	For instance,
As an example,	Then,
Another example,	In fact,
In particular,	Once,
Specifically,	One time,
To illustrate,	Another time,
Another illustration	Sometimes,
In addition,	Also,
Next,	Plus,
Furthermore,	Moreover,

On the following page, notice how three minor transitional expressions (underscored in gray) help the writer introduce an example, move smoothly from one example to another, and move from example to detail:

MAIN IDEA	Mrs. Nevis, my eleventh-grade geography teacher, was the worst teacher I've ever had. To begin with, she always picked on students and seemed to enjoy it. For example, my friend Jerry had a hard time memorizing the names of countries, so she called him a "brainless wonder." Also, she laughed at students when they made mistakes. I could never pronounce the word "Antarctic," so she always made me say it just so she could laugh at me. Her favorite way to pick on students, however, was to make us stay after school for no reason at all. Once, when I sneezed three times in a row, she assigned me one hour of detention.
Mrs. Nevis was my worst teacher.	
TRANSITIONAL EXPRESSION	
To begin with,	
SUPPORT POINT 1	
she picked on students.	
– used rude nicknames	
– laughed at students	
– made us stay after school	

ACTIVITY 12

Return to the draft of your paragraph, and add examples to your first support point. Remember the guidelines for writing examples:

- Discuss the examples *one at a time*.
- Write at least one complete sentence for each example.
- Add some specific details to the examples. (See Chapter 7 for suggestions.)
- Use *minor* transitional expressions to introduce examples, to move from one example to another, and to introduce details.

ACTIVITY 13

The following paragraphs have topic sentences, support points, and concluding sentences, but they are missing examples and specific details. For each paragraph, do the following:

- Add examples and details, being as creative as you can.
- Be sure to use minor transitional expressions to introduce examples and details. Refer to the chart on page 105 if you need to.

EXAMPLE:

All kinds of pets can improve our lives in many ways. First, dogs can comfort us by being excellent companions and guardians. *For example, Labradors and English sheepdogs are great playmates for children. They are gentle yet fun-loving and have a lot of patience. Other dogs, like German shepherds and collies, are excellent guard dogs, yet they can also be gentle friends to humans.* In addition, cats, though not always as friendly as dogs, can also be excellent companions.

For instance, many cats like to curl up on their owners' laps and purr happily, reducing stress for both human and animal. Also, cats love to play with string, rubber balls, and other toys, and it's fun for owners to both watch and participate. Finally, even cold-blooded creatures like fish and lizards can make enjoyable pets. For example, the various colors of fish can be both soothing and stimulating. Lizards also can be fascinating to watch. For instance, some species change colors to match their surroundings. Whether warm and furry or cool and scaly, pets truly can bring joy into our day-to-day lives.

1.   Spending time by any body of water can be fun, restful, and good for the soul. First, ponds and lakes have calm water that you can swim or boat in or just admire from the shore. _____

_____

_____

Second, whether fast and churning or slow and lazy, rivers are fun to watch and, of course, to fish in. _____

_____

_____

Last, but perhaps most impressive, are oceans, which blend the qualities of ponds, lakes, and rivers. _____

_____

_____

Just about any body of water has the power to soothe, entertain, and enrich us.

2.   Although the most obvious reason to get a college education is to get a job, some other benefits can be just as important. One reason to go to college is to learn about different fields and to find out what we like and don't like. _____

_____

_____

Another reason to get a college education is to meet people who can offer emotional, educational, and career support. _____

_____

_____

A final reason to go to college is to become exposed to exciting new ideas, even those not directly related to getting a job. _____

_____

_____

For all these reasons, a college education can be so much more than a gateway to the job market.

Completing the Paragraph

Now, you have only three things to do to complete your paragraph:

- Write the second support point with the related examples.
- Write the third support point with the related examples.
- Write the concluding sentence.

WRITE THE SECOND AND THIRD SUPPORT POINTS WITH THE RELATED EXAMPLES

Once you have written your first support point with its related examples (and any details about the examples), you will probably be warmed up and writing a bit faster. While you have this momentum and focus, make good use of it by moving immediately to your second support point. If you take a break now and come back to your paragraph later, you may lose valuable energy and focus.

First, introduce the second support point with a major transitional expression. Then, write the second support point and its examples, using the same instructions that you used for the first support point. When you have finished writing your second support point and the examples that go with it, write your third support point and its examples, following the same process.

ACTIVITY 14

Return to your paragraph and add your second and third support points and their related examples. Remember to introduce your support points with *major* transitional expressions. Use these guidelines for adding examples:

- Discuss the examples *one at a time.*
- Write at least one complete sentence for each example.
- Add some specific details to the examples.
- Use *minor* transitional expressions to introduce your examples, to move from one example to another, and to introduce details.

Power Tip
Some writers begin concluding sentences with expressions like "For these reasons," "In conclusion," or "To sum up." Although these are acceptable transitions, make sure that what follows them is not a mechanical restatement of your main idea; try to think of creative ways to end your paragraphs.

WRITE THE CONCLUDING SENTENCE

The last sentence of a paragraph should restate or summarize your main idea in a fresh, thoughtful manner. An unimaginative or missing concluding sentence can indicate your lack of commitment and may leave the reader unsatisfied or confused. Instead, restate your main idea in a way that expresses your sincerity and enthusiasm about the ideas discussed in the paragraph.

Follow these guidelines for writing the concluding sentence:

- Do not repeat the topic sentence in an overly simple or mechanical way.
- Do not introduce new information or go off topic.

- Find creative, persuasive ways to restate the main idea.
- Never omit the concluding sentence, even if your paragraph has met any length requirement provided by your instructor.

Now, let's look at some concluding sentences that don't work and some that do. Here is the original topic sentences:

Although I have eaten at many good restaurants, Tango stands out as my favorite.

1. Here is a concluding sentence that repeats the idea in a simple or mechanical way:

   In conclusion, I like to eat at Tango, and it is my favorite restaurant.

2. Here is a concluding sentence that goes off topic:

   That's why Tango is my favorite restaurant, but eating at home makes sense if you are on a budget.

3. Here is an effective concluding sentence that is creative and persuasive:

   While other restaurants may tempt me from time to time, my heart (and stomach) belong to Tango.

ACTIVITY 15

Read each topic sentence. Then, read the three concluding sentences, evaluating each one for possible problems. Finally, in each blank space, write one of the following: *simple and mechanical, off topic,* or *creative and persuasive.*

EXAMPLE: Topic sentence: Mrs. Nevis, my eleventh-grade geography teacher, was the worst teacher I've ever had.

Concluding sentences:

To conclude, it is worth repeating that Mrs. Nevis was the worst teacher I have ever had. *simple and mechanical*

Mrs. Nevis will stand out in my mind as a bad teacher who took pleasure in humiliating her students. *creative and persuasive*

Mrs. Nevis was the worst teacher I ever had, and Mr. Brown, who I currently have for statistics, is pretty bad too. *off topic*

1. **Topic sentence:** Music is so important in my life that I probably would not have survived college without it.

CONTINUED >

Concluding sentences:

I listen to music for all these reasons, and it's important in my life. _____

Music is important in my life, but it was more important when I was a child than it is now. _____

Music is more than just a form of entertainment for me; instead, it is a powerful force that helps me succeed in life. _____

2. **Topic sentence:** College students are facing greater and greater financial challenges.

Concluding sentences:

Clearly, the financial burden of attending college is making students reconsider their decisions. _____

College is expensive, and I am on academic probation because my grades have been so low. _____

College students have lots of money problems. _____

3. **Topic sentence:** Since I live, work, and go to school in different parts of the city, I could never survive without my car.

Concluding sentences:

I could not live without my car, and it is really important to me. _____

Although my life is very busy, I believe that I am on the road to success, and it is my car that keeps me going. _____

I could not live without my car, but I would like to trade it in for a new Hyundai that gets better gas mileage. _____

ACTIVITY 16: Teamwork

Power Tip
Notice that the rewritten concluding sentence for the Activity 16 example makes a recommendation. This is another way to end on a strong note; however, make sure that any recommendation is closely related to the main idea and support points that you have provided.

Following are several topic sentences followed by ineffective concluding sentences. With two or three classmates, discuss the problems with the concluding sentences. Then, rewrite the sentences to make them more creative and persuasive.

EXAMPLE: **Topic sentence:** Barden Hall, the oldest building on our campus, is falling apart to the point of becoming dangerous.

Concluding sentence: To sum up, Barden Hall is a mess.

Rewrite: Given the dangers that I have described, Barden Hall needs to be renovated soon, or someone could be seriously injured.

1. **Topic sentence:** Because nurses are in high demand, command good salaries, and get the satisfaction of helping others, nursing can be a great career.

   Concluding sentence: Nursing is an excellent career to pursue.

   Rewrite: _____

   _____

   _____

2. **Topic sentence:** A lot of people look down on television, but even "silly" shows can teach us about human behavior, the workings of institutions, and more.

   Concluding sentence: To restate my earlier point, television has a lot to teach us.

   Rewrite: _____

   _____

   _____

3. **Topic sentence:** It's been hard to return to college after twenty years, but age brings wisdom, patience, and a strong desire to make the most of my educational experience.

   Concluding sentence: In conclusion, going back to college has been hard but worthwhile.

   Rewrite: _____

   _____

   _____

ACTIVITY 17

Return to the draft of your paragraph and write the concluding sentence. You may have to experiment with various ideas and revise a few times to find a sentence that concludes your paragraph with enthusiasm and conviction. In other words, avoid a simple and mechanical ending, and be sure to stay on topic.

A final word: After you complete your paragraph, you'll want to reread it to make sure that you have provided all of the support that you need and that every support point and example is relevant to the main idea expressed in the topic sentence. Chapter 6 will give you specific strategies for revising your paragraph.

BRINGING IT ALL TOGETHER:
Composing the Paragraph

In this chapter, you have learned how to compose an academic paragraph with a clear topic sentence, strong examples and details, and an effective concluding sentence. Confirm your knowledge by filling in the blank spaces in the following sentences. If you need help, review the pages listed after each sentence.

✔ To be complete, a topic sentence must do two things: 1) _____
_____ and 2) _____
_____. (page 89)

✔ There are four common errors that occur when writing a topic sentence. These errors are: 1) _____,
2) _____, 3) _____, and
4) _____. (page 91)

✔ When writing the support points in a paragraph, it is important to do three things: 1) _____, 2) _____
_____, and 3) _____
_____. (page 98)

✔ When writing the examples and details in a paragraph, it is important to do four things: 1) _____, 2) _____
_____, 3) _____,
and 4) _____.
(page 102)

✔ There are two common errors that occur when writing a concluding sentence. They are: _____
and _____. (page 108)

✔ To write an effective concluding sentence for a paragraph, it is important to find _____ and _____ ways to restate the main idea. (pages 108–9)

Before you read this chapter, it's a good idea to test your understanding of revising and proofreading an academic paragraph. You may know more than you think.

For each question, select all answers that apply.

WHAT DO YOU KNOW?

1. **Which of the following are essential ingredients in an academic paragraph?**

   ___ a topic sentence

   ___ unity (all the ideas fit)

   ___ support (enough examples and details)

   ___ dialogue

2. **What does it mean to revise your writing?**

   ___ to start all over again

   ___ to give your work a quick glance to see if you still like it

   ___ to identify and fix any problems

   ___ to estimate what grade you might get

3. **When doing peer review with a classmate, which of the following are good strategies?**

   ___ Offer suggestions and ask questions.

   ___ Let your partner do all the talking.

   ___ Make yourself do all the talking.

   ___ Don't offer any opinions if your partner is sensitive or shy.

4. **What are the dangers of using electronic spelling and grammar checkers?**

   ___ They can suggest wrong words to replace your misspelled word (for example, *revel* instead of *reveal*).

   ___ They won't identify words that are misused but spelled correctly (for example, *there* instead of *their*).

   ___ They sometimes flag a sentence that has no errors.

   ___ They sometimes cause plagiarism.

5. **What are some useful strategies for proofreading your work?**

   ___ Double-space your paragraph so that it's easier to read.

   ___ Proofread on a printed page.

   ___ Read backwards.

   ___ Use a combination of pen, pencil, and highlighter to mark your errors.

Understanding the Revision Process: An Overview

The chapters preceding this one showed you how to organize and compose an academic paragraph.

> **Chapter 4** helped you to develop a careful outline for your paragraph.
>
> **Chapter 5** showed you how to follow this outline step-by-step to compose your paragraph.

When you have gained some mastery over these parts of the writing process, you will be able to produce **unified** paragraphs: paragraphs that stay on track and include only information that supports the main idea. However, the act of writing is not always orderly and predictable, and even experienced writers can get off track. Sometimes, you may become so closely involved with your ideas that you skip a key piece of your outline or get lost in your specific details. Also, you might make grammar mistakes and other errors. For these reasons, dedicated writers recognize that the final step of the writing process—**revision**—is just as important as the earlier steps.

Revision ("re" + "vision") means looking over your paragraphs with a fresh eye to identify and fix any problems with unity. You will also want to check carefully for problems with grammar, mechanics (spelling, punctuation, formatting), and word choice.

The best way to make sure that you've fixed these problems is to perform your revision as carefully as you have performed the other steps in the writing process. Many students rush their revision or skip it altogether, which can seriously harm the quality of their writing.

Revising for Unity

Again, **unity** means that a paragraph stays on track and includes only information that supports the main idea. Because unity is so important to effective writing, it's a good idea to check for it before you look for errors in individual words and sentences.

FOUR MAJOR PROBLEMS WITH UNITY

As you learned in Chapters 4 and 5, there are several ways that you can get off track when outlining and writing a paragraph. These include:

- changing your main idea when you write the topic sentence
- changing a support point, combining it with an example, or forgetting it altogether
- forgetting a transitional expression
- including information that does not fit

To see each of these problems in action, let's look at one college student's work. We'll begin by looking at her outline, which is complete and problem-free.

ASSIGNED TOPIC	*Discuss a place that makes you happy.*
MAIN IDEA	SeaWorld is a place where I feel especially happy.
TRANSITIONAL EXPRESSION	In the first place,
SUPPORT POINT 1	it has a relaxing atmosphere.

- coastal location
- people don't rush
- relieves my headaches

TRANSITIONAL EXPRESSION	In the second place,
SUPPORT POINT 2	it has my favorite sea animals.

- killer whales
- penguins
- manatees

TRANSITIONAL EXPRESSION	Finally,
SUPPORT POINT 3	it is not crowded like other theme parks.

- no long lines
- uncrowded walkways
- no waiting for tables

After writing her paragraph, the student compared it very carefully with her outline. In this revision activity, she identified four problems with her unity. The problems are numbered and underlined below, and they are discussed in more detail in the following sections.

SeaWorld in San Diego has the best entertainment of any California theme park. In the first place, I like to immerse myself in its relaxing atmosphere. Located on a seacoast, SeaWorld is full of warm sunlight and is surrounded by sparkling water. I just dive into this world of happiness, and my smile doesn't leave my face the whole day. I like its pace because people there don't rush anywhere. Life is so calm at SeaWorld that any problem seems too small to be troublesome. The magic of this place is so strong that even the headaches that I sometimes get disappear without a trace as soon as I step out of my car and breathe in the ocean air. In the second place, SeaWorld has an incredible killer-whale show. These whales are huge and potentially dangerous, but you would never guess it because in the arena they behave like house pets, listening and doing whatever their instructors tell them. And what always amazes me is how these gigantic creatures can swim as fast as a rocket. Also, I like observing penguins in an open aquarium. They have such a funny walk when they waddle slowly to the water. In addition, I like to watch how huge manatees (sea cows) consume their salad leaves from the surface of their pool. I appreciate that SeaWorld is not as crowded as other amusement

1

2

3

parks, such as Disneyland. I have never had to wait forty minutes in a long line to see a show that lasts only five minutes. Because there are four great show stadiums, there is always plenty of space for everyone. Also, the park is constructed in a smart way. All the attractions are within easy walking distance from the main entrance. You never bump into someone traveling in the opposite direction because all the walkways are wide and spacious. It is equally important that the park has several convenient cafeterias where I can relax and enjoy a peaceful meal. SeaWorld has the best hamburgers of any theme park, and the prices won't bankrupt you. One time at Knott's Berry Farm, I spent $68 for hamburgers, fries, and sodas for my husband, myself, and our two boys. Paying this amount of money for fast food ruined my whole day. When I want to enjoy a blissful experience, I just follow the tide to SeaWorld.

Problem 1: A Flawed Topic Sentence

When the student began composing her paragraph, she was excited and confident about her ideas. As a result, she wrote a bold topic sentence, praising SeaWorld:

> SeaWorld in San Diego has the best entertainment of any California theme park.

While this is a powerful claim, it misrepresents the main idea for her paragraph. According to this topic sentence, the entire paragraph should focus on the *entertainment* provided by SeaWorld. In fact, the paragraph discusses *all* the reasons why the writer has positive feelings about the park, including the relaxing atmosphere and lack of crowds. With this topic sentence, the reader will be confused by examples that are not connected to the entertainment at SeaWorld. The flawed topic sentence disrupts the unity of the entire paragraph.

Remember, the topic sentence is an especially important feature of your paragraph. If you misstate your main idea in the topic sentence, the rest of the paragraph may not make sense to your reader. Always double-check your topic sentence during the revision process.

Fix this problem by rewriting the topic sentence so that it clearly expresses your main idea for the paragraph. (For a detailed review of problems with topic sentences and how to fix them, see Chapter 5, page 91.)

Problem 2: An Unstated or Unclear Support Point

In rereading her paragraph on SeaWorld, the student noticed that something was missing: she forgot to state her second support point, skipping directly to her first example:

> In the second place, SeaWorld has an incredible killer-whale show.

This error will be quite confusing for readers, who will expect that all the examples following this sentence will relate to the killer-whale show. However, when the writer discusses the penguins and manatees, the unity will be disrupted.

Remember, each support point is a major feature of your paragraph. If you forget or misstate a support point, it can damage the unity of your writing. Always double-check your support points during the revision process.

Fix this problem by rewriting the support point so that it clearly expresses your idea and accurately sets up the examples that follow it. Often, you will need to separate the support point from the first example and rewrite them as separate sentences. (For more information on common problems with support points, see Chapter 5, page 98.)

Problem 3: A Missing Transitional Expression

The author of the SeaWorld paragraph noticed that at one point in her writing, the ideas seemed jumbled; they did not flow as smoothly as she wanted. Then, she realized that she had forgotten her third major transitional expression (introducing the third support point):

> I appreciate that SeaWorld is not as crowded as other amusement parks, such as Disneyland.

For the reader, the missing transitional expression is a large gap in the unity: the abrupt shift from the description of the manatees to the third support point (that SeaWorld is not as crowded as other parks) will be confusing.

Remember, the reader cannot anticipate when you will shift to a new support point or to a new example. You must include transitional expressions to make this shift smooth and logical for your reader. Always double-check your transitional expressions during the revision process.

Fix this problem by adding the missing transitional expression. (For more information on adding transitional expressions, see Chapter 5, page 105.)

Problem 4: Details That Do Not Fit

As the writer was describing the convenient (uncrowded) cafeterias at SeaWorld, she included an unrelated detail about the excellent hamburgers. This detail caused her to remember a time at Knott's Berry Farm when she paid too much for food:

> SeaWorld has the best hamburgers of any theme park, and the prices won't bankrupt you. One time at Knott's Berry Farm, I spent $68 for hamburgers, fries, and sodas for my husband, myself, and our two boys. Paying this amount of money for fast food ruined my whole day.

This is such a powerful memory for the student that it takes control of her writing. These details about the high price of food at Knott's Berry Farm do not fit with her support point, that SeaWorld is *not as crowded* as other theme parks.

Remember, details that do not fit can be especially confusing for your reader. When composing your paragraph, keep a close eye on your outline and don't let unrelated details get you off track. During the revision process, always double-check for details that do not fit.

Fix this problem by eliminating unrelated details. If taking out these details leaves your paragraph underdeveloped, add new details that fit your support point.

The Revised Paragraph

In her revision, the writer corrected each of the problems with unity. Take a look:

Topic sentence rewritten ——————→

The place where I forget about all my problems and feel especially happy is SeaWorld in San Diego. In the first place, I like to immerse myself in its relaxing atmosphere. Located on a seacoast, SeaWorld is full of warm sunlight and is surrounded by sparkling water. I just dive into this world of happiness, and my smile doesn't leave my face the whole day. I like its pace because people there don't rush anywhere. Life is so calm at SeaWorld that any problem looks too small to be troublesome. The magic of this place is so strong that even the headaches that I sometimes get disappear without a trace as soon as I step out of my car and breathe in the ocean air.

Missing support point (with major transition) added ——————→

In the second place, SeaWorld showcases some of my favorite sea animals. For example, it has an incredible killer-whale show. Killer whales are huge and potentially dangerous, but you would never guess it because in the arena they behave like house pets, listening and doing whatever their instructors tell them. And what always amazes me is how these gigantic creatures can swim as fast as a rocket. Also, I like observing penguins in the open aquarium. They have such a funny tread when they walk slowly to the water. In addition, I like to watch how huge manatees (sea cows) consume their salad leaves from the surface of their pool.

Transitional expression added ——————→

Finally, I appreciate that SeaWorld is not as crowded as other amusement parks, such as Disneyland. I have never had to wait forty minutes in a long line to see a show that lasts only five minutes. Because there are four great show stadiums, there is always plenty of space for everyone. Also, the park is constructed in a smart way. All the attractions are within easy walking distance from the main entrance. You never bump into someone traveling in the opposite direction because all the walkways are wide and spacious. It is equally important that the park has several convenient cafeterias where I can relax and enjoy a peaceful meal.

Detail rewritten to focus on the availability of tables in the cafeteria ——————→

I've never had to scramble for a free table or eat elbow-to-elbow with a hungry mob. When I want to enjoy a blissful experience, I just follow the tide to SeaWorld.

Caution!   A paragraph without unity can be a hazardous reading experience: the large gaps, abrupt shifts, and unexpected digressions can cause your reader to stumble and fall. To protect your reader from such hazards, always take the revision stage of the writing process seriously.

Caution: Unrevised Paragraph

ACTIVITY 1

Page 119 shows an outline and a paragraph. Do the following:

- Review the outline.
- Read the paragraph, comparing it carefully with the outline.

- Underline or highlight any problems with unity.
- In the spaces between the lines or in the margins, write in a revision to correct each problem.

The paragraph has four problems with unity.

MAIN IDEA	I try to be the best parent that I can be.
TRANSITIONAL EXPRESSION	For starters,
SUPPORT POINT 1	I try to be a good provider. – work two jobs – spend money on my kids rather than on myself – set up college fund
TRANSITIONAL EXPRESSION	Second,
SUPPORT POINT 2	I spend a lot of time with my children. – dinnertime – study and fun time after dinner – weekends
TRANSITIONAL EXPRESSION	Third,
SUPPORT POINT 3	I try to listen to and help my children. – tell them they can talk to me (and they do) – sometimes give advice – make sure they know they can count on me

It's tough being a good parent. For starters, I work two jobs. I have jobs both as a full-time administrative assistant and as a part-time salesclerk at a gift store. The hours are long, especially now that I'm in school. However, the jobs allow me to pay my expenses and those of my children, with some money to spare every month. Also, I try not to spend too much money on myself; I put my children's needs for clothing, school supplies, and occasional gifts over my own needs. Additionally, I am putting my savings into college funds for my daughter and son. I have only recently been able to afford college myself, and I don't want my kids to have to struggle for their education the same way I did. Second, I spend a lot of time with my children.

CONTINUED >

For more practice with unity and other topics covered in this chapter, visit **bedfordstmartins .com/steppingstones**.

Even though we all have busy schedules, I insist that we try to have dinner together every night so that we can talk about our days over a healthy meal. After dinner, I help my kids with their homework while I'm doing my own, and sometimes we'll watch a movie or a TV show together before bed. Our favorite shows are comedies, and we like to laugh together. Some shows are really annoying, though; I hope the reality-TV show trend dies soon! On weekends, my kids usually want to spend time with their friends, but we try to plan a special event together at least once a month, like going to the zoo or a museum. I try to listen to my children and help them with their problems as much as I can. I have told my kids that they can talk to me whenever they want, and they often come into my room before bedtime to discuss issues that are bothering them, like disagreements with friends. I give advice, but I try not to be a know-it-all. Also, I make sure they know that they can always count on me. I know I haven't always been an ideal parent, but my kids deserve my best, and I try to give that to them every day.

ACTIVITY 2

Reread one or more of the paragraphs that you developed in Chapter 5, marking any places where the unity has been disrupted. Then, fix the problems with unity, using the strategies discussed so far in this chapter.

SOME HELPFUL REVISION STRATEGIES

If you could examine your papers magnified to three times their normal size, you would probably notice every comma, every missing letter or word, and so on. You would have to move slowly across the page as well, taking in each detail as it passed before the powerful lens of your eye. With this ability, you might *really see* your writing like never before.

The following strategies are especially helpful early in the revision process, when you'll typically want to check for unity.

Revise with Fresh Eyes

If you try to revise your paragraph immediately after writing it, you may be too close to the ideas or too tired to see any problems. To see your work with fresh eyes, take a break before revising it. During this break, do something to relax your mind and take it off your writing: have a meal, get some exercise, take a nap, do some chores. If possible, wait until the next day to do your revision. Having fresh eyes will make it much easier for you to spot any mistakes in your paragraph.

During a timed, in-class writing assignment, you probably won't be able to take a break before revising your work. You can, however, pause to stretch, close your eyes, and breathe deeply for a minute or two. This brief moment of relaxation can clear your mind and boost your mental energy for the revision.

Use Your Outline

Suppose you are driving to an unfamiliar location and are relying mostly on a global positioning system (GPS) to get there. If you turn off the navigation system several miles before reaching your destination, what will happen? You might remember some of the directions, but you will probably have to guess the rest. Chances are, you will get lost.

Many students put aside their outline after composing the paragraph. This is like turning off the navigation system before reaching your final destination. In academic writing, you have not reached your final destination until you have completed the revision, using the outline to achieve unity in your paragraph.

Keep your outline beside your paragraph to check for unity during revision. Cross-check each part of the paragraph with the corresponding items in the outline. Watch for missing, misplaced, or accidentally changed features.

Get Peer Review

One of the best strategies for revising your paragraph is to exchange papers with a **peer**, a classmate or fellow student who is at the same level of English as you, to comment on each other's work. This process is known as *peer review*. Sometimes, your instructor may pair you with another student during class for peer review. If you are not given this opportunity, you can arrange to meet with another student outside of class and conduct your own peer review.

Start by inviting a fellow student who is mature and dedicated to the work. Meet in a quiet place, like the library or an empty classroom. Plan to spend at least half an hour for the peer review. You should bring your paragraph, your outline, and the peer review form on the next page. Then, follow this process:

1. Exchange paragraphs, outlines, and peer review forms with your peer.
2. Carefully examine each other's paragraphs and outlines, completing the review form as you go.
3. Exchange and discuss the review forms and the paragraphs.

A word about attitude and intellectual honesty: Remember that many people are sensitive to criticism, so try to be polite and constructive in your comments about any paper. For example, it's better to say "I think there may be a problem here" than "You messed up." Also, specific remarks are always more helpful than general ones; for example:

GENERAL	I'm confused.
SPECIFIC	I don't understand what you mean by "important reason." Can you provide more of a description?

However, remember that your job is to provide *suggestions*; it is the writer's job to make decisions and corrections. Do not try to force your opinion or act like a know-it-all. On the other hand, don't be shy or lazy about identifying potential problems. If you are overly concerned about hurting the other person's feelings, or if you aren't serious about the work, your peer review may be ineffective.

When it's your turn to get comments on your work, pay attention to what the reviewer says and try not to be defensive. If you don't understand something, ask questions. Remember, the review process is a great opportunity to improve your work, so take full advantage of it.

Power Tip

For a list of transitional expressions, see pages 98 and 105.

Power Tip

If a peer believes that your main idea is inadequately supported, you might try some of the strategies discussed in Chapter 7 to generate more details for your topic.

Power Tip

Feel free to add your own questions to the peer review form, especially if you have concerns that are specific to a certain piece of writing (for example, "Did you laugh or groan at my description of my uncle's suit?").

This peer review form is also available at bedfordstmartins.com/steppingstones.

PEER REVIEW FORM

1. Identify the topic sentence. How well does it express the main idea of this paragraph? If the topic sentence does not clearly express the main idea, what specific problems do you see?

2. Where might transitional expressions be added to the paragraph? Should any existing transitions be revised? If so, how?

3. List the support points. Is each one clearly stated in its own sentence? If not, describe the problem(s).

4. How well do the support points back up the main idea (topic sentence)? Does any support seem to be missing? If so, what type of additional support might be helpful?

5. Does the paragraph have any digressive details (details that do not fit)? If it does, identify them.

6. Did you find anything confusing? If so, what specifically?

7. What do you like best about this paragraph?

8. Do you have other recommendations for improving this paragraph?

Choose a paragraph that you wrote recently, perhaps in response to one of the activities in this book. (It should be a paragraph that you haven't yet shown to an instructor.) Then, follow these steps:

- Pair up with another student who has also chosen a paragraph.
- Trade papers and evaluate each other's writing, using the peer review form on page 122.
- Next, return the evaluations and paragraphs and ask each other any questions about the evaluations. (For example, if something isn't clear, you might say, "I'm not sure what you mean by _____. Could you please explain or give me an example?")
- Revise your paragraphs, based on the feedback.

Proofreading for Grammar, Mechanics, and Word Choice

You may recognize this scenario: An hour before class, you begin to write a paper in response to an assignment. Surprisingly, you find the topic interesting and hammer out some original ideas. With seconds left on the clock, you print your work and dash off to class. A week later, when it's time to get your paper back from your instructor, you are hopeful that the grade will reflect your original thinking. Imagine your shock when you see the paper covered in red ink, with a *C+* at the top. The instructor's comment says it all: "Great ideas, but too many errors."

What went wrong? The answer is simple: you did not proofread. That is, you did not read your writing slowly and carefully (word by word), as if with an imaginary magnifying glass, to identify mistakes. If you had reserved ten or fifteen minutes to review your composition for errors, your grade might have been significantly better.

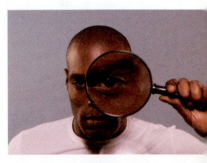

This experience is all too common in college. Because we are busy or because we see proofreading as optional, we may skip this important final step of the revision process. However, not taking the time for this step is often the number one cause of grammar, mechanical, and wording errors in student writing. Proofreading is not difficult; with even a modest effort, most writers can identify and fix many errors in their writing. More difficult is the task of training ourselves to proofread *every time we write*.

PROOFREADING FOR GRAMMAR AND MECHANICS

Grammar problems are discussed in detail in Part Three of this book, so we will not address them in depth here. However, the chart on the next page previews important errors to be aware of.

When proofreading for grammar, look at the words between periods to make sure that they are, in fact, complete, correct sentences. Also, pay

PROBLEM (and where it is covered in this book)	DEFINITION	EXAMPLE
Fragments (Chapter 10, page 246; Chapter 12, page 320; Chapter 13, page 343; Quick Guide, page R-3)	a word group that is missing a subject or a verb or that does not express a complete thought	The fastest runner. [*The fastest runner* could be the subject of a sentence, but there is no verb expressing an action.] **Corrected:** The fastest runner won.
Run-ons (Chapter 11, page 283; Quick Guide, page R-4)	joining sentences together with no punctuation or joining words	The movie ended we left. **Corrected:** The movie ended. We left. OR The movie ended, so we left. The movie ended; we left.
Comma splices (Chapter 11, page 283; Quick Guide, page R-4)	joining sentences together with just a comma	The movie ended, we left. **Corrected:** The movie ended. We left. OR The movie ended, so we left. The movie ended; we left.
Mistakes in verb usage (Chapter 15; Quick Guide, page R-6)	These include a wide variety of errors, such as using the wrong tense (time) of a verb, the wrong form of a verb, or a verb that does not agree with (match) a subject in number.	Yesterday, I go to the movies. [The sentence is in the past tense, but *go* is a present tense verb.] **Corrected:** Yesterday, I went to the movies.

close attention to verbs to make sure that they are in the correct tense and properly formed.

Mechanics issues include spelling, punctuation, and formatting (such as using double-spacing when required). Spelling is discussed on pages 130–32. For a review of punctuation, see Appendix A.

PROOFREADING FOR WORD CHOICE (AND MISSING WORDS)

When proofreading for word choice, look at every word in your writing to make sure that it exactly expresses the meaning that you intended. (When you are unsure of a word's meaning, check the definition in a dictionary.) As discussed in previous chapters, you should also make sure that your words are

- appropriate for your audience. (See Chapter 1, page 15.)
- as precise as possible. (See Chapter 7.)
- as original as possible; in other words, avoid overused expressions, or clichés. (See Chapter 7, pages 166–67.)

Also, look out for words that are often confused because they sound alike. The following chart lists words that are commonly confused. Pay special attention to these words in your writing, and check their definitions and uses against the charts on pages 125–27.

The Most Commonly Confused Words

WORDS/COMMON DEFINITIONS	EXAMPLES
its: a possessive (showing ownership) form of *it* **it's:** a combination (contraction) of *it is* or *it has*	The company lost <u>its</u> lawsuit against the town. <u>It's</u> clear that couples therapy has improved my marriage.
loose: not tight; not fully attached **lose:** to misplace; to be defeated	The <u>loose</u> shingle flapped in the wind. I <u>lose</u> a cell phone every year.
than: a word used in comparisons **then:** at another time (not now); next	Doug is funnier <u>than</u> Kyle. They were not as wealthy <u>then</u>. Peel the apples. <u>Then</u>, cut them into thin slices.
their: belonging to them **there:** at a certain location; not here **they're:** a combination (contraction) of *they are*	<u>Their</u> car broke down twice this month. Please sit <u>there</u>. <u>They're</u> still in shock about winning the lottery.
your: belonging to you **you're:** a combination (contraction) of *you are*	<u>Your</u> phone is ringing. <u>You're</u> my best friend.

Get regular practice with the most commonly confused words so that you can use them correctly every time. Take one or two quizzes a day and every day, if possible. Such quizzes are available at **bedfordstmartins.com/ steppingstones**. Also, take the time to get familiar with other words that are commonly confused by studying the additional chart that follows.

More Commonly Confused Words

WORDS/COMMON DEFINITIONS	EXAMPLES
accept: to take; to agree to **except:** excluding	I <u>accept</u> responsibility for the accident. Mara likes all vegetables <u>except</u> broccoli.
advice: a recommendation; words intended to be helpful **advise:** to give advice	We took your financial <u>advice</u>. You <u>advise</u> us to save more money.
affect: to have an impact on **effect:** an outcome or result	The storm did not <u>affect</u> our travel plans. The drugs had little <u>effect</u> on the patient.

CONTINUED >

Use the online quizzes at **bedfordstmartins.com/ steppingstones** to practice your awareness of the most commonly confused words.

WORDS/COMMON DEFINITIONS	EXAMPLES
brake: to stop or slow; a device used for this purpose	I brake my car before sharp turns.
break: to smash or cause something to stop working; a period of rest or an interruption in an activity	Be careful not to break the crystal vase. The factory workers took a break.
breath: air inhaled (taken in) and exhaled (pushed out)	I am always out of breath after the 5K race.
breathe: the act of inhaling and exhaling	It was hard to breathe in the hot, crowded room.
buy: to purchase	We buy a gallon of milk every week.
by: next to	Martino always sits by the door.
hear: to detect with the ears	I hear our neighbor's car stereo every morning.
here: present; at this location	Is Jeremy here, or did he already leave for work?
knew: past tense of *know* (see below)	Even as a child, I knew my parents were not perfect.
new: recently introduced or created	The new convertible gleamed in the sunlight.
know: to understand or comprehend; to be acquainted with	I know how to swim. You know Jim.
no: a negative expression (the opposite of *yes*)	No, I can't go to the game with you.
lie: to recline	Don't lie in the sun too long.
lay: to put something down	Lay the clothes on the bed, not on the floor.
mind: the part of a person that thinks and perceives	I couldn't get my mind around those math formulas.
mine: belonging to *me*	Those gloves on the chair are mine.
passed: went by (past tense of *pass*)	We passed the house twice before we realized it was Josie's.
past: the time before now	In the past, I drove to work every day.
peace: lack of conflict or war; a state of calm	We must work for peace in a violent world.
piece: a part of something	Have a piece of this delicious pie.
principal: the leader of a school or other organization; main or major	The principal addressed the school assembly. Our principal complaint is that we waited two hours for service.
principle: a law or standard	Professor Bates lectured on economic principles.
quiet: soundless or low in sound	The room was quiet because the children were sleeping.
quite: very; fully	We are quite happy with the decision. We are not quite there yet.
quit: to stop	Joe quit smoking a year ago.

WORDS/COMMON DEFINITIONS	EXAMPLES
right: correct; opposite of *left* **write:** to put words down in a form that can be read (on paper or on a computer screen)	Margo is <u>right</u> that our seats are on the <u>right</u> side of the concert hall. The soldier's daughter promised to <u>write</u> him an e-mail every day.
set: to put something somewhere **sit:** to be seated	I <u>set</u> the glasses on the counter. Please <u>sit</u> down.
threw: past tense of *throw* **through:** finished; going in one side and out the other	Shontelle <u>threw</u> the ball to Dave. We are <u>through</u> with exams. The Cartullos drove <u>through</u> the snowstorm.
to: in the direction of; toward **too:** also **two:** the number between one and three	Christina ran <u>to</u> the lake and back. My daughter wants to go to the movies <u>too</u>. <u>Two</u> swans glided on the pond.
use: to put into service or employ **used:** past tense of *use;* accustomed	I <u>use</u> a rubber glove to open jars that are stuck. Bill <u>used</u> butter in his cooking before his cholesterol got too high. Kent is <u>used</u> to getting up early.
weather: climate (pertaining to the absence or presence of sun, wind, rain, and so on) **whether:** a word used to present alternatives	The <u>weather</u> was beautiful during our vacation. I can't decide <u>whether</u> or not to go to the party.
whose: the possessive form of *who* **who's:** a combination (contraction) of *who is* or *who has*	I don't know <u>whose</u> car is parked in front of our house. <u>Who's</u> the actor <u>who's</u> just divorced his fifth wife?

ACTIVITY 4

For each sentence, decide which words in parentheses are correct. Then, circle your choices.

EXAMPLE: (Weather / (Whether)) or not tomorrow's ((weather) / whether) is nice, we will go on the picnic.

1. You will (loose / lose) the bracelet if the clasp on it is (loose / lose).

2. In the (passed / past), I (passed / past) your house on my daily walks.

3. If (your / you're) car isn't repaired by the weekend, (your / you're) welcome to use mine on Saturday.

4. A summer-long drought will (affect / effect) the community in many ways; the worst (affect / effect) will be limits on water usage.

CONTINUED >

5. I can't (accept / except) that every child in the neighborhood (accept / except) Martina has been invited to the party.

6. (Its / It's) likely that the citizen group will present (its / it's) petition to the city council on Wednesday.

7. After the children (quiet / quite / quit) yelling, the playground was (quiet / quite / quit) (quiet / quite / quit).

8. (Whose / Who's) the man (whose / who's) voice booms "In a world . . ." at the start of every movie preview?

9. Take my (advice / advise) and let Dan (advice / advise) you about your home renovation.

10. (Lie / Lay) your coat over the chair and (lie / lay) down for a while.

Power Tip

So that you do not overlook errors, consider proofreading for only one issue at a time. For example, you might proofread for grammar first, then for mechanics, then for word choice, then for missing words.

A final note: It is very common for writers to leave out words, especially when they are working quickly. After you have checked all of your word choices in a paragraph, read through your writing to make sure that no words are missing.

The author of the following paragraph found a number of errors through proofreading and peer review. Grammar errors are underlined, word choice or spelling problems are in bold, and places where words are missing are highlighted in yellow.

With **it's** signs of rebirth and all **it's** festivities, spring is my favorite season of the year. For one thing, spring is about celebration. My birthday is in spring. Birthdays special to me because my family and friends treat me a queen. They take me to my favorite restaurant, Café Sole, and buy me elegant like **earings** or lingerie. On the first day of May, I look forward to the party at my daughter's school. All the kids dress up and dance around the May pole. <u>Coming from a Persian family.</u> I also celebrate the Persian New Year. We welcome the summer solstice—the longest day of the year—on June 20th with a big family barbecue. Equally important, spring is time for cleaning. I get rid of my old clothes and household items that I no longer use. Sometimes, I have a yard sale with my next-door neighbor, and purge my closets of unwanted junk. <u>Spring is the time to dig out the weeds and plant new flowers I love getting my hands in the soil and clearing the ground for my new flowerbed.</u> I also like to change my eating habits in the spring, knowing that bathing **suite** season is just around the corner. I clean out the refrigerator and the cabinets, getting rid of chips, candy, and old Pop-Tarts. Most important of all, I get physically active in the spring. I start doing things that I could not do in cold **whether**. For example, I renew my monthly gym membership and take spinning classes. If I cannot make it to the gym, I go for a fast-paced with my husband when he gets home from work. With all this exercising, my energy level goes up and feel good about myself. As a result, my husband and I get more romantic. It's no surprise that both of my children were **concieved** in the month of May and born January. And if that doesn't convince you that spring is my favorite season, probably nothing will.

Through proofreading, the writer quickly discovered the two grammar errors: a fragment (the first underlined error) and a run-on (the second underlined error). She fixed these problems and was ready to hand in her work. At the last minute, she asked a peer to read her paragraph. Fortunately, her classmate spotted several places where words seemed to be missing, and she thought that a few words might be misspelled or misused. The writer decided to take action, using special strategies to strengthen her proofreading:

- She used her computer's spell checker and grammar checker to help identify errors.
- She printed her paragraph and proofread it on paper.
- She proofread her paragraph backwards.
- She used a grammar guide.
- She reviewed her spelling log to identify words that she had misspelled in the past.

As a result, the writer identified six missing words and six word choice and spelling errors!

Why did she have so much trouble seeing these twelve errors? First, missing words are often difficult to spot because we *hear* the words in our head as we read silently, even if they aren't on the page. Just as this student did, you may need to adopt special proofreading strategies to detect missing words in your writing. Also, misspelled words can be hard to identify because we get in the habit of misspelling the same words over and over again. For this reason, dedicated writers keep a spelling log in which they record these words and their correct spellings.

SOME HELPFUL PROOFREADING STRATEGIES

Next, we'll take a closer look at the proofreading strategies just discussed (and a few others). These strategies have helped thousands of students to produce better writing.

Identify Your Style of Proofreading

To a certain degree, the way you proofread is a matter of personal style and choice. Some writers proofread *as they write*: sentence by sentence, they check their grammar, spelling, punctuation, and so on. As a result, their final, overall proofreading requires less time. Other writers prefer to get their ideas down quickly, *without stopping* to proofread each sentence. For these writers, the final, overall proofreading will be a more demanding job, and they must reserve extra time for it.

Identifying your style of proofreading can help you focus your energy and manage your time during the writing process. Whatever your preference, remember that a final, overall proofreading is essential for a polished composition.

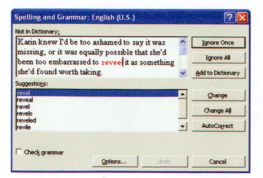

Use Spelling and Grammar Checkers — but Cautiously

Many students who compose on a computer rely on spelling and grammar checkers to eliminate errors. However, it is important to use them with caution. For example, spell checkers may not always make the right choice, as in the example on the left, in which the correct replacement should be *reveal*, not *revel*.

Do not automatically select the first word on the replacement list. Instead, examine each word until you have found the best match. If you are still unsure about the right choice, ask your instructor or a peer for advice, or check a dictionary.

Also, spell checkers will not identify words that are spelled correctly but misused, as often happens with the commonly confused words listed on pages 125–27.

Grammar checkers highlight possible grammar errors in your writing—for instance, with a green line. Often, this highlighting indicates major grammar errors, such as fragments, run-ons, comma splices, or subject-verb agreement problems. The checker also may prompt you with suggestions for fixing these errors. Once again, you should develop the habit of examining each proposed correction method. Not only will this help you make the right choice, it will build your grammar skills for those times when you do not have access to a grammar checker.

Finally, keep in mind that grammar checkers are not 100 percent accurate; they sometimes underline a sentence that is perfectly correct. Do not automatically assume that the grammar checker is right and your sentence is flawed. As your grammar awareness grows, you should begin to rely on your own judgment as much as you rely on the electronic correction tools.

Power Tip

Dictionaries are great tools for improving your spelling and for checking the definitions and proper usages of words. Invest in a portable dictionary or refer to online tools like **dictionary .com**. With **dictionary .com**, if you know the first few letters of a word but are unsure of the rest of the spelling, enter an asterisk (*) after the letters (for example, *acc** for *accidentally*). You'll get a list of words that begin with these letters, and their spellings.

Proofread in Two Views

Whenever possible, proofread your writing in *two views*: on the computer monitor and on the printed page. Each of these visual media will help you notice different details in your writing. If you proofread only on the screen, your eyes may miss quite a few errors.

After writing your composition and reading it on-screen, always print a draft and proofread *on the page*. It's a good idea to double-space your writing before you print it so that it's easier to read. Then, use a combination of pen, pencil, and/or highlighter to mark your errors. For example, you might highlight words whose spelling you need to look up in the dictionary, put a colored star by items you want to ask your instructor about, and use pencil to add missing words or make other edits. Next, go back to the computer and make any necessary corrections, consulting your instructor or other resources as needed.

Proofread Backwards

Most people would not think of riding a bicycle backwards down the street. However, it would certainly raise your awareness about your own body, the parts of your bicycle, and your surroundings. To advance safely and successfully, you would need to go slowly and pay careful attention to every part of the experience.

Similarly, most students would not think of proofreading their writing backwards. However, writers who use this strategy find that it raises their awareness about their grammar, word choice and word order, spelling, and punctuation. Proofreading one sentence at a time—starting with the *last* sentence of your composition—will force you to go slowly and pay careful attention to each sentence.

When we proofread a composition in the customary way—from top to bottom—we get caught up in the flow of our ideas. This momentum—just like the momentum of riding a bicycle forward—makes it difficult for us to slow down and pay careful attention to the fine points of our writing. When we proofread backwards, we interrupt the flow of our ideas, allowing us to focus more effectively on our sentence construction.

Power Tip

As you practice proof-reading backwards, try reading your sentences *out loud*. Pronouncing each word will force you to read more slowly and carefully, helping you to spot errors with greater ease.

Use a Grammar Guide

In proofreading your writing, have you ever *suspected* a grammar error but not felt sure? If so, you are not alone. Many college students lack confidence in identifying their grammar mistakes. For this reason, it is helpful to keep a grammar guide beside you when proofreading. This guide can be a brief list of reminders, like the one on page 124. It can also be a separate grammar handbook. If you use a handbook, you should flag or paper-clip pages that cover how to recognize and fix common and serious errors, such as fragments, run-ons, comma splices, and verb errors. Refer to these same pages every time you proofread.

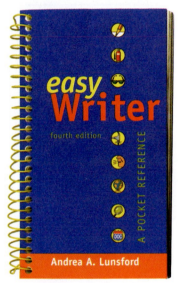

Keep Logs for Spelling, Grammar, and Vocabulary

If you frequently misspell words, keeping a spelling log is a quick and easy strategy to improve your writing. Here's how to do it: when you discover that you have misspelled a word, take a few seconds to write down *both* your incorrect spelling and the correct spelling in your log, which might be set up like the one on the next page. You should also *re-log* a word each time you misspell it; this repetition will help you master the correct spelling more quickly.

You might also keep a log of your grammar errors. Each time your instructor marks a grammar error in your writing, copy the entire incorrect sentence in the log. Then, rewrite the sentence, correcting the error. If you like, you can organize your log according to types of errors (fragments, run-ons, verb errors, and so on).

Additionally, to help build your vocabulary—an important strategy for college success—consider keeping a vocabulary log. Each time you read an unfamiliar word, look up its meaning in the dictionary. Then, write the word and its definition in your vocabulary log. You might also want to write down the sentence in which you first discovered the word.

If you've never kept a log before, start with just one, selecting the issue (spelling, grammar, or vocabulary) that is the most important for your writing.

Log of Spelling Errors			
Student _____		Course _____	
Paper Title _____		Paper Title _____	
Date _____		Date _____	
Incorrect Spelling	Correct Spelling	Incorrect Spelling	Correct Spelling
1.		1.	
2.		2.	
3.		3.	
4.		4.	
5.		5.	
6.		6.	
7.		7.	
8.		8.	
9.		9.	
10.		10.	

ACTIVITY 5: Mastery Test or Teamwork

For each paragraph below, do the following:

- Proofread backwards, starting with the last sentence and examining one sentence at a time. Edit errors that you find. (You might want to consult the brief grammar chart on page 124 or some other grammar guide.)
- Start a spelling, grammar, or vocabulary log and record the errors there.

In this paragraph, look for one fragment, one run-on, one comma splice, two verb errors, three missing words, and five misspelled or misused words.

1. Although I do not make a lot of money, I have developed habits that will ensure my financial security. First of all, I carefully monetor how much I spend. I have figured out how much extra money I have every month after necesary expenses (rent, food, utilities, and so on), and I never spend more than that, in fact, make sure that I have extra money in my bank account in case emergency expense, like a car repair bill, arises. Second, I avoids luxuries unless it is a special occasion. For example, I do not eat out unless it is my birthday, a friend's birthday, or some other special event. Also, I rented movies instead of going to the theater and spending a lot on tickets, popcorn, and soda. In addition, I do not by expensive cosmetics and face creams I make my own moisturizers with natural ingredients. Like olive oil and beeswax. Most important, I contribute regularly to my savings. I have joined company's 401(k) plan, and money for this comes directly out of my pay so that I am not tempted to spend it. Also, I try to contribute money to my savings account whenever I can. I may never be rich, but because I have excepted personal responsibility for my finances, I am confedent that I will never have to worry about money.

In this paragraph, look for two fragments, two comma splices, one run-on, three verb errors, two missing words, and three misspelled or misused words.

   2. My grandfather influenced me more than any other person in my life. In the first place, he was the role model for my life. My father die when I was four, before I could really get to know him, but my grandfather stepped write into the role of father. Teaching me Italian (my grandfather's native language), piano, and soccer, in fact, he influenced me musically that I work as a musician today, giving piano lessons and performing with musicians who come into town. In the second place, Grandpa taught me what it means to be a gentleman, he had fine manners, always listning politely to others and asking them questions about themselves. Also, he held doors open ladies, gave up his seat on the bus for pregnant women, and helping elderly neighbors in his apartment building carry groceries upstairs even when he was quiet old himself! To grandfather, dressing well was also

CONTINUED >

a form of good manners. He never went to any public place, even the grocery store, without wearing a suit and fedora hat. Because of him, I always tries to be polite to others and to dress my best. Whenever I am performing or going to any important place. Finally, Grandpa taught me the value of humor he was a quiet and dignified, but if he thought that a person was acting prejudiced or "like a big shot," he would wink at me and say to the person, "You'll have to excuse me, but I'm hard of hearing." Of course, his hearing was perfect. Although he passed away last year at ninety-two, I will always love and treasure him, and I hope that I am as good a role model to my children as he was to me.

ACTIVITY 6

Refer to the paragraph(s) you worked on for Activity 2 or to any paragraph that you developed in Chapter 5. Then, proofread your writing backwards, fixing any errors that you find. Consider recording errors in a spelling, grammar, or vocabulary log.

BRINGING IT ALL TOGETHER:
Revising

In this chapter, you have learned about revising and proofreading strategies that will help you improve your writing. Confirm your knowledge by filling in the blank spaces in the following sentences. If you need help, review the pages listed after each sentence.

✔ Paragraphs that stay on track and include only information that supports the main idea are called _____ paragraphs. (page 114)

✔ _____ means looking over your writing with a fresh eye to identify and fix any problems. (page 114)

✔ The _____ of your paragraph can be disrupted when there is a flawed topic sentence, an unstated or unclear support point, a missing transitional expression, or details that do not fit. (page 114)

✔ Some helpful revision strategies include revising with _____ eyes, using your _____ to check for unity, and getting comments from a _____. (pages 120–21)

✔ Helpful proofreading strategies include using _____ _____ cautiously and proofreading _____. You can also use a _____ guide and keep _____ to help you improve your spelling, grammar, and vocabulary. (pages 130–31)

PART TWO
Expanding Your Writing

CHAPTER 7

Developing Details

Before you read this chapter, it's a good idea to test your understanding about developing details. You may know more than you think.

For each question, select all the answers that apply.

WHAT DO YOU KNOW?

1. **What is the result of using words such as *a lot, sort of, people, stuff, things,* and *awesome* in your college writing?**

   ___ Your writing may become vague.

   ___ Your writing may contain unanswered questions.

   ___ Your writing may confuse your audience.

2. **If you copy your outline word for word when composing your paragraph, your final product will likely be:**

   ___ a paragraph with confusing and unclear details.

   ___ a paragraph with not enough details.

   ___ a paragraph with precise and colorful details.

   ___ a paragraph that sounds mechanical.

3. **If your writing has precise and colorful verbs, then it will have strong:**

   ___ action details.

   ___ concrete details.

   ___ quoted details.

4. **If your writing appeals to your audience's five senses (sight, hearing, smell, taste, touch), it will have strong:**

   ___ emotive details.

   ___ sensory details.

   ___ action details.

5. **If you use metaphors and similes in your writing, your writing is likely to have strong:**

   ___ comparative details.

   ___ concrete details.

   ___ action details.

Recognizing Imprecise and Unclear Language

In everyday conversation, we use many imprecise expressions to communicate our thoughts. These expressions are so familiar to us that we do not recognize how unclear they may be. Here are some examples:

> The teacher gives <u>a lot of</u> homework. (How much, exactly?)
> The test was <u>really</u> hard. (How hard, specifically?)
> My son <u>rarely</u> brushes his teeth. (How many times does he brush them, precisely?)
> I asked <u>someone</u> to take notes for me. (Who specifically?)
> We've got <u>stuff</u> to do. (What, exactly?)

Notice that each underlined expression is imprecise, leaving an unanswered question. When we use such expressions, we assume that the listener will understand or agree with our general meaning. However, this is not always the case. Take a look at this dialogue.

> **Jason:** My history teacher gives a lot of homework.
> **Kayla:** How much?
> **Jason:** Five pages of reading a day.
> **Kayla:** You call that a lot? My art teacher gives twenty pages plus study questions!

We can see that the expression *a lot* has a different meaning for each speaker. For Jason, five pages of reading is a lot of homework; for Kayla, it is not.

Fortunately, in a conversation, one speaker can ask the other for clarification of an idea. When you write, however, your reader may not be able to ask for clarification; therefore, you must use precise and clear language to communicate your ideas completely and effectively.

As a college writer, you should understand that imprecise expressions may weaken your writing. The following chart contains some of the most common examples. Keep in mind that you cannot avoid these words absolutely, but be aware of when you use them and think about whether you can find more precise words.

Imprecise Expressions

IMPRECISE QUANTITIES/ DEGREES	IMPRECISE OBJECTS	IMPRECISE LOCATIONS	IMPRECISE PERSONS
a couple	anything	anywhere	anybody
a few	everything	here / there	anyone
a little less	it	nowhere	no one
a little more	something	places	nobody
a lot of	stuff	someplace	people
a ton of	things	somewhere	somebody

(continued) about almost around fairly generally kind of loads of many nearly plenty of really roughly some sort of	IMPRECISE FREQUENCY always at times frequently infrequently occasionally often rarely	IMPRECISE QUALITIES bad beautiful big good happy nice okay pretty sad short small tall ugly	IMPRECISE SLANG all that awesome cool hot like that sweet totally way

slang: informal language often used between friends or within other social groups. *Dis* for *disrespect* is an example of slang.

To personalize this chart and make it more useful for you, use a highlighter to mark some of the expressions that you use most often in your speaking and writing. Also, you might add other expressions to the list.

Adding Precise Details to Your Paragraph

In Chapter 5, you learned that a well-developed paragraph should include details about the examples presented for each support point. In reality, three situations are common:

1. Some college writers add insufficient details; as a result, they end up with short, poorly developed paragraphs.
2. Other writers add imprecise or unclear details that can confuse the reader and leave many questions unanswered.
3. The best writers work hard to include precise and colorful details.

On the following pages, you will see examples of all three of these possibilities. Let's begin by looking at an outline for a paragraph. It shows where details should be added when the paragraph is written.

ASSIGNED TOPIC   *Discuss how you became a better student this semester.*

MAIN IDEA   This semester, I improved my study skills.

TRANSITIONAL EXPRESSION   First,

SUPPORT POINT 1   I was better prepared for class.
– did more homework
– studied for tests   **ADD DETAILS**
– joined study groups

TRANSITIONAL EXPRESSION	Next,
SUPPORT POINT 2	I took a more active role in class.

– did not fall asleep
– took more notes   ADD DETAILS
– asked questions

TRANSITIONAL EXPRESSION	Last,
SUPPORT POINT 3	I got help outside of class.

– a tutor
– the librarian   ADD DETAILS
– my instructors

Now, let's consider three paragraphs based on this outline. The related examples for each support point from the outline are highlighted in yellow. As you can see, these examples show varying levels of detail.

A Paragraph with Insufficient Details

This semester, I improved my study skills in college. First, I prepared more carefully for class. For instance, I did more homework than before. I started studying for tests. Also, I joined study groups. Next, I participated more actively in class. I made sure that I did not fall asleep in class. Since I was awake, I was able to take more notes. Also, I asked questions. Last, I got help from people outside of class. For example, I started working with a tutor. The librarian helped me. I also visited my instructors to get assistance. With determination and practice, I changed my study habits and became a better student in just one semester. (114 words)

Compare the examples in this paragraph to the examples in the outline above. You will see that the writer has not added any details. As a result, the paragraph lacks precise information and *personality*; we do not get a sense of a strong, individual voice behind this writing. We get the impression that the writer doesn't really care about the ideas in the paragraph.

A Paragraph with Imprecise and Unclear Details

This semester, I improved my study skills in college. First, I prepared more carefully for class. Most of the time, I tried to finish my homework assignments. I spent a lot of time studying for tests, especially the important ones. Also, I joined study groups for some of my classes. Next, I participated more actively in class. In order to do this, I had to stay awake, so I learned a few tricks that kept me from falling asleep. Then, I took better notes, writing down a lot of useful stuff. When I didn't understand something, I would ask someone a question. Last, I got help from people outside of class. I started working with a good tutor in one of the campus labs. When I needed help on a big project, I talked to a librarian. I also visited a couple of instructors during their office hours. After midterm, I visited them nearly once a week. With determination and practice, I changed my study habits and became a better student in just one semester. (175 words)

In this paragraph, the writer has added details, but the language is imprecise and unclear. As a result, many of the details leave an unanswered question:

most of the time (How much time, exactly?)
tried to finish (How much was done, specifically?)
a lot of time (How much time, precisely?)
important ones (Which ones, specifically?)
some of my classes (Which ones, exactly?)
a few tricks (What tricks, exactly?)
better notes (How were they better, exactly?)
stuff (What, specifically?)
something (What, precisely?)

someone (Who, specifically?)
good tutor (How was he or she good, exactly?)
one of the campus labs (Which one, specifically?)
big project (What project, precisely?)
a couple of instructors (Which instructors, exactly?)
nearly once a week (How often, specifically?)

A Paragraph with Precise Details

This semester, I improved my study skills in college. First, I prepared more carefully for class. I completed 80% of my homework in English, math, and geography to maintain a B average. I spent two or three hours studying for each midterm test and twice that for each final exam. To improve my math scores, I joined a study group that met twice a week. For my English class, I joined a group to practice proofreading. Next, I participated more in class. In order to stay awake, I slept eight hours on school nights and drank strong coffee before my classes. I learned to take accurate notes, writing down key examples, facts, and terms. Once, I wrote four pages of notes for my geography class! Mrs. Bosch, my English professor, taught me to raise my hand whenever I didn't understand the material, so I started asking questions in all my classes. Last, I got help from people outside of class. I met with my math tutor, Sandra, twice a week in the math lab. When I needed help finding a book on U.S. presidents, I asked the librarian for assistance. I also learned how to visit my instructors during their office hours. Mr. Vega, my math instructor, encouraged me to stop by once a week, and I did. With determination and practice, I changed my study habits and became a better student in just one semester. (236 words)

In this last paragraph, the writer has taken the time to add clear and precise details. As a result, the information is powerful, and the paragraph has *personality*: we get a sense of a strong, individual voice behind the writing. Notice that each new detail is specific or exact:

80% of my homework (an exact number)
in English, math, and geography (specific subjects)
to maintain a B average (a precise grade)
two or three hours (exact number)
each midterm / each final exam (specific tests)

to improve my math scores (a precise goal)
twice a week (an exact number)
to practice proofreading (a specific activity)
slept eight hours (a precise strategy)
drank strong coffee (a precise strategy)
accurate notes (a precise description)
four pages of notes (an exact amount)

Mrs. Bosch (a specific person)
raise my hand (a precise strategy)
my math tutor, Sandra (a specific person)
twice a week (a specific time frame)
the math lab (a precise place)

finding a book on U.S. presidents (a specific project)
the librarian (a specific person)
Mr. Vega (a specific person)
once a week (an exact number)

ACTIVITY 1

For each sentence pair below, do the following:

- Read the sentences carefully.
- Decide which sentence contains an unclear detail or details. Write "unclear" in the space after the sentence and circle the unclear word(s) or phrase(s).
- Decide which sentence contains precise details. Write "precise" in the space after the sentence and circle the precise word(s) or phrase(s).

EXAMPLE: When Juan woke up, (he felt kind of weird)   _unclear_

    When Juan woke up,
    (his head throbbed and he felt dizzy)   _precise_

1. **a.** My fresh-squeezed orange juice had pulp fibers floating in it.   _____

   b. My fresh-squeezed orange juice had something strange floating in it.   _____

2. **a.** Bernadette squeaks through her nostrils when she laughs.   _____

   b. Bernadette makes a funny noise when she laughs.   _____

3. **a.** On the desert mission, the troops covered a greater distance than they had planned on.   _____

   b. On the desert mission, the troops covered fifty kilometers more than they had planned on.   _____

4. **a.** By the time the paramedics arrived, a diabetic man in the crowd had fainted.   _____

   b. By the time the paramedics arrived, someone in the crowd had fainted.   _____

5. **a.** By Edgar's worried expression, I can tell he is nervous about his blind date.   _____

   b. By the way Edgar looks, I can tell something is wrong.   _____

ACTIVITY 2

For each pair of paragraphs below, do the following:

- Read the paragraphs carefully.
- Decide which one contains unclear details. Write "unclear" next to the paragraph and underline all the unclear details.
- Decide which paragraph contains precise details. Write "precise" next to the paragraph and underline all the precise details.

1. **Paragraph A:** _____

   Carol frowned and narrowed her eyes when her husband, Leon, came home from his manager's job at McDonald's. He had promised that he would be home at 6 P.M., but it was almost 9. Carol had been slicing, dicing, chopping, and sautéing since 10 that morning. Now, the braised beef was cold and dry, the colorful vegetable medley looked faded, and the ice cream cake was a puddle on the cake plate.

   Paragraph B: _____

   Carol looked pretty angry when her husband, Leon, came home from his job. He promised that he would be home at the usual hour, but he was a few hours late again. Carol had spent so long preparing a nice dinner, and now it was ruined.

2. **Paragraph A:** _____

   We trained a long time to prepare for the famous event. We got up early on the special day and ate some healthy food. Then we went to the place where the race starts. Other people were doing all sorts of things to get ready for the race. I did a special exercise that someone taught me a while ago. By the time the race started, I was feeling good.

   Paragraph B: _____

   My brother and I trained for five months to prepare for the New York City Marathon. We got up at 6 A.M. on race day and ate scrambled eggs and buckwheat pancakes. Then we went to Staten Island near the approach to the Verrazano-Narrows Bridge, where the race starts. A group of runners from Ethiopia was doing yoga to prepare mentally for the race. I did lunges that my trainer, Joe, taught me last summer. When the race started at 9 A.M., I felt strong and relaxed.

For more practice with choosing precise language, visit **bedfordstmartins.com/ steppingstones**.

ACTIVITY 3

Referring to the outline and paragraphs below, do the following:

- First, read the outline carefully.
- Next, read each of the three paragraphs.
- Decide which paragraph has insufficient details. On the line provided, write "insufficient details."
- Decide which paragraph has unclear details. On the line provided, write "unclear details." Then, underline or highlight all of the weak details in the paragraph.
- Last, decide which paragraph has precise details. On the line provided, write "precise details." Then, underline or highlight all the precise details in the paragraph.

ASSIGNED TOPIC	*Write about productive ways to be online.*
MAIN IDEA	Online chat rooms are an excellent way to meet people.
TRANSITIONAL EXPRESSION	To begin with,
SUPPORT POINT 1	people don't judge you.

- – your age
- – your race
- – your looks

TRANSITIONAL EXPRESSION	Second,
SUPPORT POINT 2	you can meet people with different viewpoints.

- – people from other parts of the world
- – people from different economic backgrounds
- – people in trouble

TRANSITIONAL EXPRESSION	Best of all,
SUPPORT POINT 3	it's convenient and inexpensive.

- – any time of day or night
- – don't have to go out
- – cheap

1. In my experience, online chat rooms are an excellent way to meet people. To begin with, people can't see you, so they are less likely to judge you. For example, I am young, but when I chat online, nobody judges me for my age. In "real" life, people sometimes discriminate against me because of my race, but nobody notices my race in a chat room. When I go online, I also appreciate that people don't judge me for my looks. Second, chat rooms are a great way to meet people with different viewpoints. I like to talk to people from faraway countries because they have such unique opinions about the world. I have had conversations with rich people and poor people. Sometimes, I chat with individuals who are in abusive situations. Finally, meeting people in chat rooms is convenient and inexpensive. When I need to talk to someone at an unusual time, I know that I can always find a friendly person online. It's also convenient because I don't have to leave the comfort of my own place to go out and meet someone. Best of all, meeting people online is cheaper for many reasons. For all these reasons, I'm grateful for online chats and the ways in which they have broadened and enriched my world.

2. In my experience, online chat rooms are an excellent way to meet people. To begin with, people can't see you, so they are less likely to judge you. For example, I am eighteen but I look about fifteen, so adults often treat me like a child. Online, I chat with others who take my opinions very seriously because they don't know my age. As an Asian-American, I am sensitive to the stares that I get from people who discriminate, but in a chat room my race is invisible. I also appreciate the fact that men can't judge my worth based on a glance at my figure and face. Second, chat rooms are a great way to meet people with different viewpoints. Last week, I discussed the war in Iraq with people from China, France, and India, and they helped me understand how the world views America's presence in Iraq. I chatted about globalization with a super-rich Wall Street stockbroker and a super-poor Vietnamese farmer who uses the Internet café in his village. For several months, I stayed in touch with a woman whose husband beat her, and I learned how hard it can be for a woman to escape domestic violence. Finally, meeting people in a chat room is convenient and inexpensive. Often, I wake up around 4 A.M. and can't get back to sleep. I wouldn't call my friends and wake them up, but I can go online and chat with a person who lives in England or South Africa, where it is afternoon. I don't have to get dressed or leave my house to meet people in a chat room; I love to sit in my bed with my pajamas on and chat. Best of all, I don't have to spend four dollars on a cappuccino to meet people at Starbucks; the Internet doesn't cost me a penny because my parents pay for the connection. For all these reasons, I'm grateful for online chats and the ways in which they have broadened and enriched my world.

globalization: the increasing connection among the world's peoples politically, economically, socially, and culturally as a result of advances in transport, communication technology, and so on

3. In my experience, online chat rooms are an excellent way to meet people. To begin with, people can't see you, so they are less likely to judge you. For example, nobody will know your age. Also, nobody notices your race. In addition, it never matters how you look. Second, chat rooms are a great way to meet people with different viewpoints. You can hear the experiences of people from other parts of the world. You can meet people from different economic backgrounds. Sometimes, you can learn about people who are in trouble. Best of all, meeting people in chat rooms is convenient and inexpensive. You can connect with people any time of the day or night. You don't have to go out to meet them. Since you don't have to go out, it's cheap. For all these reasons, I'm grateful for online chats and the ways in which they have broadened and enriched my world.

Power Tip
As you learned in Chapter 6, another common problem is details that do not relate to the main idea (topic sentence) of a paragraph. See page 117 to refresh your memory of this problem.

ACTIVITY 4: Teamwork

With two or three classmates, discuss the three paragraphs from Activity 3 one at a time.

- Why did each of you label the paragraphs as you did? Point to specific details in explaining your choices.
- If any of your choices differ, discuss why this might be the case.
- Consider other details that even the precise paragraph might have included.

Developing Precise and Colorful Details

As a college writer, you should aim for details that are precise and colorful.

For example, look at the two cakes pictured here. The basic ingredients and taste of each cake may be similar, but only one cake shows a professional quality of work. Although cake 1 has the main characteristics of a cake (layers and frosting), the baker has not made a special effort to create an extraordinary dessert. However, cake 2 is clearly special; the baker has added precise and creative details (different-sized layers, colors, flowers, and dancing figures) to excite the imagination and appetite of her guests.

Like a special cake, a paragraph written for college should be of professional quality. In addition to the basic characteristics of a paragraph (topic sentence, support points, and related examples), an outstanding paragraph must have something extra: it must have precise (specific) and creative details that grab readers' attention and make them hungry for more.

Although there are many strategies for developing precise and colorful details, we will focus on six in this chapter. Notice that each type of detail has a specific purpose:

1. **Concrete details:** identifying persons, places, and things
2. **Action details:** energizing your verbs
3. **Quoted details:** recording what people say
4. **Sensory details:** describing what you see, hear, smell, taste, and touch
5. **Emotive details:** exploring emotions
6. **Comparative details:** using metaphors and similes

Cake 1: Plain

Cake 2: Colorful and creative

USING CONCRETE DETAILS

Looking at the chart on pages 140–41, you will see that most of the words do not name *specific* persons, places, or things. (Notice especially the words under *Imprecise persons*, *Imprecise locations*, and *Imprecise objects*.) These words are called *abstract*. When you use abstract words in your writing, you may end up with details that are imprecise and unclear. Take a look at the underlined words in this sentence:

I want to go <u>somewhere special</u> for my birthday.

In this sentence, the phrase *somewhere special* is abstract because it does not identify a specific place; for the reader, it is unclear what this special place might be. However, we can replace this abstract phrase with a more precise detail:

I want to go to <u>an amusement park</u> for my birthday.

The phrase *amusement park* identifies a specific place. Any detail that names a specific person, place, or thing is called a *concrete* detail. Now, the reader has a clear idea about where the writer would like to go. However, the writer can make this detail even clearer by naming an actual amusement park:

I want to go to <u>Six Flags Over Georgia</u> for my birthday.

Six Flags Over Georgia tells the reader *exactly* where the writer would like to go.

Basic Guidelines for Using Concrete Details

- Avoid the abstract words in the chart on pages 140–41.
- Identify specific persons, places, and things.
- Whenever possible, use a proper noun to name specific people, places, and things.

Terminology Tip
Words that name people, places, or things are known as *nouns*. For more details, see Chapter 10, pages 228–29.

Terminology Tip
Six Flags Over Georgia is known as a *proper noun* because it names a specific (brand-name) amusement park. Proper nouns begin with capital letters. For more on proper nouns, see Chapter 10, page 228.

ACTIVITY 5

For each sentence below, do the following:
- Underline the imprecise or abstract word(s) or phrase(s).
- Rewrite the sentence, adding precise and colorful concrete details. When possible, use a proper noun to name a specific person, place, or thing. (You may find words other than nouns that can be made more specific.)

EXAMPLE: After the all-night party, Jeremy found <u>something</u> in his ear.

After the all-night party, Jeremy found a pinto bean in his ear.

1. Compared to someone who is six feet four, he is kind of short.

   _____

2. Although I generally avoid eating bad things, I occasionally have a special treat.

   _____

3. My book club is reading something new that is just okay.

   _____

CONTINUED >

4. Everyone is invited to the big event.

5. My old job was pretty cool, but my new job is awesome.

ACTIVITY 6: Teamwork

With two or three classmates, do the following:

- On a blank sheet of paper, draw a two-column list with the headings "specific details" and "details that could be more specific."

- Read each sentence of the paragraph below carefully, identifying any concrete details that are specific. Write each of these details in the column, "specific details." Then, notice if there are any details in the sentence that could be even more specific. If you find any of these, write them in the column, "details that could be more specific."

- For each detail that could be more specific, discuss with your teammates how you would change it to make it more specific.

Student Writer

Living on a tight budget isn't easy, especially when your kids want expensive gadgets. Now that the holidays are approaching, Myla, my oldest, has been asking me for a MacBook computer. Myla is planning to study something in college next year, and since Macs are supposed to be the best computers for this, I think this investment will be wise. She will be able to practice design skills on the computer and use it in college. I feel less sure about the request of my middle child, Tarik. He already has an iPod and a cell phone, but now he wants an iPhone. I can see from all the advertising that this phone has a lot of fancy features, like Internet browsing, but does a kid his age really need all of them? When Tarik is a successful executive, he can buy a phone that communicates with Mars, but until then, I think I'll just keep paying for his guitar lessons. My youngest, Daniel, wants a Wii video game, which lets him play sports like tennis, baseball, and bowling indoors. This gadget isn't cheap, but Daniel can get hyper when he's penned up, which happens often during the cold winter months here. Therefore, the Wii might actually be a gift for Mom, if you know what I mean. As much as I can, I want to make my kids' holiday dreams come true, but I also want to be practical, because that's in *all* of our best interests.

You may repeat this activity using these paragraphs by professional writers:

- paragraph 2, "The Joy of Reading and Writing: Superman and Me" (page 441)
- paragraph 1, "Comfort" (page 469)
- paragraph 1, "Passing Through" (page 476)
- paragraph 5, "Under the Influence" (page 483)

ACTIVITY 7: Teamwork

With two or three classmates, do the following:

- Read the paragraph below, underlining all the imprecise and unclear details.
- Working as a team, rewrite the paragraph, making persons, places, and things more concrete and adding other precise and colorful details.
- Have one person write the new paragraph on a separate sheet of paper.
- When all the teams in the class have finished writing, have a person from your team read the paragraph out loud to the class.

> The other night, a few of us went to a place around the corner to have some fun. When we got there, somebody had fallen several feet from a high place and was hurt really bad. One of us is in the medical field, so he volunteered to do something. A little while later, the person who fell was sitting up and feeling pretty good. We stayed way late and had an awesome time.

ACTIVITY 8

- First, look carefully at the photograph.
- Next, on a separate sheet of paper, freewrite a brief description of the photograph. Use as many concrete details as possible. (For more advice on freewriting, see Chapter 2, pages 35–37.)
- When you have finished writing, try to get together with a few of your classmates and read your descriptions out loud to one another. Decide who uses the most precise and colorful details.

ACTIVITY 9

Write a paragraph. Using as many concrete details as possible (specific persons, places, and things), discuss or describe one of the following:

- your favorite Web site
- a college class that you dislike(d) going to
- the best vacation you ever took
- the objects in your backpack or purse
- going through the security check at a busy airport

USING ACTION DETAILS

Good writing has *energy*. One of the best ways to energize your details is to use precise and colorful *verbs*. Inexperienced writers often rely on common and inexpressive verbs rather than searching for more original and powerful verbs. Take a look at the underlined verb:

> After the batter struck out, he <u>walked</u> toward the umpire.

The verb *walked* does not paint a strong picture of the batter's movement, and it tells us nothing about the batter's purpose for approaching the umpire. However, we can replace this verb with a more precise and colorful action:

> After the batter struck out, he <u>stomped</u> toward the umpire.

Here, the verb *stomped* creates a stronger image of the batter's movement; it also suggests why the batter is approaching the umpire: he's probably angry. If the writer of this sentence is especially creative, she may experiment with other powerful verbs. For example,

> After the batter struck out, he <u>stormed</u> toward the umpire.

Here, the verb *stormed* paints a powerful picture of the batter's movement. It also suggests the aggressive intention of the batter toward the umpire.

Basic Guidelines for Using Action Details

- When describing an action, close your eyes and try to imagine the specific image that you want to create in readers' minds.
- Use a portable or online thesaurus to help you find more precise and original verbs. (A thesaurus is a dictionary that, for each word, gives words with similar meanings. Remember to check with your instructor or other students if you are unsure about whether to use an unfamiliar word.)
- In a notebook, keep a list of new verbs that you would like to incorporate into your vocabulary.
- When possible, try to replace state-of-being verbs (*am, is, are, was, were*) with action verbs (like *stomped* or *stormed*). A good time to make these changes is when you are proofreading and editing your writing. (For more advice on proofreading, see Chapter 6.)

ACTIVITY 10

For each sentence below, do the following:

- Underline the inexpressive verb or verbs.
- Rewrite the sentence, adding precise and colorful action verbs.

EXAMPLE: My boyfriend <u>touches</u> my hair.
My boyfriend caresses my hair.

1. The red Corvette went around the corner.

   _____

2. When she won the $4 million lottery, Alisa smiled.

   _____

3. When my male pit bull sees another male pit bull, he always goes toward him.

   _____

4. The student who sits next to me in my geography course is overeager; every time he knows an answer, he raises his hand.

   _____

5. The nervous bank robbers asked us to get on the floor.

   _____

ACTIVITY 11: Teamwork

With two or three classmates, do the following:

- On a blank sheet of paper, draw a two-column list with the headings "specific details" and "details that could be more specific."
- Read each sentence of the paragraph below carefully, identifying any action details that are specific. Write each of these details in the column, "specific details." Then, notice if there are any details in the sentence that could be even more specific. If you find any of these, write them in the column, "details that could be more specific."
- For each detail that could be more specific, discuss with your teammates how you would change it to make it more specific.

Student Writer (This writer enters a dangerous race with a prized car, but he escapes the worst consequences — just barely.)

Monday arrived and I raced to work. As I accelerated up a hill, I approached two vehicles traveling much too slowly for me. Common traffic laws were for the weak and inexperienced; I was a man who made my own rules. I darted up the left lane; the initial vehicle posed no challenge, and I passed it with ease, the first of many victories, or so I thought. My car raced beside the second vehicle. A kid no older than sixteen looked at me with pride and contempt as he sped up. I pushed the gas pedal harder; I was flying, going almost 90 mph. The other car kept pace, and I could not catch him.

Then I saw it, cresting the top of the hill: a semi truck headed straight toward me. I panicked. I looked over to my right, and there was no room to fit between the two cars I attempted to pass. Seconds flew by; I had to react as the truck barreled closer. He approached too quickly and would crush me if I tried to brake. I jerked the steering wheel to the right, not knowing what would happen. My cherished

CONTINUED >

For more practice using action details, visit **bedfordstmartins.com/ steppingstones** and go to _Exercise Central._

possession squeezed between the two cars — surely the sign of an expert driver. Then momentum carried me on. I veered off the road, and a telephone pole did what my brakes could not: brought me to a dead halt.

You may repeat this activity using the following paragraphs by professional writers:

- paragraph 9, "Comfort" (page 469)
- paragraph 7, "The Jacket" (page 473)
- paragraph 7, "Under the Influence" (page 483)

ACTIVITY 12: Teamwork

With two or three classmates, do the following:

- Read the paragraph below, underlining all the weak verbs.
- Working as a team, rewrite the paragraph, making verbs more vivid and adding other precise and colorful details.
- Have one person write the new paragraph on a separate sheet of paper.
- When all the teams in the class have finished writing their paragraphs, have a person from your team read your work out loud to the class.

    After the concert, the crowd moved onto the stage and took the musicians' instruments. The musicians tried to exit the stage, but the crowd stopped them. At this point, someone hit one of the musicians, and the performer made a noise and fell onto the stage. Suddenly, a police officer asked everyone to get down. The crowd became quiet and stepped off the stage.

ACTIVITY 13

- First, look carefully at the photograph.
- Next, on a separate sheet of paper, freewrite a brief description of the photograph. Use as many precise and colorful action verbs as possible. (For advice on freewriting, see Chapter 2, pages 35–37.)
- When you have finished writing, try to get together with a few of your classmates and read your descriptions out loud to one another. Decide who uses the most precise and colorful verbs.

ACTIVITY 14

Write a paragraph. Using as many action details as possible, discuss or describe one of the following:

- a favorite, high-action video game
- a favorite ride at an amusement park
- an exciting sporting event
- an action-packed scene from a movie or television show
- a situation or event you were involved in where there was a lot of action

USING QUOTED DETAILS

Many writing assignments require you to discuss people—friends, family members, co-workers, historical figures, or people in the news. If the person you are writing about said something interesting or important, you might want to record that person's words in your paragraph. The more precise you are in recording a person's words, the more powerful your writing will be. Take a look at the underlined phrase in this example:

In breaking up with me, my girlfriend said <u>something that surprised me</u>.

The underlined phrase is imprecise and unclear. The reader will have to guess about what the girlfriend actually said. However, we can replace this phrase with a more precise detail:

In breaking up with me, my girlfriend said that <u>I am selfish</u>.

In this sentence, the reader has a much clearer understanding of what the girlfriend said. However, the absence of quotation marks tells us that these may not be her *actual* words. If you remember a person's actual statement—and if this statement is especially memorable—record it precisely and put it in quotation marks:

In breaking up with me, my girlfriend said, <u>"You are the most self-centered and vain man I have ever dated."</u>

The underlined section is called a **direct quotation** because it records a person's exact words. Clearly, this quotation presents powerful details that are missing in the other sentences. What the girlfriend *actually* said is much more interesting than the writer's general idea of what she said.

Basic Guidelines for Using Direct Quotations
- Put quotation marks at the beginning and end of the quotation.
- If the quotation is a complete sentence, capitalize the first word of it. For example: *Bill's father said, "Don't forget to take your lunch."*

- If the quotation is not a complete sentence, you do not need to capitalize it. For example: *All of us were told about the "mysterious green glow" that shone in Petrie Forest at night.*
- Use a comma to separate the quotation from the identification of the speaker—for example, *Tom said, "Go away." or "Go away," Tom said.* Notice that in both examples, the closing quotation mark is *after the period or comma.*

ACTIVITY 15

For each sentence below, do the following:

- Underline the imprecise or unclear detail.
- Rewrite the sentence, adding a precise and colorful *direct* quotation, with quotation marks.

EXAMPLE: Hugo said <u>something insulting</u> to me.

Hugo said, "You make money through dishonesty."

1. After the patrol officer checked Bill's license, she told him to do something.

2. At the preseason training, the coach reminded the team of an important point.

3. The palm reader whispered her gloomy prediction.

4. The professor gave a warning to students.

5. When the nurse gave the patient the wrong medicine, the doctor said something critical.

ACTIVITY 16: Teamwork

With two or three classmates, do the following:

- On a blank sheet of paper, draw a two-column list with the headings "specific details" and "details that could be more specific."

- Read each sentence of the paragraph below carefully, identifying any quoted details that are specific. Write each of these details in the column, "specific details." Then, notice if there are any details in the sentence that could be even more specific. If you find any of these, write them in the column, "details that could be more specific."

- For each detail that could be more specific, discuss with your teammates what you might do to make it more specific.

Student Writer

"I need to end this," I said one evening to Randall, who had been my boyfriend for three years. They were the hardest words for me to express, but I'm glad I was able to get them out. In many ways, Randall is a good person, and I know he loved me. However, he always was suspicious and negative about anything that might mean that I'd spend less time with him. Whenever I made new friends, he'd say something like, "I'm not sure she sounds good enough for you." When I got a promotion at my job, he complained that I'd be working late more and wouldn't be able to make dinner for both of us. The incident that finally convinced me to end the relationship was Randall's complaining about my decision to re-enter college after a break of five years. He said, "Why do you need college when you have a good job and you have me?" I tried to explain that it would be hard to advance in my profession without a degree. Also, I wanted to expand my mind and, yes, meet new people. Randall shook his head and didn't even seem to listen, and so I told him that I needed to break things off. "In time," I explained, "you might understand why I had to do it." In his next relationship, I hope Randall will learn to be more independent and less controlling. If not, he might be alone for a long time.

You may repeat this activity using the following paragraphs by professional writers:

- paragraphs 8–17, "Why Couldn't My Father Read?" (page 454)
- paragraphs 3, 4, 15–19, "Four Directions" (page 457)
- paragraphs 7–20, "As They Say, Drugs Kill" (page 480)

ACTIVITY 17: Teamwork

With two or three classmates, do the following:

- Read the paragraph below, underlining all the imprecise and unclear details.

- Working as a team, rewrite the paragraph, adding the most precise and colorful quoted details you can think of. You may want to add other details, too.

CONTINUED >

- Have one person write the new paragraph on a new sheet of paper.
- When all the teams in the class have finished writing, have a person from your team read the paragraph out loud to the class.

> This morning, my husband, Leo, said nice things to me. I asked him whether he was feeling guilty about something. He insisted that he was thinking good things about me and that I should appreciate him. I told him that it was wrong of me to be so suspicious, since he was being so nice.

ACTIVITY 18

- First, look carefully at the photograph.
- Next, on a separate sheet of paper, freewrite a brief description of the photograph. Use as many precise and colorful quoted details as possible. (For more advice on freewriting, see Chapter 2, pages 35–37.)
- When you have finished writing, try to get together with a few of your classmates and read your descriptions out loud to one another. Decide who uses the most precise and colorful quoted details.

ACTIVITY 19

Write a paragraph. Using as many quoted details as possible, discuss or describe one of the following:

- an intense argument that you had
- an interesting cell phone conversation that you had
- your favorite dialogue from a movie or television show
- a time when someone tried to make you believe something that wasn't true
- a heart-to-heart discussion you had with a parent, coach, professor, minister, or therapist

USING SENSORY DETAILS

We use our five senses (sight, hearing, smell, taste, touch) to connect with the world around us. When we read, we look for details that help our senses connect with the writer's world. These details are called **sensory** because they describe the way things look, sound, smell, taste, and feel. Unfortunately, many writers use imprecise adjectives. Look at the underlined adjective in this example:

> By the end of her shift, the nurse's uniform was <u>dirty</u>.

In this sentence, the adjective *dirty* gives an unclear picture of the nurse's uniform. The person reading this sentence will have to guess what the uniform really looked like. However, we can replace the imprecise adjective with more specific and original details:

Terminology Tip
Adjectives describe nouns (persons, places, or things). For instance, in the phrase *happy child, happy* is an adjective that describes the noun *child.* For more on adjectives, see Chapter 10, page 234.

By the end of her shift, the nurse's uniform had <u>yellow and brown stains</u> on it.

Now, the reader has a clearer picture of how the nurse's uniform actually looked. However, an especially creative writer might search for even more powerful images:

By the end of her shift, the nurse's uniform was <u>covered with dried blood, coffee stains, and a large blue spot where a pen had leaked in her pocket</u>.

In this example, we can clearly see how the addition of precise and colorful details gives the writing more *power* and *personality*. We have not only a vivid picture of the nurse's uniform, but also a snapshot of her whole workday.

Basic Guidelines for Using Sensory Details

- Close your eyes and try to imagine the sights, sounds, smells, tastes, and feelings of a situation or scene. Think of descriptions that will re-create the situation or scene in readers' minds.
- Use a portable or online thesaurus to help you find more precise and original descriptions. (Remember to check with your instructor or other students if you are unsure about whether to use an unfamiliar word.)

ACTIVITY 20

For each sentence below, do the following:

- Underline the imprecise adjective.
- Rewrite the sentence, adding precise and colorful sensory details.

EXAMPLE: Harold heard a <u>strange</u> noise outside his bedroom window.
Harold heard a high-pitched screeching and a feathery flapping outside his window, followed by a low growl.

1. My grandmother's house is full of weird smells.

2. My mother uses a sponge to wet the flaps of her envelopes because she can't tolerate the strange taste of the glue.

3. The campers saw an odd ball of light in the night sky.

4. The mechanic heard an unfamiliar noise when he pumped the brake.

5. The dermatologist felt something unusual on my back.

ACTIVITY 21: Teamwork

With two or three classmates, do the following:

- On a blank sheet of paper, draw a two-column list with the headings "specific details" and "details that could be more specific."
- Read each sentence of the paragraph below carefully, identifying any sensory details that are specific. Write each of these details in the column, "specific details." Then, notice if there are any details in the sentence that could be even more specific. If you find any of these, write them in the column, "details that could be more specific."
- For each detail that could be more specific, discuss with your teammates what you might do to make it more specific.

Student Writer

Last year, I went to a Japanese tea ceremony with my grandmother, and it was a great honor and delight. All the guests wore simple kimonos of colorful silk. My grandmother had given me a blue kimono decorated with large white flowers, and I wore it with pride, loving the feeling of the soft fabric on my skin. After we had cleansed our hands and mouths in a basin outside of the tearoom, the hostess invited us inside. We took off our shoes and entered a small, simple room with woven straw mats on the floor. Long banners with graceful Japanese writing hung from the walls, and tall ceramic vases held branches of orange blossoms. The sweet scent of the flowers perfumed the air. The room was quiet except for the low whispers of the guests admiring the decorations. As the ceremony began, we sat on the mats, feeling the cool stone of the floor beneath them. Then, we watched the hostess go through the traditional ritual of placing green tea powder in a ceramic bowl and mixing in hot water with a special whisk. When she whisked the tea, its sharp, leafy aroma filled the air. Then, carefully, the hostess passed the bowl to the first guest. The two exchanged bows, and then the guest drank from the bowl, wiped the rim, and rotated the bowl before passing it to the next guest. When it was my turn, I was a little nervous, but my grandmother had explained each step of the ritual to me. I bowed, drank the rich, bitter tea, wiped the bowl's rim, and passed the bowl to the next guest with a gentle smile. At that moment, I felt the simple beauty of the ceremony connecting me to all those present and to all of my ancestors.

kimono: traditional Japanese robe

You may repeat this activity using the following paragraphs by professional writers:

- paragraph 6, "Devotion" (page 451)
- paragraph 12, "The Jacket" (page 473)
- paragraph 6, "As They Say, Drugs Kill" (page 480)

When you want to describe something vividly, work through the five senses one at a time and think of details that appeal to each. Here are details that one writer came up with to describe a state fair:

SENSE	DETAILS
Sight	spinning rides; red-and-white tents; crowds of people in shorts, T-shirts, and swimsuit tops; tractors in muddy tractor-pull ring; cows, hogs, and sheep in pens for judging
Hearing	laughing and shouting children; rumbling rides; blaring announcements from loudspeakers; mooing and squealing from animal pens
Smell	fried dough and hot dogs; suntan lotion; diesel from tractor engines
Taste	sweet ice cream and tangy fried dough; salty hot dogs and buttery popcorn
Touch	soft fur of animals in petting zoo; vibrations of old rides

ACTIVITY 22: Teamwork

With two or three classmates, select one of the following scenes and describe it with details based on each of the five senses. Work together on one sense at a time and generate the most colorful and precise details you can. (You may not have direct experience with these particular scenes, but use your imagination.) If you'd like, use the chart before this exercise as a guide.

- Describe a busy emergency room.
- Describe being at the beach on a crowded day.
- Describe a crew of firefighters battling a raging forest fire.
- Describe being inside a packed subway train or city bus during rush hour.
- Describe the cages of an overcrowded animal shelter.

Sight: _____

Hearing: _____

Smell: _____

Taste: _____

Touch: _____

ACTIVITY 23: Teamwork

With two or three classmates, do the following:

- Read the paragraph below, underlining all the imprecise and unclear details.
- Working as a team, rewrite the paragraph, adding the most vivid sensory details you can think of, as well as any other details to bring the paragraph to life.
- Have one person write the new paragraph on a separate sheet of paper.
- When all the teams in the class have finished writing, have someone from your team read the paragraph out loud to the class.

When Mildred started her car, she heard an unusual sound coming from the engine. She waited a minute, and then she smelled a very offensive odor coming through the air conditioning. The smell was so intense that it left a strange taste in her mouth. She decided to look under the hood of the car. When she did, she saw a very surprising sight.

ACTIVITY 24

- First, look carefully at the photograph.
- Next, on a separate sheet of paper, freewrite a brief description of the photograph. Use as many precise and colorful sensory details as possible. (For more advice on freewriting, see Chapter 2, pages 35–37.)
- When you have finished writing, try to get together with a few of your classmates and read your descriptions out loud to one another. Decide who uses the most precise and colorful details.

ACTIVITY 25

Write a paragraph. Using as many sensory details as possible (taste, sight, sound, smell, touch), discuss or describe one of the following:

- an important holiday meal in your family
- a crowded food court in a shopping mall
- a beautiful natural setting that you enjoy
- the team locker room after a victorious sporting event
- a preschool filled with energetic children

For more practice using precise and colorful details, visit **bedfordstmartins.com/ steppingstones** and go to *Exercise Central.*

USING EMOTIVE DETAILS

In college, you will sometimes be asked to write on topics that bring up strong emotions for you. Good writers take the time to explore such feelings and find precise details to describe them; these details are called **emotive**. Strong emotive details capture your emotions in a powerful way that allows the reader to connect deeply with your experiences.

Once again, start by recognizing imprecise expressions that may weaken your writing. Notice the underlined words in the following example:

> As the first member of my family to graduate from college, I felt <u>very happy</u>.

In this sentence, the phrase *very happy* gives an unclear picture of the writer's feelings. The person reading this sentence will have to guess about the writer's exact emotions. However, we can replace the imprecise expression with more specific emotive details:

> As the first member of my family to graduate from college, I felt <u>a deep sense of pride and achievement</u>.

The underlined expression gives a clearer sense of the writer's feelings. However, the writer might explore even deeper levels of the emotional experience:

> As the first member of my family to graduate from college, I felt <u>the hope and pride of my ancestors, five generations of farm laborers</u>.

The underlined phrase contains powerful emotive details that help the reader connect with the writer's deepest feelings.

Basic Guidelines for Using Emotive Details
- Avoid the abstract words from the chart on pages 140–41.
- Close your eyes and recall the important memory or experience in as much detail as possible.

ACTIVITY 26

For each sentence below, do the following:

- Underline the imprecise or unclear detail.
- Rewrite the sentence, adding precise and colorful emotive details.

EXAMPLE: After her date, Margie <u>was upset</u>.

> After her date, Margie ran into her house, flung herself facedown on the couch, screamed, and beat the cushions with her fists.

1. When the television executive was sentenced to thirty years in jail, he wasn't happy.

CONTINUED >

2. The paramedic felt bad when he could not revive the drowned child.

_____

3. After dreaming of going to her state university for ten years, Julie was glad when she received her acceptance letter.

_____

4. When the star witness disappeared before the trial, the lawyer was disappointed.

_____

5. The pilot sounded normal when he announced the emergency landing.

_____

ACTIVITY 27: Teamwork

With two or three classmates, do the following:

- On a blank sheet of paper, draw a two-column list with the headings "specific details" and "details that could be more specific."

- Read each sentence of the paragraph below carefully, identifying any emotive details that are specific. Write each of these details in the column, "specific details." Then, notice if there are any details in the sentence that could be even more specific. If you find any of these, write them in the column, "details that could be more specific."

- For each detail that could be more specific, discuss with your teammates what you might do to make it more specific.

Student Writer

It happens too often in my neighborhood. You hear screaming and sirens, or maybe you don't, and later on, there's some kind of shrine on the street: prayer candles, red roses from the 7-Eleven, and teddy bears hugging stuffed hearts. Usually, there's a picture of the kid who got shot and taped-up signs from parents, brothers, sisters, and other kids: "We will always love you," "We miss you," "With Jesus." I've walked by shrines like these maybe four times, and each time I've felt a cold stone in my chest. The faces in the pictures are unfamiliar, and I can't make myself feel all the hurt I could feel. My attitude changed last week when I walked by a new shrine at Garden and Adams. My first thought when I saw the kid's picture was simply _I know that face_. It was like when you're on the bus and nod at someone you've seen around but don't know that well. Then, I realized it was Bo Robbins, a kid I went to grade school with. When I put this fact together with all the other things — the candles, the notes, and the flowers — it felt like someone kicked me in the stomach. I think I actually fell back a little. I had lost touch with Bo after we went on to separate schools, but I remembered him well. He got in trouble a lot for talking in class, but he was funny and made everyone laugh — even the teachers. You couldn't stay angry with him. In the picture at the shrine, he looked like he was getting ready to laugh. That's what got me. I felt the stone again, but this time it was in my throat; I couldn't swallow it down. I walked away from there fast, blinking and wiping my eyes.

You may repeat this activity using the following paragraphs by professional writers:

- paragraph 25, "Four Directions" (page 457)
- paragraph 10, "The Jacket" (page 473)
- paragraph 28, "As They Say, Drugs Kill" (page 480)
- paragraphs 8–9, "Under the Influence" (page 483)

ACTIVITY 28: Teamwork

With two or three classmates, do the following:

- Read the paragraph below, underlining all the imprecise and unclear details.
- Working as a team, rewrite the paragraph, adding the most precise and colorful emotive details you can think of. You may want to add other details, too.
- Have one person write the new paragraph on a separate sheet of paper.
- When all the teams in the class have finished writing, have someone from your team read the paragraph out loud to the class.

     In front of an international television audience, Christina Montero from Brazil was crowned Miss Universe. When the judge announced her name, she was surprised. The other contestants began to gather around her, which helped her feel OK. When the former Miss Universe placed the crown on her head, Christina felt special. Finally, as she walked down the runway, she felt the strongest emotion of her life.

ACTIVITY 29

- First, look carefully at the photograph.
- Next, on a separate sheet of paper, freewrite a brief description of the photograph. Use as many precise and colorful emotive details as possible. (For more advice on freewriting, see Chapter 2, pages 35–37.)
- When you have finished writing, try to get together with a few of your classmates and read your descriptions out loud to one another. Decide who uses the most precise and colorful details.

ACTIVITY 30

Write a paragraph. Using as many emotive details as possible, discuss or describe one of the following:

- the time in your life when you were most frightened
- the person you love or hate the most
- the time in your life when you cried the hardest
- a time in your life when you felt lonely or abandoned
- the time in your life when you felt the happiest

USING COMPARATIVE DETAILS: METAPHORS AND SIMILES

Metaphors are a common feature of language, and most people use them without knowing it. The best way to understand metaphors is to look at some examples.

Let's begin with a sentence that would benefit from the addition of a metaphor:

My six-year-old daughter is an excellent swimmer.

While this sentence makes a clear statement, the phrase *an excellent swimmer* does not give the reader a colorful image of the little girl as a swimmer. However, the writer might use a more creative description. Notice the underlined words:

My six-year-old daughter is <u>a dolphin in the water</u>.

In this sentence, the phrase *a dolphin in the water* is a metaphor that gives the reader an immediate and powerful image of the little girl gliding gracefully through the water. A **metaphor** is a creative comparison of two items with similar characteristics. Sometimes, creative comparisons (comparative details) use the words *like* or *as*:

My six-year-old daughter swims <u>like</u> a dolphin.
My six-year-old daughter swims as gracefully <u>as</u> a dolphin.

Comparisons that use *like* or *as* are known as **similes**.

Basic Guidelines for Using Creative Comparisons (Comparative Details)

- Do not overload your writing with these comparisons. One or two distinctive comparisons in a paragraph are usually sufficient.
- Try to avoid overused comparisons like those in the following list. (These are known as *clichés*, expressions that used to sound original and creative but have lost their spark because of overuse.)

Some Overused Comparisons (Clichés)

avoid _____ like the plague	pretty as a picture
blind as a bat	sick as a dog
cool as a cucumber	sleep like a log
dull as dishwater	smart as a whip
like a bull in a china shop	

ACTIVITY 31

For each of the following sentences, fill in the blank with a comparative detail.

EXAMPLE: In her brown dress covered with cowboy hats and fringes, Noreen looked like ___*a lampshade in a ten-year-old's bedroom*___.

1. My sister spends every free moment reading; she says that books are like _____ to her.

2. The boxer's face had been smashed so many times that it looked like

   _____.

3. After three final exams in twenty-four hours, Max's brain was as jammed with facts as _____.

4. The professor's vocabulary was so difficult that listening to his lecture was like _____.

5. After he was arrested for buying cocaine, the politician's thirty-year career ended as quickly as _____.

ACTIVITY 32: Teamwork

With two or three classmates, do the following:

- On a blank sheet of paper, draw a two-column list with the headings "specific details" and "details that could be more specific."
- Read each sentence of the paragraph below carefully, identifying any comparative details that are specific. Write each of these details in the column, "specific details." Then, notice if there are any details in the sentence that could be even more specific. If you find any of these, write them in the column, "details that could be more specific."
- For each detail that could be more specific, discuss with your teammates what you might do to make it more specific.

Student Writer

When my car broke down in the fast lane of the freeway, it was like being caught in the eye of a tornado. Other vehicles flew by at seventy miles per hour, causing my car to shake like a tin can. I felt as though my little Toyota would be picked up violently and slammed

CONTINUED >

against a nearby overpass. Car horns screeched furiously, and big rigs roared around me like toys tossed by the storm. I was sure that my end had come, that I would be ripped apart in a collision of metal and concrete. I passed out. The next thing I knew, a police officer was knocking on my window, looking like an angel of mercy.

You may repeat this activity using the following paragraphs by professional writers:

- paragraph 3, "The Joy of Reading and Writing: Superman and Me" (page 441)
- paragraphs 1–4, "The Jacket" (page 473)
- paragraphs 10–11, "Under the Influence" (page 483)

ACTIVITY 33: Teamwork

With two or three classmates, do the following:

- Read the paragraph below, underlining all the imprecise details and descriptions.
- Working as a team, rewrite the paragraph, adding the most creative comparative details that you can think of. (If you have trouble figuring out where to add comparative details, use the list of hints after the passage.)
- Have one person write the new paragraph on a separate sheet of paper.
- When all the teams in the class have finished writing, have someone from your team read the paragraph out loud to the class.

My boss has bad breath. It's so terrible that I feel sick when I smell it. The other morning, he came to work with a BIG hangover. He hadn't showered or shaved, so he looked really awful. And worst of all, his breath was a powerful force. I was standing at least six feet away from him when he spoke to me, but the blast was deadly.

Some helpful hints for creative comparisons:

His breath is like . . .

Feel sick as a . . .

His hangover was as big as . . .

He looked like . . .

A powerful force like . . .

Deadly like . . .

ACTIVITY 34

- First, look carefully at the photograph.

- Next, on a separate sheet of paper, write a creative comparison using the image in the photograph. Begin with the following sentence: "_____ is like a rattlesnake ready to strike." Then, freewrite briefly about why _____ is like a rattlesnake that is ready to strike. (For more advice on freewriting, see Chapter 2, pages 35–37.)

- When you have finished writing, try to get together with a few of your classmates and read what you have written out loud to one another. Decide who uses the most precise and vivid details.

ACTIVITY 35

Write a paragraph. Using as many comparative details as possible (metaphors or similes), discuss or describe one of the following:

- getting my driver's license was like . . .
- falling out of love is like . . .
- getting a promotion/raise at my job was like . . .
- having my first child was like . . .
- seeing _____ die was like . . .

ACTIVITY 36

Look back on one or two of the paragraphs that you developed in Chapter 4. Reread the paragraphs and underline or highlight any imprecise or unclear details. Then, using the strategies discussed in this chapter, rewrite the details to make them more precise and colorful. As a reminder, you might use one or more of the following:

- **Concrete details:** identifying persons, places, and things
- **Action details:** energizing your verbs
- **Quoted details:** recording what people say
- **Sensory details:** describing what you see, hear, smell, taste, and touch
- **Emotive details:** exploring emotions
- **Comparative details:** using metaphors and similes

BRINGING IT ALL TOGETHER:
Developing Details

In this chapter, you have explored ways of bringing your writing to life through the use of precise and colorful details. Confirm your knowledge by filling in the blank spaces in the following sentences. If you need help, review the pages listed after each sentence.

✔ When developing an academic paragraph, it is important to avoid two common problems. First, if you use _____ or _____ details, you may leave many questions unanswered and confuse your reader. If you have _____ details, your paragraph may lack personality, and your reader may think that you don't care about the ideas. (page 141)

✔ _____ details identify specific persons, places, and things. To be as specific as possible, use _____ nouns. (pages 148–49)

✔ _____ details use energetic, expressive verbs. (page 152)

✔ _____ details record the exact words spoken by people. (page 155)

✔ _____ details describe the way things look, sound, smell, taste, and feel. (page 158)

✔ _____ details describe feelings as powerfully as possible. (page 163)

✔ _____ details include metaphors and similes. (page 166)

✔ A _____ directly compares one thing to another. For example, *My six-year-old daughter is a dolphin in the water*. (page 166)

✔ A _____ uses *like* or *as* to make comparisons. For example, *My six-year-old daughter swims like a dolphin.* (page 166)

Before you read this chapter, it's a good idea to test your understanding of the patterns of development. You may know more than you think.

For each question, select all the answers that apply.

WHAT DO YOU KNOW?

1. When you speak or write, you often use *patterns of development* to express your ideas effectively. For example, if you are telling a story, the pattern you are probably using is:

   ___ description.
   ___ process.
   ___ narration.
   ___ exemplification.

2. If your paragraph includes strong sensory details (sights, sounds, smells, tastes, textures), the pattern you are probably using is:

   ___ argument.
   ___ definition.
   ___ description.
   ___ cause and effect.

3. If you are exploring the similarities and differences between two things, the pattern you are probably using is:

   ___ cause and effect.
   ___ comparison and contrast.
   ___ argument.
   ___ definition.

4. If you are explaining how to do something or how an event occurs, the pattern you are probably using is:

   ___ cause and effect.
   ___ narration.
   ___ comparison and contrast.
   ___ process.

5. If you are stating a clear position on an issue and providing strong reasons for your position, the pattern you are probably using is:

   ___ exemplification.
   ___ definition.
   ___ argument.
   ___ narration.

Terminology Tip
The patterns of development are sometimes called the *modes* or *rhetorical modes*.

Patterns of Development

In our everyday conversations, we use a number of patterns to develop our ideas and communicate them effectively. Here are some examples of basic— or, the most common—patterns:

- We can describe something (**description**).
- We can give examples of something (**exemplification**).
- We can tell a story (**narration**).
- We can explain how something happens or how to do something (**process**).
- We can explain what something means (**definition**).

If your art professor talks about the brush technique in a painting, she will probably use *description*. If you tell your family about your successes so far in college, you will probably use *exemplification*. If your friend tells you what happened in last night's episode of *Cold Case*, he will probably use *narration*. If you explain to your father how to download music to his iPod, you will probably use *process*. And if you ask the cashier at Starbucks what a "triple grande frappuccino" is, she will probably respond with a *definition*.

As you can tell from these examples, we use **patterns of development** in many instances of daily life. Just as frequently, we rely on these patterns in our writing. Successful writers are especially aware of when and how they use these patterns.

Once you understand how to use these basic patterns of development, you will be able to master the advanced ones more effectively. Here are the advanced patterns:

- We can explain the origin and outcome of an event or occurrence (**cause and effect**).
- We can identify the similarities and/or differences between things (**comparison and contrast**).
- We can state and defend a position on an issue (**argumentation**).

Basic Writing Patterns

The following pages discuss the main features of the basic writing patterns and provide examples of each pattern.

DESCRIPTION

In descriptive writing, you describe what you see, hear, smell, taste, or feel. The subject of your description might be a person, a place, or an object. **The key to good descriptive writing is finding colorful and precise adjectives and nouns that will create a strong sensory experience for your reader.** (For more on adjectives and nouns, see Chapter 10, pages 228 and 234. For more on developing powerful sensory details, see Chapter 7, page 158.)

A Student Writer Uses Description

In the following paragraph, a student describes a photograph of two giraffes. Notice the colorful and precise adjectives and nouns that she uses to create a vivid picture in words.

A beautiful day welcomes a mother giraffe and her new baby. Far back in the picture are a soothing blue sky and blue hills. The blueness is layered with shades of light and dark. The darkest part is the hills. However, some parts of the hills look lighter, as if there might be grass or trees growing in places. Closer up is a field. In the part of the field next to the hills are some shapes that are difficult to see. These might be village huts or tents. Closer to the front of the picture is green and brown grass. There are also some bushes and other dark shapes. The background is slightly blurry because the photographer is focusing on the giraffes. Both have acorn-brown spots on a cream background. There is short, bristly hair on the back of the mother's and baby's necks, and the mother is bending her head down, almost as if she is whispering in the baby's ear. The giraffes' eyes are black blurs, but you can still see the love between them. As their faces touch, they can feel each other's warmth through thin, soft fur. They can also feel the cool air lightly brushing their fur and tickling them, cooling them off on a hot day in July.

In developing her description, this student focused on one part of the image at a time. This strategy helped her organize her paragraph and describe each section in precise detail.

ACTIVITY 1

Read the previous paragraph carefully, underlining or highlighting precise and colorful details, especially adjectives and nouns. (To review adjectives and nouns, see Chapter 10, pages 228 and 234.)

ACTIVITY 2

Working from the previous paragraph, complete the following outline. (Part of it has already been filled in for you.) The outline will help you see how the writer divides her description into three major parts and then uses a series of descriptive details to develop each part.

MAIN IDEA   A beautiful day welcomes a mother giraffe and her new baby.

PART 1   background: blue sky and blue hills

layered blueness: light and dark

hills are darkest part

lighter parts within dark hills

CONTINUED >

Power Tip

Notice that some of the transitions in this paragraph (*Far back in the picture, Closer up*, and so on) move the reader through space. For more on transitions, see Chapter 5, page 105.

Power Tip

For an example of a description by a professional writer, see paragraph 10 of "The Jacket" by Gary Soto (page 473).

PART 2   closer up: field
_____
_____
_____
_____

PART 3
_____
_____
_____
_____
_____
_____
_____
_____

ACTIVITY 3

For each of the following prompts, list precise and colorful adjectives and nouns.

1. Describe your ideal bedroom (personal sanctuary) if you had unlimited money to furnish and decorate it.

2. Describe the outfit and "look" (hair, etc.) you'd wear to impress someone you're meeting for the first time.

3. Describe the most disgusting, gross, or horrible sight you've ever seen.

4. Describe the meal you'd serve to someone from another planet to introduce him or her to "great food on planet Earth."

5. Describe a place where you go when you want to feel great.

ACTIVITY 4

Select one of the photographs from the following page and write an academic paragraph in which you describe the image. Do the following:

- First, brainstorm on what you see, writing down every single detail in the photograph. (You may not be able to use them all in your paragraph, but write them down anyway so that you know your options.)

- You may want to divide the photo into major parts and brainstorm on one part at a time. This will keep you focused and help you get better results.

- Write an outline for your paragraph. Each "major part" of the photograph can be a support point. This will help your description flow logically from one "major part" of the photo to another.

- Compose your paragraph.

- Revise and proofread your paragraph.

Power Tip
You might also use other powerful images to write about. Ask your instructor if you can use a photo that you find yourself, either online or in a book or magazine.

Photo 1: After the storm

Photo 2: In the streets

Photo 3: At the bull run

EXEMPLIFICATION

With exemplification, you provide a series of examples to support or illustrate your main idea. Depending on the topic of your writing assignment, the examples may come from your personal experience or from information that you have read or studied. **The key to good exemplification writing is finding colorful and precise examples that will capture your reader's interest and imagination.**

A Student Writer Uses Exemplification

In the following paragraph, a student explains why reading is important to her, giving several examples.

> Reading is important to me because it excites my imagination as well as challenges my intelligence, and in the end it makes me forget my problems. First of all, reading excites my imagination like nothing else can. For instance, the passage I am reading becomes real to me. Things appear as if they were right in front of me, unfolding before my eyes. Also, colors come alive. Purple is not just purple; it's an electric purple. Green is like neon green but much brighter and clearer. Reading also excites my imagination when I picture myself as one of the characters. Whether it's the main character or a minor character, I just let myself go free and flow with the story. For instance, I can feel as if I'm in the midst of a battle or running through a meadow or locked in a passionate embrace. In the second place, reading challenges my intelligence and broadens my thoughts. When I read different styles of writing, I think differently. Some books challenge what I believe or what I think I believe. They may put questions in my mind and make me think hard as to what I really believe. If I am biased about a topic, I try to think the way the writer is thinking, or I try to be open about what the writer is trying to get across. Finally, reading helps me pass the time and escape all my worries and problems. Reading makes time fly on flights or during boring days at home. Once I am engrossed in a book, I don't even realize that I have sat in one place all day. Alone in my own little world of reading, I forget my problems and doubts. Without reading, my life would be much less rich.

In this paragraph, the student's examples all come from her personal experience. They are memorable examples because they reflect the student's genuine love of reading.

ACTIVITY 5

Working off of the previous paragraph, complete the following outline. (Part of it has already been filled in for you.) The outline will help you see how the student uses a series of examples to illustrate her main idea.

MAIN IDEA

EXAMPLE 1

Reading excites my imagination like nothing else can.

Things become real.

Colors come alive.

I picture myself as one of the characters.

EXAMPLE 2

EXAMPLE 3

Power Tip

For an example of exemplification by a professional writer, see paragraph 17 of "The Sanctuary of School" by Linda Barry (page 445).

ACTIVITY 6: Teamwork

With classmates, make a list of examples to support each of the following topics. Then, working individually, select one of the topics and brainstorm for ten minutes, getting down all the ideas you can.

Power Tip

For more on brainstorming, see Chapter 2, pages 26–37.

1. Give examples of ways to spend time on the Internet.
2. Give examples of food that you should avoid eating.
3. Give examples of people in a hospital emergency room with their injuries and illnesses.
4. Give examples of good (or bad) study habits.
5. Give examples of the symptoms of falling in love.

NARRATION

In narrative writing, you relate the key events and important details of a story. Depending on the topic of your writing assignment, this may be a true personal story, a fictional story, or perhaps a current event or historical episode. **The key to good storytelling is including the major events or actions of the story and using colorful details to bring the characters, settings, and actions to life.**

A Student Writer Uses Narration

The following paragraph tells one student's story of growing up with a difficult mother during a difficult time in the United States. (The student was born during the Depression, a severe economic downturn that began in 1929 and lasted through the 1930s.)

> On reflection, I can see how my relationship with my mother shaped my life. Times were tough, and my mother was very headstrong. I seemed to be the target mostly because I was sensitive. For example, although we didn't have much money, she gave me pennies once to buy candy for myself and my brothers. I was only six years old and rarely had candy, so I kept some extra hidden for myself. When my mother discovered this, she yelled, "You are a selfish, ungrateful child!" She gave me a beating. My dad said, "Oh, stop! Can't you see he's just a kid?" but he was afraid of her, too. I think my mother's abuse showed outside the home because my teacher would check my legs for bruises. Children didn't have much protection in those days. Once, when I was a teenager, my mother and I argued about how late I could stay out, and she locked me out of the house and told me not to come back. I ran away from home for a few days. In much later years, I came to realize that I needed professional help to sort things out. During this therapy, I talked about old wounds. Apparently, though my mother's anger hurt, I got enough mothering to be whole. In many ways, this time in childhood helped me to have a wonderful relationship with my own children. In other words, the old conflict taught me to deal with my own emotional issues instead of inflicting them on my son and daughter.

In developing his narration, the student first identified key events in the story. With this understanding of his narrative, he was then able to add colorful details and dialogue to bring the characters, settings, and actions to life.

ACTIVITY 7

The author of the previous piece devotes most of his paragraph to one traumatic experience. Name the experience. Then, list all the events that were part of this experience. The last event has been filled in for you.

The experience: _____

_____

Power Tip

For an example of narration by a professional writer, see "Passing Through" by Yiyun Li (page 476).

The events

1. _____

2. _____

3. _____

4. _____

5. _____

6. _____

7. Son has a good relationship with his own children.

ACTIVITY 8

For each of the following topics, list the major events in the story.

1. Tell the story of something you did that you'll never do again.

2. Tell the story of a time when someone you love disappointed you.

3. Tell the story about the proudest moment of your life.

4. Tell the story about a time when you were very scared or very excited.

5. Tell the story about a time when someone or something crushed your spirit.

ACTIVITY 9

Select one of the photographs from the following page and write an academic paragraph in which you tell a story about the image. Do the following:

- First, brainstorm about the characters in the story. Who are the people in the image? Use your imagination and have fun.

- Next, brainstorm about the setting for the story. Based on the image, where is this story taking place? Be sure to give the place a name.

- Next, brainstorm about the events that make up the story (the *plot*). Start by providing background on the characters and the situation. How did the characters come together to be in this situation? Second, explain the important action that is taking place *at this moment* in the photograph. This action will probably be the dramatic high point of your story. Finally, what *outcome* will take place after the current action in the image? You may want to resolve the action or leave it hanging. Use your imagination.

- Remember, your narrative can be tragic, dramatic, suspenseful, humorous, inspirational, or something else.

- Write an outline for your paragraph.

- Compose your paragraph.

- Revise and proofread your paragraph.

Power Tip

A basic structure for a plot is: *background + current action + outcome*.

Photo 1: Marching forward

Photo 2: At the beach

Photo 3: On the hunt

PROCESS

In process writing, you explain or describe each step in a series of actions. There are two types of process writing: the "how to" approach and the "how it happens" approach.

In the "how to" approach, you give specific instructions to the reader, teaching him or her how to do something. The following are "how to" writing topics:

> How to <u>prepare for a job interview</u>
> How to <u>apply for financial aid</u>
> How to <u>decorate a wedding cake</u>

In "how to" writing, the reader is an imaginary *participant* in the process. In order for the reader to complete the process successfully, you must provide clear step-by-step instructions and precise details.

In the "how it happens" approach, you describe how an event occurs. The following are "how it happens" writing topics:

> How <u>a solar eclipse</u> occurs
> How <u>cell division</u> occurs
> How <u>a tsunami</u> occurs

In "how it happens" writing, the reader is an imaginary *observer* of the process. In order for the reader to understand fully how the process occurs, you must provide clear step-by-step descriptions and precise details.

In both approaches, the key to good process writing is providing clear step-by-step explanations and precise details.

A Student Writer Uses Process ("How To")

In the following paragraph, a student writer explains how to get a good night's sleep.

> In today's stressful world, many of us have trouble sleeping the seven to nine hours that we need to feel rested. Fortunately, you can take some steps to become a better sleeper. First, make sure that your mattress and pillows are comfortable, and try to replace them if they are worn. Ideally, a mattress should be firm to provide support and prevent backaches. Next, try to start going to bed at the same time every night. This way, you will get your body into a routine and help it to "expect" to sleep at a certain time. When you have established your bedtime, count back two hours from it. During this two-hour period, avoid stimulating activities such as exercising, watching TV shows, listening to loud music, arguing, or thinking about work or other responsibilities. Instead, you might read in a quiet room or listen to soft music. Also, be careful about what you eat and drink before bedtime. Avoid coffee, chocolate, and other foods or beverages containing caffeine. If you want a little snack before bed, try drinking warm milk. Once

it's time for bed, make sure that your room is dark and cool. Ideally, your room should be no warmer than 65 degrees. Draw your shades or blinds to make sure that streetlights don't keep you up or wake you up prematurely. You can cover your eyes with a bandana or eye mask if your window coverings aren't adequate. Finally, turn off your light and let drowsiness wash over you. If it doesn't, try counting imaginary sheep as they leap a fence one by one. Believe it or not, this old trick works for some people!

The paragraph takes readers step-by-step through the process of preparing for a good night's sleep, providing precise details.

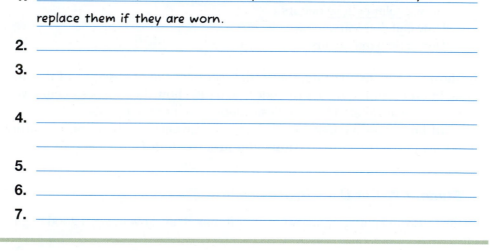

ACTIVITY 10

Working from the previous paragraph, list the major steps of preparing for a good night's sleep. The first step has been filled in for you.

1. _Make sure that your mattress and pillows are comfortable; try to replace them if they are worn._

2. _____

3. _____
   _____

4. _____
   _____

5. _____

6. _____

7. _____

A Student Writer Uses Process ("How It Happens")

In this paragraph, a student writer describes the steps in the grieving process.

Psychiatrist Elisabeth Kübler-Ross, in her 1969 book *On Death and Dying*, describes the process a person goes through when grieving. The first stage is denial or shock. At first, the loss is so overwhelming that a person cannot even believe it is happening. It's a natural defense mechanism to refuse to accept the facts. After the person goes through denial, he or she usually comes to the anger stage. For example, if the individual has lost someone to death, he or she may be angry with the person for letting it happen (even if the death was unavoidable). Survivors may also be angry with themselves and think they could have somehow prevented the death. It is important to keep this stage in mind when someone you know is going through this stage. Do not judge this anger as wrong. After anger, the person goes through the bargaining stage. He or she may want to make a deal with God or the universe or *someone*. If, for instance, the individual is terminally ill, he or she may say, "Just let me stay around long enough to see my daughter graduate from college," or "If I could just get well, I'll go to church every Sunday." In cases of romantic separation, a grieving person may say to his or her former partner, "Why don't we at least remain friends?" The next stage is depression. In this stage, the individual is filled with sadness and hopelessness and may think, "What's the use of doing anything?" This step is important because it means the person is working through to the final stage, which is acceptance. The person may not be happy about the situation, but he or she realizes that reality will not change. The loss is inescapable or unchangeable, so the best response is to be ready for it. According to Kübler-Ross, it is best to allow oneself to go through each of these stages, however long they may take.

The paragraph explains each stage of the grieving process, with examples, so that readers understand how this process happens.

ACTIVITY 11

Working from the previous paragraph, list the major steps of the grieving process.

1. _____   4. _____

2. _____   5. _____

3. _____

Power Tip

For an example of "how it happens" process writing by a professional writer, see paragraph 4 of "The Joy of Reading and Writing: Superman and Me" by Sherman Alexie (page 441).

ACTIVITY 12: Teamwork

With classmates, list the steps for each of the following processes. Then, working individually, select one of the topics and brainstorm for ten minutes, getting down all the details you can.

1. Explain how to use a Web site like Facebook, eBay, YouTube, etc.

2. Explain the steps you would take to build a successful romantic relationship.

3. Explain how to play a video or Wii game.

4. Explain how to make something that you enjoy making.

5. Explain the steps you would take to convince your parents (or boyfriend/girlfriend) to change their mind about something important.

DEFINITION

In writing a definition, you explain the meaning of a word or idea. Most people think of definitions as short, formal explanations of meaning such as those found in a dictionary. However, if you are writing a paragraph or an essay, a short dictionary-style definition will not allow you to develop your assignment adequately.

Instead, you will probably be asked to develop a more complex and creative definition. For example, a *technical* definition may require you to define the full meaning of a scientific or technical term, such as *symbiosis* or *photosynthesis*. A *personal* definition might ask you to define what a particular term, such as *success* or *love*, means for you. A *contextual* definition may ask you to define a term in a specific framework, such as *depression in postpartum women* or *capitalism in modern Russia*. In each case, **the key to good definition is discussing as many levels of meaning as possible and using precise vocabulary and examples to discuss each level.**

A Student Writer Uses Definition

In the following paragraph, a student provides a *personal* definition of the term *freedom*.

> To some people, the word "freedom" may mean freedom of speech or freedom of religion, but to me it means freedom from people telling me how to live my life. First, I choose jobs that allow me to be free to do things the way I want. For instance, I could never work at a fast-food restaurant where I'd have to weigh each burger, bean, or tomato to make a perfect cookie-cutter product every time. Currently, I work as an in-home care companion, and I can do what feels right to help each individual. No one tells me to do anything differently. Each experience is created on the spot, as a result of my sense of what's needed. Second, I don't want my parents telling me how to live my life. Now that I'm nineteen, I feel it's important to make my own choices, even if it means making mistakes. I choose my own hours to come and go, make my own choices about what classes to take, and manage my own money. While I will listen to my parents' suggestions, I make decisions that feel right for me. Finally, I enjoy being free from cultural pressure. I don't hang out with cliques, or buy the products that everyone else buys. I don't allow magazines, television, or friends to tell me how to be. I dress the way that feels true to me, regardless of this season's style. The friends I spend time with come from different social circles. The freedom I have allows me to be confident and comfortable in my own skin.

In developing her definition of *freedom*, this student identifies several levels of meaning and gives examples for each.

ACTIVITY 13

Working from the previous paragraph, complete the following outline. (Part of it has already been filled in for you.) The outline will help you see how the writer identifies different levels of meaning for *freedom* and explores each one.

MAIN IDEA _____

PART 1   I choose jobs that give me freedom. _____

I avoid jobs that require creation of a cookie-cutter

product every time. _____

I do what feels right in my current job as an in-home

companion. _____

_____

PART 2   _____

_____

_____

_____

_____

PART 3   _____

_____

_____

_____

Power Tip

For an example of a definition by a professional writer, see paragraph 4 of "Living What You Do Every Day" by Yolanda O'Bannon (page 461).

ACTIVITY 14: Teamwork

With classmates, make a list of possible definitions for the following words or ideas. Then, working individually, select one of the terms and brainstorm for ten minutes, getting down all the details you can.

1. Define beauty.
2. Define honor.
3. Define evil.
4. Define unselfishness.
5. Define self-confidence.

6. Define betrayal.
7. Define patriotism.
8. Define peace of mind.
9. Define fun.
10. Define true love.

Advanced Writing Patterns

Advanced writing patterns require more planning and careful thought to execute. The following pages discuss the main features of these patterns (cause and effect, comparison and contrast, and argument) and provide examples of each one.

Power Tip
Many of the professional readings in Part Four of this book blend causes and effects. Examples include "The Sanctuary of School" by Lynda Barry (page 445) and "As They Say, Drugs Kill" by Laura Rowley (page 480).

CAUSE AND EFFECT

In cause-and-effect writing, you explain the origin and the outcome of a particular event or occurrence. There are three approaches to this writing pattern: pure cause, pure effect, or combined cause and effect.

In pure cause, you show only the causes or origins of something. Look at these examples:

> There are several <u>causes</u> of <u>lung cancer</u>.
> Three <u>factors</u> prompted the <u>rapid development of the Internet</u>.

In pure effect, you show only the results or outcomes of something. Look at these examples:

> <u>Global warming</u> has many harmful <u>effects</u> on the planet.
> I have noticed several <u>benefits</u> from my <u>new workout routine</u>.

In combined cause and effect, you show both the origin and the outcome of something. Consider these examples:

pandemic: a disease that is prevalent throughout an entire region or population

> Several <u>factors</u> are responsible for the <u>AIDS pandemic in Africa</u>; furthermore, the <u>effects</u> of the disease are threatening the survival of the continent and its inhabitants.

> Currently, about 20% of the world's adult population is illiterate. What allows for this outrageous figure, and what does it mean to be an illiterate person in today's world? The <u>causes</u> of <u>illiteracy</u> are both political and economic, and the <u>effects</u> of <u>illiteracy</u> on the illiterate can be devastating.

The key to successful cause-and-effect writing is to clarify the main origins and/or outcomes and to provide sufficient details to illustrate them.

A Student Writer Uses Pure Cause

In the following paragraph, a student writer explains what caused him to be a poor student during his freshman year of college.

> As I look back on my freshman year of college, I now see clearly the causes for my lack of success. For one thing, I didn't pay attention to my physical health. For the first time in my life, I had total control over my eating habits, and I chose to eat only what I wanted to. I lived on beer, Domino's pizza, Oreos, and Fritos. For months, nothing green could be found on my plate. I also stayed up late watching movies and soon became sleep-deprived, which also meant that I slept during class. My poor health affected my class attendance and my concentration. Furthermore, I ignored my instructors' studying advice. I never read assignments before class, so often I couldn't follow the lecture and didn't have questions about the reading that I didn't do. Because I was ill-prepared for class, I would sit in the very back of the room, away from the blackboard. Therefore, the few notes I would take

were always incomplete. I would cram the night before exams and become overwhelmed by so much material that was new to me (but shouldn't have been). Even if I managed to pick up some information, I would feel panicked or tired during the exam and forget what little I did learn. Finally, I lacked discipline in the new social environment of college. Meeting new people or bonding with new friends always seemed more important than studying for an exam. I found a club I liked and went there almost every night. Also, I went to a lot of parties. As a result of my active social life, my grades plummeted. Poor decisions about my health, lousy study habits, and always choosing socializing over school led to a freshman-year GPA that I'm still working to make up for.

For each case of the student's lack of academic success, he provides plenty of details.

ACTIVITY 15

Working from the previous paragraph, complete the following outline. (Part of it has already been filled in for you.) The outline will help you see how the writer identifies various causes of his unsuccessful freshman year and provides details to explain each cause.

MAIN IDEA
_____
_____

CAUSE 1
I didn't pay attention to my physical health.

I ate what I wanted to (beer, pizza, and so on), not what

was healthy for me.

_____

CAUSE 2
_____

I never read assignments before class.

_____

_____

_____

CAUSE 3
_____

_____

_____

_____

_____

_____

_____

A Student Writer Uses Pure Effect

In the following paragraph, a student writer explains the effects (results or outcomes) of the AIDS pandemic in the region of Africa south of the Sahara.

> AIDS continues to have a devastating effect on sub-Saharan Africa. To begin with, AIDS is the most common cause of death there. In 2007, nearly 23 million people in the region were living with HIV, and 1.6 million of them died. Furthermore, AIDS has orphaned 11.4 million children in sub-Saharan Africa, and this number is expected to grow. Many orphaned children are forced to seek help in the streets, begging for money and food. Also, many orphaned girls turn to prostitution to survive, greatly raising their chances of contracting HIV. Finally, AIDS causes hunger. In Malawi, Zambia, and Zimbabwe, grandparents can end up caring for ten or more children because the children's parents have died of AIDS-related illness. These grandparents often can't provide enough food for everyone. Another reason that AIDS affects food availability is that it takes the greatest toll on the most productive members of the community, those who work to provide food or earn money. "AIDS kills those on whom society relies to grow the crops, work in the mines and factories, run the schools and hospitals and govern countries," said former South African president Nelson Mandela. Even when AIDS does not kill, it weakens providers in families, with serious consequences. Years after AIDS started making national headlines in the U.S., it remains a powerfully destructive force in sub-Saharan Africa.

In this paragraph, the author examines each effect of AIDS, providing details and explanations.

ACTIVITY 16

Working from the previous paragraph, complete the following outline. (Part of it has already been filled in for you.) The outline will help you see how the writer identifies and explains various effects of HIV/AIDS in sub-Saharan Africa.

MAIN IDEA   AIDS continues to have a devastating effect on sub-Saharan Africa.

EFFECT 1   It is the most common cause of death.

_____

_____

EFFECT 2   _____

_____

_____

_____

EFFECT 3

_____

_____

_____

_____

_____

_____

_____

_____

_____

_____

ACTIVITY 17: Teamwork

With classmates, list causes or effects for each of the following events or occurrences. Then, working individually, select one of the topics and brainstorm for ten minutes, getting down all the details you can.

1. Causes of getting into debt.
2. Causes of getting a bad grade or failing a college class.
3. Causes of stress in your life.
4. Causes of a relationship breakup.
5. Causes of procrastination (putting things off).
6. Effects (outcomes) of getting a college degree.
7. Effects (outcomes) of frequent absences in your college classes.
8. Effects (outcomes) of working a part-time or full-time job while going to college.
9. Effects (outcomes) of being a young parent or a single parent.
10. Effects (outcomes) of cheating in school.

COMPARISON AND CONTRAST

In comparison-and-contrast writing, you identify the similarities and/or differences between things (usually two). There are three approaches to this writing pattern: pure comparison, pure contrast, or combined comparison and contrast.

In pure comparison, you show only the similarities between items. Look at these examples:

Spanish and Italian are very similar languages.
Halloween and Day of the Dead have important similarities.

In pure contrast, you show only the differences between items. Look at these examples:

> <u>High school</u> and <u>college</u> are very <u>different</u> academic experiences.
> <u>Ancient Athens</u> and <u>ancient Sparta</u> were extremely <u>different</u> cultures.

In combined comparison and contrast, you show both the similarities and differences between items. Consider these examples:

> <u>American baseball</u> and <u>British cricket</u> are both <u>similar</u> and <u>different</u>.
> <u>Jazz</u> and <u>bluegrass</u> have some <u>similarities</u> and some <u>differences</u>.

The key to successful comparison-and-contrast writing is to clarify the main similarities and/or differences and to provide sufficient details to illustrate them.

A Student Writer Uses Pure Comparison

In the following paragraph, a student uses pure comparison to show how she is similar to Rosa Parks (1913–2005). Parks, an African American, became an inspiring figure in the U.S. civil-rights movement when, in 1955, she refused a command to give up her seat on a Montgomery, Alabama, bus to a white passenger. Parks was arrested as a result, triggering a 381-day bus boycott among African Americans and drawing national attention to the cause of ending racial segregation, the forced separation of blacks from whites.

> Rosa Parks and I are similar in various ways. First, our childhoods were similar because we were raised by a single female parent. Parks's parents separated when she was very young, after her brother was born. My father walked out when I was four years old, right after my brother was born. Both Parks and I are the older of two children, and we grew up needing a father figure, as well as having to take on more responsibilities. Parks took care of her ill grandmother and then her ill mother. When I was young, I took care of my ill grandmother and went with her to dialysis. Having many responsibilities made me grow up at a young age. Second, both Parks and I have a positive attitude toward life. Although Parks faced segregation and obstacles to getting an education, she didn't give up. In fact, she took advantage of all the opportunities she could to become educated. When I was young, negative people around me told me that I could not go to college, yet I did. I've tried to learn as much as I can. Like Parks, I pursued my dreams. Finally, Parks stood up for her beliefs: she took a stand that started the Alabama bus boycott, even though it caused her to lose her job and receive threatening phone calls. I have also stood up for what is important to me. When I was young, I loved going to the Christian church with my grandmother, although I knew my mother hated that religion. When I would get home from church, she would yell at me. Yet I kept going to that church. Both Parks and I were successful in our

Power Tip
Many of the professional readings in Part Four of this book blend comparison and contrast. Examples include "Caring Makes Us Human" by Troy Chapman (page 467) and "The Jacket" by Gary Soto (page 473).

Rosa Parks's arrest in Alabama, 1955

dialysis: a blood-cleaning procedure used in patients with kidney failure

efforts: the bus boycott that Parks started helped to end segregation on Alabama buses. After five years of my prayers, my mother gave me her blessing to attend church. Although Parks and I lived at different times, all of our struggles and accomplishments have shaped our personalities in similar ways.

Notice that the author of this paragraph lays out three different points of similarity. For each point, she compares herself fully to Rosa Parks before moving on to the next point. This is known as *point-by-point comparison.* (As you will see, the Albert Einstein paragraph on page 192 uses point-by-point contrast.) Another way to organize the paragraph would have been to describe only Parks's qualities in the first part of the paragraph and then present the author's similar qualities in the second part of the paragraph.

ACTIVITY 18

Working from the previous paragraph, complete the following outline. (Part of it has already been filled in for you.) The outline will help you see how the writer identifies various similarities between herself and Rosa Parks and then provides details to illustrate these similarities.

MAIN IDEA _____

SIMILARITY 1 _____

_____

_____

_____

_____

SIMILARITY 2   Both Parks and I have a positive attitude toward life.

We both pursued an education despite obstacles and

negative influences.

SIMILARITY 3 _____

_____

_____

_____

A Student Writer Uses Pure Contrast

In the following paragraph, a student uses pure contrast to show how he is different from Albert Einstein (1879–1955), a German-born physicist best known for his theories of relativity.

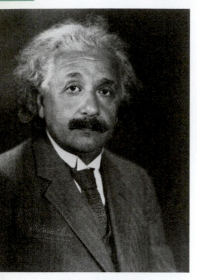

Albert Einstein

Terminology Tip

The Theory of Relativity says that measurements of time and distance vary with the speed at which the observer is traveling relative to what is being observed. Einstein's study of relativity led to his famous formula describing the conversion of energy into mass and vice versa: $E = mc^2$. This formula was the scientific basis for the development of the atomic bomb.

Although I, like Albert Einstein, have a strong interest in mathematics, he and I are different in several important ways. To begin with, Einstein was a free thinker; he was not bound by the limits set by his colleagues or by books. He was able to think "outside the box," like a visionary. He could not be taught like ordinary children; he did better when he was self-taught. I, on the other hand, do better when things are explained or taught to me. For example, in college math, I do exceptionally well and find many solutions for one problem, but I use the rules put before me. I do not question why the rules are there as long as they can be proven. Another way that I am different from Einstein is in our backgrounds. Einstein was a Jewish man from Germany who traveled to faraway places such as Milan, Italy; Zurich, Switzerland; and Princeton, New Jersey, where he eventually settled. In contrast, I have never been anywhere besides Southern California. Additionally, I was raised Roman Catholic. The final difference between Einstein and me is that he became famous, while I am not—not yet, anyway. Einstein is widely known for his theory of relativity, which led to his formula $E = mc^2$. He also won the Nobel Prize for physics. His work has aided understanding of time and space. I have taken only a small step by going to college. I have taken Calculus 1 but have not yet scratched the surface of Calculus 2. However, I hope to further my studies in science and mathematics, allowing me to better understand Einstein's theory of relativity.

ACTIVITY 19

Working from the previous paragraph, complete the following outline. (Part of it has already been filled in for you.) The outline will help you see how the writer identifies various differences between himself and Albert Einstein and then provides details to illustrate these differences.

MAIN IDEA

_____

_____

DIFFERENCE 1

Einstein was a free thinker, while I am not.

Einstein wasn't bound by colleagues or books;

he could think outside the box and did better when

he was self-taught.

_____

_____

DIFFERENCE 2

_____

_____

_____

_____

DIFFERENCE 3

ACTIVITY 20: Teamwork

With classmates, list similarities and/or differences for each of the following pairs of topics. Then, working individually, select one of the topics and brainstorm for ten minutes, getting down all the details you can.

1. Compare and/or contrast shopping in stores and shopping online.

2. Compare and/or contrast two of your college classes. (For example, compare two classes that you like or dislike. Or, contrast one class that you like with one that you dislike.)

3. Compare and/or contrast two people who have impacted your life, either positively or negatively.

4. Compare and/or contrast living with family and having your own apartment. (If you have never had your own apartment, imagine what it would be like.)

5. Compare and/or contrast two activities, one that you are highly motivated to do and one that you resist doing.

ACTIVITY 21

Select one *pair* of photographs from the following pages and write a paragraph in which you compare and/or contrast the images. Do the following:

- Decide on the pair of photographs you would like to write about.
- Decide if you want to write a pure comparison. This can work well if the two images have strong similarities.
- Decide if you want to write a pure contrast. This can work well if the two images have strong differences.
- Decide if you want to write a combination of comparison and contrast. This can work well if the images have strong similarities *and* differences.
- Write an outline for your paragraph. Each major similarity or difference will be a support point in your outline.
- Compose your paragraph.
- Revise and proofread your paragraph.

Power Tip

In discussing similarities, your topic sentence might be something like, *Although each image shows a different child, their similarities are very striking.*

Power Tip

If you decide to write a combination of comparison and contrast, your topic sentence might be something like, *The two images of extreme sports have important similarities and differences.*

Pair 1

A Pakistani girl with her dog.

A Kazakhstani boy with his hawk.

Pair 2

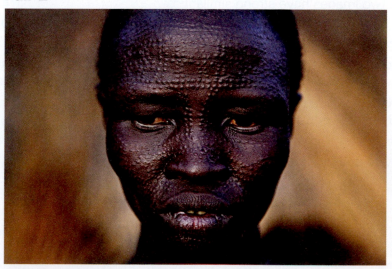

A Sudanese woman.

A New York woman.

Pair 3

A surfer on the waves.

A motorcyclist on the dunes.

ARGUMENTATION

In argumentation, you state and defend your position on an issue. Look at the underlined issues in the following examples:

I am against underline{experimentation on animals}.
underline{Steroid use in professional sports} should be legalized.
underline{College professors} should be required to underline{dress professionally}.
I am in favor of underline{granting driver's licenses to illegal immigrants}.

Defending your position means providing your *best reasons* for being for or against an issue. Look at the reasons given for this position on steroid use:

Steroid use in professional sports should be legalized underline{because} . . .
— it results in better performance.
— it helps athletes recover from injuries.
— it helps athletes have longer careers.

When explaining your reasons, try to keep in mind *counterarguments* that might be used to challenge your position. Anticipating how others might oppose your argument can help you explain your position more carefully.

For example, some readers might have concerns about the negative health effects of steroids. The writer might acknowledge these concerns in a statement like the following:

Although some people are concerned about the negative health effects of steroids, moderate use of them can actually help athletes recover from injuries.

The key to successful argumentation is to state your position clearly, to give sufficient reasons for it, and to provide precise details to illustrate your reasons.

A Student Writer Uses Argumentation

In the following paragraph, a student writer makes a convincing argument for workplace-provided daycare.

To benefit workers and improve performance, businesses should provide onsite daycare. First, onsite daycare reduces absenteeism and improves productivity. According to a report by the National Conference of State Legislatures (NCSL), 80 percent of the companies they surveyed said that child care problems cause reduced workdays among their employees. With onsite daycare, employees would be able to work full, productive days. Also, knowing that a company cares enough to provide daycare is a morale booster. When morale is high, workers tend to be more productive and more willing to work harder in their jobs. Second, onsite daycare helps to attract and retain workers. In a personal interview, Helen Dobbs, president of Maywood Technology, said, "There's no question that our daycare facility has helped us to attract top talent, both men and women. It sets us apart from the competition in a tight market for highly skilled technology workers." Dobbs and other employers report that onsite daycare also contributes to worker satisfaction, meaning less employee turnover. Finally, onsite daycare may actually benefit companies' financial health. The biggest argument against such a benefit has been that it is too expensive and that only the biggest and most profitable businesses can afford it. However, in their recent book *Kids at Work: The Value of Employer-Sponsored On-Site Child Care Centers*, Rachel Connelly, Deborah S. DeGraff, and Rachel A. Willis argue that onsite daycare can actually be profitable for companies. Two daycare-providing companies studied by the authors saved $150,000 and $250,000 in wages. The authors also found that workers were willing to contribute up to $225 per year to help pay for company daycare, whether or not they themselves would make use of it. These workers seemed to realize that onsite daycare would help to make everyone happier and more productive. Although setting up onsite daycare facilities certainly takes effort, the evidence suggests that it pays off in the long run—in both human and financial terms.

Notice that the writer mentions an important counterargument. You might want to underline this counterargument and then the reasons and details that the writer provides to address it.

ACTIVITY 22

Working from the previous paragraph, complete the following outline. (Part of it has already been filled in for you.) The outline will help you see how the writer clearly states a position, provides reasons for the position, and then gives detailed explanations for each reason.

MAIN IDEA _____

_____

REASON 1   Onsite daycare reduces absenteeism and improves

productivity.

An NCSL study indicates that child care problems

cause reduced workdays; onsite daycare would

eliminate this problem, improving productivity.

_____

_____

REASON 2 _____

_____

_____

_____

Power Tip
Several of the professional readings in Part Four make arguments. Examples include "About Men; One Man's Kids" by Daniel Meier (page 463), "Caring Makes Us Human" by Troy Chapman (page 467), and "As They Say, Drugs Kill" by Laura Rowley (page 480).

CONTINUED >

REASON 3

_____

_____

_____

_____

_____

_____

_____

ACTIVITY 23: Teamwork

With classmates, list reasons to support each of the following arguments. Then, select one of the topics and brainstorm for ten minutes, getting down all the details you can.

1. College students should (or should not) have an attendance requirement because . . .

2. America is (or is not) the greatest country because . . .

3. Medical marijuana use should (or should not) be legalized because . . .

4. Magazines should (or should not) discuss the private lives of celebrities because . . .

5. Non-math majors should (or should not) be required to take math classes in college because . . .

Mixing the Patterns

Sometimes, you may need to use more than one of the patterns to communicate your ideas effectively. Let's see how one writer uses a combination of patterns for her topic.

ASSIGNED TOPIC   _Report on a town that was hit by a category five hurricane._

To give an accurate and helpful account of this event, the writer may need to use a combination of patterns. For example, she might:

1. explain the origin and path of the hurricane (narration)
2. describe the town after it has been hit by the hurricane (description)
3. explain what makes a hurricane a category five (definition)
4. list the damages and injuries caused by the hurricane (exemplification)
5. explain how people can prepare for a category five hurricane (process)

Of course, the writer does not have to use all five of the strategies. However, sometimes a combination of patterns will communicate the information more effectively than a single pattern.

As a beginning college writer, it is a good idea to decide on a **primary pattern** for a writing assignment and one or two **supporting patterns** that will help you to develop your ideas. Here is an example:

ASSIGNED TOPIC	*Discuss what success means to you.*
PRIMARY PATTERN	Definition (I will define *success*.)
SUPPORTING PATTERN	Exemplification (I will give examples of *success* to back up my definition.)
SUPPORTING PATTERN	Description (In my examples, I may need to describe *success*.)

ACTIVITY 24: Teamwork

With your classmates, discuss the following topics. How would you use each of the suggested patterns to communicate the information effectively? In the spaces provided, briefly describe how you would use each pattern. Then, identify the primary pattern that you would use and explain why.

1. **Topic:** Explain to a foreigner the U.S. high school tradition of a "senior prom."

   Patterns that will help you communicate your ideas effectively:

   Definition (What would you need to define?):

   _____

   Exemplification (What examples would you give?):

   _____

   Description (What would you describe?):

   _____

   Primary Pattern (Which strategy is most important to the success of this assignment?): _____

   Explain your answer: _____

   _____

   _____

2. **Topic:** Write an accident report at your job.

   Patterns that will help you communicate your ideas effectively:

   Narration (What story would you tell?):

   _____

   Description (What would you describe?):

   _____

   Exemplification (What examples would you give?):

   _____

CONTINUED >

Primary Pattern (Which strategy is most important to the success of this assignment?): _____

Explain your answer: _____

3. **Topic:** Give a clear picture of the costumes used in a production of *The Lion King.*

   Patterns that will help you communicate your ideas effectively:

   Description (What would you describe?):

   _____

   Exemplification (What examples would you give?):

   _____

   Definition (What would you need to define?):

   _____

   Primary Pattern (Which strategy is most important to the success of this assignment?): _____

   Explain your answer: _____

ACTIVITY 25: Teamwork

For each of the following topics, discuss with your classmates which patterns of development would help you communicate the ideas most effectively. Then, decide which pattern would be your **primary pattern** and write it in the space provided. Next, decide which **supporting patterns** would work best for the topic and write them in the spaces provided. **Note:** You do not have to agree with your classmates on your final choices.

1. **Topic:** Explain your idea of a "beautiful" person.

   Patterns of development for the writing:

   Primary Pattern: _____

   Supporting Pattern: _____

   Supporting Pattern: _____

2. **Topic:** Discuss the most embarrassing thing that ever happened to you.

   Patterns of development for the writing:

   Primary Pattern: _____

   Supporting Pattern: _____

Supporting Pattern: _____

3. **Topic:** Explain how a tsunami happens.

   Patterns of development for the writing:

   Primary Pattern: _____

   Supporting Pattern: _____

   Supporting Pattern: _____

BRINGING IT ALL TOGETHER:
Patterns of Development

In this chapter, you have learned about eight patterns of development for your college writing. Confirm your knowledge by filling in the blank spaces in the following sentences. If you need help, review the pages listed after each sentence.

✔ The key to good _____ is finding precise and colorful adjectives and nouns that will create a strong sensory experience for your audience. (page 172)

✔ The key to good _____ is finding precise and colorful examples that will capture your audience's interest and imagination. (page 176)

✔ The key to good _____ is including the major event or actions of the story and using colorful details to bring the characters, settings, and actions to life. (page 177)

✔ The key to good _____ writing is providing clear step-by-step explanations and precise details. With the "how to" approach, you provide _____ for the reader. With the "how it happens" approach, you describe _____. (page 181)

✔ The key to good _____ writing is discussing as many levels of meaning as possible and using precise vocabulary and examples to discuss each level. (page 184)

✔ The key to good _____ writing is to clarify the main origins and/or outcomes of the issue and to provide sufficient details to illustrate them. You must also decide whether to use pure _____ or pure _____ or a combination of these. (page 186)

CONTINUED >

✔ Another word for "cause" is _____. Another word for "effect" is _____ or _____. (page 186)

✔ The key to good _____ writing is to clarify the main similarities and/or differences and to provide sufficient details to illustrate them. You must decide whether to use pure _____ or pure _____ or a combination of these. (pages 189–90)

✔ Another word for "comparison" is _____. Another word for "contrast" is _____. (page 189)

✔ The key to good _____ writing is to state your position clearly, to give sufficient reasons for it, and to provide strong examples to support your reasons. (page 196)

CHAPTER 9

Moving from Paragraphs to Essays

Before you read this chapter, it's a good idea to test your understanding about moving from paragraphs to essays. You may know more than you think.

For each question, select all the answers that apply.

WHAT DO YOU KNOW?

1. **An academic essay includes which of the following?**
   ___ An introduction and a conclusion.
   ___ Only one body paragraph.
   ___ Two or more body paragraphs.
   ___ Either an introduction or a conclusion.

2. **In the introduction (or opening paragraph) of an essay, what two things must the writer accomplish?**
   ___ Restate the writing assignment word for word.
   ___ Grab the reader's attention.
   ___ Present a thesis.
   ___ Present a conclusion.

3. **If you begin writing a paragraph, but then decide to write a full essay, what are two ways that you might reuse your original paragraph?**
   ___ It could become one body paragraph in the essay.
   ___ It must become the introduction.
   ___ It could be split up and expanded into two or more body paragraphs.
   ___ It must become the conclusion.

4. **A topic sentence (paragraph) and a thesis statement (essay) are similar in some ways. What are they?**
   ___ They identify the general topic.
   ___ They express your original point about the topic.
   ___ They summarize the support points.
   ___ They avoid using key words from the topic.

5. **One of the following sentences is more appropriate for a topic sentence. The other is more appropriate for a thesis statement. In the blank spaces, write "topic" or "thesis" to identify them correctly.**
   College textbooks are much more expensive than I had imagined.
   _____
   The cost of a college education is more expensive than I had imagined. _____

Understanding the Difference between Paragraphs and Essays

So far, you have learned the basic features of an academic *paragraph*:

- It is well developed, with usually more than five *sentences*.
- It is carefully organized, with a main idea and a series of support points.
- It is grammatically correct.

Notice now that the academic *essay* (a freshman-level college essay) has similar features:

- It is well developed, with usually three or more *pages*.
- It is carefully organized, with a main idea and a series of support points.
- It is grammatically correct.

In addition, most instructors will require a standard college essay to include the following:

- **an introduction:** an opening paragraph that includes the main idea, known as the **thesis statement**
- **two or more "body" paragraphs:** fully developed academic paragraphs that develop the support points
- **a conclusion:** a paragraph that may restate the main idea or make some other observation

Because you have already mastered the basics of the academic paragraph, you have an important head start in mastering the academic essay.

MOVING FROM PARAGRAPH TO ESSAY: TWO METHODS

There are two common methods for moving from an academic paragraph to a complete essay. The first method involves expanding each part of the paragraph; the second method involves expanding the main idea of the paragraph. The following pages will introduce you to these two methods.

Method 1: Expand the Parts of Your Paragraph

The first method for moving from paragraph to essay is to expand each part of the paragraph into a complete and separate paragraph in the essay. In the example below, notice how each part of the paragraph (*the topic sentence, support point 1, support point 2, support point 3, and the concluding sentence*) becomes a separate and complete paragraph in the essay. Each highlighted section of the paragraph corresponds to a separate paragraph in the essay, highlighted in the same color.

The Paragraph

Although I am not a perfect son or brother, I believe I am a responsible member of my family. First, I help out financially whenever I can. For example, from the pay for my part-time job, I give my parents $100 each month to help with the rent. Also, on the weekends, I pay for movie rentals and take-out pizza because I know that my parents can't afford extras. In an emergency, my family can always count on me. Last year, when my father's car got impounded, I took all the money from my savings account so he could get it back and drive to work. Second, I am a good role model for my younger siblings. For instance, I sit with them every night and do my college homework while they do their homework. In addition, my brother needs lots of advice about women, and since I am an expert, I always tell him how to treat the ladies with respect. I also change my schedule when possible to drive my sister to school and soccer practice so she doesn't have to take the bus. Last, I respect my parents. I try never to argue with them about things like yard work or girlfriends. I obey their rules, like the midnight curfew on weekends, because I know that the rules are for my benefit. Plus, I honor their religious beliefs even though I don't worship with them anymore. I know that my parents and siblings love me and appreciate my contributions to our family.

— Topic sentence

— Support point 1

— Support point 2

— Support point 3

— Concluding sentence

The Essay

What if you woke up one day and you had no family? How would your life change if all of the love and support that you receive from your family members were suddenly gone? I never forget for a second that my family is the greatest treasure I have in life. By giving them financial support, being a role model for my siblings, and respecting my parents, I demonstrate that I am a responsible family member.

— Introduction

— Thesis

Although I work only part-time at Office Depot, I try to help my family financially whenever I can. To begin with, I contribute to the rent. When I got my first paycheck three years ago, I was very proud to give half of it to my mother for the rent. One year ago, we had to move to a new apartment, and the rent almost doubled. That was when I increased my monthly contribution to $100. I also helped pay the security deposit, which was two months' rent. Second, I like to buy some "extras" that I know my parents can't afford. For instance, every Friday night I go to Blockbuster and rent two movies. Then, I get take-out pizza on the way home. When my brother or sister needs to buy school supplies or soccer uniforms, I tell them to ask me for the money so my parents won't feel added pressure. Last, I always support my family in a financial emergency if I can. Last year, when my father's car was impounded, I didn't hesitate to take out all my savings and help him get back his car. Also, my mother was suffering once with a horrible toothache. She didn't want to spend the money to see the dentist, but I drove her there anyway and paid the bill myself. Spending money on my family is always the right thing to do.

— Body paragraphs

Power Tip
Notice that you start a new paragraph by indenting, that is, adding space before the first sentence. This space shows readers that you are beginning a new block of related ideas.

Body paragraphs

Conclusion

Another way I am responsible in my family is by being a good role model for my younger siblings. To begin with, since I am the first person in our family to attend college, I try to demonstrate good study habits to my brother and sister. Every night after dinner, I sit down with Alfred and Hilaria, and we do our homework together. I show them my techniques of reviewing the assignments, organizing my materials, and planning my time. I also enjoy tutoring Alfred when he needs help with his Algebra homework. Next, I give advice to my siblings in matters of love. Because Alfred is fifteen, he needs lots of advice about women, and I always tell him how to treat the ladies with respect. My sister Hilaria always asks me what boys are thinking, and I warn her about how men are different from women. Finally, I try to set a good example of unselfishness for my brother and sister. I get them to help me pick up around the house so my parents don't have to come home to a messy environment. Also, I change my schedule when I can to drive my sister to school and soccer practice. I enjoy being a role model for my siblings because I can see them maturing into thoughtful and considerate people.

Respecting my parents is a third way I am a responsible family member. In the first place, I have a record of not arguing with my parents, no matter what. For example, if my dad is tired when he gets home, he sometimes complains about my yard work. I could argue that my priorities are school and work, but I just keep a positive attitude and tell him I'll try to do better. Since my mother wants me to marry a Latina woman, she came up with this crazy rule that the only girls I can invite to the house are Latinas. I could argue, but I just smile and say that *Cupido* will decide whom I marry. In the second place, I obey the rules that my parents set. I stay enrolled as a full-time student and keep my work hours to twenty or fewer per week because my parents ask me to. On weekends, I am always home before the midnight curfew. Last, I honor my parents' beliefs as much as possible. The belief that is most important to them is their faith in God. I no longer worship with them, but I show respect for their religious practices. Even though I'm a typical American teenager, I've taken classes on Latin America, and I keep up with news about Guatemala on the Internet to support my parents' views and heritage. One value that I have no trouble embracing is my parents' work ethic. They know, and I know, that the only way for us to attain the American dream is through hard work and determination.

I always consider it a privilege to be a responsible family member—not a burden. If it were not for my family, I would not be the happy and successful person I am today. Writing this essay only reminds me of how precious my family is to me, and it renews my conviction to always do more for them.

Although the organization of an essay mirrors the organization of a paragraph, we use different names to identify the features of a paragraph and the features of an essay. Although the names are different, the basic purpose of each feature remains the same.

FEATURE	. . . IN A PARAGRAPH	. . . IN AN ESSAY
Main idea ⟶	Topic sentence ⟶	Thesis statement
Support point 1 ⟶	Support point 1 ⟶	Topic sentence 1
Support point 2 ⟶	Support point 2 ⟶	Topic sentence 2
Support point 3 ⟶	Support point 3 ⟶	Topic sentence 3
Conclusion ⟶	Concluding sentence ⟶	Concluding paragraph

ACTIVITY 1: Teamwork

Working with a few of your classmates, answer the following questions about the paragraph and essay used to illustrate method 1.

1. In the essay's first body paragraph (light green), what new information and details have been added? Identify at least three new items.

2. In the essay's second body paragraph (medium green), what new information and details have been added? Identify at least three new items.

3. In the essay's third body paragraph (darker green), what new information and details have been added? Identify at least three new items.

4. Identify the topic sentence (in the paragraph) and the thesis statement (in the essay). Explain how these two sentences are similar and different. What new information has been added to the essay's first paragraph? Discuss whether you think this additional information begins the essay in an interesting, effective manner.

5. What new information and details have been added to the essay's conclusion? Explain how the concluding sentence (in the paragraph) and the concluding paragraph (in the essay) are similar and different. Discuss whether you think this information ends the essay in an interesting, effective manner.

Power Tip
For a detailed discussion of topic sentence versus thesis statement, see page 214 in this chapter.

In the two outlines on page 208, you can see how the transition from a paragraph to an essay is very logical. Take a closer look:

- The main idea in the paragraph outline becomes the thesis in the essay outline.

- Each support point in the paragraph outline becomes a topic sentence for each body paragraph in the essay outline.

- Each related example in the paragraph outline becomes a support point in the essay outline.

Paragraph Outline

MAIN IDEA	I am a responsible family member.
TRANSITIONAL EXPRESSION	First,
SUPPORT POINT 1	I help out financially. – rent – extras – emergencies
TRANSITIONAL EXPRESSION	Second,
SUPPORT POINT 2	I am a good role model for my siblings. – study habits – advice on love – unselfish acts
TRANSITIONAL EXPRESSION	Last,
SUPPORT POINT 3	I respect my parents. – no arguing – obey their rules – honor their beliefs

Essay Outline

THESIS	I am a responsible family member.
TOPIC SENTENCE 1	I help out financially.
SUPPORT POINT 1	I contribute to the rent. – gave half of first paycheck for rent – increased rent contribution to $100 – helped with security deposit
SUPPORT POINT 2	I pay for "extras." – movies and pizza – school supplies/ uniforms
SUPPORT POINT 3	I help out in emergencies. – father's car impounded – mother's dental work
TOPIC SENTENCE 2	I am a good role model for my siblings.
SUPPORT POINT 1	I teach them good study habits. – study together – organization, time planning – tutor my brother
SUPPORT POINT 2	I give them advice on love. – respect women – tell sister about boys
SUPPORT POINT 3	I try to act unselfishly. – pick up the house – drive sister places
TOPIC SENTENCE 3	I respect my parents.
SUPPORT POINT 1	I don't argue with them. – about yard work – about the girls I date
SUPPORT POINT 2	I obey their rules. – school and work – curfew
SUPPORT POINT 3	I honor their beliefs. – religion – Guatemalan culture – work ethic

When you write an essay outline, it's a good idea to state main ideas (both the thesis statement and topic sentences) and support points as complete sentences. Doing so will help you to focus your ideas and express them accurately as you draft your essay. Your examples do not need to be stated as complete sentences.

ACTIVITY 2

Select a paragraph that you have already written for this class and expand it into an essay using method 1. In other words, do the following:

- Select a paragraph whose ideas you can expand easily.
- Expand the topic sentence into an opening paragraph. (See pages 204–8.)
- Expand each support point into a separate and complete body paragraph.
- Expand the concluding sentence into a concluding paragraph. (See pages 204–8.)

Power Tip

For help writing opening and concluding paragraphs, see pages 213–19 of this chapter.

Method 2: Expand the Main Idea of Your Paragraph

The second method for moving from paragraph to essay is to expand the main idea of your paragraph and add new support points that were not part of your original composition. In this way, your original paragraph stays a body paragraph within the essay. The colored highlighting in the samples below will help you see this transition more clearly. Notice that the second body paragraph stays exactly the same in the essay, while the new paragraphs (in rust, light and dark green, and purple) provide related ideas and information that was not part of the original paragraph.

The Paragraph

One thing that really motivated me in school was finding a mentor in my friend Jocelyn. To begin with, Jocelyn motivated me by sharing her many experiences in life and in college. For example, she had been divorced and coped with her depression by drinking. In time, she turned these negative behaviors, but her first attempt at college was not successful. She skipped classes and fell behind in her work. The turning point was when she was put on academic probation. Jocelyn was brave to share her mistakes with me. By doing this, she helped me avoid similar errors. Another way that Jocelyn supported me was by making me feel intelligent. She volunteered to read my assignments and provided tough but sensitive criticism. No matter how poor my efforts were that first semester, she praised my ability and encouraged me to stick with it. Finally, Jocelyn taught me so much about taking care of my health while going to college. She introduced me to the campus recreation center, and we started meeting there after class to run on the treadmill. She also told me that dieting was a waste of time, and that it

Topic sentence

Support point 1

Support point 2

Support point 3

Support point 3

Concluding sentence

was better to eat small portions throughout the day. I took her advice, and I have lost weight and gained energy. I am so grateful for Jocelyn's mentorship, and I hope that one day I can be a mentor for another student who is just starting out in college.

The Essay

Introduction

Thesis

Thinking about attending college was intimidating to me. I wondered whether I could make it through the classes, and I often wondered whether I was "college material." However, once I began taking classes at City College, three things motivated me to stick with my education. Taking a career assessment test, finding a helpful mentor, and writing in my English class all motivated me to work hard in college.

Support point 1

First of all, when I started college, my counselor told me to identify my goals by taking a career placement exam. The exam did not sound interesting to me, but I took it anyway. I was surprised by how much fun I had answering the questions about where I wanted to work (inside or outside), what hours I wanted to work (day, evening, or night), and where I wanted to live. I had never thought about many of these preferences, and the test helped me imagine jobs that I had never considered, like being a veterinary assistant or a landscape architect. I could work with animals in the wild, specimens in a lab, or children in a cancer ward. I did not have to be an accountant—my parents' preferred career for me. Finally, the exam helped me see that some careers would require me to leave Tucson and live somewhere else, away from my parents. I always wanted to live in a place where there are four seasons, with snow in the winter, colorful leaves in the autumn, and flowers in the springtime. Now, college and career could be my ticket to a new hometown. Taking the career placement exam turned out to be a great motivator for my college success.

Support point 2

One thing that really motivated me in school was finding a mentor in my friend Jocelyn. To begin with, Jocelyn motivated me by sharing her many experiences in life and in college. For example, she had been divorced and coped with her depression by drinking. In time, she changed these negative behaviors, but her first attempt at college was not successful. She skipped classes and fell behind in her work. The turning point was when she was put on academic probation. Jocelyn was brave to share her mistakes with me. By doing this, she helped me avoid similar errors. Another way that Jocelyn supported me was by making me feel intelligent. She volunteered to read my assignments and provided tough but sensitive criticism. No matter how poor my efforts were that first semester, she praised my ability and encouraged me to stick with it. Finally, Jocelyn taught me so much about taking care of my health while going to college. She introduced me to the campus recreation center, and we started meeting there after class to run on the treadmill. She also told me that dieting was a waste of time, and that it was better to eat small portions throughout the day. I took her advice, and I have lost weight and gained energy. I am so grateful for Jocelyn's mentorship, and I hope that one day I can be a mentor for another student who is just starting out in college.

Support point 2

One of the most important ways I became motivated in college was by writing in my first English class. In high school, writing essays always bored me. However, my college English instructor, Ms. Ezell, encouraged me to write on topics that meant a lot to me. These assignments allowed me to reflect on important events in my life. For example, I had never accepted how hard it was when my brother left to serve in the Afghan war. Even though I tried not to think about him getting hurt or killed, it distracted me in my personal life and at school. I realized that my poor academic performance was not caused by a lack of intelligence but by anxiety. Another time, Ms. Ezell asked me to write an essay about smoking on campus. I figured it was just another boring topic. However, when I started brainstorming, I realized how much I resent the smell of smoke on my clothes and how lethal secondhand smoke can be. This started me thinking about what was most important—the right to breathe safe air or the right to feed a nicotine addiction. Then I got angry, and became more involved on campus. Finally, I had to write a research paper on homelessness and interview real homeless people near our campus. Learning about these people's struggles helped me see the importance of the lessons in my history and economics classes. I learned that when I write about topics that matter, writing can be powerful.

Support point 3

If you are a new college student, and your motivation is low, take my advice: Go take a career placement test, immediately! Then, identify another student (one who has more experience than you and is successful) and ask that person to be your mentor. You will probably get a positive response. Last, go visit your English instructor and say that you would like to write on a topic that has personal meaning for you. If you are lucky, you may get another positive response that will boost your motivation and allow you to enjoy your college work.

Conclusion

ACTIVITY 3: Teamwork

Working with a few of your classmates, answer the following questions about the paragraph and essay used to illustrate method 2.

1. What is the topic sentence in the paragraph? What is the thesis statement in the opening paragraph of the essay? How are these sentences similar or different? Why is the thesis statement more appropriate for a full essay?

CONTINUED >

2. What two new topic sentences have been added to the essay (in the first and third body paragraphs)? How are the ideas in these topic sentences related to the topic sentence of the second body paragraph?

3. Are any of the supporting points or examples in the new body paragraphs present in the original paragraph? If so, what are they?

If you use method 2 when moving from paragraph to essay, you will need to know how to expand your main idea. Here are a few examples:

Main Idea (paragraph):	Anger is an emotion that has played an important role in my life.
Thesis (essay):	Several powerful emotions have ruled my life.
Main Idea (paragraph):	Credit cards have been a cause of my financial ruin.
Thesis (essay):	Irresponsible money management has led to my financial ruin.
Main Idea (paragraph):	Internet gambling has become a wide-spread addiction among Americans.
Thesis (essay):	The Internet has provided an array of new addictions for Americans, including social media, gambling, and shopping.

ACTIVITY 4

Select a paragraph that you have already written for this class and expand it into an essay using method 2. In other words, do the following:

- Expand your main idea into a broader thesis that will allow you to add new support points that were not part of your original paragraph.

- Brainstorm until you have gathered enough ideas for your new body paragraphs. Write a detailed outline. Compose your new body paragraphs. Include your original paragraph as a body paragraph in the essay.

- Write an opening paragraph (with the thesis) and a short concluding paragraph.

Power Tip
For help writing opening and concluding paragraphs, see pages 213–19 of this chapter.

Adding an Introduction and Thesis

If your instructor asks you to write an essay with two or more body paragraphs, you will need to add an introduction and a conclusion to make that essay complete. Also, if you start out writing a single paragraph but decide to divide that paragraph into two or more separate body paragraphs, you will need to add an introduction and a conclusion.

The introduction (opening paragraph) for an academic essay has two basic purposes:

1. to "hook" your reader
2. to "pop" (present) your thesis

HOOKING THE READER

When you "hook" your reader, you get him or her interested in your topic by opening with a clever idea. You can usually develop this hook in a few carefully crafted sentences; you do not want the hook to get out of control and become a distraction for the reader.

Here are five strategies that are especially effective in hooking readers:

- starting with a series of questions
- starting with a story (about yourself or someone else)
- starting with a comparison (x is like y)
- starting with an imaginary scenario (What if . . . , Imagine if . . .)
- starting with a quotation

Now, let's look at some sample opening paragraphs. Pretend that your essay discusses the benefits and frustrations of working with other students in a small group. As you read the following samples, consider which one might "hook" the reader most effectively, getting him or her interested in your topic.

Starting with a Series of Questions

Are two heads better than one? What about three or four heads, or more? If everyone has an opinion, isn't it more trouble than it's worth to work in a group? Isn't it just easier to work alone? (Pop the thesis here.)

Starting with a Story (about yourself or someone else)

Mark was a bright student who planned to transfer to UCLA after two more semesters at his community college. So far, he had a 4.0 average. He worked hard studying, meeting with his instructors, and staying up late writing papers to keep his high average. But when his history instructor put the class into groups, some of the students seemed lazy, and some disagreed with his plans for how to carry out group projects. Suddenly, he worried that the group might hurt his chances of keeping straight A's. (Pop the thesis here.)

Starting with a Comparison (x is like y)

Working with other students in a group is like a team sport. In baseball, for example, if the left outfielder and the first baseman are both goofing off, there is a good chance that the other team can hit some fly balls or grounders and score some runs. Similarly, in a geography class, if two members of a discussion group are talking about the parties they went to on Saturday night instead of analyzing the features of a glacier, they may cause the group to "drop the ball" in the learning opportunity. When the instructor asks the group to share its ideas with the whole class, the group may strike out. (Pop the thesis here.)

Starting with an Imaginary Scenario (What if . . . , Imagine if . . .)

Imagine that you're sitting in class and the instructor says, "Get into groups of three or four students to discuss the impact that television has had on education." You're excited because you have so many ideas on that subject. However, when you join your group, things don't go so well: One person thinks the topic is dumb, one doesn't say a word, one disagrees with your ideas, and another agrees with your ideas but for different reasons than you had in mind. Suddenly, group work has become group clash. (Pop the thesis here.)

Starting with a Quotation

Martina Horner, the president of Radcliffe College, observes, "What is important is to keep learning, to enjoy challenge, and to tolerate ambiguity. In the end, there are no certain answers." When I work with other students in small groups, there are always a few students who think they know it all. But, like Martina Horner, I think group learning should allow everyone to have an opinion. People should forget about getting the right answer to impress the teacher. Most teachers want students to explore more complex issues that don't have simple answers or solutions. (Pop the thesis here.)

Power Tip

If you start with a quotation, remember that the quotation cannot stand alone. You must explain how the quotation relates to your introduction. Also, note that you can consult special reference books and Web sites for quotations. For instance, you might type the term *popular quotations* into a search engine.

POPPING THE THESIS

Once you have hooked your reader, it's time to "pop" your thesis, stating *boldly* and *clearly* the main idea for your essay. As a beginning college writer, it is a good strategy to write your thesis in one complete sentence; this will help you focus your ideas and express them precisely. Also, it is a good habit for beginning writers to make the thesis statement the last sentence of the introduction. This way, it will be easy to verify that you have a thesis every time you write an essay.

Thesis Statement versus Topic Sentence

A basic thesis statement is like a topic sentence in that it should always do two things: 1) identify the general topic, and 2) express your original point or opinion about the topic.

The major difference, then, between a topic sentence and a thesis statement is <u>the scope</u> of the idea. For example, you should be able to develop the idea in a topic sentence fully in one academic paragraph. To develop the idea in a thesis statement, you will need two or more body paragraphs, plus an introduction and a conclusion.

Let's return to some earlier examples of topic sentences and thesis statements. In each example, the assigned topic is underlined <u>once</u>. The original point or opinion about the topic is underlined <u>twice</u>.

ASSIGNED TOPIC	*Discuss what emotion(s) have been important in your life.*
Topic Sentence (paragraph):	<u>Anger</u> is an emotion that <u><u>has played an important role in my life</u></u>.
Thesis Statement (essay):	<u>Several powerful emotions</u> <u><u>have ruled my life</u></u>.
ASSIGNED TOPIC	*Discuss your financial challenges.*
Topic Sentence (paragraph):	<u>Credit cards</u> have been a <u><u>cause of my financial ruin</u></u>.
Thesis Statement (essay):	<u>Irresponsible money management</u> has <u><u>led to my financial ruin</u></u>.
ASSIGNED TOPIC	*Discuss a form or forms of addiction caused by the Internet.*
Topic Sentence (paragraph):	<u>Internet gambling</u> has become <u><u>a widespread addiction among Americans</u></u>.
Thesis Statement (essay):	<u>The Internet</u> has provided an <u><u>array of new addictions for Americans, including socializing, gambling, and shopping</u></u>.

Power Tip

If you are writing an essay in response to an assigned topic, it is important that your thesis (and the entire essay) respond directly to the topic. For example, you might use key words from the assignment. For more information, see Chapter 2, page 22, and Chapter 5, page 89.

ACTIVITY 5: Teamwork

In each pair of sentences, underline the assigned topic and double underline the original point or opinion. Then, write either "topic sentence" or "thesis statement" in the space provided. (For examples, see above.)

1. **ASSIGNED TOPIC**   *Discuss a problem you've had with your parents.*
   a. My expensive cell phone bills have caused me problems with my parents. _____
   b. My cell phone usage habits have caused me problems with my parents. _____

2. **ASSIGNED TOPIC**   *Discuss how you succeed in your college work.*
   a. When I prepare for my college classes, I use a variety of study skills. _____

CONTINUED >

b. When I read assignments for my college classes, I use a variety of critical reading strategies. _____

3. **ASSIGNED TOPIC**   *Discuss last night's episode of* Dancing with the Stars.
   a. Jennifer Grey and Derek Hough gave a flawless performance on *Dancing with the Stars* last night. _____
   b. The three remaining couples gave strong performances on *Dancing with the Stars* last night. _____

4. **ASSIGNED TOPIC**   *Discuss your favorite Web site(s).*
   a. My favorite Web sites are Facebook, eBay, and YouTube.
   _____
   b. My favorite Web site is YouTube. _____

5. **ASSIGNED TOPIC**   *Discuss how to decorate a home successfully.*
   a. Successful home decorating requires a variety of skills.
   _____
   b. Successful home decorating requires a good sense of color.
   _____

For a foolproof introduction, remember that it's a good idea to make the thesis *the last sentence* of the opening paragraph. Here's an example based on the introduction shown on page 213. Notice how the first few sentences *hook the reader*, and the last sentence *pops the thesis*.

> Are two heads better than one? What about three or four heads, or more? If everyone has an opinion, isn't it more trouble than it's worth to work in a group? Isn't it just easier to work alone? Although collaborating with others may seem difficult at first, small-group work has many benefits, and the obstacles that sometimes arise can be handled successfully.

ACTIVITY 6

Read the body paragraphs below. Then, do the following:

- On a separate sheet of paper, write *three different* introductions for the essay, using your three favorite strategies for "hooking" the reader. (These strategies are discussed on page 213.)
- Formulate a thesis statement that identifies the assigned topic and expresses an original point or opinion about the topic.
- Add the thesis as the last sentence of each introduction.
- Exchange introductions with a few classmates. Discuss which of the introductions would be most likely to hook the reader effectively and which thesis statements "pop" loudly and clearly.

> Most of my friends love their cell phones and BlackBerries, but I think these devices are harmful to good communication. For starters, people allow their devices to interrupt important conversations. One

thing that irritates me is that my study partners answer their cell phones even if we're reviewing for an exam. Furthermore, I recently quit dating a woman because she would answer her cell phone no matter what, as if any call were more important than our relationship. My sales job is tougher, too, because of electronic communication devices. Clients don't hesitate to answer their phones during my sales pitch. Sometimes, they even use a call as an excuse to walk away and not come back. In addition, electronic communication can mislead or confuse people. For example, I have sent e-mails or text messages to friends in a joking tone, but my friends thought I was being weird or rude. There is no "body language" with electronic communication, which has the potential to cause confusion and hurt feelings. Last, I believe that these devices trivialize communication. The juvenile text messages that my friends send to one another are a good example. Another example is the nonstop, shallow conversations people have — talking just to be talking. It's clear that cell phones and BlackBerries are here to stay, but we should not abuse them or allow them to replace good old-fashioned face-to-face conversations.

— Body paragraph 1

    Portable electronic music devices, such as MP3 players and iPods, make it more difficult to meet people. For one thing, it's harder to meet people in public places. For example, at the bus stop, I used to talk to strangers while waiting for the bus. I actually met my roommate this way. But nowadays, everyone at the bus stop listens to an MP3 player. The same is true for the school cafeteria. Just a few years ago, strangers would share a table and strike up a conversation. Now, you can look like a loser if you sit at a table by yourself without an iPod plugged into your ear. Furthermore, electronic music devices have made it harder for people with similar interests to meet. For instance, I remember when the gym was a great place to meet other people interested in health and fitness. We would trade tips and stories on the workout floor. Now, it seems like earbuds and MP3 players have become mandatory equipment; instead of sharing training tips, people sing to themselves. Similarly, one time, on the train to San Diego, I wanted to continue a conversation with a woman I'd just met. She wanted to listen to music instead, so she put in her earbuds and kept listening until her stop. She could have been the woman of my dreams, but I'll never know. It seems to make some people feel important to be constantly attached to their portable music device. However, they don't know what social interactions they're missing out on!

— Body paragraph 2

Adding a Conclusion

After you have written two or more body paragraphs and an introduction, you will need to complete your essay with a conclusion. If you do not add a conclusion, your last body paragraph will leave readers hanging, and they will not have the sense of a satisfying finish.

The conclusion for an academic essay can be short or long, depending on the specific requirements of the assignment. Many instructors are satisfied if you briefly restate your main idea; other instructors expect the conclusion to be a well-developed paragraph in which you consolidate and explore the best ideas from the essay. Because instructors have different expectations for the conclusion, be sure to ask for clarification if you are uncertain about what to include.

Here are five strategies for writing a brief conclusion:

- giving advice to the reader
- making a prediction
- ending with some thought-provoking questions
- making a personal growth statement
- finishing the story that you used in your introduction (if you began with a story)

Following are sample conclusions for each strategy. The conclusions are for the previously developed essay on small-group work in college.

Strategy 1: Giving Advice to the Reader

If you are a student, remember that group work can be one of the most powerful learning opportunities available to you. Defending your ideas, listening to others, and in some cases teaching others all provide a mental workout that your brain won't get if you are snoozing through a lecture. If you are an instructor, remember that group work is effective only if students are given clear objectives and an occasional helping hand when the discussion gets off track or overheated.

Strategy 2: Making a Prediction

I predict that by the year 2050, most colleges and universities will have a "group learning" requirement and general education courses such as "Group Learning 101." The reason for this is the growing recognition among educators and employers that collaborative skills are essential for personal and professional success. In the United States, we live in a democracy whose future depends on the ability of its citizens to work together effectively. As such, developing collaborative learning skills seems at least as important as understanding the Pythagorean theorem or the process of photosynthesis.

Strategy 3: Ending with Some Thought-Provoking Questions

What if college professors were no longer allowed to lecture in class? What if every minute of class time had to be spent in small-group work with other students? Do you think college students would rise to the challenge and take more responsibility for their intellectual growth and education? Or would they just goof off and cheat themselves and their peers of a meaningful learning opportunity? What would you do?

Strategy 4: Making a Personal Growth Statement

Before writing this essay, I generally had a bad attitude about working in groups with other students. In my experience, college students aren't responsible enough to engage in independent intellectual discussion, and college professors aren't dedicated enough to ensuring productivity within the groups. However, because group work is clearly here to stay, I've decided to be a model participant and leader, guiding my peers to meaningful collaboration. Even if they don't reciprocate, I'll be sharpening my management skills for my future career in international business.

Strategy 5: Finishing the Story That You Used in Your Introduction

(For the first part of this story, see page 213.)

Remember Mark and his fears about small-group work in history class? Well, his group experience turned out to be a near disaster. Two students disappeared from the class without doing their share of the work. Another student worked hard but produced mediocre results. Therefore, the bulk of the work fell on Mark and Dana, who resented having to do the work of five people but were determined to get an A. The professor refused to give any special allowances to the group for the troubles they were having. In the end, the group received a B for the project. Fortunately, Mark's other grades in the class brought his average up to an A. Although the experience was difficult for Mark, he learned a valuable lesson about the challenges of working with others—a lesson that he believes will benefit him later in college and beyond.

ACTIVITY 7

Review the introductions that you wrote for Activity 6. Then, do the following:

- Write *three different* conclusions for the essay, using your favorite three strategies.
- Exchange your conclusions with a few classmates. Discuss which of the conclusions would be most effective in leaving the reader thinking about the topic.

Revising and Proofreading

To revise and proofread your essay, use the strategies presented in Chapter 6 of this book (pages 120–22 and 129–32). Keep in mind that the revising and proofreading process will take longer for an essay than for a paragraph, and plan accordingly.

BRINGING IT ALL TOGETHER:
Moving from Paragraphs to Essays

In this chapter, you have learned about the differences between academic paragraphs and complete essays, and you have seen how to develop the various parts of an essay. Confirm your knowledge by filling in the blank spaces in the following sentences. If you need help, review the pages listed after each sentence.

✔ An academic paragraph and an essay are similar because they both have a main idea and a series of support points. However, the essay includes three things that are not part of an academic paragraph. These are: 1) _____, 2) _____, and 3) _____. (page 204)

✔ There are two common methods for moving from a paragraph to an essay. With the first method, you must expand _____ _____. With the second method, you must expand _____. (page 204)

✔ With method 1, the topic sentence becomes _____. Each support point becomes a _____. The concluding sentence becomes _____. (page 207)

✔ With method 2, the original paragraph stays _____. You must add new _____ that were not part of the original paragraph. (page 209)

✔ There are five effective strategies for "hooking" the reader in your introduction. These strategies are: 1) _____, 2) _____, 3) _____, 4) _____, and 5) _____. (page 213)

✔ A thesis statement is similar to a topic sentence. They both must do two things: 1) _____ and 2) _____ _____. (page 214)

✔ The major difference between a thesis statement and a topic sentence is
_____. (page 215)

✔ There are five effective strategies for writing a brief conclusion. These
strategies are: 1) _____, 2) _____,
3) _____, 4) _____
_____, and 5) _____.
(page 218)

PART THREE
Grammar for Academic Writing

CHAPTER 10

The Simple Sentence

Before you read this chapter, it's a good idea to test your understanding of simple sentences. You may know more than you think.

WHAT DO YOU KNOW?

Circle "Yes" if each word group below is a complete, correct sentence. Circle "No" if it is incomplete. Then, explain your choice.

1. **He blinked.**

   Yes   No

   Explanation: _____

   _____

2. **A hungry prairie dog wandering across the wilderness of Wyoming.**

   Yes   No

   Explanation: _____

   _____

3. **The special effects in the new sci-fi movie beyond belief.**

   Yes   No

   Explanation: _____

   _____

4. **Looking inside the aquarium with a flashlight for her lost earring.**

   Yes   No

   Explanation: _____

   _____

5. **After the four-alarm fire on Thursday night, the firefighters slept all day on Friday.**

   Yes   No

   Explanation: _____

   _____

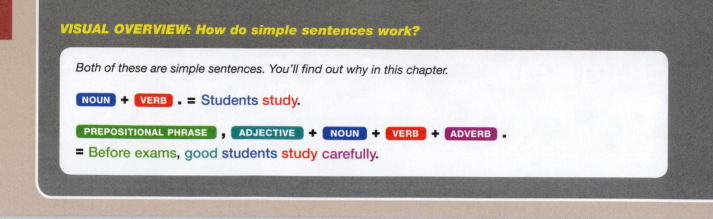

Both of these are simple sentences. You'll find out why in this chapter.

NOUN + **VERB** . = Students study.

PREPOSITIONAL PHRASE , **ADJECTIVE** + **NOUN** + **VERB** + **ADVERB** .
= Before exams, good students study carefully.

The Building Blocks of Language

From infancy into childhood, we learn language in stages. Each stage gives us new building blocks with which to express our ideas, eventually in complete sentences.

The first stage generally takes place between the ages of one and two. In this stage, infants use single words to identify *things* (**nouns**) and *actions* (**verbs**). We call these **foundation words** because they are the foundation of all verbal communication.

With just nouns and verbs, infants begin to build simple "sentences." Take a look:

NOUN   **VERB**
baby   sit
dog   run

In the next stage of language building, children find words to *describe* things and actions (**adjectives** and **adverbs**). Take a look:

good baby sit

The **adjective** *good* describes *baby*.

dog run fast

The **adverb** *fast* describes *run*.

We call these **descriptive words**, and we use them to <u>add onto</u> the foundation of nouns and verbs. (Notice that **adjective** and **adverb** both begin with the prefix *ad-*, showing that they are an *added* layer.)

In the third stage, children discover words that connect all the other words (**prepositions** and **conjunctions**). Take a look:

good baby sit in chair

The **preposition** connects *sit* to *chair*.

dog **and** cat run fast

The **conjunction** connects *dog* and *cat.*

At this point, a child possesses the main building blocks of language. As you will see in the next chapter, every sentence that we speak or write is a combination of these six building blocks:

PREPOSITIONS
CONJUNCTIONS
ADVERBS
ADJECTIVES
VERBS
NOUNS

> *Connecting Words*

> *Descriptive Words*

> *Foundation Words*

The chapters in this part of the book include a color-coded key that identifies foundation, descriptive, and connecting words. This color-coding will help you understand how words combine to form sentences. The key is shown here in the margin. Watch for it as you work through the chapters in Part Three.

BUILD IT: Short Simple Sentences

In the following sections, you will build longer and longer simple sentences using the building blocks of nouns, verbs, adjectives, adverbs, conjunctions, and prepositions.

BUILDING SHORT SIMPLE SENTENCES

Did you know that a complete, correct sentence may have as few as **two words**? One of these words must be a noun, and the other must be a verb. The noun is also called the **subject**. In sentences with just two words, you can think of the subject as the *actor* and the verb as the *action*. Here's an example:

SUBJECT   VERB

Athletes   compete.

This is a complete, correct sentence because it has a subject and a verb, and it expresses a complete thought. Yes, it could contain more information, but it does not have to.

KEY TO CHALLENGE METER
WARMUP
EASY
MODERATE
ADVANCED
MASTERY

Identify the difficulty level of each activity using the key above.

WARMUP

ACTIVITY 1

Create ten simple sentences, matching subjects and verbs from the columns below. Begin by creating five sentences from the two columns on the left. Then, create five more sentences from the two columns on the right. Remember to start each sentence with a capital letter and end it with a period. The first sentence has been written for you.

Subject	Verb	Subject	Verb
cells	heals	smoke	procrastinate
we	sings	Elvis	hurts
Beyoncé	infect	reading	rises
love	divide	jealousy	lives
viruses	collaborate	I	enlightens

Cells divide.

FOUNDATION WORDS: NOUNS

A **noun** is a word that identifies a person, place, or thing. There are three types of nouns (concrete, proper, and abstract) and a noun substitute (pronoun).

Concrete nouns identify physical objects that can be seen or touched, such as _desk, pencil, laptop, shirt, dress, shoe,_ and so on. Simply look around you: Any object that you can see or touch has a name for it, and that name is a concrete noun.

Abstract nouns do not identify physical objects. Instead, they identify feelings or sensations (_love, fear, sadness, hunger,_ and so on), ideas (_fun, trouble, intelligence, success,_ and so on), or activities (_shouting, thinking, jogging, lying,_ and so on). Remember: Because you can't touch any of these things, they are considered abstract.

Proper nouns are the names given to specific people, places, or things, such as _Michael Jackson, Philadelphia,_ or _Toyota._ Proper nouns always begin with a capital letter.

Pronouns are convenient <u>substitutes</u> for the other types of nouns. The most common pronouns are _personal_ pronouns: _I, you, he, she, it, they,_ and _we._ As an example, _she_ could be a convenient substitute for _the woman._ Remember: Pronouns can be the subject or _actor_ in a sentence.

ACTIVITY 2

In the blank spaces provided, add additional examples to each of the following lists.

Concrete Nouns	**Abstract Nouns**	**Proper Nouns**	**Pronouns**
bike	friendship	New York	you
fingernail	shame	Shaq	
star	intelligence	Burger King	
phone	joy	Honda	

ACTIVITY 3

Return to Activity 1. For each sentence, identify whether the subject is a concrete, abstract, or proper noun, or a pronoun. Write one of the following beside each sentence: *concrete*, *abstract*, *proper*, or *pronoun*.

In some sentences, the verb must be followed by another noun in order to express a complete thought and make sense. The second noun usually answers the question "What?" Take a look:

NOUN **VERB** **NOUN**
Teachers give _____ [What?]

In this case, the simple sentence must have at least three words to be complete. The second noun is called the *object*, and it receives the action. Here is the complete sentence:

SUBJECT **VERB** **OBJECT**
Teachers   give   homework.

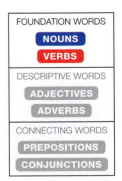

FOUNDATION WORDS
NOUNS
VERBS

DESCRIPTIVE WORDS
ADJECTIVES
ADVERBS

CONNECTING WORDS
PREPOSITIONS
CONJUNCTIONS

ACTIVITY 4

MODERATE

Create ten simple sentences, combining subjects, verbs, and objects from the columns below. Begin by creating five sentences from the three columns on the left. Then, create five more sentences using the three columns on the right. Remember to start each sentence with a capital letter and end it with a period. The first sentence has been written for you.

Subject	Verb	Object	Subject	Verb	Object
children	outsells	teams	vitamins	take	diplomas
fans	diagnose	a murder	they	defeated	charge
she	support	affection	Serena	improves	illness
Honda	crave	disease	leaders	received	concentration
doctors	witnessed	Toyota	sleep	prevent	Venus

Children crave affection.

_____   _____

_____   _____

_____   _____

_____   _____

ACTIVITY 5

MODERATE

Go back to your answers for Activity 4. For each sentence that you wrote, underline the subject (the actor), circle the verb (the action), and draw a rectangle around the object (the recipient of the action). Then, above each subject and object, write _concrete_, _proper_, _abstract_, or _pronoun_ to identify the noun type.

ACTIVITY 6: Teamwork

ADVANCED

For each of the following pairs of words, decide whether the verb _must be followed_ by another noun in order to make sense. If another noun is required, add the noun and a period to complete the sentence. If the two words already express a complete thought, just add a period.

EXAMPLE: We expect _____ _results._ _____

1. Microsoft makes _____

2. It dissolved _____

3. Robert E. Lee surrendered _____

4. Exercise improves _____

5. She bought _____

6. Texting saves _____

7. Wildfires cause _____

8. The World Trade Center collapsed _____

9. An iPod costs _____

10. The Patriots won _____

FOUNDATION WORDS: VERBS

So far in this chapter, we have looked at verbs that express actions. These are called **action verbs**. Most of the verbs in the English language are action verbs, and they are easy to recognize. However, a few verbs do not express an action, so they are more difficult to recognize as verbs. These are called **linking** and **helping** verbs. Take a look:

| NOUN | LINKING VERB | (not an action) |

Deirdre   is . . .

| NOUN | HELPING VERB | (not an action) |

Students   should . . .

As you can see from these examples, linking and helping verbs do not express an action, nor do they express a complete thought. They must be followed by more information to make sense. This additional information comes in the form of either an adjective (with linking verbs) or another verb (with helping verbs).

| NOUN | LINKING VERB | ADJECTIVE |
Deirdre   is   distracted.

| NOUN | HELPING VERB | ANOTHER VERB |
Students   should   study.

Common Linking Verbs

am, is, are, was, were (states of being)

appear, become, feel, get, grow, look, seem, smell, sound, taste

Common Helping Verbs

am, is, are, was, were

do, does, did

have, has, had

can, could, may, might

must, shall, should, will, would

ACTIVITY 7

WARMUP

Fill in the blank spaces to complete each sentence. Refer to the boxes of common linking and helping verbs above for more help.

Add a linking verb.

EXAMPLE: The spider _____*is*_____ hairy.

1. They _____ sad.
2. The soldier _____ frightened.
3. I _____ disgusted.
4. Intelligence _____ useful.
5. The pie _____ good.

Add a helping verb.

EXAMPLE: We _____*will*_____ study.

6. He _____ laugh.
7. Tourists _____ visit.
8. The judge _____ rule.
9. The box _____ opened.
10. They _____ escape.

Power Tip

A *linking* verb is often followed by a word that describes the subject. A *helping* verb is always followed by another verb, which is considered the *main verb* of the sentence. Together, the helping verb and the main verb make up the complete verb.

ACTIVITY 8

EASY

Fill in the blank spaces to complete each sentence.

Add a linking verb and an adjective.

EXAMPLE: Miguel ___sounded sick___.

1. We _____.
2. The roses _____.
3. Jeremy _____.
4. The drink _____.
5. The house _____.

Add a helping verb and another verb.

EXAMPLE: Our neighbors ___should come___.

6. It _____.
7. The employee _____.
8. Jessica _____.
9. The pilot _____.
10. We _____.

Power Tip
Remember that an adjective describes a noun. For example, in the phrases, "The good baby," or "The cute dog," *good* and *cute* are adjectives.

ACTIVITY 9

MODERATE

In each of the following sentences, underline the subject and circle the verb. Then, in the space provided, write *action, linking,* or *helping* to identify the verb type. (Note: If you find a helping verb, circle it, but do not circle the verb that follows it.)

EXAMPLE: The deadline (will) expire. _helping_

1. Pyramids are ancient. _____
2. The president appears hopeful. _____
3. Cigarettes cause cancer. _____
4. Chrysanthemums smell bitter. _____
5. Consumers need protection. _____
6. Racism is contagious. _____
7. It looks threatening. _____
8. Thoughtfulness becomes habitual. _____
9. She should confess. _____
10. Violence might erupt. _____

For more practice with nouns and verbs, go to **bedfordstmartins.com/ steppingstones**.

ACTIVITY 10: Teamwork

For each of the following word groups, decide if more information is needed to express a complete thought. If so, add <u>one more word</u> and a period. If not, just add a period. Then, in the space provided, write *action, linking,* or *helping* to identify the verb type.

EXAMPLE: The flu might ____*spread.*____   Verb type: _*helping*_

1. Counselors should _____   Verb type: _____

2. We seem _____   Verb type: _____

3. Bombs _____   Verb type: _____

4. Nelson Mandela ended _____   Verb type: _____

5. The Beatles sounded _____   Verb type: _____

6. You must _____   Verb type: _____

7. The hurricane damaged _____   Verb type: _____

8. The spaceship landed _____   Verb type: _____

9. Dreams can _____   Verb type: _____

10. The boxer won't _____   Verb type: _____

Power Tip
You may use very short sentences in your college writing, but do not overuse them. Too many might suggest that your thinking and writing are simplistic. Effective writers save very short sentences for special emphasis.

BUILD IT: Longer Simple Sentences

You already know that a sentence may have as few as two or three words. However, we usually write longer sentences that contain some of the other building blocks of language.

DESCRIPTIVE WORDS: ADJECTIVES AND ADVERBS

FOUNDATION WORDS
NOUNS
VERBS

DESCRIPTIVE WORDS
ADJECTIVES
ADVERBS

CONNECTING WORDS
PREPOSITIONS
CONJUNCTIONS

As human beings, we like to describe things, and we use a lot of descriptive words to do this. Descriptive words—**adjectives** and **adverbs**—also add length to our sentences. As an example, let's start with a very short simple sentence:

NOUN   **VERB**
Surgeons operate.

Now, let's add an **adjective** to describe *what type* of surgeons operate:

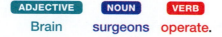

ADJECTIVE   **NOUN**   **VERB**
Brain   surgeons   operate.

Now, let's add an **adverb** to describe *how* brain surgeons operate.

Power Tip
Remember that *adverbs* and *adjectives* *add* meaning to verbs and nouns.

ADJECTIVE	NOUN	VERB	ADVERB
Brain	surgeons	operate	cautiously.

Adjectives describe nouns and pronouns. Take a look:

reliable employee

healthy appetite

blind date

messy clothes

successful student

Adverbs describe actions (verbs). Take a look:

think carefully

sleep late

jump high

dance gracefully

study hard

ACTIVITY 11
EASY

In each sentence, circle the word(s) that describe(s) the underlined word(s). Then, in the space provided, write *adjective* or *adverb* to identify the type of descriptive word(s) that you have circled.

EXAMPLE: Jeremy has (neat) handwriting. *adjective*

1. It <u>hurts</u> deeply. _____
2. <u>Soccer</u> has become popular. _____
3. College <u>will cost</u> more. _____
4. The singer <u>will appear</u> nightly. _____
5. Soap <u>operas</u> exaggerate life. _____
6. Socrates taught critical <u>thinking</u>. _____
7. Thomas Jefferson owned many <u>slaves</u>. _____
8. Fame <u>may not satisfy</u> you completely. _____
9. Good <u>reputations can be lost</u> quickly. _____, _____
10. Absolute <u>power corrupts</u> absolutely. _____, _____

ACTIVITY 12

MODERATE

Select any five of the following word pairs and write a short sentence. You will need to add a subject and a verb.

EXAMPLE: drunk, happily _The drunk man sang happily._

1. nervous, suddenly _____
2. smart, carefully _____
3. heartbroken, endlessly _____
4. talented, gracefully _____
5. rich, stylishly _____
6. competitive, aggressively _____
7. beautiful, proudly _____
8. angry, loudly _____
9. old, wisely _____
10. shy, softly _____

ACTIVITY 13: Teamwork

ADVANCED

As sentences become longer, we still need to be able to recognize the subject and the verb. In the following sentences, cross out the descriptive words (adjectives and adverbs). Then, underline the subject and circle the verb. (Note: hyphenated terms count as one word.)

EXAMPLE: ~~College~~ graduates (have) a ~~better~~ chance at ~~career~~ success.
(Cross out three descriptive words.)

1. The magician performed unbelievable magic tricks. (Cross out two descriptive words.)

2. Political awareness has increased nationally. (Cross out two descriptive words.)

3. Crossword puzzles are educational and fun. (Cross out three descriptive words.)

4. Memorization techniques include flash cards and rhyming games. (Cross out three descriptive words.)

5. Martin Luther King Jr. spoke courageously to government leaders and ordinary citizens. (Cross out three descriptive words.)

6. Good study habits make college success easier. (Cross out four descriptive words.)

For more practice with adjectives and adverbs, go to **bedfordstmartins.com/ steppingstones.**

7. The international diplomatic team met again recently. (Cross out four descriptive words.)

8. The now-famous Rosa Parks bravely defied ignorant, racist laws. (Cross out four descriptive words.)

9. Talented athletes can become rich, famous, and even heroic. (Cross out five descriptive words.)

10. Experienced pilots can easily identify weather patterns and safely fly large aircraft. (Cross out five descriptive words.)

CONNECTING WORDS: CONJUNCTIONS

Some simple sentences have *more than one* subject or *more than one* verb. We use **conjunctions** (*and, or, but*) to join **compound subjects** and **compound verbs**. Take a look:

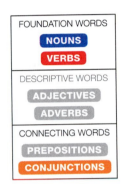

> **SUBJECT**   **VERB**
>
> Jason   laughed.

Now, let's add another subject:

> **COMPOUND SUBJECT**   **VERB**
>
> Emily and Jason   laughed.

Now, let's add another verb:

> **SUBJECT**   **COMPOUND VERB**
>
> Jason   laughed and cried.

Note that a sentence can have *both* a compound subject and a compound verb.

> **COMPOUND SUBJECT**   **COMPOUND VERB**
>
> Emily and Jason   laughed and cried.

The conjunctions *but* and *or* are also used to form compound subjects and verbs. Take a look:

> **COMPOUND SUBJECT**
>
> A cold or the flu is making me ill.

> **COMPOUND VERB**
>
> Roger skipped lunch but ate a snack.

compound: made up of two or more parts
conjunction: a connector between words, phrases, or clauses

FOUNDATION WORDS
NOUNS
VERBS
DESCRIPTIVE WORDS
ADJECTIVES
ADVERBS
CONNECTING WORDS
PREPOSITIONS
CONJUNCTIONS

ACTIVITY 14

EASY

In each of the following sentences, complete the compound subjects and compound verbs by filling in the blanks.

EXAMPLE: <u>Halloween</u> and <u>St. Patrick's Day</u> are my favorite holidays.

Add two nouns.

1. _____ or _____ will win the game.

2. _____ and _____ don't go well together.

3. _____ and _____ will keep fighting forever.

4. _____ or _____ will be my major in college.

5. _____ and _____ are popular Web sites.

Add two verbs.

6. Airport security officers _____ and _____ passengers.

7. Many people _____ but still _____ weight.

8. To stay healthy, people should _____ and _____ .

9. The tennis player _____ the first game but _____ the match.

10. On *Dancing with the Stars*, the contestants _____ and _____ .

ACTIVITY 15

MODERATE

Select any five of the following word pairs and write a simple sentence with a compound subject or a compound verb. Use the conjunctions *and, or,* or *but* to connect the subjects and the verbs.

EXAMPLE (NOUN): football, baseball <u>Football and baseball are America's favorite sports</u>.

EXAMPLE (VERB): riot, loot <u>Citizens rioted and looted in Baghdad</u>.

Nouns

1. diabetes, heart disease _____ .

2. MySpace, Facebook _____ .

3. exercise, diet _____ .

4. men, women _____ .

5. spinach, broccoli _____ .

Verbs

6. win, lose _____ .

7. love, forgive _____ .

8. struggle, survive _____ .

9. cheat, fail _____ .

10. think, decide _____ .

ACTIVITY 16: Teamwork

ADVANCED

In each sentence, underline the subject and circle the verb. The clue in the parentheses will tell you when there are compound subjects and/or compound verbs.

EXAMPLE: <u>Meatloaf and lasagna</u> (are) good leftovers. (compound subject)

1. Politicians and voters often disagree. (compound subject)

2. Garlic can reduce cholesterol and boost the immune system. (compound verb)

3. Wedding and funerals, no matter when they happen, are emotional events for most people. (compound subject)

4. While in prison, Malcolm X read many books and copied the entire dictionary. (compound verb)

5. Turmeric and cayenne pepper will kill bacteria. (compound subject)

6. Republicans and Democrats meet in Congress and write bills. (compound subject and compound verb)

7. Mohandas K. Gandhi and Martin Luther King Jr. both read Thoreau's essay *Civil Disobedience.* (compound subject)

8. Fashion advertisements promote false beauty standards and mislead young girls. (compound verb)

9. Environmentalists, conservationists, and animal rights activists endorse environmental awareness and encourage eco-friendly behavior. (compound subject and compound verb)

10. Soccer, basketball, and tennis are the most popular sports in the world and have the largest number of fans. (compound subject and compound verb)

BUILD IT: Even Longer Simple Sentences

As you have seen, sentences become longer when we add descriptive words, compound subjects, and compound verbs. Even longer simple sentences usually have one or more prepositional phrases that tell us *when, where,* and sometimes *how* an action occurs.

For more practice with building simple sentences, visit this book's Web site at **bedfordstmartins.com/ steppingstones**.

Terminology Tip
The noun at the end of a prepositional phrase is known as the *object of the preposition*.

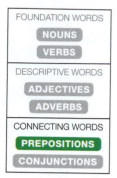

Power Tip
Because the phrase *in the water* describes the verb *fell*, it is functioning as an adverb. Prepositional phrases can also function as adjectives, as in this sentence: *The cat on the bed is friendly.* The phrase *on the bed* serves as an adjective describing the noun *cat*.

CONNECTING WORDS: PREPOSITIONS

Let's start with a short simple sentence:

SUBJECT	VERB

The book   fell.

You already know that this is a complete, correct sentence. However, we might want to add more information about where, when, or how the book fell. So, let's add a preposition:

SUBJECT	VERB	PREPOSITION

The book   fell   in . . .

Now that we have added the preposition *in*, we must complete the thought. If we do not complete the thought, the sentence will not make sense.

SUBJECT	VERB	PREPOSITIONAL PHRASE

The book   fell   in the water.

The preposition *in* connects the verb *fell* with information about *where* the book fell. The preposition **plus** the words that complete the thought are called the **prepositional phrase**. A prepositional phrase always begins with a preposition (a single word) and usually ends with a noun.

PREPOSITION   NOUN

The book fell   in the water.

COMMON PREPOSITIONS				
about	before	except	off	throughout
above	behind	for	on	to
across	below	from	onto	toward
after	beneath	in	out	under
against	beside	inside	outside	until
along	between	into	over	up
among	beyond	like	past	upon
around	by	near	since	with
as	down	next	than	within
at	during	of	through	without

📶 **ACTIVITY 17**
WARMUP

In each sentence, circle the preposition (one word), and then complete the prepositional phrase.

EXAMPLE: The plane flew (over) *our house* .

1. The actor hid behind _____.
2. The average college student hopes to earn a degree in _____.
3. On our vacation, we will take a cruise around _____.
4. When filing their tax return, many people forget to put their check in

   _____.

5. I watch the evening news on _____.

ACTIVITY 18
WARMUP

In each of the following sentences, add a single preposition to complete the sentence. Use the chart on page 240 to find prepositions.

EXAMPLE: The dentist's best patient brushes his teeth __*for*__ ten minutes.

1. The poker champion put three red chips _____ the table.
2. When you drink alcohol, you should never get _____ the wheel of a car.
3. My first class begins promptly _____ 7:45 A.M.
4. Before modern banking, many people kept their money _____ a mattress.
5. We want to make our Halloween costumes _____ October 31.

ACTIVITY 19
EASY

In each of the following sentences, add a prepositional phrase. (Hint: To write a prepositional phrase, start with a preposition from the chart on page 240 and then complete the thought.)

EXAMPLE: We drove __*to the hospital.*__ (Where?)

1. The White House and the U.S. Capitol are _____. (Where?)
2. During the Gold Rush, miners searched _____. (What?)
3. Thousands of communication satellites fly _____. (Where?)
4. America celebrates its national independence _____. (When?)
5. The play *Hamlet* was written _____. (Who?)

Power Tip

The preposition "to" followed by a verb does *not* create a prepositional phrase. Rather, it expresses the infinitive form of a verb, such as "to run," "to think," "to dream," or "to read."

Power Tip
Remember that many prepositional phrases have only two words: the preposition and a noun. For example, "*before* midnight," "*of* wood," "*on* Tuesday," "*in* time," "*at* work," or "*with* love."

ACTIVITY 20

EASY

To complete each of the following sentences, add a prepositional phrase at the beginning. Use the chart on page 240 to construct each phrase.

EXAMPLE: _On my birthday_, I always celebrate.

1. _____, my boss rewards the employees.
2. _____, our house finally sold.
3. _____, my professor canceled class.
4. _____, the newlyweds took a flight.
5. _____, three puppies were adopted.

ACTIVITY 21

MODERATE

In the spaces provided, rewrite each of the sentences from Activity 20, adding another prepositional phrase *at the end* of the sentence.

EXAMPLE: On my birthday, I always celebrate _with my friends_.

1. _____, my boss rewards the employees _____.
2. _____, our house finally sold _____.
3. _____, my professor canceled class _____.
4. _____, the newlyweds took a flight _____.
5. _____, three puppies were adopted _____.

In some sentences, two or more prepositional phrases may also be connected to make a string of prepositions. Take a look:

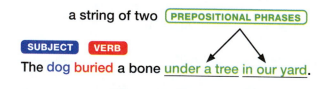

a string of two   (PREPOSITIONAL PHRASES)

SUBJECT   VERB

The dog buried a bone under a tree in our yard.

ACTIVITY 22: Teamwork

ADVANCED

Working with other students, underline the complete string of prepositional phrases. Then, circle the preposition that begins each prepositional phrase. Last, carefully count the exact number of prepositional phrases in the string and write that number in the blank space.

EXAMPLE: Each nation needs a flag (as) a symbol (of) its independence. 2

1. Betsy Ross sewed the first flag for the United States of America. ___

2. Ross was a widow with her own sewing business at the time of America's new independence. ___

3. She worshipped with George and Martha Washington at Christ Church in Philadelphia. ___

4. Washington came to her with a design for a flag with a six-pointed star. ___

5. She completed the flag in late May or early June of 1776. ___

Power Tip

Remember that *or* is a conjunction, not a preposition.

IDENTIFYING SUBJECTS WHEN THERE ARE PREPOSITIONAL PHRASES

Sometimes, a prepositional phrase may come between the subject and the verb. Take a look:

The man in my dream was handsome.

FOUNDATION WORDS
NOUNS
VERBS
DESCRIPTIVE WORDS
ADJECTIVES
ADVERBS
CONNECTING WORDS
PREPOSITIONS
CONJUNCTIONS

ACTIVITY 23
EASY

Add a prepositional phrase between the subject and the verb. (Hint: you may use the suggested preposition in parentheses.)

EXAMPLE: A can <u> of Diet Coke </u> came out of the drink machine. (of)

1. A pair _____ was drying on the clothesline. (of)

2. A police officer _____ pulled me over. (in)

3. A loud sound _____ disturbed the class. (from)

4. The TV series _____ was my favorite this year. (with)

5. The passengers _____ complained about an odor. (on)

ACTIVITY 24
MODERATE

In each of the following sentences, cross out the prepositional phrase between the subject and the verb. Then, underline the subject and circle the verb.

EXAMPLE: A <u>bouquet</u> ~~of roses~~ (arrived) from the florist.

1. The can of spray paint exploded.

2. A pedestrian on the sidewalk waved for help.

3. A professor in the Biology Division received a teaching award.

4. The rollercoasters at Six Flags are the fastest.

5. The laptop with a 17-inch screen costs $500.

Power Tip

Remember that the noun in a prepositional phrase can never be the subject of the sentence.

ılıl   **ACTIVITY 25: Teamwork**
ADVANCED

In each of the following sentences, cross out all the prepositional phrases. Then, in the spaces provided, write the subject and the verb.

EXAMPLE: A tsunami is a sequence ~~of gigantic, destructive waves in a sea or ocean.~~ (Cross out two prepositional phrases.) Subject: _tsunami_
Verb: ___is___

1. In March of 2011, an earthquake occurred off the coast of Japan. (Cross out four prepositional phrases.) Subject: _____
   Verb: _____

2. The magnitude of this earthquake, at 9.0 on the Richter scale, was the greatest on record in Japan's recent history. (Cross out five prepositional phrases.) Subject: _____ Verb: _____

3. After the earthquake, a tsunami hit the coast of Japan. (Cross out two prepositional phrases.) Subject: _____ Verb: _____

4. With waves over 30 feet-high, the tsunami destroyed house, cars, and almost everything in its path. (Cross out three prepositional phrases.) Subject: _____ Verb: _____

5. The earthquake also triggered explosions in several of the reactors at a nuclear power plant. (Cross out three prepositional phrases.) Subject: _____ Verb: _____

6. Operators injected water into the nuclear reactors in an attempt to avoid a meltdown. (Cross out two prepositional phrases.) Subject: _____ Verb: _____

7. Within one week, estimates of the death toll of the earthquake and tsunami had surpassed 10,000. (Cross out three prepositional phrases.) Subject: _____ Verb: _____

8. Hundreds of thousands of victims were displaced in shelters across the country.(Cross out four prepositional phrases.) Subject: _____ Verb: _____

9. Japan, which is among the most earthquake-prone countries on the planet, has the most advanced earthquake warning system in the world. (Cross out three prepositional phrases.) Subject: _____ Verb: _____

10. After the disaster, the prime minister of Japan vowed to rebuild the country. (Cross out two prepositional phrases.) Subject: _____ Verb: _____

IDENTIFYING SUBJECTS AND VERBS IN WHOLE PARAGRAPHS

To build your awareness of complete sentences, it's a good idea to practice identifying subjects and verbs in whole paragraphs. The following activity will give you practice with this skill.

For more practice with prepositions, go to bedfordstmartins.com/ steppingstones.

MASTERY **ACTIVITY 26: Mastery Test**

In each sentence of the following paragraphs:

- Underline the subject and circle the verb. Watch for compound subjects and compound verbs.
- If you have trouble identifying a subject or verb, remember to cross out any prepositional phrases in the sentence.
- If you are still having trouble, try crossing out any descriptive words.

The first sentence has been marked for you.

1. (1) <u>Carlos</u> (wants) an office job. (2) He applied for one on Tuesday. (3) The position is with a real estate company. (4) The company has an excellent reputation. (5) It pays its employees well and offers great benefits. (6) His girlfriend wrote a cover letter for him. (7) In it, she emphasized his work qualities. (8) For example, he is punctual. (9) He is a strong team player and respects others. (10) His experience with computers and copy machines will be valuable in an office. (11) Carlos has a good attitude. (12) Companies usually love these qualities. (13) His friends send good wishes to him. (14) Maybe he will get the job. (15) He would be a model employee.

2. (1) A rite of passage celebrates a progression in a person's life. (2) For instance, some girls celebrate their fifteenth birthday. (3) This celebration occurs in some Latin American cultures. (4) It is called a Quinceañera. (5) Jewish children celebrate their twelfth or thirteenth birthday with a Bar or Bat Mitzvah. (6) At this time, the children become responsible for their actions. (7) In Christianity, baptism is a purification ritual. (8) The minister immerses the individual in water or sprinkles water on the forehead of the person. (9) In Native American culture, an adolescent boy must perform a vision quest. (10) During the quest, the boy goes into nature and survives by himself for several days.

FIX IT: Solving Problems in Simple Sentences

FOUNDATION WORDS
NOUNS
VERBS

DESCRIPTIVE WORDS
ADJECTIVES
ADVERBS

CONNECTING WORDS
PREPOSITIONS
CONJUNCTIONS

You already know that a complete sentence must have a *subject* and a *verb* and express a complete thought. If a sentence is **missing a subject or a verb**, it will be a **fragment** (an incomplete sentence).

FIXING FRAGMENTS THAT ARE MISSING VERBS

Take a look at the following word groups and see if you notice a problem.

> The runner.
>
> My job.
>
> A person.

Each of these fragments is **missing a verb**. We don't know what is happening to the runner, the job, or the person. It is easy to recognize and fix this problem. Just add a verb to each subject:

> The runner collapsed.
>
> My job ended.
>
> A person shouted.

Some fragments can also be quite long, making it more difficult to recognize a missing verb. The following fragments contain descriptive words and prepositional phrases, but are missing a verb.

> At the finish line, the fastest runner in the New York marathon.
>
> My extremely boring job behind a desk at an accounting firm.
>
> In the ticket line at the movie theater, a rude person behind me.

To fix these longer fragments, we need to add a verb:

> At the finish line, the fastest runner in the New York marathon collapsed.
>
> My extremely boring job behind a desk at an accounting firm ended.
>
> In the ticket line at the movie theater, a rude person behind me shouted.

Power Tip

If necessary, cross out the descriptive words and the prepositional phrases to help you find the subject.

ACTIVITY 27
EASY

In each of the following fragments, underline the subject. Then, rewrite the entire fragment, adding a verb and any additional information that you want in order to make a complete sentence.

EXAMPLE: The small <u>dog</u> in the dark cage at the animal shelter.

The small dog in the dark cage at the animal shelter barked

all night.

1. A man with a white T-shirt and dirty blue jeans.

_____

_____

2. Too many people with unresolved anger.

_____

3. At the end of her shift, the exhausted waitress from Red Lobster.

_____

_____

4. The Chunky Monkey ice cream in the refrigerator.

_____

_____

5. Some tourists from France.

_____

FIXING FRAGMENTS THAT HAVE INCOMPLETE VERBS

Sometimes, a sentence will contain only part of a verb. Any sentence with an **incomplete verb** is also a **fragment**. Take a look at the following examples and see if you notice a problem.

> John laughing at his brother.
>
> The police chasing a suspect.

Each of these examples is a fragment because the verb is incomplete. A verb ending with -*ing* is not a complete verb by itself. It needs one of the following helping verbs to make it complete: *am, is, are, was, were*. Take a look:

> John was laughing at his brother.
>
> The police are chasing a suspect.

Each of these sentences is now complete and correct because it contains a subject and a complete verb (a helping verb plus the main verb). Now, take a look at the following examples and see if you notice a problem.

> The kids lost in the mall.
>
> Martha questioned by security.

Each of these sentences is also a fragment because the verb is incomplete. To fix this type of incomplete verb, add one of the same helping verbs: *am, is, are, was, were.*

> The kids were lost in the mall.
>
> Martha was questioned by security.

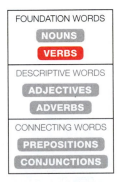

FOUNDATION WORDS

NOUNS

VERBS

DESCRIPTIVE WORDS

ADJECTIVES

ADVERBS

CONNECTING WORDS

PREPOSITIONS

CONJUNCTIONS

Power Tip

The kids lost . . . could be the start of a complete sentence if the meaning is that the kids lost something: *The kids lost their mother in the mall.* However, the meaning here is that the kids themselves *were* lost. Therefore, another helping verb (*were*) needs to connect the kids to the description (*lost*). For more on using verbs, including *was* and *were*, see Chapter 15.

For more practice with fixing fragments, go to **bedfordstmartins.com/ steppingstones.**

ACTIVITY 28

Turn each of the following word groups into a sentence by adding *am, is, are, was,* or *were* to complete the verb. If you are unsure of what form of the verb (*am, is, are,* and so on) to use with each subject, see Chapter 15, page 386.

EXAMPLE: The letter mailed. *The letter was mailed.*

1. Dogs barking. _____

2. Wilma studying. _____

3. I caught. _____

4. The tent destroyed. _____

5. Voters complaining. _____

ACTIVITY 29

In each of the following fragments, underline the subject and circle the incomplete verb. Then, turn each fragment into a sentence by completing the verb.

EXAMPLE: Some <u>spices</u> (becoming) popular because of their many uses.
   Some spices are becoming popular because of their many uses.

Power Tip
If necessary, cross out the descriptive words and the prepositional phrases to help you find the subject.

1. The spice turmeric known as one of nature's most powerful substances.

   _____

   _____

2. Turmeric been used medicinally for over 2,500 years in India.

   _____

   _____

3. The Chinese treating depression with turmeric.

   _____

4. Arthritis reduced by turmeric in food.

   _____

5. Turmeric also helping people with weight management.

   _____

   _____

FIXING FRAGMENTS THAT ARE MISSING SUBJECTS

FOUNDATION WORDS
NOUNS
VERBS
DESCRIPTIVE WORDS
ADJECTIVES
ADVERBS
CONNECTING WORDS
PREPOSITIONS
CONJUNCTIONS

Remember that if a sentence is **missing a subject**, it will also be a **fragment**. Take a look at the following examples and see if you notice a problem.

> Running to first base.
>
> To earn her degree.
>
> Hurt by his girlfriend.

Each of these examples is a fragment because there is **no subject**. We don't know *who* or *what* runs to first base, earns her degree, or was hurt by his girlfriend. To correct each fragment, add a subject and adjust the verb so that it is complete and correct:

> The batter runs to first base.
>
> Elizabeth will earn her degree.
>
> My brother was hurt by his girlfriend.

ACTIVITY 30
WARMUP

Add a subject to turn each of the following fragments into a complete sentence. You do not need to change the verb.

EXAMPLE: Played minor-league baseball. _Luis played minor-league baseball._

1. Ran the race. _____
2. Likes classical music. _____
3. Will reschedule his appointment. _____
4. Wants to go home. _____
5. May borrow money. _____

Once again, if the fragment is long, it may be more difficult to recognize that a subject is missing. Here's an example:

> To improve her dance steps before the regional competition on Friday night.

This long group of words provides a lot of information, but there is no subject. (We don't know *who* or *what* is improving her dance steps.) Therefore, this is not a complete, correct sentence. To fix the problem, simply add a subject and adjust the verb so that it is complete and correct:

> Marie improved her dance steps before the regional competition on Friday night.

ACTIVITY 31

EASY

Turn each of the following fragments into a complete sentence by adding a subject and adjusting the verb.

EXAMPLE: Learned his lesson about the dangers of an unhealthy diet.

Miguel learned his lesson about the dangers of an unhealthy diet.

1. Eating fast food six or seven times in a week.

    _____

2. Gave him high cholesterol and high blood pressure and made him gain weight.

    _____

    _____

3. To prevent heart disease and diabetes.

    _____

4. Stopped eating junk food, went on a diet, and started an exercise program.

    _____

    _____

5. Today, feeling better, looking better, and getting better reports from his doctor.

    _____

    _____

In order to master your understanding of the simple sentence, it is important to remember two key rules:

1. A grammatically correct sentence must have a subject and a verb, and it must express a complete thought.
2. A complete, correct sentence may be very short or quite long; the length of a sentence has nothing to do with its completeness and correctness.

ACTIVITY 32: Teamwork

ADVANCED

Working with some of your classmates, explain why each of the following word groups is or is not a complete, correct sentence. Then, discuss how you would fix the problem.

EXAMPLE: One of the most important Academy Awards for best direction of a film. _missing verb_____

1. The Academy Award given to some famous directors but not to others. _____

2. Alfred Hitchcock never received. _____

3. Hitchcock's many successful films, including *Rebecca, Rear Window, Vertigo,* and *Psycho.* _____

4. In 1940, Hitchcock nominated for Best Director for *Rebecca.*

_____

5. He lost. _____

_____

6. However, the film won the award for Best Picture. _____

_____

7. Throughout his career, a total of five nominations for the Oscar.

_____

8. Finally, in 1968, late in his career as a successful Hollywood director.

_____

9. Hitchcock honored with a special award for consistent high-level achievement. _____

10. His entire acceptance speech to the Academy was, "Thank you."

_____

_____

FIXING FRAGMENTS IN WHOLE PARAGRAPHS

The following activity will give you practice with recognizing and fixing fragments in whole paragraphs—a valuable skill for improving your own writing.

ACTIVITY 33: Mastery Test or Teamwork

Read the following paragraph carefully, looking for fragments. Then, do the following:

- Each time you find a fragment, write an "F" above it.
- Then, rewrite each fragment, turning it into a complete sentence. (You may need to add a subject or verb, or you may need to complete a verb. However, do not join any sentences together in this practice.)
- If a sentence is already complete and correct, write "OK" above it.

The first sentence of each paragraph has been edited for you.

The following paragraph has 10 fragments, including the one that has been edited for you.

           F   was
1. (1) Jack going to pitch in the big game. (2) Had practiced

for three months. (3) His pitching arm looking good. (4) The coach

helped him with his form. (5) Videotaped Jack pitching the ball.

(6) They studied the video. (7) Jack corrected his posture and angle.

CONTINUED >

(8) Lifted weights to improve his strength. (9) Felt more confident than ever before. (10) The night of the big game, Jack. (11) The accident happened on the way to the game. (12) Tripping over a stump. (13) He landed on his left wrist. (14) As a result, unable to pitch in the game. (15) Fortunately, won anyway.

The following paragraph has 11 fragments, including the one that has been edited for you.

2. (1) Last summer, ^F **Maya and her mother** traveled to Canada. (2) Hoping to save money. (3) Stayed in bed-and-breakfasts and inexpensive hotels. (4) Also, cooked many of their own meals. (5) To take advantage of free attractions. (6) One afternoon, they (7) Another day, they went to a town festival. (8) They also looked for stores with inexpensive souvenirs. (9) Sold postcards and lapel pins. (10) Sometimes, just enjoying sipping coffee at outdoor cafes. (11) Surprised by all the fun they had for so little money. (12) Realizing that great vacations do not have to be expensive. (13) Already, excited about taking another trip next summer.

The following paragraph has 11 fragments, including the one that has been edited for you.

3. (1) Confident people have a number of character traits. (2) First, ^F **they believe** ~~believing~~ in themselves. (3) Accepting themselves the way they are. (4) They also evaluate themselves realistically. (5) Know they are not perfect but feel okay about that. (6) Not needing to be critical of others to boost their ego. (7) People with strong confidence are straightforward and honest. (8) To hide nothing about their personal beliefs. (9) Look other people in the eye. (10) In addition, accept responsibility for their actions. (11) Learning from their mistakes. (12) Accepting life's ups and downs is another characteristic

For more practice fixing fragments, go to bedfordstmartins.com/ steppingstones.

that conveys confidence. (13) For instance, seeing life as a series

of challenges and opportunities. (14) Not defeated by setbacks.

(15) Also accepting change as a normal part of life. (16) People with

self-confidence are open to themselves, to others, and to life.

BRINGING IT ALL TOGETHER:
The Simple Sentence

In this chapter, you have learned about the building blocks of language, the simple sentence, and fragments. Confirm your knowledge by filling in the blank spaces in the following sentences. If you need help, review the pages listed after each sentence.

✔ ＿＿＿＿＿＿＿ and ＿＿＿＿＿＿＿ are known as foundation words because they are the foundation of all verbal communication. (page 226)

✔ A noun is a word that identifies a person, place, or thing. There are three types of nouns—＿＿＿＿＿＿＿, ＿＿＿＿＿＿＿, and ＿＿＿＿＿＿＿—and a noun substitute: ＿＿＿＿＿＿＿. (page 228)

✔ There are three types of verbs. An ＿＿＿＿＿＿＿ verb expresses an action and is easy to identify. A ＿＿＿＿＿＿＿ verb must be connected to more information, usually a descriptive word. A ＿＿＿＿＿＿＿ verb must be connected to another verb. (page 231)

✔ ＿＿＿＿＿＿＿ and ＿＿＿＿＿＿＿ are descriptive words. ＿＿＿＿＿＿＿ describe nouns, and ＿＿＿＿＿＿＿ describe verbs. (pages 234–35)

✔ ＿＿＿＿＿＿＿ and ＿＿＿＿＿＿＿ are used to connect the other building blocks of language. (pages 237, 240)

✔ A complete, correct sentence must have a ＿＿＿＿＿＿＿ and a ＿＿＿＿＿＿＿, and it must express a ＿＿＿＿＿＿＿. (page 250)

CONTINUED >

✔ Some sentences have more than one subject or more than one verb. More than one subject is called a _____. More than one verb is called a _____. (page 237)

✔ The longest simple sentences usually have one or more _____ _____. (page 239)

✔ The subject of a sentence will *never* be found in a _____ _____. (page 243)

✔ A sentence fragment may be caused by any one of the following problems: _____, _____, or _____. (pages 246–49)

✔ The _____ of a sentence has nothing to do with its completeness or correctness. (page 250)

CHAPTER 11

The Compound Sentence

Before you read this chapter, it's a good idea to test your understanding of compound sentences. You may know more than you think.

WHAT DO YOU KNOW?

Circle "Yes" if each word group below is a complete, correct sentence. Circle "No" if it is incomplete. Then, explain your choice.

1. **Heavy meals make people feel hot, light meals can keep people cool.**

   Yes   No

   Explanation: _____

   _____

2. **Dolphins swim, and eagles fly.**

   Yes   No

   Explanation: _____

3. **Fruits and vegetables make excellent snacks for children, parents should have plenty available.**

   Yes   No

   Explanation: _____

   _____

4. **Professional cyclist Lance Armstrong won the Tour de France seven times in a row, he was accused of doping.**

   Yes   No

   Explanation: _____

   _____

5. **Michael Jackson is known as the King of Pop; Aretha Franklin is referred to as the Queen of Soul.**

   Yes   No

   Explanation: _____

   _____

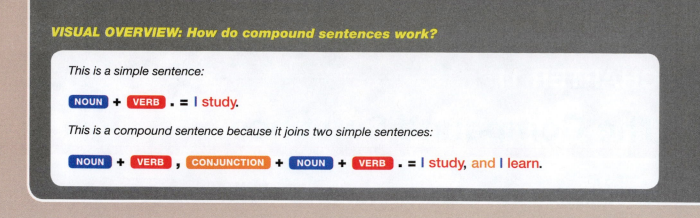

This is a simple sentence:

NOUN + **VERB** . = I study.

This is a compound sentence because it joins two simple sentences:

NOUN + **VERB** , **CONJUNCTION** + **NOUN** + **VERB** . = I study, and I learn.

BUILD IT: Short Compound Sentences

In the previous chapter, you learned that a **simple sentence** may have as few as two words: a subject (noun) and a verb. Here are two examples:

We walked. They drove.

In this chapter, you will learn how to write and recognize compound sentences. A **compound sentence** is two or more related simple sentences joined together. Often, these sentences are joined using **a comma and a conjunction**. Take a look:

SIMPLE SENTENCE 1   **SIMPLE SENTENCE 2**
We walked, and they drove.

COMMA AND CONJUNCTION

In the short compound sentence above, the coordinating conjunction *and* functions like glue to hold the two simple sentences together. In the English language, there are just seven coordinating conjunctions: *and, or, but, so, yet, nor,* and *for*. Each conjunction expresses a *different type of relationship* between two simple sentences. The most common are *and, but, so,* and *or*.

- Use **and** to <u>combine</u> two similar ideas:

    IDEA 1   **IDEA 2**
    Food nourishes, and exercise strengthens.

    These two ideas both express healthy influences on the body.

- Use **but** to <u>contrast</u> two different ideas:

    IDEA 1   **IDEA 2**
    Blanca forgot, but Edgar remembered.

    Each idea expresses a contrasting action.

- Use **so** to show <u>a result</u>:

IDEA 1   IDEA 2

The team won, so we celebrated.

Here, the second idea is a result of the first idea.

• Use **or** to show <u>alternatives</u>:

IDEA 1   IDEA 2

We can drive, or we can walk.

These two ideas express alternative options or possibilities.

Coordinating Conjunctions

and, but, or, so (for, nor, yet)

To sum up, the four types of relationships are **combination** (*and*), **contrast** (*but*), **result** (*so*), and **alternatives** (*or*). The following exercise will help you recognize the different relationships between two ideas in compound sentences.

📶 **ACTIVITY 1**
WARMUP

First, add a conjunction (**and**, **but**, **so**, or **or**) to complete each compound sentence. Then, circle which type of relationship the conjunction suggests between the two ideas.

EXAMPLE: You clean the bathroom, ___*and*___ I will clean the kitchen.   (⟨combination⟩, contrast, result, alternatives)

1. Jonah inherited money, _____ he bought a house.   (combination, contrast, result, alternatives)

2. Ida must stop gambling, _____ she will go broke.   (combination, contrast, result, alternatives)

3. Asad dislikes peas, _____ he refuses to eat them.   (combination, contrast, result, alternatives)

4. I will make a pie, _____ Dennis will bring cupcakes.   (combination, contrast, result, alternatives)

5. Joan called Eric three times, _____ he did not call back.   (combination, contrast, result, alternatives)

In a compound sentence, the conjunction that you use will determine the idea in the second sentence. For example:

COMBINATION	They painted their garage, and they re-roofed the house.
CONTRAST	They painted their garage, but they did not paint the house.
RESULT	They painted their garage, so the neighbors stopped complaining.

In each sentence, the first idea is the same. However, the second idea changes according to the conjunction used.

For more practice with compound sentences, go to **bedfordstmartins.com/steppingstones**.

KEY TO CHALLENGE METER

WARMUP	
EASY	
MODERATE	
ADVANCED	
MASTERY	

Identify the difficulty level of each activity using the key above.

Power Tip

In this chapter, we will discuss *and, or, but,* and *so.* The remaining conjunctions—*yet, for,* and *nor*—are used less frequently. If you would like to learn more about these three conjunctions, go to **bedfordstmartins.com/ steppingstones**.

ACTIVITY 2

First, add a conjunction (*and, but, so,* or *or*) that makes sense to complete each compound sentence. Do not use a conjunction more than once in a set. Then, circle which type of relationship the conjunction suggests between the two ideas.

EXAMPLE:

    a. Milo lost the race, ___*but*___ he won the championship. (combination, (contrast), result, alternatives)

    b. Milo lost the race, ___*so*___ he didn't receive a medal. (combination, contrast, (result), alternatives)

    c. Milo lost the race, ___*and*___ he wrecked his car. ((combination), contrast, result, alternatives)

1. a. Selena wrote a poem, _____ she was too shy to share it with others. (combination, contrast, result, alternatives)

    b. Selena wrote a poem, _____ she had it published in the college newspaper. (combination, contrast, result, alternatives)

    c. Selena wrote a poem, _____ she calls herself a poet now. (combination, contrast, result, alternatives)

2. a. Robert is a salesperson, _____ he loves his work. (combination, contrast, result, alternatives)

    b. Robert is a salesperson, _____ he doesn't make much money. (combination, contrast, result, alternatives)

    c. Robert is a salesperson, _____ he travels often. (combination, contrast, result, alternatives)

3. a. Carolyn may go on a trip to Europe, _____ she may travel to South America. (combination, contrast, result, alternatives)

    b. Carolyn may go on a trip to Europe, _____ first she has to save her money. (combination, contrast, result, alternatives)

    c. Carolyn may go on a trip to Europe, _____ she is shopping for new luggage. (combination, contrast, result, alternatives)

4. a. Arturo wants a bachelor's degree, _____ he enrolled in college. (combination, contrast, result, alternatives)

    b. Arturo wants a bachelor's degree, _____ he can't afford college. (combination, contrast, result, alternatives)

    c. Arturo wants a bachelor's degree, _____ he wants to teach school. (combination, contrast, result, alternatives)

5. a. Felicia is a single, working mother, _____ she has two children. (combination, contrast, result, alternatives)

    b. Felicia is a single, working mother, _____ she has to watch her budget carefully. (combination, contrast, result, alternatives)

    c. Felicia is a single, working mother, _____ she receives child support from her ex-husband. (combination, contrast, result, alternatives)

ACTIVITY 3: Teamwork

MODERATE

With classmates, discuss what type of idea is necessary to complete each compound sentence. Then, write a simple sentence in the space provided to complete each sentence.

EXAMPLE:

a. Leandra forgot Tim's birthday, so *she called him to apologize*.

b. Leandra forgot Tim's birthday, but *she always remembered his anniversary*.

c. Leandra forgot Tim's birthday, and *she missed his party*.

1. a. The dentist found cavities, and _____.

   b. The dentist found cavities, so _____.

   c. The dentist found cavities, but _____.

2. a. I found a new job, but _____.

   b. I found a new job, and _____.

   c. I found a new job, so _____.

3. a. Tamika likes the outdoors, so _____.

   b. Tamika likes the outdoors, but _____.

   c. Tamika likes the outdoors, and _____.

4. a. The team must score, or _____.

   b. The team must score, but _____.

   c. The team must score, and _____.

5. a. The professor was absent, so _____.

   b. The professor was absent, but _____.

   c. The professor was absent, and _____.

Sometimes, *and* and *but* can both make sense in a compound sentence:

> **Planes fly, and boats float.**
>
> **Planes fly, but boats float.**

The first sentence suggests that planes and boats are <u>similar</u> because they are both modes of transportation. However, the second sentence suggests that planes and boats are <u>different</u> in the particular ways they move.

Let's consider another example:

> **My husband votes Republican, and I vote Democrat.**
>
> **My husband votes Republican, but I vote Democrat.**

The first sentence suggests that the husband and wife are <u>similar</u> because they both vote for a political party. The second sentence suggests that the husband and wife are <u>different</u> in the party they vote for. The writer would have to decide whether to highlight the similarity or the difference between the husband and wife.

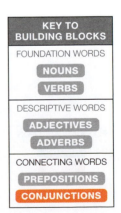

KEY TO
BUILDING BLOCKS

FOUNDATION WORDS

NOUNS

VERBS

DESCRIPTIVE WORDS

ADJECTIVES

ADVERBS

CONNECTING WORDS

PREPOSITIONS

CONJUNCTIONS

ACTIVITY 4: Teamwork

With classmates, discuss how the sentences with *and* express a similarity and how the sentences with *but* express a difference. Then, write a brief explanation in the space provided.

EXAMPLE:

a. The soccer team runs two miles, **and** the cross country team runs eight miles.
   Similarity: *Running is a part of both teams' training.*

b. The soccer team runs two miles, **but** the cross country team runs eight miles.
   Difference: *The cross country team runs six miles more than the soccer team.*

1. a. My sister jogs, **and** I run.
   Similarity: _____

   b. My sister jogs, **but** I run.
   Difference: _____

2. a. Blake drives a minivan, **and** Iris drives a pickup truck.
   Similarity: _____

   b. Blake drives a minivan, **but** Iris drives a pickup truck.
   Difference: _____

3. a. Duane dislikes spinach, **and** he hates liver.
   Similarity: _____

   b. Duane dislikes spinach, **but** he hates liver.
   Difference: _____

DISTINGUISHING COMPOUND SUBJECTS/VERBS AND COMPOUND SENTENCES

In Chapter 10, you learned about compound subjects and verbs. In this chapter, you are learning about compound sentences. It is very important that you do not confuse these two things. Compound <u>subjects and verbs</u> can appear in **one simple sentence**. On the other hand, compound <u>sentences</u> must contain **two or more simple sentences**.

First, let's review compound subjects and verbs found in **one simple sentence**.

FOUNDATION WORDS
NOUNS
VERBS
DESCRIPTIVE WORDS
ADJECTIVES
ADVERBS
CONNECTING WORDS
PREPOSITIONS
CONJUNCTIONS

- A compound <u>subject</u>:

   <u>Rhonda</u> and <u>Bill</u> danced.

Two subjects are performing the *same* action. Notice that when the conjunction (*and*) joins two simple subjects, **no comma is used**.

- A compound <u>verb</u>:

   Rhonda <u>danced</u> and <u>sang</u>.

One subject is performing *two* connected actions. Notice that when the conjunction (*and*) joins two simple verbs, **no comma is used**.

- A compound <u>subject</u> and a compound <u>verb</u>:

ONE COMPOUND SUBJECT	ONE COMPOUND VERB
Rhonda and Bill	danced and sang.

Here, *two* subjects are both performing *two* actions. Notice that when the conjunction (*and*) joins two simple <u>subjects</u> or two simple <u>verbs</u>, **no comma is used**.

Next, let's look at a **compound sentence**, which must contain two or more simple sentences.

SENTENCE 1		SENTENCE 2	
Rhonda	danced, and	Bill	sang.
1ST SUBJECT	1ST VERB	2ND SUBJECT	2ND VERB

In a compound sentence, there will always be at least <u>two separate</u> subjects involved in at least <u>two separate</u> actions. Notice that when a conjunction joins two simple <u>sentences</u>, **a comma is required**. Here's another example, with the conjunction *but*:

Kent smoked, but he quit.

Power Tip

Note that you can also create compound adjectives (***Beautiful and talented*** *Rhonda danced*), compound adverbs (*Rhonda danced **smoothly and gracefully***), and compound prepositional phrases (*Rhonda danced **at home and at the ballet studio***).

ACTIVITY 5
EASY

For each simple sentence below, do the following:

- Underline the subjects and circle the verbs.
- Rewrite the sentences, turning them into compound sentences by matching each subject to its own verb. Make sure to put a comma before the conjunction.

EXAMPLE:

Simple sentence: The <u>husband</u> and <u>wife</u> (cleaned) the house and (cooked) dinner.

Compound sentence: The husband cleaned the house, and the wife cooked dinner.

1. **Simple sentence:** Jennifer and Minh swam laps and played tennis.

   Compound sentence: _____

2. **Simple sentence:** The demonstrators and the police clashed and yelled.

   Compound sentence: _____

3. **Simple sentence:** Bekka and Thomas enjoyed the picnic but left early.

   Compound sentence: _____

CONTINUED >

4. **Simple sentence:** The children and the adults like roller coasters but get sick on them.

   Compound sentence: _____

   _____

ACTIVITY 6

MODERATE

Rewrite the following simple sentences, turning each of them into compound sentences. You will need to invent a second subject to complete the compound sentence. Remember to add a comma when you write the compound sentence.

EXAMPLE:

Simple sentence: The bartender spilled a drink and got soaked.

Compound sentence: _The bartender spilled a drink, and a customer_ _got soaked._

1. **Simple sentence:** My sister told a joke and laughed.

   Compound sentence: _____

2. **Simple sentence:** The tennis star missed the ball and became angry.

   Compound sentence: _____

   _____

3. **Simple sentence:** Marcus swerved off the road but did not crash.

   Compound sentence: _____

   _____

4. **Simple sentence:** Jorge dressed in a chicken costume and put on a cowboy hat.

   Compound sentence: _____

   _____

5. **Simple sentence:** Nina walked into the room and yelled, "Surprise!"

   Compound sentence: _____

   _____

ACTIVITY 7

MODERATE

Rewrite the following simple sentences, turning each of them into compound sentences. You will need to invent a second verb to complete the compound sentence. Remember to add a comma when you write the compound sentence.

EXAMPLE:

Simple sentence: The clown and his dog rode a bike.

Compound sentence: *The clown rode a bike, and his dog barked.*

1. **Simple sentence:** Kristoff and his wife danced.

   Compound sentence: _____

2. **Simple sentence:** The apartment building and the library burned down.

   Compound sentence: _____
   _____

3. **Simple sentence:** Clea and her husband told the truth.

   Compound sentence: _____

4. **Simple sentence:** The brownies and cookies were rich.

   Compound sentence: _____
   _____

5. **Simple sentence:** The president and vice president traveled.

   Compound sentence: _____
   _____

In some cases, you can express the same ideas as *either* a simple sentence *or* a compound sentence. For example:

- A simple sentence:

  ONE SUBJECT **ONE COMPOUND VERB**
  Andrea called but hung up.

This sentence has only <u>one</u> simple subject and <u>one</u> compound verb.

- A compound sentence:

This sentence has <u>two separate</u> subjects and <u>two separate</u> verbs. The pronoun *she* refers to *Andrea*, but it counts as a separate subject.

   If both of these sentences express the same ideas, and both of them are grammatically correct, which is the best choice? The simple sentence states matter-of-factly that Andrea called and hung up; perhaps she never really intended to talk to the person she was calling. In the compound sentence, special emphasis is given to the fact that Andrea hung up; the author may be suggesting that Andrea changed her mind after calling and decided to hang up.

Power Tip

Notice that the second part of the sentence uses the singular (one person) feminine pronoun *she* to refer to *Andrea*. Whenever you include a pronoun in the second part of a compound sentence, make sure that it matches the subject in the first part: feminine pronouns for singular feminine subjects, masculine pronouns for singular masculine subjects, and so on. (For more on pronouns, see Chapter 10, page 228, and Chapter 16.)

ıll **ACTIVITY 8**
MODERATE

From the two simple sentences provided, create (1) a simple sentence with a compound verb and (2) a compound sentence with a pronoun for the second subject. Make sure to include the required comma in the compound sentence.

EXAMPLE:

Simple sentences: Derek buys hats. Derek never wears them.

Simple sentence with compound verb: Derek buys hats but never wears them.

Compound sentence: Derek buys hats, but he never wears them.

1. **Simple sentence:** Victoria buys fabric. Victoria makes quilts.

    Simple sentence with compound verb: _____

    _____

    Compound sentence: _____

2. **Simple sentence:** Farad plays the guitar. Farad does not sing.

    Simple sentence with compound verb: _____

    _____

    Compound sentence: _____

3. **Simple sentence:** The Jacobsons volunteer. The Jacobsons donate money.

    Simple sentence with compound verb: _____

    _____

    Compound sentence: _____

4. **Simple sentence:** The waiter dropped the tray. The waiter got fired.

    Simple sentence with compound verb: _____

    _____

    Compound sentence: _____

5. **Simple sentence:** The skier fell. The skier did not break her leg.

    Simple sentence with compound verb: _____

    _____

    Compound sentence: _____

ıll **ACTIVITY 9: Teamwork**
ADVANCED

Rewrite each of the following simple sentences as a compound sentence expressing the same idea. You will need to do the following:

- Add a pronoun as the second subject.
- Add a second verb, and make sure that this verb is complete.
- Add the required comma to the compound sentence.

EXAMPLE:

Simple sentence: You must floss your teeth or face health consequences.

Compound sentence: You must floss your teeth, or you may face health consequences.

1. **Simple sentence:** Many people floss their teeth but do not realize that flossing might help prevent heart disease.

   Compound sentence: _____

   _____

2. **Simple sentence:** Researchers suspected a connection between gum disease and heart disease and eventually found a link.

   Compound sentence: _____

   _____

3. **Simple sentence:** Mouth bacteria can build up and travel to the heart.

   Compound sentence: _____

   _____

4. **Simple sentence:** Pregnant women can be affected and deliver premature babies.

   Compound sentence: _____

   _____

5. **Simple sentence:** Flossing can prevent tooth and gum disease and improve one's overall health.

   Compound sentence: _____

   _____

USING A SEMICOLON IN PLACE OF A CONJUNCTION

Conjunctions are the most common type of "glue" used to form compound sentences. However, there is one other type of glue to form compound sentences: the **semicolon** (;).

Consider the following pair of ideas:

SENTENCE 1   SENTENCE 2

Watching basketball is fun. Playing it is better.

The period between the sentences above creates a full stop, suggesting that the two ideas are not closely related. However, since we know that the ideas *are* closely related, we can join them to make a compound sentence. There are just two ways to do this:

1. With a related idea (preceded by a comma):

   SENTENCE 1   SENTENCE 2

   Watching basketball is fun, but playing it is better.

2. With a semicolon:

| SENTENCE 1 | SENTENCE 2 |

Watching basketball is fun; playing it is better.

The semicolon <u>joins</u> the two ideas, suggesting that there is a special relationship between them. This relationship is reinforced by the lack of capitalization of the first word in the second sentence.

The most important rule to remember as you start to use the semicolon is this: It must always *follow* a complete sentence. Semicolons (and often periods) must also *be followed* by another complete sentence.

| SENTENCE 1 | SENTENCE 2 |

The music started. The dancers appeared.

| SENTENCE 1 | SENTENCE 2 |

The music started; the dancers appeared.

Power Tip
Although the semicolon has other uses as described in Appendix A, its main use is to connect two sentences. We recommend that you master this use of the semicolon before attempting others.

Many students try to use the semicolon to replace commas. **Avoid this mistake!** As a "soft" period, the semicolon is nearly as powerful as a "hard" period (a full stop), and you must respect its authority.

ACTIVITY 10

MODERATE

Form compound sentences from each pair of simple sentences by (1) using a comma and a conjunction and (2) using a semicolon.

EXAMPLE:

Simple sentences: Thunderstorms are frightening. Hurricanes are terrifying.

Compound sentence with a conjunction: Thunderstorms are frightening, but hurricanes are terrifying.

Compound sentence with a semicolon: Thunderstorms are frightening; hurricanes are terrifying.

1. **Simple sentences:** Some people will do anything to win. They may cheat.

   Compound sentence with a conjunction: _____

   _____

   Compound sentence with a semicolon: _____

   _____

2. **Simple sentences:** Cheating is dishonest. Covering it up is worse.

   Compound sentence with a conjunction: _____

   _____

Compound sentence with a semicolon: _____

_____

3. **Simple sentences:** I cheated at cards. I regret it.

Compound sentence with a conjunction: _____

_____

Compound sentence with a semicolon: _____

_____

4. **Simple sentences:** Cheating seems easy. Dishonesty hurts the cheater.

Compound sentence with a conjunction: _____

_____

Compound sentence with a semicolon: _____

_____

5. **Simple sentences:** Poker players may stack the deck. They may use marked cards.

Compound sentence with a conjunction: _____

_____

Compound sentence with a semicolon: _____

_____

Power Tip

When joining two simple sentences, use a semicolon _only if_ the relationship between the two sentences is absolutely clear. If it's not, use a comma and a joining word to clarify the relationship.

Many students have difficulty deciding when a semicolon is a better choice than a conjunction. Take a look at these two sentences:

Slot machines require luck, **but** poker requires skill.

Slot machines require luck; poker requires skill.

Some writers would say that the contrast between slot machines and poker is absolutely clear, so the conjunction _but_ is not necessary. Other writers would say that the conjunction emphasizes the contrast. Both versions are appropriate. If you were faced with this choice, you would have to decide which version you like best.

Power Tip

Avoid using a semicolon to replace _so_ (a result), _or_ (alternatives), and _but_ (when it expresses a strong contrast). In general, you will not use semicolons very often. In fact, most writers use many more conjunctions than semicolons.

ACTIVITY 11: Teamwork

ADVANCED

For each item below, do the following:

- Work individually to form two compound sentences from each pair of simple sentences. Do this in two ways: (1) with a conjunction, and (2) with a semicolon. Make sure the conjunction is preceded by a comma.
- Working with classmates, decide which compound sentence is more effective.

CONTINUED >

For more practice with conjunctions and semicolons, go to **bedfordstmartins.com/ steppingstones**.

EXAMPLE:

Simple sentences: Jamie loves baseball. His parents take him to many games.

Compound sentence with a conjunction: Jamie loves baseball, so his parents take him to many games.

Compound sentence with a semicolon: Jamie loves baseball; his parents take him to many games.

1. **Simple sentences:** Jamie likes a lot of teams. The Orioles are his favorite.

   Compound sentence with a conjunction: _____

   _____

   Compound sentence with a semicolon: _____

   _____

2. **Simple sentences:** Jamie wanted a birthday surprise. His parents threw him a "baseball" party.

   Compound sentence with a conjunction: _____

   _____

   Compound sentence with a semicolon: _____

   _____

3. **Simple sentences:** Jamie's mother baked a baseball-shaped cake. Jamie loved it.

   Compound sentence with a conjunction: _____

   _____

   Compound sentence with a semicolon: _____

   _____

4. **Simple sentences:** It rained. The party guests played baseball.

   Compound sentence with a conjunction: _____

   _____

   Compound sentence with a semicolon: _____

   _____

5. **Simple sentences:** Jamie wanted an autographed baseball. His parents got one from his favorite player.

   Compound sentence with a conjunction: _____

   _____

   Compound sentence with a semicolon: _____

   _____

BUILD IT: Longer Compound Sentences

So far, the sentences that you've written in this chapter have been rather short. In your academic writing, the compound sentences will sometimes be much longer. As with shorter sentences, it is important that you select the appropriate conjunction and use correct punctuation when writing longer compound sentences.

A compound sentence can become longer for three reasons:

1. The two simple sentences in it include descriptive words and prepositional phrases.
2. The two simple sentences contain a compound subject and/or a compound verb.
3. Three simple sentences are connected instead of two.

ADDING DESCRIPTIVE WORDS AND PREPOSITIONAL PHRASES

First, let's review how simple sentences become longer. In Chapter 10, you learned that a simple sentence can have as few as two words (a subject and a verb). When a writer adds descriptive words (adjectives and adverbs) and prepositional phrases, the simple sentence becomes longer. (As a reminder, a prepositional phrase begins with a preposition and typically ends with a noun. For more information, see Chapter 10, page 240.)

The longest simple sentences can have three or more prepositional phrases. Look at the following example:

SUBJECT AND A VERB INCLUDED	The bell rings.
DESCRIPTIVE WORDS ADDED	The tardy bell rings promptly.
PREPOSITIONAL PHRASES ADDED	The tardy bell rings promptly at eight o'clock in the morning.
ANOTHER PREPOSITIONAL PHRASE ADDED	At my high school, the tardy bell rings promptly at eight o'clock in the morning.

Similarly, compound sentences can contain descriptive words and prepositional phrases. Take a look:

> SENTENCE 1
>
> At my high school, the tardy bell rings promptly at eight o'clock in the morning, and late students complain loudly to each other.
> SENTENCE 2

FOUNDATION WORDS

NOUNS

VERBS

DESCRIPTIVE WORDS

ADJECTIVES

ADVERBS

CONNECTING WORDS

PREPOSITIONS

CONJUNCTIONS

Power Tip

For a list of common prepositions, see Chapter 10, page 240.

ACTIVITY 12

MODERATE

For each pair of simple sentences below, do the following:

- Add a prepositional phrase to the end of each simple sentence.
- Use a conjunction to join the two sentences that you have created, making sure to precede it with a comma.

Even though the compound sentence will be longer, you will have only one comma, and it will be before the conjunction.

EXAMPLE:

Simple sentences: The truck broke down. The driver called.

Add a prepositional phrase to sentence 1: *The truck broke down on the highway.*

Add a prepositional phrase to sentence 2: *The driver called for help.*

Combine the two previous sentences to make a compound sentence:
The truck broke down on the highway, so the driver called for help.

1. **Simple sentences:** Randall lost his cell phone. He found it.

   Add a prepositional phrase to sentence 1: _____

   _____

   Add a prepositional phrase to sentence 2: _____

   _____

   Combine the two previous sentences to make a compound sentence:

   _____

   _____

2. **Simple sentences:** Anna had a minor car accident. She missed her flight.

   Add a prepositional phrase to sentence 1: _____

   _____

   Add a prepositional phrase to sentence 2: _____

   _____

   Combine the two previous sentences to make a compound sentence:

   _____

   _____

3. **Simple sentences:** The pitcher threw the baseball. The batter hit the ball.

   Add a prepositional phrase to sentence 1: _____

   _____

   Add a prepositional phrase to sentence 2: _____

   _____

For more practice with compound sentences, go to **bedfordstmartins .com/steppingstones.**

Combine the two previous sentences to make a compound sentence:

_____

_____

ACTIVITY 13: Teamwork

ADVANCED

First, write down each compound sentence from the previous exercise in the space provided. Then, make the sentence longer by

- adding another prepositional phrase to the beginning of the sentence, and
- adding another prepositional phrase to the end of the sentence.

NOTE: When a prepositional phrase starts a sentence, you usually put a comma after it. Therefore, each compound sentence will have two commas: one after the first prepositional phrase and one before the conjunction. Be sure to place your commas in the correct position.

EXAMPLE:

Compound sentence: The truck broke down on the highway, so the driver called for help.

Add a prepositional phrase to the beginning and to the end: During rush hour, the truck broke down on the highway, so the driver called for help on his phone.

1. **Compound sentence:** _____

   _____

   Add a prepositional phrase to the beginning and to the end: _____

   _____

   _____

2. **Compound sentence:** _____

   _____

   Add a prepositional phrase to the beginning and to the end: _____

   _____

   _____

3. **Compound sentence:** _____

   _____

   Add a prepositional phrase to the beginning and to the end: _____

INCLUDING COMPOUND SUBJECTS AND VERBS

Earlier in this chapter, you studied the difference between two sentence types:

1. a simple sentence that contains a **compound subject** and/or a **compound verb**

2. a **compound sentence** that contains two simple sentences

Now, if we put these two types together, we get a third possibility:

3. a compound sentence made up of two simple sentences, each of which contains a compound subject and/or a compound verb

Let's take a closer look.

Here is a simple sentence with a compound subject and a compound verb:

> **A COMPOUND SUBJECT**   **A COMPOUND VERB**
>
> The players and the fans rushed to the field and embraced.

<u>Both</u> subjects are involved in <u>two</u> connected actions. Notice that <u>no comma</u> is used to join a compound subject or a compound verb.

Here is a compound sentence:

> **SENTENCE 1**   **SENTENCE 2**
>
> The fans rushed to the field, and the players embraced.
>
> **1ST SUBJECT** **1ST VERB** **CONJUNCTION** **2ND SUBJECT** **2ND VERB**

These are <u>two separate</u> subjects involved in <u>two separate</u> actions. As you know, a comma is required when joining two simple sentences with a conjunction.

Here is a compound sentence in which each simple sentence has a compound subject and a compound verb:

> **1ST COMPOUND SUBJECT**   **1ST COMPOUND VERB**
>
> The winning players and their fans rushed to the field and embraced,
> but the losing team and its coaches sat in silence and watched them.
>
> **CONJUNCTION** **2ND COMPOUND SUBJECT** **2ND COMPOUND VERB**

When we join simple sentences that have compound subjects and compound verbs, the resulting compound sentence can be quite long. Notice, however, that there is still only <u>one</u> comma in the previous sentence; we do not need a comma to join a compound subject or a compound verb.

ACTIVITY 14

MODERATE

Form a compound sentence from each pair of simple sentences, using an appropriate conjunction or a semicolon. (If you use a conjunction, remember to put a comma before it.) Write the compound sentence in the space provided.

EXAMPLE:

Simple sentences: Katie and Jessica go to the same school and spend a lot of time together. They have poor judgment and sometimes get into trouble.

Compound sentence: *Katie and Jessica go to the same school and spend a lot of time together, but they have poor judgment and sometimes get into trouble.*

1. **Simple sentences:** Katie and Jessica skipped class on Thursday and claimed that they had the flu. Mrs. Fiskall listened to their excuse but didn't believe them.

   Compound sentence: _____

   _____

   _____

2. **Simple sentences:** The Rag Dolls were in Denver and played only one concert Thursday night. Katie and Jessica had to see their favorite band.

   Compound sentence: _____

   _____

   _____

3. **Simple sentences:** Katie and Jessica cut class and drove to Denver. They arrived late and had terrible seats in the back.

   Compound sentence: _____

   _____

   _____

4. **Simple sentences:** They left the concert at midnight and made up the flu story for the next day. They forgot one small detail and didn't realize it.

   Compound sentence: _____

   _____

   _____

5. **Simple sentences:** Mrs. Fiskall and the other students noticed and were surprised by the "Rag Dolls" stamps on Katie's and Jessica's hands. Mrs. Fiskall smirked and asked the girls if they enjoyed the concert.

   Compound sentence: _____

   _____

   _____

ACTIVITY 15: Teamwork

ADVANCED

With classmates, do the following for each set of simple sentences:

- Discuss how to combine each pair of simple sentences to make one simple sentence with a compound subject and/or a compound verb. Write the simple sentences in the spaces provided.

- Select a conjunction (or use a semicolon) to form a compound sentence from the simple sentences. Write the compound sentence in the space provided, making sure to place the comma correctly.

EXAMPLE:

Simple sentences:

a. Snorkeling is a lot of fun. Scuba diving is a lot of fun.

b. Both activities can be dangerous. Both activities require special training.

Combined to form compound subjects/verbs:

a. Snorkeling and scuba diving are a lot of fun.

b. Both activities can be dangerous and require special training.

Compound sentence: Snorkeling and scuba diving are a lot of fun, but both activities can be dangerous and require special training.

1. **Simple sentences:**

   a. Snowboarding is great exercise. Skiing is great exercise.

   b. These sports can be expensive. These sports often require travel.

   Combined to form compound subjects/verbs:

   a. _____

   b. _____

   Compound sentence: _____

   _____

2. **Simple sentences:**

   a. Shawn's truck was old. Shawn's truck needed a new engine.

   b. Shawn worked double shifts. Shawn bought a new truck.

   Combined to form compound subjects/verbs:

   a. _____

   b. _____

   Compound sentence: _____

   _____

3. **Simple sentences:**

   a. The murder suspect struggled on the grass. The police officer struggled on the grass.

   b. The suspect broke free. The suspect escaped in a getaway car.

For more practice with compound sentences, go to **bedfordstmartins.com/ steppingstones**.

Combined to form compound subjects/verbs:

a. _____

b. _____

Compound sentence: _____

_____

_____

4. **Simple sentences:**

   a. The bride exited the church and waved to the guests. The groom exited the church and waved to the guests.

   b. The bridesmaids threw rice and cheered. The ushers threw rice and cheered.

Combined to form compound subjects/verbs:

a. _____

b. _____

Compound sentence: _____

_____

_____

5. **Simple sentences:**

   a. Two gorillas escaped from the zoo and fled to a suburban neighborhood. One baboon escaped from the zoo and fled to a suburban neighborhood.

   b. Zoo officers sped to the scene and captured the animals. Police sped to the scene and captured the animals.

Combined to form compound subjects/verbs:

a. _____

_____

b. _____

Compound sentence: _____

_____

_____

JOINING THREE SIMPLE SENTENCES INSTEAD OF TWO

Most compound sentences join two simple sentences. Sometimes, however, a compound sentence will join three simple sentences. In this case, the sentence will have three separate subjects and three separate verbs. Also, two conjunctions will be needed to join the three sentences. In some instances, you may use a semicolon to replace one of the conjunctions.

FOUNDATION WORDS
NOUNS
VERBS
DESCRIPTIVE WORDS
ADJECTIVES
ADVERBS
CONNECTING WORDS
PREPOSITIONS
CONJUNCTIONS

Consider this example:

SIMPLE SENTENCE 1	Beth left early for the airport on Friday morning.
SIMPLE SENTENCE 2	The traffic was heavier than usual.
SIMPLE SENTENCE 3	She missed her flight and had to reschedule for the following day.
COMPOUND SENTENCE	Beth left early for the airport on Friday morning, but the traffic was heavier than usual, so she missed her flight and had to reschedule for the following day.
WITH SEMICOLON	Beth left early for the airport on Friday morning, but the traffic was heavier than usual; she missed her flight and had to reschedule for the following day.

📶 **ACTIVITY 16**
ADVANCED

Select appropriate conjunctions (or use a semicolon) to connect the following simple sentences. Start by joining the first two sentences, and then the third sentence should be easier to add. Write the complete compound sentence in the space provided.

NOTE: Each compound sentence will have at least two commas, unless you want to use a semicolon in place of one of the conjunctions. If the compound sentence begins with a prepositional phrase, the sentence will have an additional comma. Be sure that your commas are in the correct places.

EXAMPLE: Lakwon is a talented singer. His friend Brandon is an experienced guitar player. They formed a band.

Compound sentence: <u>Lakwon is a talented singer, and his friend</u>
<u>Brandon is an experienced guitar player, so they formed a band.</u>

1. Joan is a professional dancer. Her boyfriend is clumsy. They never go dancing together.

   Compound sentence: _____

   _____

2. We have to water the yard. The grass and the plants will die. Our house will be the disgrace of the neighborhood.

   Compound sentence: _____

   _____

   _____

3. Joseph's new college will not allow him to work during the semester. He can apply for a government loan. He can ask his family for tuition aid.

   Compound sentence: _____

   _____

   _____

4. Some people like to rest and relax on their vacation. Other people want to climb mountains or scuba dive. Still other people prefer sight-seeing and cultural activities.

   Compound sentence: _____

   _____

   _____

5. During the long drought, the mayor and city officials were concerned about the water supply. They restricted the city's water use and banned citizens from watering their lawns. They threatened fines against violators.

   Compound sentence: _____

   _____

   _____

   _____

ACTIVITY 17

ADVANCED

Complete each of the following compound sentences by adding another conjunction (if needed) and a third simple sentence.

EXAMPLE: Jocelyn has an SUV, and she must drive 50 miles a day to and from her office, *so she decided to start a carpool with co-workers.*

1. Erika needed a gift for her boyfriend's birthday, and she had only one hour to shop, _____

2. Jon and Lori needed a new front porch and wanted a new car, but they couldn't afford both, _____

3. Randall's term paper was due on Monday, but his computer and printer were broken, _____

4. After their company's expansion, Denise and Jacqueline might be promoted, or they might get higher-paying positions in the company's new offices; _____

5. During the blaze at the electronics factory, firefighters brought all the workers to safety and delivered first aid to the injured, so no one perished, _____

ACTIVITY 18: Mastery Test or Teamwork

With classmates, unscramble each set of three simple sentences, following these steps:

- Discuss the sentences and put them in the correct order.
- Decide which conjunctions will join the sentences smoothly. You might use a semicolon in place of a conjunction.
- Working individually, write the compound sentence in the space provided. Make sure your commas are correctly placed.

EXAMPLE: We put our camping gear in the car and drove there. The tickets were too expensive. We waited until the last minute to look online for a flight to Alaska.

Compound sentence: We waited until the last minute to look online for a flight to Alaska, and the tickets were too expensive, so we put our camping gear in the car and drove there.

1. Yvonne felt more at ease. Yvonne was nervous about her job interview. The interviewer was friendly and kind.

   Compound sentence: _____

   _____

2. It will be towed. You can park in the garage next to the bank. You can't leave your car on the street.

   Compound sentence: _____

   _____

3. Pamela's doctor advised her to become more active. She also signed up for a yoga class. She began walking two miles every morning.

   Compound sentence: _____

   _____

   _____

4. He replaced their meals and gave them a complimentary dessert. William and Christine ordered steak. The waiter served them chicken by mistake.

   Compound sentence: _____

   _____

   _____

5. Sleeping restfully is difficult. Mr. Cobb and Mrs. Brien argue loudly on the street every Saturday morning. Sleeping late is impossible.

   Compound sentence: _____

   _____

   _____

RECOGNIZING CORRECT PUNCTUATION IN SIMPLE AND COMPOUND SENTENCES

So far, you have learned four rules for punctuating simple and compound sentences. The following is a review, with examples.

- If a sentence begins with a prepositional phrase, a comma usually follows this phrase:

  PREPOSITIONAL PHRASE

  At three in the morning, the telephone started ringing.

  ↑ **COMMA**

- No comma is used when forming a compound subject or a compound verb:

  COMPOUND SUBJECT, NO COMMA **COMPOUND VERB, NO COMMA**

  Liz and Ryan collect antiques and restore furniture.

- When a conjunction is used to join two simple sentences, a comma should precede the conjunction:

  SENTENCE 1   **SENTENCE 2**

  My brother can have my old car, or he can buy a new one.

  ↑ ↑ **COMMA & CONJUNCTION**

- The semicolon follows a complete sentence, so it should not be used to replace a comma:

  INCORRECT   I returned to college; and my grades improved.

  CORRECT   I returned to college, and my grades improved.

  I returned to college. My grades improved.

  I returned to college; my grades improved.

  ↑ **SEMICOLON REPLACES A PERIOD**

ACTIVITY 19

ADVANCED

In this activity, you will need to add missing commas to compound sentences. For each sentence, do the following:

- Underline the subjects and circle the verbs. There will be some compound subjects and compound verbs.
- Decide whether the sentence is simple or compound. If the sentence is compound, write **C** next to it and add the missing comma to the sentence.

CONTINUED >

EXAMPLE: Dietary <u>changes</u> (can be) difficult, but <u>they</u> (are) possible. C

1. For years, Marcus and his friends ate a lot of meat and liked it.

2. Negative news reports about meat-heavy diets changed Marcus's views and he became a vegetarian last spring.

3. He has lost ten pounds since then so he is pleased about making the change.

4. At first, Marcus's parents and sister were puzzled by his vegetarianism and they teased him.

5. After a month or so, Marcus's mother searched the Internet and found some information on the health benefits of vegetarian diets.

6. She found and read an interesting article about the pros and cons of different diets and it linked plant-based diets to reduced risks of heart disease and cancer.

7. After reading the article, Marcus's mother grew concerned about her family's meat-rich diet so she and her husband decided to make a change.

8. For each meal, Marcus's mother and father now prepare and serve more vegetables and whole grains but minimize portions of meat.

9. Marcus's parents and sister feel better so they are grateful to Marcus for helping them to change their lifestyle and he is happy too.

10. Now, Marcus has begun an exercise program so he might start another trend in his family.

ACTIVITY 20: Teamwork

ADVANCED

Carefully examine and discuss each of the following groups of sentences. Only one sentence has the correct punctuation. Put a check mark beside it.

EXAMPLE:

a. Modern life is demanding; and many people seek relief from stress.

b. Modern life is demanding, and many people seek relief from stress. ✓

c. Modern life is demanding and many people seek relief from stress.

1. a. In today's busy world many people fill their lives with too many activities.

   b. In today's busy world, many people fill their lives with too many activities.

   c. In today's busy world; many people fill their lives with too many activities.

2. a. At home and at work; people struggle to find happiness.

   b. At home and at work people struggle to find happiness.

   c. At home and at work, people struggle to find happiness.

For more practice with punctuation in compound sentences, go to **bedfordstmartins.com/ steppingstones**.

3. a. They bring work home and they have little energy left for family and hobbies.

    b. They bring work home; and they have little energy left for family and hobbies.

    c. They bring work home, and they have little energy left for family and hobbies.

4. a. Good time-managers say "no" to extra commitments, they are not ashamed of this response.

    b. Good time-managers say "no" to extra commitments; they are not ashamed of this response.

    c. Good time-managers say "no" to extra commitments they are not ashamed of this response.

5. a. Employees should leave work at closing time everyone needs relaxation time.

    b. Employees should leave work at closing time, everyone needs relaxation time.

    c. Employees should leave work at closing time; everyone needs relaxation time.

6. a. Employees can spend less time at work; but that time can be more productive.

    b. Employees can spend less time at work, but that time can be more productive.

    c. Employees can spend less time at work but that time can be more productive.

ACTIVITY 21: Mastery Test or Teamwork

In the following paragraph, form seven compound sentences, using **and**, **or**, **but**, or **so**. First, identify each pair of sentences that can be joined, and then decide which conjunction will join the sentences most effectively. The first one has been done for you.

Why is it important for children to play outside? Years ago,
children played outdoors all the time. ~~Now~~ , but now many children spend
much less time in nature. There are many reasons for this. Some
parents fear for their children's safety. Others fear lawsuits over
other children's injuries on their land. Also, there is little outdoor area
left for play due to urban development. However, being outdoors
provides many opportunities for children. They can burn off energy
and engage their imaginations. Staying indoors keeps children

CONTINUED >

inactive. Their energy has no outlet. Inactivity can lead to depression

and anxiety disorders. It can also lead to childhood obesity. Backyards

and fenced-in parks are a poor substitute for open meadows

and wild woods. Many studies now reveal the importance of

unstructured play for children. One author, Richard Louv, wrote a book

called *Last Child in the Woods*. He recommends more time in nature

for children. Parents should take their children for hikes, fishing

trips, and long walks in the woods. Louv's book may encourage more

outdoor activity. Parents may also come to this conclusion by

themselves. The reunion with nature could decrease emotional

problems in children. It could lead to healthier children.

ACTIVITY 22: Mastery Test

In the following paragraph, form seven compound sentences, using **and**, **or**, **but**, or **so**. First, identify each pair of sentences that can be joined, and then decide which conjunction will join the sentences most effectively. The first one has been done for you.

, and it

Yosemite National Park is located in east central California. It

stretches between the western slopes of the Sierra Nevada

Mountains. This national park offers so much. Close to four million

people a year visit the park. Most of them stay in less than one percent of

the park's massive acreage. People from around the world come

to see its waterfalls, rock cliffs, crystal-clear streams, and giant

sequoia trees. They also marvel at the diversity of wildlife that includes

mountain lions, wolves, coyotes, and black bears. California

has around seven thousand plant species. More than 20 percent of those

can be found in the park. In addition, Yosemite offers a wealth

of recreational opportunities. Visitors may go backpacking and camping. More adventurous types may want to try rock climbing.

In the summer, it's fun to picnic and ride horses, Winter offers many

options as well, including skiing, snowboarding, and ice skating. Yosemite

has a Mediterranean climate. The winter is mild. The other seasons

are relatively dry. This means that people can visit this beautiful

park year-round. Visiting Yosemite also helps people to slow

down and appreciate life.

FIX IT: Solving Problems in Compound Sentences

So far in this chapter, you have learned that there are just two types of "glue" to form compound sentences: a **conjunction** (preceded by a comma) and a **semicolon**. Remember that there are only seven coordinating conjunctions (*and, or, but, so, yet, nor, for*), and that <u>no other words can be glue</u>. Let's review:

and
or
but
so
▪
,

A conjunction with a comma as glue:

SENTENCE 1   SENTENCE 2

Class ended, so we left.

A semicolon as glue:

Class ended; we left.

UNDERSTANDING HOW RUN-ONS AND COMMA SPLICES OCCUR

If you forget to use glue when joining two simple sentences—or, if you try to use other words or punctuation as glue—you will create a **run-on** or a **comma splice**. Take a look:

1. Trying to join two sentences with no glue:

   Class ended we left.
         ↑

Although these sentences are very short, they are two separate sentences with two separate subjects and two separate verbs. If we <u>run them together</u> without glue, we have a **run-on**.

2. Trying to use a comma as glue:

Class ended, we left.

Because these sentences are so short, some writers believe that they can be joined with a comma. However, remember that a comma by itself is never glue. If we "splice" (join) these two sentences with a comma only, we have a **comma splice**.

Power Tip

A run-on and a comma splice are really the same grammatical error. In both cases, two separate sentences are joined without glue. In the case of a comma splice, the writer has added a comma as glue, but you now know that a comma by itself is never glue.

3. Trying to use other words as glue:

Class ended **then** we left.

Class ended, **then** we left.

In English, there are many words that seem like glue but are not. In this example, *then* has been used in place of a conjunction, but it is not glue. As a result, the first example is a **run-on**. The second example is a **comma splice**. In both cases, the sentences do not have the glue they need to be joined correctly.

ACTIVITY 23
MODERATE

Carefully examine each of the following items. Then, decide whether each is

- a correct compound sentence,
- a run-on, or
- a comma splice.

Write the appropriate label in the space provided. Then, fix incorrect sentences by adding glue (a comma and conjunction or a semicolon) or by forming two separate sentences.

EXAMPLE:

Staying focused on some tasks is not easy, it is especially hard for
                                               ;
unpleasant chores. <u>comma splice</u>
                              ^

1. Most people resist unpleasant chores, distractions can occur more

   easily. _____

2. Let's take the chore of laundry it seems simple enough. _____

3. You separate the clothes into piles, and you put one load into the

   washing machine. _____

4. You see a stain on your red shirt you need a stain remover. _____

5. On the top shelf of the laundry room closet, you find the stain remover,

   but the bottle is empty. _____

For more practice with fixing run-ons and comma splices, go to **bedfordstmartins.com/ steppingstones**.

6. The store is nearby, you get in your car and drive toward town.

   _____

7. At the store, you find great bargains, so you fill your shopping cart

   with everything from lip balm to sandals. _____

8. Electric ice-cream makers are on sale, you buy one and all the ingredi-

   ents for vanilla and mocha-almond ice cream. _____

9. You drive home with a smile on your face and with plans for ice cream

   parties with your friends life is good, very good. _____

10. You walk in the door and see the washing machine you have forgotten

   the bottle of stain remover. _____

UNDERSTANDING WORDS THAT CAN CAUSE RUN-ONS AND COMMA SPLICES

Many run-ons and comma splices are caused when we try to use <u>words that are not conjunctions</u> as glue. As you already know, there are only seven words that can truly be used as glue: *and, but, or, so, for, nor,* and *yet.* However, what often confuses students is that there are lots of other words that *seem* like glue.

Below are some words that are commonly *misused* as glue. They are divided into four groups to help you remember them.

PERSONAL PRONOUNS	DEMONSTRATIVE PRONOUNS	ADDITIVE EXPRESSIONS	TRANSITIONAL EXPRESSIONS
I	this	also	as a result
you	that	for example	consequently
he	these	for instance	furthermore
she	those	next	however
it		plus	in addition
we		then	instead
they			moreover
			nevertheless
			otherwise
			therefore

Power Tip
The additive expressions listed here can also be used as transitional expressions. However, we distinguish them here because they cause run-ons and comma splices in a particular way.

Let's look at each of these groups individually to understand why the words often *seem like* glue.

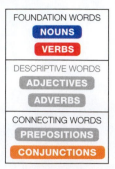

FOUNDATION WORDS
NOUNS
VERBS

DESCRIPTIVE WORDS
ADJECTIVES
ADVERBS

CONNECTING WORDS
PREPOSITIONS
CONJUNCTIONS

Personal Pronouns

The personal pronouns in the previous list cause more run-ons and comma splices than any other group of words. Therefore, it is very important that you understand why. Take a look at the following run-on:

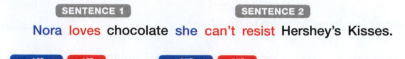

| SENTENCE 1 | SENTENCE 2 |

Nora loves chocolate she can't resist Hershey's Kisses.

| 1ST SUBJECT | 1ST VERB | 2ND SUBJECT | 2ND VERB |

Notice that there are two separate sentences here with two separate subjects and two separate verbs. Therefore, we need some glue to join them.

Many of the sentences we write are about people. If the sentence is compound, the first subject will often name a person or persons. Then, the second subject will often be a <u>personal pronoun</u> that <u>refers back</u> to the first subject. Take a look:

Nora loves chocolate she can't resist Hershey's Kisses.

Because *she* refers to *Nora*, many writers believe that it is glue that can join the two simple sentences. However, *she* is the subject of the second simple sentence, even though it refers back to Nora. Therefore, we still need some glue to join these two sentences, or we need to break them into separate sentences:

COMMA AND COORDINATING CONJUNCTION ADDED	Nora loves chocolate, so she can't resist Hershey's Kisses.

or

SEMICOLON ADDED	Nora loves chocolate; she can't resist Hershey's Kisses.

or

PERIOD ADDED	Nora loves chocolate. She can't resist Hershey's Kisses.

The last option (using a period) does correct the run-on; however, it does not <u>join</u> the two simple sentences to form a compound sentence.

Remember: When you write a compound sentence with a <u>personal pronoun</u> as one of the subjects, <u>the pronoun is not glue</u>; you still need a conjunction or a semicolon to join the sentences.

![Activity 24 bar chart icon] **ACTIVITY 24**

MODERATE

For each of the run-ons or comma splices below, do the following:

- Circle the personal pronoun.
- Draw an arrow connecting the pronoun to the subject to which it refers.
- Rewrite the run-on or comma splice in the space provided, adding a conjunction or a semicolon to make it a correct compound sentence. If you use a conjunction, don't forget to add the required comma.

EXAMPLE:

Dining out should be enjoyable (it) can be unpleasant.

Dining out should be enjoyable, but it can be unpleasant.

1. Ted and Louisa were celebrating their tenth anniversary, they chose a special restaurant.

_____

_____

2. The Blue Sail served elegant dinners it was located close to the ocean.

_____

_____

3. Ted and Louisa enjoyed the food, they will never go to the Blue Sail again.

_____

_____

4. The reason was not the food or service it was the other patrons.

_____

5. Three small children were seated with their family nearby, they were noisy throughout the evening.

_____

_____

6. The father ignored the children's behavior he was more interested in the messages on his cell phone.

_____

_____

CONTINUED >

7. From time to time, the mother snapped at the children she annoyed Ted and Louisa with her sharp voice.

_____

_____

8. The children ignored their mother, they ran around the restaurant and bumped into other tables and diners.

_____

_____

9. At another nearby table, a woman held her cell phone to her ear and laughed repeatedly and loudly she did not see the cold stares from the serving staff and from other patrons in the restaurant.

_____

_____

_____

10. For their next anniversary, Ted will make a fancy meal for two, he and Louisa will dine alone in the peacefulness of their backyard.

_____

_____

FOUNDATION WORDS

NOUNS
VERBS

DESCRIPTIVE WORDS

ADJECTIVES
ADVERBS

CONNECTING WORDS

PREPOSITIONS
CONJUNCTIONS

Demonstrative Pronouns

Demonstrative pronouns (_this, that, these, those_) work in a similar way as personal pronouns except that they refer to <u>things, places, or ideas</u> instead of people. Demonstrative pronouns do not cause as many run-ons and comma splices as personal pronouns do, but they are often more difficult to spot. Take a look at the following comma splice:

SENTENCE 1	SENTENCE 2

My teacher didn't read my essay, that upset me.

1ST SUBJECT **1ST VERB**   **2ND SUBJECT** **2ND VERB**

This example also contains two separate sentences with two separate subjects and two separate verbs. However, it may be difficult to recognize the pronoun _that_ as a separate subject.

When a demonstrative pronoun is used as a subject in a compound sentence, it often <u>refers back</u> to a thing, a place, or an idea in the first part of the sentence. This thing, place, or idea may consist of more than one word. Take a look:

My teacher didn't read my essay, that upset me.

That is a pronoun, and just like all pronouns, it refers to something else (a person, place, thing, or idea). To understand what *that* refers to, ask yourself, "What upset me?" What upset you was the fact that your teacher did not read your essay. Because the pronoun *that* refers back to the idea in the first part of the sentence, many writers believe that it is glue, but it is not. We still need some glue to join these sentences, or we need to break them into separate sentences:

COORDINATING CONJUNCTION ADDED	My teacher didn't read my essay, and that upset me.
or	
SEMICOLON USED	My teacher didn't read my essay; that upset me.
or	
PERIOD USED	My teacher didn't read my essay. That upset me.

The last option (the use of a period) does correct the comma splice; however, it does not <u>join</u> the two simple sentences to form a compound sentence.

Power Tip
If there is any chance that a reader might not understand what you are referring to with a demonstrative pronoun, replace it with more specific words. For example, take a look at this replacement for *that*: *My teacher didn't read my essay, and <u>her lack of interest in my work</u> upset me.*

ACTIVITY 25
MODERATE

For each of the run-ons or comma splices below, do the following:

- Circle the demonstrative pronoun.
- Underline the thing, place, or idea to which the demonstrative pronoun refers.
- Rewrite the run-on or comma splice in the space provided, adding a conjunction or a semicolon to make it a correct compound sentence. If you use a conjunction, don't forget the required comma.

EXAMPLE:

On Sundays, my father brings home <u>jelly doughnuts</u> (these) are my favorite treats.

On Sundays, my father brings home jelly doughnuts; these are

my favorite treats.

1. My boss yelled at me every day that was only one reason behind my decision to quit.

_____

_____

2. I don't usually like mussels, these are the best I've tasted.

_____

_____

CONTINUED >

3. My boyfriend buys me flowers for every special occasion this always makes me happy.

_____

_____

4. Brian took out an expensive mortgage on a new home, that became his financial downfall.

_____

_____

5. For the holidays, I will make my famous mouse-shaped chocolates, those are big hits with my friends and family.

_____

_____

Additive Expressions

Sometimes, we write a sentence and then decide to add more information to it. We often use additive expressions (*also*, *for example*, *next*, *plus*, *then*, and so on) to join this information to our sentence. However, if this additional information is expressed with a separate subject and a separate verb, it cannot be joined to the first simple sentence with an additive expression. <u>Additive expressions are never glue.</u> Look at the following comma splice:

| SENTENCE 1 | | SENTENCE 2 | |

My new job has great insurance, plus we get paid holidays.

| 1ST SUBJECT | 1ST VERB | | 2ND SUBJECT | 2ND VERB |

| FOUNDATION WORDS |
| NOUNS |
| VERBS |
| DESCRIPTIVE WORDS |
| ADJECTIVES |
| ADVERBS |
| CONNECTING WORDS |
| PREPOSITIONS |
| CONJUNCTIONS |

Additive expressions are tricky because they seem so much like glue! However, you know that in English, the <u>only glue</u> for joining sentences is (1) a conjunction (*and*, *but*, *or*, *so*, *for*, *nor*, or *yet*) preceded by a comma or (2) a semicolon. To fix the previous comma splice, you could use a conjunction in place of the additive expression or use a semicolon followed by the additive expression. If a conjunction is used, a comma must precede it. If an additive expression is used, a comma usually follows it. Take a look:

CONJUNCTION USED   My new job has great insurance, and we get paid holidays.

or

SEMICOLON AND ADDITIVE   My new job has great insurance; plus,
EXPRESSION USED   we get paid holidays.

In some cases—most commonly with *then*—you can use both a conjunction and an additive expression. Take a look:

I left my home in Dallas, and then I moved to San Francisco.

⊞⊞ ACTIVITY 26

MODERATE

For each of the run-ons or comma splices below, do the following:

- Circle the additive expression (*also*, *for example*, *next*, *plus*, *then*, and so on).
- Rewrite the run-on or comma splice in the space provided, using the correction methods described previously. (If you add a conjunction, make sure to put a comma before it. If you use a semicolon followed by an additive expression, make sure that a comma follows this expression.)

EXAMPLE:

Scott is an adventurous person, (for example,) he likes traveling to distant places.

Scott is an adventurous person; for example, he likes traveling to

distant places.

1. Scott quit his job at Burger Bun, then he went on the road.

_____

_____

2. He wanted a new start also he wanted to live in the West.

_____

_____

3. Scott had heard about the beauty of California, for example, California is home to the Sierra Nevada mountain range.

_____

_____

4. He gave his landlord thirty days' notice next he sold all his unneeded possessions at a yard sale.

_____

_____

5. Scott earned quite a bit of money from his yard sale, plus he had saved money from his job.

_____

_____

6. On a cool September morning in Atlanta, Scott packed his remaining possessions in his truck then he turned west and headed for the mountains of California.

_____

_____

_____

CONTINUED >

7. Along the way, Scott visited some interesting attractions for example, he stopped at the Grand Canyon in Arizona and spent one night in glittering Las Vegas.

_____

_____

8. After driving across the country, Scott eventually stopped in a small town in a valley to the west of the Sierra Nevada Mountains then he smiled.

_____

_____

_____

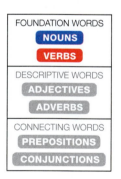

| FOUNDATION WORDS |
| NOUNS |
| VERBS |
| DESCRIPTIVE WORDS |
| ADJECTIVES |
| ADVERBS |
| CONNECTING WORDS |
| PREPOSITIONS |
| CONJUNCTIONS |

Transitional Expressions

You already know that we use a conjunction to join two related simple sentences. Transitional expressions (*as a result, consequently, furthermore, however, in addition,* and so on) do exactly the same thing; in fact, transitional expressions are really just "grown-up" conjunctions. The only difference is that <u>transitional expressions are never glue</u>. A transitional expression by itself can never join two separate sentences. Take a look at this run-on:

SENTENCE 1   SENTENCE 2

My uncle refused to pay his gas bill furthermore he wrote a rude

1ST SUBJECT   1ST VERB   2ND SUBJECT   2ND VERB

letter to the gas company.

First, notice that this example consists of two separate sentences with two separate subjects and two separate verbs. The writer has tried to use *furthermore* as glue to join the two simple sentences, but we know that a transitional word can never be glue. Often, a writer will add a comma with the transitional word:

My uncle refused to pay his gas bill, <u>furthermore</u> he wrote a rude letter to the gas company.

COMMA & TRANSITIONAL EXPRESSION

However, you already know that a comma can never be glue. Even though the student has used a comma and a transitional word together here, there is still <u>no glue</u> to hold the two simple sentences together. <u>If you want to use a transitional expression in a compound sentence, the best way to do so is with a semicolon.</u> Take a look:

My uncle refused to pay his gas bill; furthermore, he wrote a rude letter to the gas company.

This sentence is now a correct compound sentence; the semicolon provides the glue that joins the two simple sentences. Now, notice the added comma after *furthermore.*

New comma rule: When a transitional expression begins a sentence (including a sentence that is part of a compound sentence), this expression should be followed by a comma. (Remember that this same rule applies to a prepositional phrase when it begins a sentence.) Also, recall that a comma usually follows an additive expression when it begins a sentence.

Power Tip

Transitions are an important tool for helping readers to follow your ideas. For more advice on using them, see Chapter 4, page 76, and Chapter 5, pages 98 and 105.

ACTIVITY 27

MODERATE

For each of the following run-ons or comma splices, do the following:

- Circle the transitional expression (*as a result, consequently, furthermore, however, in addition,* and so on).

- Rewrite the run-on or comma splice in the space provided, turning it into a correct compound sentence. Use a semicolon as glue, and remember to put a comma after the transitional expression.

EXAMPLE:

Greedy people may save money, (however) they may lose friends and respect.

Greedy people may save money; however, they may lose friends and

respect.

1. John has been called greedy, as a result people avoid him.

2. At restaurants with friends, he "forgets" his wallet, therefore someone else must pay his bill.

3. He rarely bought dinner for his former girlfriend instead he bought her a drink at happy-hour prices and "treated" her to the free appetizers.

4. In the office lunchroom, he helps himself to co-workers' lunches and snacks, in addition he takes office supplies home on a regular basis.

5. For a long time, John's friends have recommended counseling to him however John seems unaware of his problem and would find a counselor's fees too expensive anyway.

For more practice with run-ons and comma splices, go to **bedfordstmartins.com/ steppingstones.**

The following chart shows that conjunctions and transitional expressions are used to show the same *four types of relationships* between ideas.

Relationships Shown by Conjunctions and Transitional Expressions

	COMBINATION	CONTRAST	RESULT	ALTERNATIVES
Coordinating conjunctions	and (nor)	but (yet)	so (for)	or
Transitional expressions	furthermore in addition moreover	however nevertheless	as a result consequently therefore	instead on the other hand otherwise

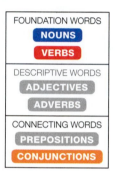

FOUNDATION WORDS
NOUNS
VERBS
DESCRIPTIVE WORDS
ADJECTIVES
ADVERBS
CONNECTING WORDS
PREPOSITIONS
CONJUNCTIONS

Let's take a closer look:

Combination

My sister was accepted to Stanford, and the university offered her a scholarship.

My sister was accepted to Stanford; furthermore, the university offered her a scholarship.

In the first sentence, the conjunction is the glue. In the next sentence, the semicolon is the glue, not the transitional expression.

Both compound sentences mean the same thing. Just like the conjunction *and*, the transitional expressions *furthermore, in addition,* and *moreover* **combine** two **similar** ideas.

Contrast

My sister was accepted to Stanford, but she decided to go to a local college.

My sister was accepted to Stanford; however, she decided to go to a local college.

In the first sentence, the conjunction is the glue. In the next sentence, the semicolon is the glue, not the transitional expression.

Both compound sentences mean the same thing. Just like the conjunction *but*, the transitional expressions *however, instead,* and *nevertheless* **contrast** two **different** ideas.

Result

My sister was accepted to Stanford, so she declined UCLA's offer.

My sister was accepted to Stanford; as a result, she declined UCLA's offer.

In the first sentence, the conjunction is the glue. In the next sentence, the semicolon is the glue, not the transitional expression.

Both compound sentences mean the same thing. Just like the conjunction *so*, the transitional expressions *as a result, consequently,* and *therefore* show a **result** of one idea from another.

Alternatives

My sister might accept Stanford's offer, or she might wait for a better one.

My sister might accept Stanford's offer; otherwise, she might wait for a better one.

Power Tip
If you were the writer of any of these pairs of sentences, you would have to choose the version you like best; it is a matter of personal style and taste.

In the first sentence, the conjunction is the glue. In the next sentence, the semicolon is the glue, not the transitional expression.

Both compound sentences mean the same thing. Just like the conjunction *or*, the transitional expressions *instead* and *otherwise* show **alternative** options or possibilities.

As a beginning writer, you should not feel pressured to use transitional expressions or semicolons. If you are more comfortable using conjunctions, focus your practice on writing compound sentences with conjunctions. Many excellent writers do not use transitional expressions or semicolons.

MODERATE

ACTIVITY 28

Correct each of the following run-ons or comma splices in two ways:

- For the first correction, add a conjunction. Make sure that a comma precedes the conjunction.
- For the second correction, add a semicolon and a transitional expression. Make sure that a comma follows the transitional expression.

EXAMPLE:

We can't avoid noise, we can avoid some of its unhealthy effects.

We can't avoid noise, but we can avoid some of its unhealthy effects.

We can't avoid noise; however, we can avoid some of its unhealthy effects.

1. This world is a busy place it is filled with noise.

2. At home, the television blares, appliances beep and buzz.

3. In our cars, we listen to the radio, we talk on our cell phones.

4. For many of us, solitude is not easy to find in our hectic lives, we must seek silence for the sake of our mental health.

CONTINUED >

5. At busy times, we can take a walk in a peaceful place, we can just sit in a quiet room and close our eyes for a few minutes.

REVIEWING CAUSES AND CORRECTIONS OF RUN-ONS AND COMMA SPLICES

In this part of the chapter, you have learned about four groups of words that often cause run-ons and comma splices when used incorrectly as "glue":

1. personal pronouns (*I, you, he, she, it, we, they*)

2. demonstrative pronouns (*this, that, these, those*)

3. additive expressions (*also, for example, for instance, next, plus, then*)

4. transitional expressions (*as a result, consequently, furthermore, however, in addition, instead, moreover, nevertheless, otherwise, therefore*)

▎ACTIVITY 29: Teamwork

ADVANCED

For each of the run-ons or comma splices below, do the following:

- Circle the word or words that cause the problem.
- Above this expression, write **PP** for personal pronoun, **DP** for demonstrative pronoun, **ADD** for additive expression, or **TRANS** for transitional expression.
- Decide how to correct the error, and write the correct compound sentence on the line provided.

Try not to use a hard period; however, if you are not comfortable with any of the other methods, you may use a hard period. Be sure that commas are placed correctly.

EXAMPLE:

ADD

Many consumers are concerned about gas mileage, for example more people are buying higher-mileage vehicles.

Many consumers are concerned about gas mileage; for example,

more people are buying higher-mileage vehicles.

1. Marianna was spending too much money on gasoline she did research on gas mileage.

   _____

   _____

2. She found and tried many ideas for improving her gas mileage, these helped her save a significant amount of money.

   _____

   _____

3. Marianna's mechanic checked her engine's efficiency, then he tuned up her engine in an effort to improve the gas mileage.

   _____

   _____

4. On the freeway, Marianna avoids speeding moreover she accelerates and brakes her car more gently.

   _____

   _____

5. She keeps her tires inflated to the recommended pressure, otherwise, her gas mileage will be decreased.

   _____

   _____

FIXING RUN-ONS AND COMMA SPLICES IN WHOLE PARAGRAPHS

Remember, when you find a run-on or a comma splice in your writing, it is easy to fix:

Just add glue!

and, but, or, so (+ for, nor, yet) *or* **;**

The following activity will give you practice with recognizing and fixing run-ons and comma splices in whole paragraphs—a valuable skill for improving your own writing.

ACTIVITY 30: Mastery Test or Teamwork

Read each of the following paragraphs carefully, looking for run-ons and comma splices. Then, rewrite each error to fix the problem, using one of the following methods: (1) adding a conjunction (with a comma, if one is missing), (2) adding a semicolon alone, (3) adding a semicolon followed by an additive or transitional expression and a comma, or (4) using a period. The first sentence of each paragraph has been edited for you.

This paragraph has five comma splices (including the one that has been edited for you) and three run-ons.

1. (1) Most of us would prefer a clutter-free place for paying bills and
doing other tasks, _{but} many of us suffer from messy workspaces.

(2) Efficiency experts offer several ideas for reducing clutter, anyone can get more organized by trying them. (3) A filing cabinet offers valuable storage space furthermore the different drawers can help with organizing documents. (4) Hanging folders can be used for more than just letters and bills they can hold recipes, photographs, maps, and other documents. (5) Wire baskets are also useful for organizing materials, they can be stacked to save room on a desktop. (6) Shelves and drawers in the workspace should hold items commonly used for paperwork and studying, these items include envelopes, stamps, a calculator, a dictionary, pens, pencils, and paper clips. (7) Time management also plays a role in clutter control you should look at each piece of mail only once and act on it or throw it away.

(8) With this practice, papers will not pile up, you will spend less time looking for important documents.

This paragraph has six comma splices (including the one that has been edited for you) and five run-ons.

2. (1) The Greece Athena High School basketball team was
winning, _{and} it was the last game of the season. (2) With four minutes left in the game, the team had a comfortable lead spirits were high.

(3) Coach Jim Johnson sent autistic student Jason McElwain onto the court this was Jason's first and only chance to play for his team. (4) Jason was only five feet, six inches tall, he was too small to make the team. (5) In spite of his size, he loved basketball and served as the team's manager also, he was one of the team's biggest fans. (6) Jason charged onto the court with enthusiasm, he shot an air ball and a layup that also missed. (7) Jason's teammates wanted him to make at least one basket they kept passing him the ball. (8) Then, something magical happened, it stunned the crowd. (9) Jason sunk one two-point basket and six three-point shots, within three minutes, he had scored twenty points for his team. (10) The news spread rapidly around the country, Jason quickly became a national hero. (11) He appeared on numerous television news programs he even met President Obama.

This paragraph has five comma splices and seven run-ons (including the one that has been edited for you).

3. (1) Sarah Breedlove Walker was a successful businesswoman**;** moreover**,** she became a role model for many African American women. (2) Sarah Breedlove was the daughter of freed slaves, she grew up in Louisiana at a very difficult time for African Americans. (3) After losing her parents and then her husband, Breedlove went north, in her new home, she worked as a washerwoman for little pay. (4) Eventually, Breedlove started selling beauty products for another woman she got restless and started her own beauty-products business in Denver, Colorado.

(5) In Denver, she met advertising expert Charles J. Walker he became her second husband. (6) Charles Walker helped his wife create attractive advertisements for her products, he convinced her to use the fancy name "Madam C. J. Walker." (7) Advertising drew thousands of people to Sarah Breedlove Walker's products, it was the key to her

CONTINUED >

success. (8) By the early 1900s, she had a 3,000-person sales force and yearly sales of more than $200,000 she had won the admiration of many. (9) In a relatively short time, Breedlove Walker became one of the largest employers of African American women, this is one of her most famous achievements. (10) She eventually purchased a large home and obtained other luxuries she never forgot the less fortunate. (11) Her generosity benefited many causes for example, she contributed to schools, orphanages, and civil-rights groups. (12) By the time of her death in 1919, Breedlove Walker had become an astonishing success she continues to inspire others.

BRINGING IT ALL TOGETHER:
The Compound Sentence

In this chapter, you have learned how to build compound sentences and punctuate them correctly. You have also learned how to avoid two common problems in these sentences: run-ons and comma splices. Confirm your knowledge by filling in the blank spaces in the following sentences. If you need help, review the pages listed after each sentence.

✔ A compound sentence is two or more related simple sentences joined together. In the English language, there are just two types of "glue" used to form compound sentences. These two types of glue are _____ and _____. (pages 256, 265)

✔ There are seven coordinating conjunctions in the English language. They are _____, _____, _____, _____, _____, _____, and _____. (page 256)

✔ Each coordinating conjunction expresses a specific type of relationship between the two simple sentences. _____ combines two similar ideas. _____ contrasts two different ideas. _____ shows a result. _____ shows alternatives. (pages 256–57)

✔ In a compound sentence, there must always be two separate
_____ and two separate _____. When punctuating
a compound sentence, a _____ must always come before the
conjunction. (pages 260–61)

✔ A semicolon can be used to join two simple sentences that have a special
connection, but it must always follow a _____. (page 266)

✔ If you try to join two simple sentences with no glue (without a conjunction or a semicolon), the result will be a _____, a major
grammatical error. (page 283)

✔ If you try to join two simple sentences with only a comma, the result will
be a _____, a major grammatical error. (page 284)

✔ Four groups of words are often used *incorrectly* as glue when joining
simple sentences. These groups of words are: _____,
_____, _____, and
_____. (page 285)

CHAPTER 12

The Complex Sentence

Before you read this chapter, it's a good idea to test your understanding of complex sentences. You may know more than you think.

WHAT DO YOU KNOW?

Circle "Yes" if each word group below is a complete, correct sentence. Circle "No" if it is incomplete. Then, explain your choice.

1. **When the moon blocks the light of the sun; there is a solar eclipse.**

   Yes   No

   Explanation: _____

   _____

2. **Unless this country begins to take care of those in need.**

   Yes   No

   Explanation: _____

   _____

3. **If you leave, I'll cry.**

   Yes   No

   Explanation: _____

   _____

4. **After the sun rose slowly over the mountaintop this morning Eddie went for a run.**

   Yes   No

   Explanation: _____

   _____

5. **Since I woke up on time, I was late for work today.**

   Yes   No

   Explanation: _____

   _____

Both of these are complex sentences. They have the same basic meaning, but are different in important ways. You'll learn why in this chapter.

CONJUNCTION + **NOUN** + **VERB** , **NOUN** + **VERB** . = Because I study, I learn.

NOUN + **VERB** + **CONJUNCTION** + **NOUN** + **VERB** . = I learn because I study.

BUILD IT: Complex Sentences

In the previous chapter, you learned that **coordinating conjunctions** (*and, but, or,* and *so,* and less commonly *for, nor,* and *yet*) work like glue to join simple sentences into **compound** sentences.

SIMPLE SENTENCES	SENTENCE 1 SENTENCE 2	
	Our team won. We celebrated.	
COMPOUND SENTENCE	SENTENCE 1 SENTENCE 2	
	Our team won, so we celebrated.	

↑
COORDINATING CONJUNCTION PRECEDED BY COMMA

In this chapter, you will study **subordinating conjunctions**, another group of words that work like glue to join simple sentences into what are known as **complex sentences**.

SIMPLE SENTENCES	SENTENCE 1 SENTENCE 2	
	Our team won. We celebrated.	
COMPLEX SENTENCE	SENTENCE 1 SENTENCE 2	
	Since our team won, we celebrated.	

↑
SUBORDINATING CONJUNCTION

From these examples, you can already see that coordinating and subordinating conjunctions work in a very similar way. However, you should keep some differences in mind:

- There are **more** subordinating conjunctions than coordinating conjunctions.
- Subordinating conjunctions have different rules for **punctuation**.
- If you do not correctly punctuate sentences with subordinating conjunctions, you can create a **sentence fragment**.

Subordinating conjunctions are like a **glue gun**. Whenever you use a glue gun instead of using glue from a bottle, you need to be especially

Common Subordinating Conjunctions

after, although, as, because, before, even though, even if, if, since, unless, until, when, while

careful because you have more power and more risk of making a mistake. Likewise, when you use subordinating conjunctions instead of coordinating conjunctions, you also have more power and more risk of making a mistake.

UNDERSTANDING COORDINATING VERSUS SUBORDINATING CONJUNCTIONS

In Chapter 11, you learned that we use coordinating conjunctions to

- combine similar ideas
- contrast different ideas
- show a result
- show alternatives

This chart reviews the relationships shown by coordinating conjunctions, and those shown by subordinating conjunctions. Examples of these relationships follow.

Relationships Shown by Conjunctions

	COMBINATION	CONTRAST	RESULT	ALTERNATIVES/ POSSIBILITIES
Coordinating conjunctions	and (nor)	but (yet)	so (for)	or
Subordinating conjunctions	after as before when while	although even though	because since	if (even if) unless (until)

In each of the following sentence pairs, both sentences express the same idea. However, the first sentence uses a **coordinating conjunction**, and the second uses a **subordinating conjunction**. In the second (complex) sentence, the subordinating conjunction comes at the <u>beginning</u> of the sentence. The comma is in the <u>middle</u> of both sentences.

Combining two similar ideas

The clouds passed, and the moon appeared.
After the clouds passed, the moon appeared.

Contrasting two different ideas

Blanca always remembers, but Bert always forgets.
Although Blanca always remembers, Bert always forgets.

Showing a <u>result</u>

Our team won, **so** we celebrated.

Because our team won, we celebrated.

Showing <u>alternatives</u> or <u>possibilities</u>

You must study, **or** you will fail.

Unless you study, you will fail.

Note that the parts of a sentence joined by a coordinating conjunction have equal weight:

You must study, or you will fail.

However, when you begin one sentence part with a subordinating conjunction, it often has less weight (emphasis) than the other part. In other words, it becomes *subordinate* (less important).

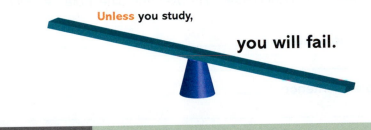

Unless you study,

you will fail.

📶 ACTIVITY 1
EASY

Combine each pair of simple sentences in two ways:

- as a compound sentence, using a coordinating conjunction, and
- as a complex sentence, using a subordinating conjunction.

For a list of conjunctions, see the chart on page 304.

EXAMPLE: Greg is shy. He likes parties.

Compound sentence: Greg is shy, but he likes parties.

Complex sentence: Even though Greg is shy, he likes parties.

1. It was Greg's birthday. We baked him a cake.

Compound sentence: _____

_____

Complex sentence: _____

_____

CONTINUED >

KEY TO
CHALLENGE
METER

WARMUP

EASY

MODERATE

ADVANCED

MASTERY

Identify the difficulty
level of each activity
using the key above.

2. Greg's favorite flavor is pineapple. We baked him a chocolate cake.

   Compound sentence: _____

   _____

   Complex sentence: _____

   _____

3. We called Greg's friends. We surprised him with a party.

   Compound sentence: _____

   _____

   Complex sentence: _____

   _____

4. Greg walked into his apartment. We all jumped up and yelled,
   "Surprise!"

   Compound sentence: _____

   _____

   Complex sentence: _____

   _____

5. Greg loved the chocolate cake. He loved the pineapple ice cream even
   more.

   Compound sentence: _____

   _____

   Complex sentence: _____

   _____

ACTIVITY 2

First, complete each compound sentence. Then, rewrite each compound sentence as a complex sentence, using a subordinating conjunction at the beginning. For a list of subordinating conjunctions, see page 304.

EXAMPLE:

Compound sentence: Don't shake the bottle, or it _will explode_.

Complex sentence: _If you shake the bottle, it will explode._

1. **Compound sentence:** We must leave by noon, or _____

   _____

   Complex sentence: _____

   _____

2. **Compound sentence:** The exam was long, but _____

   _____

   Complex sentence: _____

   _____

For more practice with
complex sentences, go to
**bedfordstmartins.com/
steppingstones**.

3. **Compound sentence:** You should close the door, or _____

_____

Complex sentence: _____

_____

4. **Compound sentence:** Beverly drove too fast, so _____

_____

Complex sentence: _____

_____

5. **Compound sentence:** We lost power on campus, so _____

_____

Complex sentence: _____

_____

UNDERSTANDING RELATIONSHIPS SHOWN BY SUBORDINATING CONJUNCTIONS

Different subordinating conjunctions signal different meanings and relationships in complex sentences. The following sections describe some of the most important relationships.

Expected and Unexpected Results

In the examples below, we will start with the simple sentence: *My alarm clock did not ring.*

To show an <u>expected result</u>

<u>Since</u> my alarm clock did not ring, I overslept.

When we use *since* or *because* to form a complex sentence, we want to show an **expected** result. For example, when your alarm clock does not ring, you generally expect that you will oversleep.

Note that *since* and *because* mean the same thing. It does not matter which one you use.

<u>Because</u> my alarm clock did not ring, I overslept.

To show <u>an unexpected result (contrast)</u>

<u>Although</u> my alarm clock did not ring, I woke up on time.

When we use *although* or *even though* to form a complex sentence, we want to show an **unexpected** result (a contrast). For example, when your alarm clock does not ring, you generally do not expect to wake up on time.

KEY TO
BUILDING BLOCKS

FOUNDATION WORDS

NOUNS

VERBS

DESCRIPTIVE WORDS

ADJECTIVES

ADVERBS

CONNECTING WORDS

PREPOSITIONS

CONJUNCTIONS

Note that *although* and *even though* mean the same thing. It does not matter which one you use.

Even though my alarm clock did not ring, I woke up on time.

ACTIVITY 3

MODERATE

Examine each of the following pairs of complex sentences and decide whether each sentence shows an <u>expected</u> result or an <u>unexpected</u> result (a contrast). Then, use **since/because** or **although/even though** to complete the sentence.

EXAMPLE:

    a. _____Since_____ my car ran out of gas, I was late for work.

    b. _____Although_____ my car ran out of gas, I was on time for work.

1. a. _____ the watch was very expensive, I bought it.

    b. _____ the watch was very expensive, I did not buy it.

2. a. _____ the weather was cold, we did not go to the football game.

    b. _____ the weather was cold, we went to the football game.

3. a. _____ the key lime pie looked delicious, we turned it down.

    b. _____ the key lime pie looked delicious, we each had a slice.

4. a. _____ the weather forecast calls for a hurricane, we canceled our beach plans.

    b. _____ the weather forecast calls for a hurricane, we went for a walk on the beach.

5. a. _____ Apple's latest iPhone has had so many problems, consumers have been quite unhappy.

    b. _____ Apple's latest iPhone has had so many problems, consumers continue to purchase it.

6. a. _____ Joanne's dreams are disturbing, she refuses to see a therapist.

    b. _____ Joanne's dreams are disturbing, she decided to consult a psychic.

7. a. _____ sweet potatoes are good for one's skin, Marcy began to eat them for dinner.

    b. _____ sweet potatoes are good for one's skin, Marcy won't eat them.

8. a. _____ driving while texting is against the law, Cindy keeps both hands on the wheel while driving to school.

    b. _____ driving while texting is against the law, Cindy continues to text her friends while driving to school.

9. a. _____ Al loves Louise, he refuses to marry her.

    b. _____ Al loves Louise, he hopes to marry her.

10. a. _____ I dislike grammar, I sometimes avoid studying it.

    b. _____ I dislike grammar, I know that it is important for my college success.

ACTIVITY 4
MODERATE

For each of the following items, complete the first sentence with an expected result. Complete the second sentence with an unexpected result (a contrast).

EXAMPLE:

a. Because Alexis lost her cell phone, *she could not call her parents.*

b. Even though Alexis lost her cell phone, *she was able to reach her parents by pay phone.*

1. a. Since the bridge was under construction, _____

    _____

    b. Although the bridge was under construction, _____

    _____

2. a. Because there was a terrible storm, _____

    _____

    b. Although there was a terrible storm, _____

    _____

3. a. Because Steven skipped lunch, _____

    b. Although Steven skipped lunch, _____

4. a. Because this restaurant has a dress code, _____

    _____

    b. Even though this restaurant has a dress code, _____

    _____

5. a. Because your apple pie is burned, _____

    _____

    b. Even though your apple pie is burned, _____

6. a. Because I am expected to graduate this spring, _____

    _____

    b. Although I am expected to graduate this spring, _____

    _____

7. a. Since she forgets birthdays, _____

    b. Even though she forgets birthdays, _____

8. a. Because Adam does not like arriving late, _____

    _____

    b. Although Adam does not like arriving late, _____

CONTINUED >

9. a. Since James always wins at card games, _____

_____

b. Although James always wins at card games, _____

_____

10. a. Because I work in a hospital, _____

_____

b. Even though I work in a hospital, _____

_____

Conditions and Outcomes

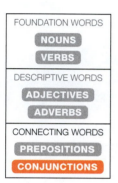

We use the subordinating conjunctions *if* and *unless* to set up a condition:

If you do this, then . . .

Unless you do this, then . . .

A **condition** can be a requirement or a hypothesis. It indicates a situation or task that must occur in order for a particular result or outcome to take place. While this may sound complicated, most of us use *if* and *unless* frequently in our conversations to state conditions. Take a look:

If you clean up your room, you can go to the arcade.

Unless you clean up your room, you can't go to the arcade.

Most writers have no difficulty using the conjunctions *if* and *unless*. Just be sure that the outcome makes sense given the condition.

ACTIVITY 5

MODERATE

Examine each of the following pairs of complex sentences and decide which should begin with the conjunction *if* and which should begin with *unless*. Write your answers in the spaces provided.

EXAMPLE:

a. _____If_____ I set my alarm clock tonight, I will wake up early enough to eat breakfast.

b. _____Unless_____ I set my alarm clock tonight, I will be late for school tomorrow.

1. a. _____ you take me to the new vampire film, I will bite you on the neck and suck your blood.

b. _____ you take me to the new vampire film, I will wash your black Mercedes.

2. a. _____ we study together, I will have a better chance of passing the exam.

b. _____ we study together, I will probably fail the exam.

3. a. _____ the athletes confess to doping, fans will wonder about their honesty.

   b. _____ the athletes confess to doping, fans can finally move forward and stop wondering about them.

4. a. _____ someone claims the wallet with $400, I'm keeping it!

   b. _____ someone claims the wallet with $400, the owner will need to identify it.

5. a. _____ I'm wrong about the warning signs of a tornado, we should get into the cellar quickly!

   b. _____ I'm wrong about the warning signs of a tornado, then we can relax and go for a walk.

6. a. _____ the phone lines went down in the storm, we should be able to reach the fire department.

   b. _____ the phone lines went down in the storm, we won't be able to reach the fire department.

7. a. _____ the nurse gets here quickly, Uncle Morty may go into toxic shock!

   b. _____ the nurse gets here quickly, Uncle Morty may survive his toxic shock.

8. a. _____ everyone recycles, we can fix the landfill problems that our country has.

   b. _____ everyone recycles, landfills will overflow beyond our ability to deal with them.

9. a. _____ teachers are made aware that many children have peanut allergies, they might be more watchful for allergic reactions in their students.

   b. _____ teachers are made aware that many children have peanut allergies, students may continue to suffer allergic reactions at school.

10. a. _____ the new Batman film really impresses me, I'll probably walk out in the middle of it.

   b. _____ the new Batman film really impresses me, I may watch it again next week with my boyfriend.

ACTIVITY 6

MODERATE

Complete each of the following sentences. In order to determine a logical outcome for each sentence, pay close attention to the subordinate conjunction that begins the sentence.

EXAMPLE:

   a. If Simon asks me to the dance, _I will buy a dress tomorrow._

   b. Unless Simon asks me to the dance, _I am not going._

CONTINUED >

1. a. Unless Gregory stretches before the game, _____

   _____

   b. If Gregory stretches before the big match, _____

   _____

2. a. If my husband uses all the right ingredients in the recipe, _____

   _____

   b. Unless my husband uses all the right ingredients in the recipe,

   _____

3. a. Unless Jaime talks to his professor, _____
   b. If Jaime talks to his professor, _____

4. a. Unless someone calls 911, _____
   b. If someone calls 911, _____

5. a. If I apply for financial aid, _____
   b. Unless I apply for financial aid, _____

Review

Relationships Shown by Subordinating Conjunctions

COMBINATION	CONTRAST	RESULT	ALTERNATIVES/ POSSIBILITIES
after as before when while	although even though	because since	if (even if) unless (until)

The following activity will give you additional practice with these different conjunctions.

ACTIVITY 7

ADVANCED

Complete each of the following complex sentences.

EXAMPLE:

   a. Since the movie is sold out, *we can go to the arcade.*
   b. Although the movie is sold out, *my friend has extra tickets.*
   c. Unless the movie is sold out, *we can buy our tickets at the last minute.*

1. a. Since it is raining outside, _____
   b. Even though it is raining outside, _____
   c. If it is raining outside, _____

For more practice with subordinating conjunctions, go to **bedfordstmartins.com/steppingstones**.

2. **a.** After the house burned down, _____

    b. Unless the house burned down, _____

    c. Even though the house burned down, _____

3. **a.** Before you go to Germany, _____

    b. If you go to Germany, _____

    c. After you go to Germany, _____

4. **a.** Because Jackie's flight from Miami was late, _____

_____

    b. Although Jackie's flight from Miami was late, _____

_____

    c. Unless Jackie's flight from Miami was late, _____

_____

5. **a.** When I forgot Aaron's birthday, _____

    b. Because I forgot Aaron's birthday, _____

    c. Although I forgot Aaron's birthday, _____

RECOGNIZING CORRECT PUNCTUATION IN COMPLEX SENTENCES

So far in this chapter, you have seen one way to form a complex sentence: by <u>beginning</u> the sentence with a subordinating conjunction:

> **Because** we were delayed at security, we missed our flight.

However, you could also put a subordinating conjunction <u>in the middle</u> of a sentence:

> We missed our flight **because** we were delayed at security.

Most students would write the second version of this sentence because it is more conversational or **informal**. The first version is more **formal**. However, both sentences emphasize the fact that the flight was missed. (For more on emphasis in sentences with subordinating conjunctions, see page 305.)

Now, notice the important difference in punctuation:

CONJUNCTION AT THE BEGINNING   **+**   **COMMA**

FORMAL   **Because** we were delayed at security, we missed our flight.

CONJUNCTION IN THE MIDDLE; NO COMMA

INFORMAL   We missed our flight **because** we were delayed at security.

When you <u>begin</u> a complex sentence with a subordinating conjunction, you must put a comma in the middle of the sentence. When the subordinating conjunction comes in the middle of the sentence, a comma doesn't usually need to come before it.

FOUNDATION WORDS

NOUNS

VERBS

DESCRIPTIVE WORDS

ADJECTIVES

ADVERBS

CONNECTING WORDS

PREPOSITIONS

CONJUNCTIONS

Note that a comma never follows a subordinating conjunction regardless of this conjunction's position in a sentence:

INCORRECT

Because, we were delayed at security, we missed our flight.

INCORRECT

We missed our flight because, we were delayed at security.

ACTIVITY 8
EASY

Examine each of the following sentences and determine whether the punctuation is correct. Write **C** next to the sentence if the punctuation is correct. Otherwise, rewrite the sentence, correcting the punctuation.

EXAMPLE: If, you don't call me I will call you.

If you don't call me, I will call you.

1. If you sleep until eleven you will miss the beautiful sunrise.

2. Felicia did not go to class; because she had the flu.

3. Unless the computer goes on sale, it is too expensive for my budget.

4. Elizabeth will forgive Bobby if, he apologizes.

5. Life became much more complicated and stressful for Jeremy; after he won the lottery.

ACTIVITY 9
MODERATE

Rewrite each of the following complex sentences, putting the conjunction at the beginning of the sentence if it's in the middle of the original sentence. Put the conjunction in the middle if it's at the beginning of the original sentence. Add or delete commas as necessary.

EXAMPLE: If it's up to me, I will never go on another family cruise.

I will never go on another family cruise if it's up to me.

1. Our cruise to Mexico was a disappointment although we had expected to have a great time.

2. Our cabin was not ready because the ship was understaffed.

_____

3. Before we could enter our cabin, we had to wait two hours.

_____

4. Because the seas were rough, Aunt Anna and Uncle Rick became ill.

_____

5. While she was taking a yoga class, Aunt Anna fell over a railing.

_____

6. She was quite embarrassed when she landed in the swimming pool.

_____

7. After we arrived on the island of Cozumel, Uncle Rick disappeared.

_____

8. We were all worried until he returned to the ship with jewelry and pottery for everyone.

_____

_____

9. After Aunt Anna was served an overdone steak, she marched into the kitchen to complain.

_____

_____

10. I am not ready for another family cruise even if Aunt Anna and Uncle Rick stay home.

_____

_____

BUILDING SENTENCE VARIETY

In Chapter 11, you learned about two ways to form **compound** sentences: (a) with a coordinating conjunction and a comma, or (b) with a semicolon (alone or with a transitional expression followed by a comma):

> **COMMA AND COORDINATING CONJUNCTION**
>
> **(a) Tom added lighter fluid, but the charcoal would not ignite.**

> **SEMICOLON WITH TRANSITIONAL EXPRESSION AND COMMA**
>
> **(b) Tom added lighter fluid; however, the charcoal would not ignite.**

In this chapter, you have learned to form **complex** sentences in two ways: (c) formally, by placing a subordinating conjunction at the beginning of

a sentence, and (d) informally, by placing a conjunction in the middle of a sentence.

> **SUBORDINATING CONJUNCTION AT BEGINNING**

(c) Although Tom added lighter fluid, the charcoal would not ignite.

> **SUBORDINATING CONJUNCTION IN MIDDLE**

(d) The charcoal would not ignite although Tom added lighter fluid.

In a basic sense, all four of these sentences express the same ideas. So which one is best for your writing? While there is no simple answer to this question, you should consider two things:

1. **Style:** If you like a more <u>casual</u> style of writing, you will probably prefer sentences **a** and **d**. Both of these sentences reflect the way we speak; they are more conversational in tone. If you like a more <u>formal</u> style of writing, you might prefer sentences **b** and **c**.

2. **Meaning:** Very thoughtful writers might notice a small difference in meaning among these sentences. Sentences **c** and **d** give a special emphasis to the fact that the charcoal would not ignite. Perhaps the writer wants to express surprise or frustration about this fact.

However, the best recommendation is to <u>use a variety</u> of these sentence types in your writing. Varied sentence patterns keep readers interested in the same way that music with varied rhythms keeps listeners interested. The more you practice and use these four sentence types, the more dynamic your writing will become.

Let's review conjunctions and transitional expressions that can be used to create sentence variety. See Chapter 11, page 285, to read more.

Words Used for Sentence Variety

	COMBINATION	CONTRAST	RESULT	ALTERNATIVES/ POSSIBILITIES
Coordinating conjunctions	and (nor)	but (yet)	so (for)	or
Subordinating conjunctions	after as before when while	although even though	because since	if (even if) unless (until)
Transitional expressions (see Chapter 11)	furthermore in addition moreover	however nevertheless	as a result consequently therefore	instead on the other hand otherwise

ACTIVITY 10

ADVANCED

Combine each pair of sentences in the four ways shown in the example. Remember: Correct punctuation is necessary for the success of your sentences. To help you get started, the type of relationship for each pair of sentences has been provided in parentheses.

EXAMPLE: The bookshelf shook in the earthquake. Two books fell down. (combination)

    a. Compound—with coordinating conjunction and comma:
       The bookshelf shook in the earthquake, and two books fell down.

    b. Compound—with semicolon and transitional expression:
       The bookshelf shook in the earthquake; consequently, two books fell down.

    c. Complex—with subordinating conjunction at beginning of sentence: When the bookshelf shook in the earthquake, two books fell down.

    d. Complex—with subordinating conjunction in the middle of sentence: Two books fell down when the bookshelf shook in the earthquake.

1. My uncle loves cars. He hates driving. (contrast)
    a. Compound: _____
    b. Compound: _____
    c. Complex: _____
    d. Complex: _____

2. The light suddenly turned red. I had to slam on the brakes. (result)
    a. Compound: _____
    _____
    b. Compound: _____
    c. Complex: _____
    _____
    d. Complex: _____
    _____

3. Mrs. Sanchez retired. She took up golfing. (combination)
    a. Compound: _____
    b. Compound: _____
    c. Complex: _____
    d. Complex: _____

CONTINUED >

For more practice with compound and complex sentences, go to **bedfordstmartins.com/ steppingstones**.

4. The patient must watch his sugar intake. His diabetes will flare up. (condition)

    a. **Compound:** _____

    _____

    b. **Compound:** _____

    _____

    c. **Complex:** _____

    _____

    d. **Complex:** _____

    _____

BUILDING COMPLEX SENTENCES IN WHOLE PARAGRAPHS

Use your knowledge of subordinating conjunctions to create new complex sentences in the following paragraphs.

ACTIVITY 11: Mastery Test or Teamwork

In the following paragraph, form eight complex sentences, using the subordinating conjunctions from the chart on page 312. First, identify each pair of sentences that can be joined, and then decide which conjunction will join the sentences most effectively. Remember that the conjunction may be placed at the beginning of the complex sentence or in the middle between the two simple sentences. The first one has been done for you.

    Many people are concerned about the Great Pacific Garbage Patch.

It is made up of about 3.5 million tons of garbage and has become

twice the size of Texas. ~~The~~ *Because the* field of waste is so enormous/ ~~It~~ *, it* can be

seen from planes on the way to Hawaii. It's in the ocean. Only

one-fifth of the garbage comes from ship dumping. The rest comes

from human land trash. According to environmental researchers,

90 percent of the trash in this ocean dump comes from nonbiodegradable

plastic, such as plastic bags. Plastic bags are so cheap to produce

and so sturdy. Eighty percent of grocery stores use them. The presence

of plastic creates enormous problems in the entire ecosystem.

Birds and sea creatures eat the minute plastic particles. They die.

Their systems are unable to digest the plastic. The plastic consumed by fish is tiny. It still moves up the food chain. We eat fish. We're eating plastic. Drastic efforts toward recycling begin soon. The world may lose an invaluable resource—a healthy Pacific Ocean. Individuals could simply use canvas bags for shopping instead of plastic ones. It would be a start in the right direction. We must take this issue seriously. It's too late.

ACTIVITY 12: Mastery Test

In the following paragraph, form up to seven complex sentences, using the subordinating conjunctions from the chart on page 312. First, identify each pair of sentences that can be joined, and then decide which conjunction will join the sentences most effectively. Remember that the conjunction may be placed at the beginning of the complex sentence or in the middle between the two simple sentences. The first one has been done for you.

The feminist movement works to reform many areas of society, including reproductive rights, maternity leave, equal pay for equal work, voting rights, sexual harassment, and domestic violence. ~~Feminism~~ *Although feminism* existed before the eighteenth century*, the* ~~The~~ roots of the modern movement can be found in the mid-eighteenth century. Some women were conservative Christians. Others were highly radical. So many women pulled together and worked so hard. They gained many rights. The territory of Wyoming passed a law in 1869. Women began to serve on juries. The National Women's Trade Union League was established in 1903. Working conditions for women began to improve. The nineteenth amendment was passed in 1919. Women were granted the right to vote. In 1996, the Supreme Court ruled that the Virginia Military School had to admit women. The school would not receive public funding. It admitted both males and females. In 2009, President Obama signed the Lilly Ledbetter Fair Pay Restoration Act. The act allowed victims of pay discrimination to file a complaint against their

CONTINUED >

employers. The act came about. A Goodyear employee was being paid 15 to 40 percent less than her male co-workers who were doing the same job. Individuals stand up for women's rights. They will continue to struggle for equality.

FIX IT: Solving Problems in Complex Sentences

In Chapter 10, you learned about an error that writers occasionally make when writing simple sentences: fragments. A fragment is a word group that is missing a subject or verb, or that doesn't express a complete thought. Fragments can also occur in complex sentences. The following sections explain common causes of fragments in complex sentences and how you can fix these errors.

FIXING FRAGMENTS CAUSED BY A MISPLACED PERIOD

By now, you know that the following simple sentence is complete and correct:

> **SUBJECT** **VERB**
> I love you.

However, take a look at the following example:

> I love you because.

Few people would write this fragment. It is obvious that this group of words is not a complete thought. Most writers would automatically complete the thought by adding more information:

> I love you because you are beautiful.

On the other hand, many writers get confused when they <u>begin</u> a sentence with a subordinating conjunction. They might create the following fragment:

> Because you are beautiful.

When we <u>begin</u> a simple sentence with a subordinating conjunction, we must add a comma and complete the thought:

> Because you are beautiful, I love you.

Writers can create fragments accidentally when they add <u>an unnecessary period</u>. Take a look:

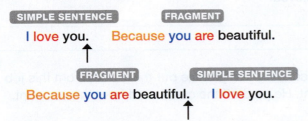

> SIMPLE SENTENCE   FRAGMENT
>
> I love you.   Because you are beautiful.

> FRAGMENT   SIMPLE SENTENCE
>
> Because you are beautiful.   I love you.

Fortunately, this type of fragment is very simple to correct. Just remove the period or replace it with a comma:

INFORMAL: Remove the period.

I love you because you are beautiful.

FORMAL: Replace the period with a comma.

Because you are beautiful, I love you.

ACTIVITY 13

In each of the following items, mark an **F** above the fragment. Then, correct the fragment by connecting it to a simple sentence. Remember to (1) remove the period between the fragment and the simple sentence to which you want to connect the fragment or (2) replace this period with a comma. Leave the other simple sentence alone.

EXAMPLE:

Credit-card debt can be frightening. Some cannot get free of it. Even though they try.

Credit-card debt can be frightening. Some cannot get free of

it even though they try.

1. Doug was in debt. Because he had a large balance on his credit card. He felt depressed.

_____

_____

2. Doug needed help. While visiting his friend Bill. He asked for advice.

_____

3. Bill needed help with a construction job. Doug could work for Bill. Until the job was done.

_____

_____

4. Since the construction job was during the day. Doug could keep his night job. He was relieved.

_____

_____

5. After Doug took the construction job. He put the money from this job in a separate account. He paid off the credit card from this account.

_____

_____

ACTIVITY 14: Teamwork

MODERATE

In each of the following items, mark an **F** above the fragment. Then, correct the fragment by connecting it to a simple sentence. Remember to (1) remove the period between the fragment and the simple sentence to which you want to connect the fragment or (2) replace this period with a comma. Leave the other simple sentence(s) alone.

EXAMPLE:

                           F

Since our math professor is hard to understand. Many students are struggling in the class. My friend and I decided to hire a tutor. This should help us with the work.

Since our math professor is hard to understand, many students are

struggling in the class. My friend and I decided to hire a tutor. This

should help us with the work.

1. Visitors should not feed chipmunks in the park. If chipmunks become dependent on humans for food. They can starve during a long, cold winter. Then, the population may be lower in the spring.

_____

_____

_____

2. The volcanic mountain Mount St. Helens was once 9,677 feet high. After it erupted violently on May 18, 1980. It lost more than 1,000 feet in height.

_____

_____

3. Even though fast food seems modern. Remains of fast-food restaurants have been found in ancient Roman ruins. People could sit down and eat at these restaurants or get their food "to go."

_____

_____

_____

4. Unfortunately, scandals have been common. Since sports have been popular. A very famous scandal occurred during the 1919 World Series. That year, members of the Chicago White Sox agreed to lose games in return for money.

_____

_____

_____

_____

5. Levi Strauss invented denim jeans for miners in California. Because these workers wore through trousers quickly. They needed something more durable. Strauss made tough trousers from canvas and sold them to the miners.

_____

_____

_____

_____

FIXING FRAGMENTS CAUSED BY A MISPLACED SEMICOLON

Complex sentences can be informal (conversational) or formal:

INFORMAL	I won't go unless you drive.
FORMAL	Unless you drive, I won't go.

As noted earlier, less experienced writers sometimes add unnecessary periods to both types of sentences.

FRAGMENT

INCORRECT   I won't go. Unless you drive.

FRAGMENT

INCORRECT   Unless you drive. I won't go.

Another common error when writing such sentences is to add a semicolon:

FRAGMENT

INCORRECT   I won't go; unless you drive.

FRAGMENT

INCORRECT   Unless you drive; I won't go.

Just like a misplaced period, a misplaced semicolon in a complex sentence causes a fragment. The rule is very simple: <u>never use a semicolon in a complex sentence</u>. You can correct the previous fragments in the following ways:

FOUNDATION WORDS
- NOUNS
- VERBS

DESCRIPTIVE WORDS
- ADJECTIVES
- ADVERBS

CONNECTING WORDS
- PREPOSITIONS
- CONJUNCTIONS

For more practice with fixing fragments, go to **bedfordstmartins.com/ steppingstones**.

Remove the semicolon.

I won't go *unless* you drive.

Replace the semicolon with a comma.

Unless you drive, I won't go.

ACTIVITY 15

MODERATE

In each of the following items, mark an *F* above the fragment. Then, correct the fragment by connecting it to a simple sentence. Remember to (1) remove the semicolon between the fragment and the simple sentence to which you want to connect the fragment or (2) replace this semicolon with a comma. Leave the other simple sentence alone.

EXAMPLE: *F*

We hid in the dark; until the birthday girl arrived. Then, we yelled, "Surprise!"

We hid in the dark until the birthday girl arrived. Then, we yelled,

"Surprise!"

1. It was snowing heavily. We drove very slowly up the mountain; because the roads were icy.

   _____

   _____

2. Martin's tax return is due soon. He must mail his return by Monday; unless he files for an extension.

   _____

   _____

3. We worked in the yard until noon. Even though we were tired; we finished the mowing and the weeding.

   _____

   _____

4. Before Amalia leaves her apartment; she turns on the television for her cat. The cat loves cartoons.

   _____

   _____

5. Marianne handles the department budget; since she has a talent for math. Lorenzo handles creative decisions.

   _____

   _____

FIXING FRAGMENTS IN WHOLE PARAGRAPHS

The following activity will give you practice with recognizing and fixing fragments in whole paragraphs—a valuable skill for improving your own writing. You can complete it individually or with classmates.

ACTIVITY 16: Mastery Test or Teamwork

In each of the following paragraphs, mark an **F** above any fragments that you find. Then, correct each fragment by connecting it to another sentence. Remember to remove incorrect periods or semicolons and replace them with commas when necessary.

The following paragraph has five fragments, including the one that has been marked for you.

1. (1) In October of 1973, Peter Jenkins began a long walk across
   because   F
   America. ~~Because~~ he wanted to understand his country and himself
   ^

   better. (2) He was a disillusioned young man. (3) It was a time of racial   **disillusioned:** deeply
                                                                                  disappointed
   tensions and drug use among his peers. (4) Jenkins was also troubled

   about the Vietnam War. Although it was nearly over. (5) His journey

   began in New York and ended; when he reached New Orleans. (6) For

   companionship and safety, he took his loyal dog, Cooper. (7) While

   Jenkins was on the road; he met many kind and interesting people.

   (8) His faith in America was eventually restored. (9) After he completed

   his long journey. He wrote a book called *A Walk Across America.*

The following paragraph has seven fragments, including the one that has been marked for you.

                                                     F   , your
2. (1) Since competition for good jobs can be fierce. ~~Your~~ résumé
                                                         ^
   must be correct, clear, and professional. (2) Although you may be well

   qualified for the position; your résumé can easily end up in the

   wastebasket. (3) Personnel managers become annoyed at several

   kinds of mistakes. (4) If your résumé is submitted on brightly colored or

   decorated paper. You might be seen as unprofessional. (5) Even a

   carelessly chosen e-mail address can cost you an interview. (6) While an

   e-mail address such as KutiePie or PartyBoy may seem clever. Such

CONTINUED >

names might reflect unfavorably on your personality. (7) Before you submit your résumé; proofread it very carefully for errors. (8) Some applicants misspell the company's name or the city where the company is located. (9) Because an employee represents the company to others. Employers look for applicants with a command of the English language.

(10) A poorly written résumé can be your worst enemy; even if you are the best person for the job.

The following paragraph has eight fragments, including the one that has been marked for you.

3. (1) When TV personality Oprah Winfrey opened a school for disadvantaged girls near Johannesburg, South Africa. She made worldwide headlines. (2) She opened the Oprah Winfrey Leadership Academy for Girls in January of 2007; after she promised former South African President Nelson Mandela to give young women a brighter future. (3) Even though this academy cost about $40 million. Winfrey believes that the money is well spent. (4) She wants to help young girls in South Africa. Because many live in poverty and cannot afford an education. (5) Many schools in South Africa are overcrowded and cannot even provide books. (6) Even if girls can afford to go to school; they face gang violence and drugs there. (7) Also, HIV and AIDS have affected more than 5 million people in South Africa. (8) Many of the victims are female. (9) If girls are educated; they are less likely to become infected. (10) Winfrey considers this academy her best achievement. Although she has received criticism from some people. (11) Unless Winfrey can first help the children of America, some say, she should not donate so much money to another country. (12) Winfrey dismisses the criticism; since she has donated millions to American charities.

BRINGING IT ALL TOGETHER:
The Complex Sentence

In this chapter, you have learned what subordinating conjunctions do, how they are used, and how they can cause problems in academic writing. Confirm your knowledge by filling in the blank spaces in the following sentences. If you need help, review the pages listed after each sentence.

✔ To form complex sentences, we use a powerful glue called a _____ conjunction. (page 303)

✔ Like coordinating conjunctions, subordinating conjunctions can show four kinds of relationships between ideas. These are _____, _____, _____, and _____. (page 304)

✔ The conjunctions *since* and *because* show an _____ outcome. The conjunctions *although* and *even though* show an _____ outcome. (page 307)

✔ In a complex sentence, the subordinating conjunction will be placed either at _____ of the sentence or in _____ of the sentence. (page 313)

✔ Punctuation rule: If a complex sentence <u>begins</u> with a subordinating conjunction, a _____ is required in the middle of the sentence. (page 313)

✔ Punctuation rule: If a complex sentence has the subordinating conjunction <u>in the middle</u> of the sentence, no _____ is required. (page 313)

✔ Punctuation rule: A misplaced _____ or a misplaced _____ can cause a subordinating clause fragment. Never use a _____ in a complex sentence. (pages 320–21, 323)

CHAPTER 13

More Complex Sentences

Before you read this chapter, it's a good idea to test your understanding of complex sentences with descriptive clauses. You may know more than you think.

WHAT DO YOU KNOW?

Circle "Yes" if each word group below is a complete, correct sentence. Circle "No" if it is incomplete. Then, explain your choice.

1. **The shelves that I built fell.**

   Yes   No

   Explanation: _____

   _____

2. **The actress who was nominated for three Emmy awards in one season.**

   Yes   No

   Explanation: _____

   _____

3. **The essay, that I worked on all night, was accidentally deleted.**

   Yes   No

   Explanation: _____

   _____

4. **The mayor, who lied on several important issues, resigned.**

   Yes   No

   Explanation: _____

   _____

5. **The algebra class which has fifty students in it and not enough seats for everyone is required.**

   Yes   No

   Explanation: _____

   _____

Descriptive clauses add more information to sentences. Also, they are another way to "glue" sentences together. You'll learn how to use them in this chapter.

NOUN + DESCRIPTIVE CLAUSE + VERB . = The students who study succeed.

NOUN , DESCRIPTIVE CLAUSE , VERB .

= The evening students, who are at school until 10 P.M., get home late.

BUILD IT: Complex Sentences with Clauses

In the previous two chapters, you learned that **coordinating conjunctions** (*and*, *but*, *or*, *so*, and so on) and **subordinating conjunctions** (*although*, *because*, *since*, *unless*, and so on) work like glue to join simple sentences. Here are some examples:

SENTENCE 1   SENTENCE 2

Our team won. We celebrated.

Joined with a Coordinating Conjunction

Our team won, so we celebrated.

Joined with a Subordinating Conjunction

Since our team won, we celebrated.

In this chapter, you will study other words that work like glue to join simple sentences. Here's an example:

SENTENCE 1   SENTENCE 2

The team won. The team celebrated.

Joined with a Pronoun

The team that won celebrated.

You can think of this as putting one sentence within another. The main idea (expressed in the **main clause**) is that the team celebrated. The **descriptive clause** tells us *which* team celebrated.

DESCRIPTIVE CLAUSE

The team that won celebrated.

MAIN CLAUSE

Power Tip

Because the clause *that won* describes the noun *team*, it is functioning as an adjective. For more on adjectives, see Chapter 10, page 234. Descriptive clauses are also known as **modifiers**.

329

Note that the descriptive clause always comes right after the word it describes (in this case, *team*). Like a jigsaw puzzle, a complex sentence formed with a descriptive clause must have all of its pieces connected in the right order to make sense.

KEY TO CHALLENGE METER	
WARMUP	
EASY	
MODERATE	
ADVANCED	
MASTERY	

Identify the difficulty level of each activity using the key above.

ACTIVITY 1
EASY

Join the following sentence pairs by making one a descriptive clause beginning with **that** and the other a main clause. Follow these steps:

- First, underline the repeated item in each simple sentence. Use this to begin your complex sentence.
- Form a descriptive clause using *that*, and put this in the middle of your new sentence.
- Underline the descriptive clause in your new sentence and double-underline the main clause.

EXAMPLE: The bird sings. The bird flew away.

The bird that sings flew away.

1. The vase fell. The vase broke.

2. The cars sped. The cars crashed.

3. The monster breathes fire. The monster terrifies me.

4. The puppy became tired. The puppy slept.

5. A marriage is based on trust. A marriage succeeds.

The word *which* is another glue word used to create descriptive clauses. When you use *which*, the descriptive clause must be set off by commas. Take a look:

SENTENCE 1   SENTENCE 2

The panda was born in captivity. The panda is now three months old.

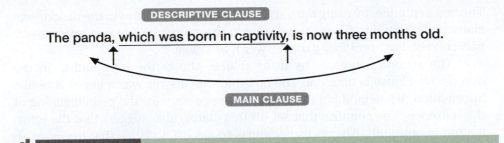

DESCRIPTIVE CLAUSE

The panda, which was born in captivity, is now three months old.

MAIN CLAUSE

ACTIVITY 2
EASY

Combine each pair of simple sentences using **which**. Remember to use commas to set off the descriptive clause.

EXAMPLE: The headphones were expensive. The headphones are not comfortable.

The headphones, which were expensive, are not comfortable.

1. The diamond ring looks real. The diamond ring is a fake.

2. The car has several tickets. The car now has a boot on it.

3. My first class meets at 8:00 A.M. My first class is English.

4. The security camera usually runs around the clock. The security camera was off last night.

5. The crime was reported. The crime will be investigated.

THAT AND *WHICH* CLAUSES

Many students have difficulty deciding when to use *that* or *which* to form a descriptive clause. However, the rule is actually quite simple:

1. Use *that* for information that is essential (absolutely necessary) for the main meaning of your sentence.
2. Use *which* for information that is optional (not absolutely necessary) for the main meaning of your sentence.

Now, look at the following two sentences, each with a descriptive clause (underlined):

The answer <u>that I gave</u> was correct.

The answer, <u>which was a guess</u>, was correct.

Terminology Tip

If the information in a descriptive clause is essential for the main meaning of the sentence, the clause is called *restrictive*. If the information is optional, the clause is called *nonrestrictive*.

The first sentence, by using *that*, shows that the information in the descriptive clause is essential to the main meaning in the sentence: Not just *any* answer was correct, but *specifically* the answer that I gave.

The second sentence, by using *which*, shows the information in the descriptive clause is optional. The fact that the answer was a guess is bonus information: It's helpful but not absolutely necessary for the main meaning of the sentence. The commas that set off this clause also suggest that the information is optional. (Always use commas to set off a clause that begins with *which*.)

ACTIVITY 3

MODERATE

Combine each pair of simple sentences to make a complex sentence.

- First, underline the repeated item in each simple sentence. Use this noun to begin your complex sentence.
- Form a descriptive clause using **that** or **which**, and put this descriptive clause in the middle of the sentence.
- If you use **which**, set off the descriptive clause with commas.
- Circle the descriptive clause in your complex sentence.

EXAMPLE: My homework was a masterpiece. My homework fell in the water.

My homework, which was a masterpiece fell in the water.

1. Markeese's computer was overloaded. Markeese's computer crashed.

2. The truck has red stripes. The truck was the one my aunt chose.

3. Pauline's vacuum cleaner was cheap and unreliable. Pauline's vacuum cleaner chewed up her rug.

4. The boat hit our boat. The boat was speeding.

5. The fireworks were loud and colorful. The fireworks made the children cheer.

ACTIVITY 4

Combine each pair of simple sentences to make a complex sentence.

- First, form a descriptive clause using **that** or **which**, and put this descriptive clause at the end of the sentence.
- If you use **which**, set off the descriptive clause with a comma.
- Circle the descriptive clause in your complex sentence.

EXAMPLE: Ricardo bought the coat. The coat was on sale.

Ricardo bought the coat (that was on sale).

1. We took the subway. The subway is cheaper than a taxi.

_____

2. Rebecca saw the movie. The movie was recommended by her best friend.

_____

_____

3. We ate the pizza. The pizza was left over from the party.

_____

4. I try to avoid spiders and snakes. Spiders and snakes have frightened me since I was a child.

_____

_____

5. I like dark chocolate. Dark chocolate is bolder in flavor than milk chocolate.

_____

_____

UNDERSTANDING GLUE WORDS USED IN CLAUSES

That and *which* are just two glue words that are used in descriptive clauses. The following chart reviews other words and their uses. Notice that in the joined sentences in the third column, the descriptive clauses come right after the words they describe.

Terminology Tip

The glue words *that*, *which*, and *who* are known as **relative pronouns**, and descriptive clauses formed with them are known as **relative clauses**.

For more practice with *that* and *which*, go to **bedfordstmartins.com/ steppingstones.**

GLUE WORD	COMMON USE	SAMPLE SENTENCE COMBINATIONS (descriptive clauses are underlined and main clauses are double-underlined)
that	**Refers to things:** The <u>house</u> that . . . ; The <u>test</u> that . . . Describes *which one* is meant	**Two sentences:** The pipe broke. The pipe was frozen. **Joined:** <u>The pipe</u> that broke <u>was frozen</u>. *Which* pipe was frozen? The one that broke.
which	**Refers to things:** The <u>bill</u>, which I received . . . ; The <u>holidays</u>, which . . . Adds details about things	**Two sentences:** The cookbook was a birthday gift. The cookbook has many color photos. **Joined:** <u>The cookbook</u>, which was a birthday gift, <u>has many color photos</u>. *What about* the cookbook? It was a birthday gift.
who	**Refers to people:** The <u>woman</u> who . . . ; The <u>coach</u> who . . . Specifies *who* is meant	**Two sentences:** The patient fainted. The patient fell down. **Joined:** <u>The patient</u> who fainted <u>fell down</u>. *Who* fell down? The patient who fainted.
where	**Refers to places:** The <u>restaurant</u> where . . . ; The <u>college</u> where . . . Describes *which place* or *where*	**Two sentences:** We danced at the club. The club closed down. **Joined:** <u>The club</u> where we danced <u>closed down</u>. *Which* club closed down? The one where we danced.
when	**Refers to time:** The <u>moment</u> when . . . ; The <u>season</u> when . . . Describes a particular time/which time	**Two sentences:** I graduated in the summer. That summer was fantastic. **Joined:** <u>The summer</u> when I graduated <u>was fantastic</u>. *Which* summer was fantastic? The one when I graduated.

PLACING CLAUSES IN SENTENCES

Descriptive clauses can appear in the middle or at the end of a sentence. The important thing is that they appear <u>directly after</u> the word they describe.

Take a look at the following examples. The descriptive clause appears first in the middle and then at the end of the sentence. The descriptive clause is underlined. An arrow indicates the word being described.

DESCRIPTIVE CLAUSE IN THE MIDDLE   The pipe <u>that broke</u> was frozen.

DESCRIPTIVE CLAUSE AT THE END   We cannot fix the pipe <u>that broke</u>.

DESCRIPTIVE CLAUSE IN THE MIDDLE	Monopoly, <u>which I hate</u>, is my in-laws' favorite game.
DESCRIPTIVE CLAUSE AT THE END	My in-laws like to play Monopoly, <u>which I hate</u>.
DESCRIPTIVE CLAUSE IN THE MIDDLE	The club <u>where we danced</u> closed down.
DESCRIPTIVE CLAUSE AT THE END	I recommended the club <u>where we danced</u>.

Power Tip
Notice that when a *nonrestrictive* clause is in the middle of a sentence, commas are used both <u>before</u> and <u>after</u> it. However, when a *nonrestrictive* clause is at the end of a sentence, we need <u>only one</u> comma: the one <u>before</u> the clause.

WHO CLAUSES

The word *who* is used to form descriptive clauses about people. Take a look:

SENTENCE 1   SENTENCE 2

The woman lost her job. The woman filed for unemployment.

DESCRIPTIVE CLAUSE

The woman <u>who lost her job</u> filed for unemployment.

ACTIVITY 5
EASY

Combine each of the following pairs of simple sentences using **who**. No commas are needed.

EXAMPLE: The graffiti artist lived quietly. The graffiti artist worked at night.

The graffiti artist who lived quietly worked at night.

1. The girl saw a mouse. The girl screamed.

2. The astronaut walked on the moon. The astronaut is from Ohio.

3. The pie eater ate the most pies. The pie eater threw up.

4. The waiter dropped a tray of drinks. The waiter was fired.

5. The student studied all night. The student received the highest score.

Just like the words *that* and *which*, the glue word *who* can introduce essential or optional information in a sentence. Take a look:

> DESCRIPTIVE CLAUSE
>
> The runner who won the marathon was from Ethiopia.

> DESCRIPTIVE CLAUSE
>
> The runner, who claimed to be steroid-free, won the marathon.

Even though both of these descriptive clauses begin with *who*, the second one is set off by commas. This shows that the information in the clause is optional; it is not absolutely necessary for the main meaning of the sentence.

However, in the first sentence, the information in the clause is essential for the main meaning: Not just *any* runner was from Ethiopia but *specifically* the runner who won the marathon.

ACTIVITY 6

MODERATE

Combine each pair of simple sentences to make a complex sentence.

- First, underline the repeated item in each simple sentence. Use this noun to begin your complex sentence.
- Form a descriptive clause using **who**, and put this clause in the middle of the sentence.
- If the information in the descriptive clause is essential, do not use commas. If the information in the descriptive clause is optional, set off the descriptive clause with commas.
- Circle the descriptive clause in your complex sentence.

EXAMPLE: The fireman retired. The fireman received a lifetime achievement award.
The fireman who retired received a lifetime achievement award.

1. Yolanda quit. Yolanda was the best player on our team.

2. The child painted the classroom walls. The child was sent home.

3. Babies are not shown affection. Babies can grow up with emotional problems.

4. Milo was the most popular student in high school. Milo became the mayor of our town.

5. Billy is terrified of clowns and performing animals. Billy refuses to go to the circus.

_____

_____

ACTIVITY 7

MODERATE

Combine each pair of simple sentences to make a complex sentence.

- Turn the second sentence into a descriptive clause beginning with **who**, and put it <u>at the end</u> of your complex sentence.
- If the information in the descriptive clause is essential, do not use a comma. If the information in the descriptive clause is optional, set off the descriptive clause with a comma.
- Circle the descriptive clause.

EXAMPLE: I made the cake for John. John is the birthday boy.

I made the cake for John, (who is the birthday boy).

1. I will plan the party for Taki. Taki is my best friend.

_____

2. We will not put peanuts in the cookies for Betty. Betty is allergic to nuts.

_____

3. I want to pay the kid. The kid shoveled our driveway after the snowstorm.

_____

4. The fraud charges will be a blow to the president. The president has already been accused of misusing funds.

_____

_____

5. The detective gave the crime-scene information to the officer. The officer was in charge of investigating the murder.

_____

_____

Power Tip

Remember that when *who* is followed by a noun or another pronoun, it usually becomes *whom*. Take a look: *Hillary Clinton, <u>whom my mother</u> admires, was first lady from 1993 to 2001.* For more practice with *who* and *whom*, go to **bedfordstmartins.com/ steppingstones**.

WHEN AND *WHERE* CLAUSES

The word *when* is used to form descriptive clauses about time (hours, days, dates, and so on). The word *where* is used to form descriptive clauses about places. In the following examples, the noun that appears in both simple sentences has been underlined. This noun or pronoun then begins the complex sentence, and it is followed immediately by *when* or *where*.

I got fired on a <u>Friday</u>. That <u>Friday</u> was a nightmare.

DESCRIPTIVE CLAUSE

The Friday <u>when I got fired</u> was a nightmare.

The soldiers fell on <u>the battlefield</u>. <u>The battlefield</u> is now a memorial park.

DESCRIPTIVE CLAUSE

The battlefield <u>where the soldiers fell</u> is now a memorial park.

ACTIVITY 8
MODERATE

Combine each pair of sentences using **when** or **where**. No commas are needed. (*Hint:* First, underline the noun that appears in both simple sentences. Then, begin your complex sentence with this noun followed by **when** or **where**.)

EXAMPLE: I eat lunch in this <u>park</u> every day. The <u>park</u> is full of oak trees.

The park where I eat my lunch every day is full of oak trees.

1. I work in the restaurant. The restaurant has roaches.

   _____

2. We met on the day. The day was the Fourth of July.

   _____

3. Denise works out at the gym. The gym was closed after the earthquake.

   _____

4. You both arrived at the exact time. The exact time escapes my memory.

   _____

5. My father parks in the garage. The garage has a security guard.

   _____

Descriptive clauses formed with *where* and *when* can also contain essential or optional information. Again, punctuation helps us understand which ideas are necessary to the main meaning of the sentence and which ideas are optional. Take a look:

DESCRIPTIVE CLAUSE

My father eats at the restaurant <u>where my mother works</u>.

DESCRIPTIVE CLAUSE

I'll never forget the Saturday night <u>when you proposed to me</u>.

In these sentences, there are **no commas**, so we know that the information contained in the descriptive clauses is essential to understand the main meaning of the sentence. In the first sentence, the father doesn't eat at just *any* restaurant; he eats *specifically* at the restaurant where the mother works. In the second sentence, it's not just *any* Saturday night that the writer will never forget but *specifically* the Saturday night when the writer was proposed to.

Now, look at these sentences:

> **DESCRIPTIVE CLAUSE**
>
> The restaurant, <u>where people sit for hours,</u> never has an empty table.

> **DESCRIPTIVE CLAUSE**
>
> On Saturday nights, <u>when most of my friends go out,</u> I study.

In these sentences, the writer has set off the descriptive clauses **with commas**, telling us that the information in these clauses is optional. In the first sentence, the fact that people sit in the restaurant for hours is interesting but not essential to the writer's main point: that the restaurant is always full. In the second sentence, the fact that most of the writer's friends go out on Saturday night is interesting but not essential to the writer's main point: that she studies on Saturday nights.

ACTIVITY 9

MODERATE

Combine each pair of simple sentences to make a complex sentence.

- Turn the second sentence into a descriptive clause beginning with **where** or **when**, and put it in the middle or at the end of your complex sentence.
- If the information in the descriptive clause is essential, do not use commas. If the information in the descriptive clause is optional, set off the descriptive clause with commas.
- Circle the descriptive clause.

EXAMPLE: The library has Internet access. We study at the library.

The library ⟨where we study⟩ has Internet access.

1. Nauset Beach is home to Nauset Lighthouse. My sister was married on Nauset Beach.

2. Sarah arrived at that instant. I opened the door at that instant.

3. On Saturdays, Jack works long hours. Many people relax on Saturdays.

4. We rented an apartment on Bridge Street. You live on Bridge Street.

5. Dan plays guitar at the bar. His brother works at the bar.

BUILD IT: Longer Sentences with Clauses

We started this chapter by looking at complex sentences with few words. Let's go back to an earlier example:

TWO SENTENCES	The team won. The team celebrated.
JOINED WITH A DESCRIPTIVE CLAUSE	The team <u>that won</u> celebrated.

KEY TO BUILDING BLOCKS

FOUNDATION WORDS

NOUNS

VERBS

DESCRIPTIVE WORDS

ADJECTIVES

ADVERBS

CONNECTING WORDS

PREPOSITIONS

CONJUNCTIONS

We can make complex sentences more informative by adding descriptive words (adjectives and adverbs) and prepositional phrases to the different parts of the sentence.

The team	that won	celebrated.
WHICH TEAM?	**HOW DID IT WIN?**	**HOW DID IT CELEBRATE?**
The varsity football team	narrowly by one point	late into the night.

Now, let's put the pieces of the puzzle together:

The varsity football team that won narrowly by one point celebrated late into the night.

For a review of adjectives and adverbs, see Chapter 10, page 234. For more on prepositions and prepositional phrases, see Chapter 10, page 240.

ACTIVITY 10: Teamwork

ADVANCED

Working in a group of three students, expand each of the sentences below, following these steps:

- Each student should take one part of the sentence.
- Working individually, each student should think of descriptive words and/or a prepositional phrase to add to that part of the sentence.
- Starting at the beginning of the sentence, each student should read his or her part aloud, including the added words.
- When everyone has finished, each student should write down the complete sentence, being sure to include any necessary commas.

EXAMPLE: The car + that crashed + exploded.

The bright red sports car that crashed violently into a tree exploded into a ball of flames.

1. The night + when we danced + is a happy memory.

_____

_____

2. The building + where we work + was evacuated.

_____

_____

3. The moon + that rose + dazzled us.

_____

_____

4. Adam, + who exercises, + is healthy.

_____

_____

5. Danice + will make fish and chips, + which she cooked for last year's picnic.

_____

_____

_____

ACTIVITY 11: Teamwork

ADVANCED

Combine each pair of sentences into one complex sentence. If helpful, follow these steps:

- First, underline the phrase that is repeated in both sentences.
- Next, connect the appropriate glue word (*that*, *which*, *who*, *where*, *when*) to the phrase you have underlined.
- Use this phrase and glue word to turn one of the sentences into a descriptive clause.
- Join the descriptive clause with the other sentence.

EXAMPLE: The publishers of the literary magazine awarded the poetry prize to a young author. The young author had never been published before, other than a short poem in a local newspaper.

The publishers of the literary magazine awarded the poetry prize

to a young author who had never been published before, other

than a short poem in a local newspaper.

1. The odd-looking man ran into a waiting car and left the scene. The odd-looking man left the mysterious little package on our front porch.

_____

_____

2. The children's spring play left the audience sweaty, thirsty, and exhausted. The children's spring play lasted for three long hours in a hot gym with no air-conditioning.

_____

_____

CONTINUED >

3. The angry note made me hop up and down with fury. My nosy neighbor left the angry note on my car windshield in the morning.

_____

_____

4. The long summer was full of thrilling discoveries about flowering plants, towering trees, and creepy bugs. I went to science camp in the long summer.

_____

_____

5. Detective Daniels ducked into the dark, smoke-filled club. The famous actress was last seen at the dark, smoke-filled club before she disappeared.

_____

_____

BUILDING COMPLEX SENTENCES IN WHOLE PARAGRAPHS

ACTIVITY 12: Mastery Test or Teamwork

In the following paragraph, form eight complex sentences, using *that*, *which*, *who*, *when*, or *where*. First, identify each pair or group of sentences that can be joined, and then decide which word will join the sentences most effectively. The first one has already been done for you.

According to the *Atlantic Monthly* magazine, a number of individuals stand out as the most important figures in American history. The magazine's list includes one hundred people. The people have made significant contributions to humanity. Number one on the list is Abraham Lincoln. He abolished slavery in America in 1863. Martin Luther King Jr. also appears on the list for bringing the dream of racial equality closer to reality. Alexander Graham Bell invented the telephone. The telephone expanded the possibilities of communication. Another important inventor on the list is Henry Ford. Ford's invention was a 26-horsepower automobile. He tested the automobile himself by racing it. Of course, the genius Albert Einstein is on the list. Einstein grew up in Europe. Europe is where he made his early scientific breakthroughs.

For more practice with *that*, *which*, *who*, *when*, and *where*, go to **bedfordstmartins.com/ steppingstones**.

However, the Nazi threat in the 1930s required Einstein to emigrate to the United States. In the United States, he quickly became a celebrity. Others made the list. Women such as birth-control advocate Margaret Sanger, and writers such as Mark Twain and Walt Whitman. In more modern times, Bill Gates contributed to the invention of the computer. The computer transformed global connections and accelerated mathematical calculations. It is astounding to consider what a powerful effect these individuals have had on American culture.

FIX IT: Solving Problems in Complex Sentences with Clauses

In this section, you will learn how to find and fix fragments in complex sentences that contain descriptive clauses. Remember from earlier chapters that fragments are word groups that are missing a subject or verb or that do not express a complete thought.

FIXING FRAGMENTS

By now, you know that the following sentence is complete and correct:

> **SUBJECT** **VERB**
> The phone rang.

Now, decide whether the following example is a complete, correct sentence:

> The phone that rang.

The answer is *no.* By adding *that,* we have created a **descriptive clause**: it is part of a sentence, but it can't stand alone as a sentence. In other words, it is a **fragment**.

To fix this fragment, we must complete the thought by adding a verb to the main clause:

> **MISSING VERB**
> The phone [that rang]

In other words, we must answer the question, *What happened with the phone that rang?* Take a look:

> The phone [that rang] interrupted the teacher.

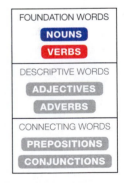

FOUNDATION WORDS
NOUNS
VERBS

DESCRIPTIVE WORDS
ADJECTIVES
ADVERBS

CONNECTING WORDS
PREPOSITIONS
CONJUNCTIONS

Power Tip
You might be wondering why this sentence needs another verb in addition to *rang.* The reason is that *rang* is no longer the main verb in the sentence. The words *that rang* function as an adjective describing the phone: *What phone? The phone that rang.*

To check whether you have successfully completed the complex sentence, cover the descriptive clause and read the main clause:

> The phone [   ] interrupted the teacher.

This makes sense. The main clause has been completed successfully.

Notice that you cannot correct a descriptive clause fragment by adding descriptive words:

> The phone [that rang] repeatedly.

To see why, remove the descriptive clause and read the main clause:

> The phone [   ] repeatedly.

This does not make sense. The word *repeatedly* describes how the phone *rang*, so it belongs in the descriptive clause:

> The phone [that rang repeatedly] _____.

To complete this sentence, add a verb to the main clause:

> The phone [that rang repeatedly] interrupted the teacher.

Also, you cannot complete a descriptive clause fragment with a prepositional phrase:

> The phone [that rang] during the lecture.

To see why, remove the descriptive clause and read the main clause:

> The phone [   ] during the lecture.

This does not make sense. The prepositional phrase *during the lecture* describes when the phone *rang*, so it belongs in the descriptive clause:

> The phone [that rang during the lecture] _____.

To complete this sentence, add a verb to the main clause:

> The phone [that rang during the lecture] interrupted the teacher.

ACTIVITY 13
EASY

For each item below, do the following:

- First, put brackets around the descriptive clause.
- Then, decide whether the word group is a complete sentence or a fragment.
- If the word group is a complete sentence, write **correct** on the line provided.

- If the word group is a fragment, rewrite it as a complete, correct sentence on the line provided.

EXAMPLE: The majorette [who marched in the Fourth of July parade.]

The majorette who marched in the Fourth of July parade dropped
her baton.

1. The hiker who was trapped under the boulder.

   _____

2. Cape Cod, where I first met my husband.

   _____

3. The concert ticket that I purchased online is a fake.

   _____

4. Florence, who lives in the big yellow house.

   _____

5. The summer when we lived in the cabin.

   _____

6. Nelson, which is my father's name.

   _____

7. The fast-food restaurant where we worked has been closed by the health department.

   _____

   _____

Remember that the *length* of a word group does not determine whether it is a complete and correct sentence. When descriptive clause fragments are long, they can be tricky to recognize. Take a look:

> The National Rifle Association headquarters, [where the congressman gave his famous speech on the right to bear arms].

If we remove the descriptive clause, we can see that the word group that is left is not a complete sentence:

> The National Rifle Association headquarters, [   ].

Now, let's form a complete sentence by adding a verb and other words to complete the thought:

> The National Rifle Association headquarters, [where the congressman gave his famous speech on the right to bear arms], is hosting a rally in support of the Second Amendment.

ACTIVITY 14

For each item below, do the following:

- First, put brackets around the descriptive clause.
- Then, decide whether the word group is a complete sentence or a fragment.
- If the word group is a complete sentence, write **correct** on the line provided.
- If the word group is a fragment, rewrite it as a complete, correct sentence on the line provided.

EXAMPLE: The new president of the college, [whom the board of trustees approved in a unanimous vote on Tuesday,] will be sworn into office on Friday. _correct_

1. The fragile old dinosaur skeleton, which the researchers found in a narrow cave in the desert.

2. The cold and rainy week when we took our family vacation at the beach.

3. For lunch, my aunt, who caught ten pounds of fresh trout in the stream.

4. Talented poet and essayist Chris Santos, whom you met at the college's literary awards dinner in May.

5. The empty riverbed, where high school students used to race cars dangerously on Saturday nights.

6. After digging in the yard for several hours, my oldest son discovered a small metal box that someone had buried under a rosebush on the side of the house.

Often, writers create descriptive clause fragments accidentally, by putting a period where it does not belong. Take a look:

DESCRIPTIVE CLAUSE FRAGMENT

INCORRECT   My father and I cleaned out the garage. <u>Where we found a squirrel's nest with two baby squirrels in it.</u>

When you find a descriptive clause fragment in your writing, usually the easiest way to fix it is to join it to another sentence—either the sentence that comes before it or the sentence that comes after it.

CORRECT   My father and I cleaned out the garage, where we found a squirrel's nest with two baby squirrels in it.

Sometimes, when you connect the fragment to another sentence, you may have to remove an extra word. For example:

DESCRIPTIVE CLAUSE FRAGMENT

INCORRECT   <u>The stadium where we played our final game.</u> It had bad lighting and old Astroturf.

When joining this fragment to the sentence that follows, we must remove the extra subject *it*. Take a look:

CORRECT   The stadium where we played our final game had bad lighting and old Astroturf.

ACTIVITY 15

ADVANCED

For each item below, do the following:

- First, mark an **F** above the fragment.
- Then, correct the fragment by connecting it to a simple sentence. Remember to remove the period or replace the period with a comma. Also, you may need to remove an extra word.
- Leave the other simple sentence alone.

EXAMPLE: The paint that we bought. It was the wrong kind. We needed a weather-resistant paint.

The paint that we bought was the wrong kind. We needed

a weather-resistant paint.

1. I like to swim. When it's warm outside. The pool is the perfect temperature.

   _____

   _____

2. The hall where we met to plan the party. It had a leaky roof. Therefore, we met at my house.

   _____

   _____

CONTINUED >

For more practice correcting fragments in complex sentences, go to **bedfordstmartins.com/ steppingstones**.

3. Dan likes stamps. Which he has collected since he was a child. He gets stamps for every birthday.

_____

_____

_____

4. The people who live next door. They have loud parties every Friday night. We have had to call the police.

_____

_____

_____

5. My daughter and I shop at Marconi's. Where we find many good bargains. Last week, we both bought shoes there.

_____

_____

_____

Power Tip

In descriptive clauses, the glue words are *that, which, where, when,* and *who.*

Sometimes, you will not be able to fix a descriptive clause fragment by joining it to another sentence. Take a look:

> **DESCRIPTIVE CLAUSE FRAGMENT**
>
> Our coach asked for volunteers to pick up lunch. <u>Ernie, who was the first to volunteer.</u> However, the coach had another job for him.

If we try to connect this descriptive clause fragment to one of the other sentences, the results will not make sense. In this case, there are two other methods for correcting the fragment. First, we could simply delete the glue word *who:*

> **CORRECT SIMPLE SENTENCE**
>
> Our coach asked for volunteers to pick up lunch. <u>Ernie was the first to volunteer.</u> However, the coach had another job for him.

The second method is to add more information to the fragment to make it a complete, correct sentence:

> Our coach asked for volunteers to pick up lunch. Ernie, who was the first to volunteer, <u>was not chosen.</u> The coach had another job for him.
>
> **ADDED INFORMATION**

ACTIVITY 16: Teamwork

ADVANCED

In each item below, do the following:

- First, mark an **F** above the fragment.

- Then, correct the fragment by (1) deleting the glue word or (2) adding more information to make the fragment a complete sentence.
- Leave the other simple sentence(s) alone.

EXAMPLE: For my physical education requirement, I chose tae kwon do. Martial arts, which build strength and discipline. Also, my brother has enjoyed taking karate.

For my physical education requirement, I chose tae kwon do.

Martial arts build strength and discipline. Also, my brother has

enjoyed taking karate.

1. In September, we pick apples at my uncle's farm. The apples that fall to the ground. We pick them up and save them for applesauce.

_____

_____

_____

2. Miklos's debt, which is growing and growing. He plans to see a credit counselor. Also, he has gotten rid of two of his credit cards.

_____

_____

_____

3. The media are blamed for many wrongs. My friend Portia, who writes for our local paper. She is upset by people's criticism.

_____

_____

_____

4. When we moved to our new apartment. The mechanic across the street worked on cars until midnight. The children down the street played loudly throughout the day.

_____

_____

_____

5. My mother goes jogging every morning before work. Exercise that gets her blood flowing. She also lifts weights at the gym.

_____

_____

_____

CONTINUED >

6. Our math professor is hard to understand. Some students who are struggling in the class. They have decided to hire a tutor. This assistance should improve their grades.

_____

_____

_____

7. Where the stolen car was hidden. Branches had been placed on top of it. A tarp covered the side closest to the street. I called the police.

_____

_____

_____

8. We found many talented people to perform at the benefit concert. Sam, who sings in his church choir every Sunday. Madeleine will play the piano. Her sister Maria will dance to a song that she composed herself.

_____

_____

_____

_____

9. Cucumbers, which do not agree with me. They hurt my stomach and make me burp. I do not put them in salads. Also, I ask waiters to leave them out of my meals.

_____

_____

_____

10. The party was a disaster. First, the host split his pants up the seam. Then, a potted plant that fell from a shelf. Finally, the cake collapsed in the oven.

_____

_____

_____

FIXING FRAGMENTS IN WHOLE PARAGRAPHS

The following activity will give you practice with recognizing and fixing fragments in whole paragraphs—a valuable skill for improving your own writing.

ACTIVITY 17: Mastery Test or Teamwork

MASTERY

Read each of the following paragraphs carefully, looking for fragments. Then, rewrite each error to fix the problem, using one of the following methods:

- Connect the fragment to another sentence.
- Delete the glue word.
- Add more information to make the fragment a complete sentence.
- If the revised sentences require commas, be sure to include them.

The first item in each paragraph has been edited for you.

Power Tip
In descriptive clauses, the glue words are *that*, *which*, *where*, *when*, and *who*.

The following paragraph has six fragments (including the first one that has been edited for you).

1. (1) The number of Americans who have been asked to make sacrifices in the wars in Iraq and Afghanistan / (2) ~~It~~ has been relatively small. (3) Soldiers and their families have carried the full burden. (4) Which many people believe to be unfair. (5) In other wars, however, when more Americans were asked to contribute. (6) For example, during World War II, citizens were asked to limit their use of gasoline, sugar, certain cloth, and other materials. (7) Which helped the government supply troops and the defense industry with necessary goods. (8) Also, the "Victory Gardens" that many private citizens grew. (9) They accounted for about 40 percent of vegetables consumed during the war. (10) Most significant, a draft required all eligible men to register for military service. (11) As a result, not just thousands but millions of Americans who faced the possibility of losing a loved one — or their own life.

The following paragraph has six fragments (including the first one that has been edited for you).

2. (1) People who have a positive, optimistic outlook on life / (2) ~~They~~ are likely to be healthier than negative people, researchers report. (3) Studies have found that optimistic people are less likely to get infectious diseases, heart disease, and other illnesses than people with a negative outlook. (4) One study, which was done among college students. (5) It found that

CONTINUED >

positive students reported having more energy and fewer minor illnesses than negative students. (6) When researchers looked for the reasons for the better health of positive people. (7) They found a few possible answers. (8) First, positive people tend to be more connected to others. (9) Which makes it easier for them to get the help and support that they need. (10) Also, negative emotions that can cause high blood pressure, harm the immune system, and even raise blood sugar. (11) In other words, negative emotions may wear down the body over time. (12) Regardless of the reason for the link between optimism and health, it is a good idea to adopt a positive attitude toward even bad events. (13) That come our way.

The following paragraph has eight fragments (including the first one that has been edited for you).

3. (1) Most of us know people/ (2) ~~Who~~ *who* like to collect certain objects, like dolls, baseball cards, or stamps. (3) However, some people feel compelled to fill their homes with things. (4) That many others would consider worthless — even garbage. (5) These people, who are known as *hoarders*. (6) Psychologists are learning more about what causes hoarding. (7) It may be a response to stress or isolation from others. (8) It may also occur. (9) When people become unusually attached to objects. (10) Additionally, some hoarding may result from a chemical imbalance in the brain. (11) Whatever the cause, hoarding is a serious problem. (12) That can cause difficulties in the lives of sufferers and their families. (13) For example, some hoarders have lost important papers or other valuable possessions. (14) Others have even been buried under piles of boxes. (15) That were stacked dangerously high. (16) Mental health professionals who can help hoarders with their problem. (17) For example, these professionals can recommend psychotherapy. (18) Which can help hoarders explore and change their behavior. (19) Also, doctors can prescribe helpful medications, such as antidepressants.

MISPLACED MODIFIERS

As you already know, a descriptive clause adds information to a sentence. Whether this information is essential or optional, it changes, or "modifies," the meaning of the main clause. For example, look at the following simple sentence:

My father married a woman.

Now, when we add a descriptive clause to this sentence, it modifies the meaning of the main clause:

DESCRIPTIVE CLAUSE

My father married a woman <u>who was pregnant</u>.

In this sentence, the descriptive clause modifies *woman*. However, suppose that you were writing quickly and put the modifier in the wrong place:

My father <u>who was pregnant</u> married a woman.

In this funny example, the descriptive clause modifies *father*. Clearly, the writer did not want to say that his father was pregnant. Instead, the descriptive clause must be placed right next to the item it is modifying (in other words, right after *woman*).

If you put a descriptive clause in the wrong place, you can end up with a **misplaced modifier** and possibly a very strange sentence.

ACTIVITY 18: Teamwork

MODERATE

For each sentence below, do the following:

- First, put brackets around the descriptive clause.
- Next, decide where the descriptive clause needs to be placed.
- Then, rewrite the sentence with the descriptive clause in the correct place.

If the sentence requires commas, be sure to include them.

EXAMPLE: The scout lost his way [who led the hike.]

The scout who led the hike lost his way.

1. The lion roared that we saw at the zoo.

2. In spring, where we live the farm is full of baby animals.

3. Valerie takes care of five horses whom you met at my wedding.

4. The eggs were served on a silver dish that I ate for breakfast.

CONTINUED >

For more practice with fixing fragments and misplaced modifiers, go to **bedfordstmartins.com/ steppingstones.**

Power Tip
You will learn about other types of misplaced modifiers in Chapter 14.

5. The restaurant is next to a jail where we had our first date.

_____

6. Boris, which is Anna's favorite treat, hates rice pudding.

_____

7. The thief was captured by police who stole the jewels.

_____

8. The field was full of big, ripe pumpkins where the spaceship landed.

_____

9. The answer disappointed the audience, which took almost ten minutes.

_____

10. The deep and comfortable bathtub is next to a large window, which is my favorite place to relax, with a view of the park.

_____

_____

BRINGING IT ALL TOGETHER:
More Complex Sentences

In this chapter, you have learned what descriptive clauses are, how they are used, and how they can cause problems in academic writing. Confirm your knowledge by filling in the blank spaces in the following sentences. If you need help, review the pages listed after each sentence.

✔ To form complex sentences with descriptive clauses, we can use five glue words. They are _____, _____, _____, _____, and _____. (page 334)

✔ Descriptive clauses can be placed both in _____ of a sentence and at _____ of a sentence. (page 334)

✔ A descriptive clause that is *not* set off by commas contains information that is _____ to the main meaning of the sentence. (page 336)

✔ A descriptive clause that *is* set off by commas contains information that is _____ for the main meaning of the sentence. (page 336)

✔ When a descriptive clause begins with the word _____, it must always be set off by commas. (page 332)

✔ A descriptive clause by itself does not express a complete thought, so it cannot be a _____. (page 343)

✔ A descriptive clause that is used as a complete sentence is a _____, a major grammatical error. (page 343)

✔ To correct a descriptive clause fragment, you must add a _____ to complete the main clause. (page 343)

✔ In whole paragraphs, descriptive clause fragments are sometimes caused by putting a _____ where it does not belong. (page 347)

✔ In whole paragraphs, there are three ways to correct a descriptive clause fragment. These ways are: 1) _____, 2) _____, and 3) _____. (pages 347–48)

✔ If you put a descriptive clause in the wrong place, you can end up with a _____ and possibly a very strange sentence. (page 353)

CHAPTER 14

Sentences with Modifiers

Before you read this chapter, it's a good idea to test your understanding of sentences formed with modifying phrases. You may know more than you think.

WHAT DO YOU KNOW?

Circle "Yes" if each word group below is a complete, correct sentence. Circle "No" if it is incomplete. Then, explain your choice.

1. **Running, I tripped.**

   Yes   No

   Explanation: _____

2. **Dialing the number, my cell phone wouldn't work.**

   Yes   No

   Explanation: _____
   _____

3. **To survive, they ate bugs.**

   Yes   No

   Explanation: _____

4. **To win in her final event, the balance beam required all her concentration.**

   Yes   No

   Explanation: _____
   _____

5. **Trained to climb Mount Everest, the last half mile almost defeated the experienced climber.**

   Yes   No

   Explanation: _____
   _____

Modifying words and phrases offer other ways to add information to different sentence parts. You'll learn how to use them in this chapter.

[MODIFYING PHRASE] **,** [NOUN] **+** [VERB] **. = Prepared for the exam, I succeeded.**

[NOUN] **,** [MODIFYING PHRASE] **,** [VERB] **.**

= The students, studying together for long hours, succeeded.

BUILD IT: Sentences with Modifiers

In Chapters 11 through 13, you learned how to combine simple sentences into compound or complex sentences. In this chapter, you will learn a new and useful method of combining simple sentences. Let's begin with a brief review.

[SIMPLE SENTENCE 1]   [SIMPLE SENTENCE 2]

My dog howls at the moon. He wakes up all the neighbors.

You already know that these two simple sentences can be combined to form a **compound** sentence. Take a look:

My dog howls at the moon, <u>and</u> he wakes up all the neighbors.

My dog howls at the moon<u>; as a result,</u> he wakes up all the neighbors.

Or, you can combine the two simple sentences to make a **complex** sentence:

<u>When</u> my dog howls at the moon, he wakes up all the neighbors.

My dog, <u>who howls at the moon,</u> wakes up all the neighbors.

As you have learned, both compound and complex sentences always have two separate subjects and two separate verbs. However, if we do not want to repeat a subject, we can combine the two simple sentences by turning one of them into a **modifying phrase**.

[MODIFYING PHRASE]   [SIMPLE SENTENCE]

<u>Howling at the moon,</u> my dog wakes up all the neighbors.

[SUBJECT BEING DESCRIBED]

When you begin a sentence with a phrase, the phrase works like a coat hanger: You will "hang" the rest of your sentence on it.

Terminology Tip
A **phrase** is a word group that does not have both a subject and a verb. *Howling at the moon* is a phrase because it is missing a subject — we don't know who or what is howling at the moon.

In the first part of this chapter, you will learn to begin sentences with three types of modifying phrases:

- an *-ing* phrase (*present participle* phrase)
- a *to* phrase (*infinitive* phrase)
- an *-ed* phrase (*past participle* phrase)

These phrases all work in the same basic way, but their meanings vary somewhat. Later in this chapter, you will learn how to use *-ing*, *to*, and *-ed* phrases in the middle or at the end of sentences.

PLACING MODIFYING PHRASES AT THE BEGINNING OF A SENTENCE

Beginning a sentence with a modifying phrase is a good way to add variety to your writing, especially if a lot of your sentences start with subjects and verbs.

Read these two examples aloud. Can you hear a difference between them?

The criminal entered the courtroom. He smiled at the jury.

Entering the courtroom, the criminal smiled at the jury.

The first example sounds almost robot-like. The second example sounds more musical. The following sections of this chapter will help you make your writing more "musical" by showing you how to begin sentences with different modifying phrases.

Beginning a Sentence with an *-ing* Phrase

Verbs ending in *-ing* (*dancing, sleeping, driving,* and so on) are typically used for one action that is **ongoing** at the same time as another. In the following sentence, the *-ing* verb (*Running*) leads into or sets up the second action, so the *-ing* verb comes first, followed by the second action (*tripped*) that occurs while the first action is taking place.

Running for the bus, Dominic tripped on a garden hose.

If you wish to combine two simple sentences by turning one of the sentences into an *-ing* phrase, begin by identifying the verb in each simple sentence:

Dominic ran for the bus. He tripped on a garden hose.

Next, use the base form of the first verb (*run* in this case) and add *-ing* to it. Begin your sentence with the *-ing* phrase:

Running for the bus . . .

Power Tip
Some writers prefer to add the word *while* to the beginning of an *-ing* phrase. For example: *While running for the bus, Dominic tripped on a garden hose.*

Now, add a comma and "hang" the rest of your sentence onto the phrase:

Running for the bus, Dominic tripped on a garden hose.

The second part of the sentence begins with the subject *Dominic* instead of *he* because *Dominic* doesn't appear in the first part of the sentence, and it is a more specific name for the subject.

	KEY TO CHALLENGE METER
WARMUP	
EASY	
MODERATE	
ADVANCED	
MASTERY	

Identify the difficulty level of each activity using the key above.

ACTIVITY 1
WARMUP

Complete each sentence below by following these steps:

- Add a verb to the subject.
- Add any additional information to complete the thought.

EXAMPLE: Sliding into second base, Jason *twisted his ankle* .

1. Opening the door to his apartment, Dewayne _____
   _____ .

2. Seeing a strange light in the sky, the farmer _____ .

3. Making lasagna for dinner, Stephen _____ .

4. Jogging around the block, Jolina _____ .

5. Chasing the neighbor's cat, my dog _____ .

ACTIVITY 2
EASY

Combine each pair of simple sentences by turning the first sentence into an *-ing* phrase. Follow these steps:

- Underline the verb in each simple sentence.
- Put the first verb in the *-ing* form and use it to write an *-ing* phrase that will begin your new sentence.
- Add a comma after the phrase.
- Hang the rest of your sentence onto the phrase. (You may need to change the subject of the second part of the sentence.)

EXAMPLE: Nicole <u>noticed</u> a problem. She <u>sprung</u> into action.

Noticing a problem, Nicole sprung into action.

1. Nicole heard screeching tires. She looked out her window.

   _____

2. She saw a badly damaged car in the ditch. She called 911.

   _____

3. Nicole wanted to help. She grabbed her first aid kit.

   _____

CONTINUED >

For more practice with using modifiers, go to **bedfordstmartins.com/ steppingstones.**

4. Nicole arrived at the crash site. She calmed the injured driver.

_____

5. The driver trembled with fear. He thanked Nicole for her help.

_____

ACTIVITY 3: Teamwork

MODERATE

For each of the following items, use the two verbs and subject provided to write a sentence that begins with an -*ing* phrase. Follow these steps:

- Put the first verb in the -*ing* form and use it to begin your sentence with a phrase.
- Add a comma after the phrase.
- Use the subject and the second verb to complete the thought. (You may put the second verb in the past, present, or future tense.)

Power Tip
For advice on forming various verb tenses, see Chapter 15.

EXAMPLE:

First verb: sneak   Subject: Laura   Second verb: surprise

Sneaking into the house, Laura surprised her roommates.

1. **First verb:** drive   **Subject:** Miguel   **Second verb:** listen

_____

2. **First verb:** wash   **Subject:** Blake   **Second verb:** cut

_____

3. **First verb:** investigate **Subject:** detective **Second verb:** question

_____

4. **First verb:** sip   **Subject:** Melinda   **Second verb:** burn

_____

5. **First verb:** throw   **Subject:** pitcher   **Second verb:** hurt

_____

Beginning a Sentence with a *to* Phrase

Terminology Tip
A verb that is written in the *to* form is called an **infinitive**. The *to* in an infinitive should not be confused with the preposition *to*, which typically shows direction: *I went to the store.*

When a verb is written in the *to* form (*to dance, to sleep, to drive,* and so on), it often shows a **desired action** or goal. In such cases, you will find a desired action or goal (the *to* phrase) in the first part of the sentence and a necessary action in the second part of the sentence:

DESIRED ACTION   ACTION THAT MUST BE TAKEN

To get to work on time, I catch the six o'clock train.

When you begin sentences like these with a *to* phrase, it is the same as beginning the sentence with *In order to* . . . Take a look:

> To get to work on time, I catch the six o'clock train.

> <u>In order to</u> get to work on time, I catch the six o'clock train.

Both of these sentences are correct, and they have the same meaning. You may use either form you prefer.

If you wish to combine two simple sentences by turning one of the sentences into a *to* phrase, begin by identifying the *to* + verb combination in the first simple sentence:

> My cousin wants <u>to find</u> a girlfriend. He tried an online dating service.

Use this combination to form the phrase that will begin your new sentence:

> To find a girlfriend . . .

Now, add a comma and "hang" the rest of your sentence onto the phrase:

> To find a girlfriend, my cousin tried an online dating service.

The second part of the sentence begins with *my cousin* instead of *he* because *my cousin* doesn't appear in the first part of the sentence, and it is a more specific name for the subject.

ıl|l ■ **ACTIVITY 4**
WARMUP

Complete each sentence below by following these steps:

- Add a verb to the subject.
- Add any additional information to complete the thought.

EXAMPLE: To teach the spoiled child a lesson, the babysitter <u>took away his</u>
<u>PlayStation</u> .

1. To get to work on time, Frank _____
_____ .

2. To receive a free coupon, the customer _____
_____ .

3. To repair the broken lamp, you _____
_____ .

4. To comfort the lost child, the police officer _____
_____ .

5. To learn her lines, the actress _____
_____ .

ACTIVITY 5

Combine each pair of simple sentences by turning the first sentence into a *to* phrase. Follow these steps:

- Underline the *to* + verb combination in the first simple sentence.
- Use this combination to form the phrase that will begin your new sentence.
- Add a comma after the phrase.
- Hang the rest of your sentence onto the phrase. (You may need to change the subject of the second part of the sentence.)

EXAMPLE: Many people like to live close to their work. They move into a new home.

To live close to their work, many people move into a new home.

1. Aaron wanted to spend less time commuting. He found a house that was very close to his job.

_____

_____

2. Aaron wanted to get more exercise. He rode his bicycle to work in nice weather.

_____

_____

3. Aaron decided to save money on lunch. He sometimes went home to eat during his lunch hour.

_____

_____

4. Aaron liked to socialize with his co-workers outside of work. He invited them over to watch movies.

_____

_____

5. Aaron needed to get to work early on Wednesdays. He set his alarm a half hour earlier than normal.

_____

_____

ACTIVITY 6: Teamwork

For the following items, use the two verbs and subject provided to write a sentence that begins with a *to* phrase. Follow these steps:

- Put the first verb in the *to* form and use it to begin your sentence with a phrase.
- Add a comma after the phrase.

- Use the subject and the second verb to complete the thought. (You may put the second verb in the past, present, or future tense.)

EXAMPLE:

First verb: improve   **Subject:** the high school senior   **Second verb:** hire

To improve his SAT scores, the high school senior hired a tutor.

1. **First verb:** save   **Subject:** Ben   **Second verb:** make

2. **First verb:** find   **Subject:** Tim and Holly   **Second verb:** ask

3. **First verb:** learn   **Subject:** many people   **Second verb:** take

4. **First verb:** get   **Subject:** Adela   **Second verb:** eat

5. **First verb:** enroll   **Subject:** students   **Second verb:** pay

Beginning a Sentence with an *-ed* Phrase

When a verb in a modifying phrase is written in the *-ed* form (*embarrassed, married, angered,* and so on), it indicates the **condition** of someone or something. In a sentence that begins with an *-ed* phrase, you will find the description of the condition in the first part of the sentence and the person or thing being described, and what the person/thing did, in the last part of the sentence:

CONDITION   **PERSON DESCRIBED**   **PERSON'S ACTION**

Injured during the tryouts, the gymnast could not compete in the Olympics.

Injured is known as a *past participle*. Keep in mind that not all past participles end in *-ed*. (You will learn more about the irregular forms in Chapter 15.) Take a look:

PAST PARTICIPLE OF *LOSE*

Lost in the amusement park, the child started to cry.

PAST PARTICIPLE OF *STEAL*

Stolen on New Year's Day, my car was never found.

If you wish to combine two simple sentences by turning one of the sentences into an *-ed* phrase (or other past-participle form), begin by identifying the complete verb in the first simple sentence:

Our antique clock was damaged during the move. It will not keep the correct time.

Power Tip

For more on identifying complete verbs (including helping verbs and the verbs that follow them), see Chapter 10, page 231, and Chapter 11.

Drop the helping verb *was* and use the part participle to form the phrase that will begin your new sentence:

> **Damaged during the move . . .**

Now, add a comma and "hang" the rest of your sentence onto the phrase:

> **Damaged during the move, our antique clock will not keep the correct time.**

The second part of the sentence begins with the subject *our antique clock* instead of *it* because *our antique clock* doesn't appear in the first part of the sentence, and it is a more specific name for the object.

ACTIVITY 7

WARMUP

Complete each sentence by following these steps:

- Add a verb to the subject.
- Add any additional information to complete the thought.

EXAMPLE: Punctured by a nail, the tire *flapped loudly* _____.

1. Confused by the numerous signs, the driver _____.

2. Exhausted by the huge engagement party, the mother of the bride

   _____.

3. Excited about his new job, Isaac _____.

4. Annoyed by the noisy children, the neighbor _____.

5. Frightened by the large spider, Professor Stevens _____

   _____.

ACTIVITY 8

EASY

Combine each pair of simple sentences by turning the first sentence into an *-ed* phrase. Follow these steps:

- Underline the complete verb in the first simple sentence.
- Drop the helping verb and use the past participle to form the phrase that will begin your new sentence.
- Add a comma after the phrase.
- Hang the rest of your sentence onto the phrase. (You may need to change the subject of the second part of the sentence.)

EXAMPLE: Some students <u>are motivated</u> by a desire to improve their skills. They seek help.

> *Motivated by a desire to improve their skills, some students*
>
> *seek help.*

1. Gregory was discouraged about his poor writing skills. He talked to his instructor.

   _____

   _____

2. Professor Adams was pleased about Gregory's dedication. He recommended a tutor.

   _____

   _____

3. Gregory was determined to pass his writing course. He made an appointment with the tutor.

   _____

   _____

4. The tutor was talented in language skills. She helped Gregory with grammar.

   _____

   _____

5. Gregory was convinced that he could pass the course. He thanked the tutor and his instructor.

   _____

   _____

ACTIVITY 9: Teamwork

MODERATE

For each of the following items, use the two verbs and subject provided to write a sentence that begins with an *-ed* phrase.

- Put the first verb in the *-ed* form and use it to begin your sentence with a phrase.
- Add a comma after the phrase.
- Use the subject and the second verb to complete the thought. (You may put the second verb in the past, present, or future tense.)

EXAMPLE:

First verb: identify   **Subject:** the suspect   **Second verb:** confess

Identified in a lineup, the suspect confessed to the robbery.

1. **First verb:** surprise   **Subject:** Corey   **Second verb:** jump

   _____

2. **First verb:** satisfy   **Subject:** the customer   **Second verb:** buy

   _____

3. **First verb:** frustrate   **Subject:** Ellen   **Second verb:** call

   _____

CONTINUED >

4. **First verb:** exhaust   **Subject:** the truck driver   **Second verb:** pull

5. **First verb:** anger   **Subject:** the student   **Second verb:** drop

---

The following activities mix the three different modifying phrases that we have discussed so far: *-ing* phrases, *to* phrases, and *-ed* phrases.

ACTIVITY 10

ADVANCED

Combine each pair of simple sentences by turning the first sentence into an *-ing* phrase, a *to* phrase, or an *-ed* phrase. Follow these steps:

- Decide whether the beginning phrase should express an ongoing action, a desired action, or a condition.
- Create this phrase using the guidance provided earlier in this chapter. (Use *-ing* phrases for ongoing actions, *to* phrases for desired actions, and *-ed* phrases for conditions.)
- Add a comma after the phrase.
- Hang the rest of your sentence onto the phrase. (You may need to change the subject of the second part of the sentence.)

EXAMPLE: Many employees are faced with difficult co-workers. These employees may not know what to do.

Faced with difficult co-workers, many employees may not know what to do.

1. Employees can follow a few tips. They can deal with most difficult colleagues.

2. Employees can recognize that a difficult person may be insecure. They can acknowledge his or her positive traits.

3. A difficult co-worker will be encouraged by such praise. He or she may become less defensive.

For more practice with using modifiers, go to bedfordstmartins.com/ steppingstones.

4. Employees need to deal with a know-it-all. They should recognize that arguing with such a person is useless.

_____

_____

5. It is a good idea to avoid misunderstandings through e-mail. Employees should discuss difficult situations face to face.

_____

_____

PLACING MODIFYING PHRASES IN OTHER PARTS OF A SENTENCE

So far in this chapter, you have practiced placing modifying phrases <u>at the beginning</u> of sentences.

An *-ing* phrase at the beginning

<u>Listening to classical music</u>, Deirdre fell into a deep sleep.

A *to* phrase at the beginning

<u>To enlist in the army</u>, my cousin visited his local recruiting office.

An *-ed* phrase at the beginning

<u>Annoyed by the attorney</u>, the judge called a recess.

However, modifiers can also appear <u>in the middle</u> or <u>at the end</u> of sentences. Consider the following examples:

A modifying phrase in the middle

Deirdre, <u>listening to classical music</u>, fell into a deep sleep.

The judge, <u>annoyed by the attorney</u>, called a recess.

A modifying phrase at the end

Deirdre fell into a deep sleep <u>listening to classical music</u>.

My cousin visited his local recruiting office <u>to enlist in the army</u>.

Notice that when a modifying phrase is in the middle of a sentence, commas are used before and after it. When a modifying phrase comes at the end, commas generally are not used.

You will have to decide on the best position for a modifying phrase. In most cases, though, it is a good idea to place the modifying phrase right before or right after the word(s) it is describing. Otherwise, you may create a problem known as a *misplaced modifier*. (For more information, see page 353 of Chapter 13.)

ACTIVITY 11

MODERATE

For each of the following modifying phrases, write different sentences that place the phrase as directed. Remember these rules:

- When a modifying phrase starts a sentence, a comma comes after it.
- When the phrase is in the middle of a sentence, commas are used before and after it.
- When a modifying phrase comes at the end, commas generally are not used.

EXAMPLE:

Modifying phrase: to get to Phoenix by 5 A.M.

Phrase at the beginning: To get to Phoenix by 5 A.M., we'll have to fly overnight.

Phrase at the end: We'll have to fly overnight to get to Phoenix by 5 A.M.

1. **Modifying phrase:** driving to the dinner party

   Phrase at the beginning: _____

   _____

   Phrase at the end: _____

   _____

2. **Modifying phrase:** wounded in a fight with another dog

   Phrase at the beginning: _____

   _____

   Phrase in the middle: _____

   _____

3. **Modifying phrase:** to get tickets to the concert

   Phrase at the beginning: _____

   _____

   Phrase at the end: _____

   _____

4. **Modifying phrase:** jumping into the pool

   Phrase at the beginning: _____

   _____

   Phrase at the end: _____

   _____

BUILDING SENTENCES WITH MODIFIERS IN WHOLE PARAGRAPHS

ACTIVITY 12: Mastery Test or Teamwork

MASTERY

In each of the following paragraphs, combine pairs of simple sentences by turning one of the simple sentences into a modifying phrase. First, identify a pair of sentences that can be combined, and then decide which one will become a modifying phrase.

1. (*Hint:* Combine two pairs)

    Helen Keller's name often comes up in stories about overcoming obstacles, but few realize how truly amazing she was. She was born in Tuscumbia, Alabama. She was the daughter of a Confederate army veteran and the editor of the local newspaper. At the young age of 19 months, she became seriously ill. The doctors described her illness as "brain congestion." Her illness was probably what later became known as meningitis or scarlet fever. Although Keller's illness did not last too long, it left her both deaf and blind (hearing and sight impaired).

2. (*Hint:* Combine four pairs)

    Keller managed to break through her isolation from the world with the help of her teacher Anne Sullivan. Keller learned Braille in only three years. She could then read and write. Keller then wanted to learn to speak in a voice others could understand. Keller attended the Horace Mann School for the Deaf in Boston. She went on to attend the Wright-Humason School for the Deaf. She interpreted lectures with the help of Anne Sullivan. From there, she went on to a prep school, The Cambridge School for Young Ladies. She graduated from Radcliffe with honors. Keller became the first person who was both deaf and blind to earn a Bachelor of Arts degree.

CONTINUED >

3. (*Hint:* Combine five pairs)

Despite her disability, Keller became an enormously important voice. Keller wrote extensively. She was outspoken in her opposition to war. She also campaigned for women's right to vote. She was also concerned about blindness in prostitutes. She believed they contracted syphilis (a common cause of blindness) because of what she referred to as "wrong industrial conditions, often caused by the selfishness and greed of employers." Keller also fought for the rights of laborers. She joined the IWW (Industrial Workers of the World). In 1920, she became one of the founders of the ACLU (American Civil Liberties Union). In addition, she also campaigned for the rights of those with disabilities. She also spoke out for socialism. She was attacked by the newspapers that once praised her courage, strength, and intelligence. They suggested that her radical views stemmed from her disabilities.

FIX IT: Fixing Problems in Sentences with Modifiers

In this section, you will learn how to recognize and fix a common problem in sentences with modifying phrases: dangling modifiers. (For more on misplaced modifiers, see Chapter 13, page 353.)

RECOGNIZING DANGLING MODIFIERS

Take a look at the following sentence and see if you can spot a problem with its meaning:

Delayed in traffic, the sun got hotter and hotter.

There is something odd about this sentence, but you may have to look very closely to figure out the problem. Let's begin by examining a simple sentence:

The sun got hotter and hotter.

The meaning of this sentence is clear and simple. However, if we add a modifying phrase to the beginning of the sentence, we have to be sure that the two parts of the sentence fit together. Sometimes, especially when we are writing quickly, we may write a sentence where the two parts do not fit together. As a result, the sentence will not make perfect sense:

Delayed in traffic, the sun got hotter and hotter.

According to this sentence, who or what was delayed in traffic? While your imagination may tell you that a *person* was delayed in traffic, the sentence actually says that *the sun* was delayed in traffic. This is an odd idea.

To be absolutely clear, we must add a subject that makes sense:

Delayed in traffic, Mark felt the sun get hotter and hotter.

When you begin a sentence with a modifier, remember two rules:

- The subject of the sentence must come immediately after the comma.
- This subject must connect with the action in the modifier.

Take a look:

A. Waking up on Friday morning, my blanket was on the floor.

B. Waking up on Friday morning, I discovered my blanket on the floor.

According to sentence A, the *blanket* woke up, which doesn't make sense. When we write or read such a sentence, we usually allow our imagination to fill in the *real* subject of the action. Instead, we should recognize that the sentence does not make sense and needs to have an appropriate subject added. Sentence B is correct because it tells us that *I* woke up on Friday morning. In this case, the subject of the action is 100 percent clear.

When an appropriate subject is missing or unclear, we cannot be 100 percent sure who or what is connected to the action in the modifier. So, the action is left **dangling** or *unattached* to a subject that makes sense.

 ACTIVITY 13: Teamwork

EASY

Working with two or three classmates, do the following for each group of sentences below:

- Read all three sentences.
- In the space provided, write a question that will help you identify the correct subject. (See the example below.)
- Circle the subject or subjects that fit with the action in the modifier. If none of the subjects fit, write "none" in the margin.

CONTINUED >

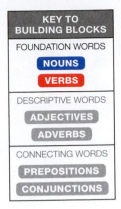

KEY TO BUILDING BLOCKS

FOUNDATION WORDS

NOUNS

VERBS

DESCRIPTIVE WORDS

ADJECTIVES

ADVERBS

CONNECTING WORDS

PREPOSITIONS

CONJUNCTIONS

For more practice with correcting dangling modifiers, go to **bedfordstmartins.com/ steppingstones**.

EXAMPLE:

Locked out of the house, Antonia's keys would not work.

Locked out of the house, an open window was Antonia's only option.

Locked out of the house, Antonia's luck ran out.   none

Question: Who or what was locked out of the house?

1. Seated in the dentist's chair, the dentist prepared to drill.

   Seated in the dentist's chair, the patient nervously awaited the drill.

   Seated in the dentist's chair, the drill came closer.

   Question: _____

2. Barking wildly, Jennifer told the dog to be quiet.

   Barking wildly, the dog's owner told the dog to be quiet.

   Barking wildly, Jennifer's patience with the dog was wearing thin.

   Question: _____

3. Returning to the car, one of the tires was flat.

   Returning to the car, a slash had flattened one of the tires.

   Returning to the car, Jake and I discovered a flat tire.

   Question: _____

4. Injured during a football tackle, Victor's grandmother forbade him to play again.

   Injured during a football tackle, Victor's shoulder required surgery.

   Injured during a football tackle, Victor suffered a broken shoulder.

   Question: _____

5. Landing the airplane during a storm, the passengers were nervous.

   Landing the airplane during a storm, the flight attendants calmed the passengers.

   Landing the airplane during a storm, the pilot avoided an accident.

   Question: _____

When we write a sentence that begins with an *-ing* phrase, a *to* phrase, or an *-ed* phrase, the subject of the sentence is really connected with two actions. Take a look:

To memorize the new vocabulary, the students used flash cards.

You already know that *used* must be the verb in this sentence because the verb can never appear within a modifier. However, the subject (*students*) is still connected to two related actions: *memorizing* and *using*. Understanding this idea will help you to control the sentences that you write with modifiers.

ACTIVITY 14
EASY

For each sentence below, do the following:

- First, circle the subject.
- Next, underline the two actions that are connected to the subject.
- Last, draw arrows from the subject to each of the actions.

EXAMPLE: <u>Hiding</u> in the tall grass, the (crocodile) <u>waited</u> for lunch.

1. Concerned about the rash on his arm, Kevin called his physician.

2. Pouring hot fudge sauce on her ice cream, Michelle licked her lips.

3. To save money on airline tickets, you should fly in the middle of the week.

4. Overwhelmed by the wedding plans, Ann hired a wedding planner.

5. To enter the building, employees must have a valid identification card.

ACTIVITY 15
EASY

Complete each of the following sentences by adding a verb and any additional information that you want.

EXAMPLE: Swollen to twice its normal size, my ankle *throbbed with pain* .

1. Running backwards to catch a fly ball, the right-fielder _____
   _____ .

2. Excited about his vacation plans in Las Vegas, Grandpa _____
   _____ .

3. Turning left onto Colorado Avenue, the taxi driver _____
   _____ .

4. To train for the marathon, Chris _____ .

5. Stung by an angry hornet, the small child _____ .

▂▃▅ ACTIVITY 16
MODERATE

Complete each of the following sentences by adding a subject, a verb, and any additional information that you want. Be sure that your subject fits with the action in the modifier.

EXAMPLE: To reach his desired body weight, *the body builder ate only tuna for lunch* .

1. Frightened by the loud thunder, _____ .
2. Wearing a brand-new suit, _____ .
3. To save money for a house, _____ .
4. Wanting to impress his girlfriend, _____ .
5. Opening up the morning newspaper, _____

_____ .

FIXING DANGLING MODIFIERS

If you find that you have written a dangling modifier, you will need to do *one* of the following things:

1. Change the <u>second part</u> of the sentence by adding a subject.
2. Change the <u>first part</u> of the sentence (the modifier) by adding a subject and a complete verb.

Let's consider these options one at a time.

Changing the Second Part of the Sentence

Take a look at a new example:

> Standing in line, the hours seemed to drag.

Clearly, it does not make sense to say that *the hours* stood in line. As you read sentences like this, *do not let your imagination do the work that the sentence should be doing*. The first way to fix this error is to leave the modifier the same but <u>change the second half of the sentence</u>. In doing this, we must <u>add a subject</u> that fits with the action *standing*. For example:

MODIFIER STAYS THE SAME	NEW SUBJECT

<u>Standing in line,</u> Bill felt the hours dragging.

Now it is clear that *Bill* was standing in line. This makes perfect sense. Notice, too, that the new subject, *Bill*, requires a new verb, *felt*. Bill did what? He felt the hours dragging.

ACTIVITY 17

Correct each dangling modifier below by following these steps:

- Copy the modifying phrase that opens the sentence, leaving it the same.
- Put a comma after this phrase.
- Add a subject that fits with the action in the modifier.
- Add a verb and complete the thought.

Note: You may need to change other words in the second part of the sentence.

EXAMPLE: Entering the subway, a huge *Shrek* poster caught my attention.

Entering the subway, I noticed a huge Shrek poster.

1. Walking to work one morning, a briefcase fell from a skyscraper onto the sidewalk.

2. To repair the engine, the valves must be changed.

3. Seated in the back row, the performers were difficult to see and hear.

4. Riding a skateboard down the street, a rock hit me in the face.

5. Exhausted by the long drive, the hotel bed looked inviting.

Changing the Modifier

The second method for correcting a dangling modifier is to <u>change the modifier</u> but leave the second half of the sentence the same. In doing this, we must <u>add a subject</u> that fits with the action in the modifier. We must also make sure that there is a complete verb. Let's return to a familiar example:

> Standing in line, the hours seemed to drag.

Now, we will <u>add a subject</u> to the first part of this sentence. We will also add the helping verb *was* before *standing* to make the verb complete. (For more on helping verbs, see Chapter 10, page 231.) Notice that the second half of the sentence remains unchanged:

> **NEW SUBJECT** **COMPLETE VERB**
>
> While **Bill** **was standing** in line, the hours seemed to drag.

Notice also that the subordinating conjunction *while* has been added to the opening phrase. By adding this information to the modifier, we have created a complex sentence with two separate subjects and two separate verbs.

1ST SUBJECT   **1ST VERB**   **2ND SUBJECT**   **2ND VERB**

While Bill was standing in line, the hours seemed to drag.

Now it is clear that *Bill* was standing in line.

ACTIVITY 18

ADVANCED

Correct each dangling modifier below by following these steps:

- Rewrite the modifier, adding a subordinating conjunction (see the Subordinating Conjunctions box at left) and a new subject. Change the verb as necessary.
- Add a comma.
- Leave the second half of the sentence the same.

Subordinating Conjunctions

after	if
although	since
as	unless
because	until
before	when
even if	while
even though	

EXAMPLE: Putting out the campfire at the end of the night, it sizzled.

When Lynn put out the campfire at the end of the night, it sizzled.

1. Fishing for salmon, Matt's line became snagged on a branch.

2. Crossing a shallow stream, Betty's foot slipped on a rock.

3. Setting up the tent properly, the stakes were secure in the ground.

4. Going to sleep, the forest was quiet.

5. Making hot chocolate, their first stop was to buy marshmallows.

ACTIVITY 19: Mastery Test

MASTERY

Correct each of the following dangling modifiers in two ways:

- First, leave the opening modifier the same but change the second half of the sentence.
- Next, add more information to the opening modifier but leave the second half of the sentence the same.

For more practice with correcting dangling modifiers, go to **bedfordstmartins.com/ steppingstones.**

EXAMPLE: **Dangling modifier:** Sledding downhill, a wolf appeared behind a snow bank.

First revision: Sledding downhill, Maria saw a wolf appear behind a snow bank.

Second revision: As Maria was sledding downhill, a wolf appeared behind a snow bank.

1. Writing the last paragraph of his essay, his cat stepped on the delete key.

   First revision: _____

   _____

   Second revision: _____

   _____

2. Covered with hot fudge and whipped cream, the guests admired the dessert.

   First revision: _____

   _____

   Second revision: _____

   _____

3. To be eligible for the athletic scholarship, a college coach must recommend the athlete.

   First revision: _____

   _____

   Second revision: _____

   _____

FIXING DANGLING MODIFIERS IN WHOLE PARAGRAPHS

The following activity will give you practice with recognizing and fixing dangling modifiers in whole paragraphs—a valuable skill for improving your own writing.

ACTIVITY 20: Mastery Test or Teamwork

Read each of the following paragraphs carefully, looking for dangling modifiers. Then, rewrite each error to fix the problem, using one of the following methods:

- Leave the opening modifier the same, but change the second half of the sentence.

CONTINUED >

- Add more information to the opening modifier, but leave the second half of the sentence the same.

Be sure to put any commas in the correct places. The first error in each paragraph has been edited for you.

The following paragraph has five dangling modifiers (including the one that has been edited for you).

1. (1) My best friend, Marta, a full-time security guard and mother, has great ideas for eating well on a budget. (2) First, she's a smart shopper. (3) To get the best deals, ~~bulk purchases are essential~~ *she purchases items in bulk*. (4) Marta looks for sales on spaghetti sauce, ground turkey, toilet paper, and other common items and then buys large quantities to get the best price. (5) Driving to the store, a snack of carrot sticks or peanut butter on crackers keeps her from shopping while hungry, a major cause of over-purchasing. (6) Committed to her family's health and her budget, chips and soda are a no-no. (7) She knows that junk food is not only bad for the body but costlier than healthier foods. (8) At home, Marta saves time and money by cooking meals in advance and saving them in a large freezer. (9) On busy nights when she's too tired to cook, she defrosts a pre-cooked meal instead of spending money on fast-food takeout. (10) Stretching meat portions by adding rice or beans, her meals are flavorful, nutritious, and economical.

(11) To save more money, Marta is a role model for me.

The following paragraph has six dangling modifiers (including the one that has been edited for you).

2. (1) The Apple iPod is the most recognizable of all portable digital music players. (2) Dissatisfied with existing digital music players, *a team of engineers invented* a better design ~~was invented by a team of engineers~~ with a more seamless user interface. (3) First launched in October of 2001, one year was how long it took them to develop the iPod. (4) Holding five gigabytes of music, advertisements touted the first iPods as

"1,000 songs in your pocket." (5) Citing a quote from the movie *2001: A Space Odyssey*, the iPod was named by Vinnie Chieco, a freelance copywriter. (6) The iPod has won many awards and still receives many positive customer reviews. (7) People like its design, usability, looks, and functionality. (8) With over 70 percent of the market, all other digital music players are dominated by iPod sales. (9) Sometimes even being used in business settings, Glasgow's Western Infirmary teaching hospital now uses iPods as part of their training program. (10) Even with complaints and various recalls of the product over the years, the popularity of iPods still remains extremely high. (11) Apple continues to improve on its original invention that is now the biggest-selling digital music player of all time.

BRINGING IT ALL TOGETHER:
Sentences with Modifiers

In this chapter, you have learned about sentences formed with modifying phrases. You have also learned how to avoid common problems caused by modifying phrases. Confirm your knowledge by filling in the blank spaces in the following sentences. If you need help, review the pages listed after each sentence.

✔ One way to combine two simple sentences is to turn one of them into a modifying phrase. Three common modifying phrases are _____ phrases, _____ phrases, and _____ phrases. (pages 357–58)

✔ Modifying phrases can be placed at _____ of a sentence, in _____ of a sentence, or at _____ of a sentence. (page 367)

CONTINUED >

✔ One common problem in sentences with modifying phrases is the _____ modifier. When this problem occurs, the _____ of the sentence is not clear. (pages 370–71)

✔ There are two basic ways to correct a dangling modifier. They are:

1) _____, and

2) _____

_____. (page 374)

CHAPTER 15

Using Verbs Correctly

Before you read this chapter, it's a good idea to test your understanding of verbs. You may know more than you think.

WHAT DO YOU KNOW?

Circle "Yes" if each word group below is a complete, correct sentence. Circle "No" if it is incomplete. Then, explain your choice.

1. **Two years ago, my brother and I build a sailboat from a kit.**

   Yes   No

   Explanation: _____

   _____

2. **If Emily had been given the chance, she would of gone to college.**

   Yes   No

   Explanation: _____

   _____

3. **The title of the new television series are *Househusbands*.**

   Yes   No

   Explanation: _____

   _____

4. **He do whatever his girlfriend tell him to do.**

   Yes   No

   Explanation: _____

   _____

5. **The tornado touched down at 6:00 P.M. and three people are injured.**

   Yes   No

   Explanation: _____

   _____

Verbs tell us when something happens or happened. You'll learn more details in this chapter.

PRESENT TENSE

The students study.

PAST TENSE

The students studied.

PRESENT PERFECT TENSE

The students have studied for many hours.

PAST PERFECT TENSE

The students had studied for many hours by the day of the exam.

BUILD IT: Sentences with Correct Verbs

As you have learned, **verbs** often express actions, although some of them have other functions. (See Chapter 10 for a review.) In this chapter, you will learn about how verbs change form to express different times, and you will also learn about some problems that can occur with verbs.

RECOGNIZING STANDARD AND NONSTANDARD VERBS

When we speak, we sometimes use *nonstandard English*, which does not follow the rules of written academic English. Take a look at this example:

NONSTANDARD ENGLISH   Alex be smart. He don't need to study.

STANDARD ENGLISH   Alex is smart. He doesn't need to study.

You may hear nonstandard English in conversation, television shows, movies, and music. Rap and hip-hop artists, for example, often mix standard and nonstandard English in their songs. Look at the lyrics of "Hard Times," by hip-hop group Run-D.M.C. (Nonstandard verbs—and their standard versions—appear in red.)

(standard English: are spreading)

Hard times spreading just like the flu

Watch out, homeboy, don't let it catch you

P-p-prices go up, don't let your pocket go down

(standard English: have)

When you got short money you're stuck on the ground

Turn around, get ready, keep your eye on the prize

And be on point for the future shock

Hard times are coming to your town

So stay alert, don't let them get you down

They tell you times are tough, you hear that times are hard

But when you work for that ace you know you pulled the right card

Hard times got our pockets all in chains   (standard English: have)

I'll tell you what, homeboy, it don't have my brain   (standard English: doesn't)

All day I have to work at my peak

Because I need that dollar every day of the week

Hard times can take you on a natural trip

So keep your balance, and don't you slip

Hard times is nothing new on me   (standard English: are)

I'm gonna use my strong mentality   (standard English: going to)

Like the cream of the crop, like the crop of the cream

B-b-beating hard times, that is my theme

Hard times in life, hard times in death

I'm gonna keep on fighting to my very last breath   (standard English: going to)

This song communicates a powerful message, and Run-D.M.C. shows that breaking the rules of grammar can sometimes be empowering in our personal and artistic lives. However, if you know *only* nonstandard English, you may be limiting your opportunities for personal and professional success.

Standard English (which follows the rules of written academic English) helps you to express your ideas with great precision and clarity, and it is the form of English expected in most school and work settings. Therefore, as a college writer, you should commit to learning and using standard English. Doing so will help you achieve academic success and allow you to communicate more effectively in your personal and professional lives.

If you are more comfortable with nonstandard English than with standard English, you can improve your academic writing simply by focusing on verbs, as you'll do in this chapter.

KEY TO
BUILDING BLOCKS

FOUNDATION WORDS

NOUNS

VERBS

DESCRIPTIVE WORDS

ADJECTIVES

ADVERBS

CONNECTING WORDS

PREPOSITIONS

CONJUNCTIONS

THE "MYTH" OF LEARNING VERBS

Many students mistakenly believe that learning standard verb usage is very difficult. Some students are even convinced that they will *never* learn to use verbs correctly because they've been embarrassed by verb errors throughout their school years, and their grades may have suffered. In truth, however, learning correct verb usage doesn't have to be difficult; it just requires some *awareness* and *self-discipline* based on the following principles:

1. **Some memorization** will be necessary. Many students dislike memorization because it can be dull. In this chapter, however, you will learn memorization strategies that minimize the dullness while providing faster results. Keep in mind that the memorization will not go on forever; after mastering the most common verbs, you can look up the rest in your textbook or in a dictionary as needed.

2. **Daily practice** with verbs is the key to your success. A small amount of practice each day (about ten minutes) is the quickest and most effective way to build your skills. If you do an hour's worth of practice only one day a week, the information won't "stick." If possible, try to do your ten minutes at the same time every day—right after breakfast or lunch, for example. Once you sit down, you'll see that the ten minutes will fly by, and you will improve quickly.

3. **Online exercises** are the best resource for your daily practice. Unlike exercises in your textbook, online practices can provide immediate feedback on your answers and almost endless practice. Plenty of exercises on verbs and other topics are available on this book's Web site at **bedfordstmartins.com/steppingstones**, and immediate feedback is provided. If you do not have a computer at home, plan to use one at your school or local public library.

Once you understand these principles, it is time for you to make a personal decision. Are you ready to dedicate yourself to learning correct verbs? Keep in mind that you can dramatically improve your skills if you are willing to follow the principles. To ensure your success, check each of the following statements that apply to you:

_____ Yes, I want to use correct verbs in my writing.

_____ Yes, I will use the memorization strategies in this chapter.

_____ Yes, I will find ten minutes each day to practice my verbs.

_____ Yes, I will use online exercises for my practice. If necessary, I will use a computer at my school or public library.

BUILD IT: Basic Verb Usage, Present and Past Tenses

As you have learned, every sentence must have a subject and a verb. The verb must be in the correct form to match

- the tense (time) of the action in a sentence *and*
- the subject. (More on this later.)

The simple present tense is used for

- regular actions (*I **take** the train every day*),
- facts (*Jonas **likes** rich desserts*), and
- actions happening right now (*I **hear** the doorbell*).

The simple past tense is used for actions completed in the past (*I **walked** four miles every day*).

The correct form of a verb is determined by the spelling. About 90 percent of all verb problems are caused by two simple errors: the absence or unnecessary addition of an **-s** or an **-ed** ending. You will learn more about these problems and other common mistakes later in this chapter.

USING THE PRESENT TENSE

Again, the simple present tense is used for regular actions, for facts, and for actions happening right now. Present tense verbs follow a very simple spelling rule. Take a look:

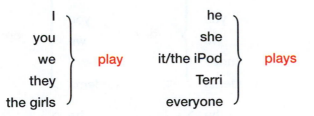

I you we they the girls } **play**	he she it/the iPod Terri everyone } **plays**

Grabbing onto the Slippery -s

Notice that the only difference in the two forms of the verb *play* is that an **-s** comes at the end when the subject is *he*, *she*, or *it* (or some equivalent). We call this "the slippery **-s**" because, like a snake or a lizard, it can slip out of sight easily when we are not paying attention. Most students know how to spell verbs in the present tense, but they sometimes forget to write the **-s**. (And sometimes they add it when it's not needed.) Because the slippery **-s** is a major cause of verb errors, you should grab a hold of it in your mind and not let go.

The Slippery -s

KEY TO CHALLENGE METER

WARMUP
EASY
MODERATE
ADVANCED
MASTERY

Identify the difficulty level of each activity using the key above.

ACTIVITY 1
WARMUP

For each sentence below, do the following:

- In the space provided, write the correct present tense form of the verb in parentheses.
- If the verb ends in -s, circle the s or mark it with a highlighter.

EXAMPLE: We _____*need*_____ (need) six sources for our research project.

1. Enrico _____ (walk) three miles every day.
2. We _____ (believe) Bradley's wild story.
3. The city park _____ (remain) open from dawn until dusk.
4. Petra _____ (want) a satisfying career.
5. The Rodriguez sisters _____ (visit) Mexico every summer.

Recognizing Irregular Present Tense Verbs: Be, Have, and Do

You should be aware of three "irregular" verbs that we use frequently. These verbs are irregular because they follow different spelling rules from regular verbs (like *play*, *walk*, and *bake*). Fortunately, most students use and spell them correctly.

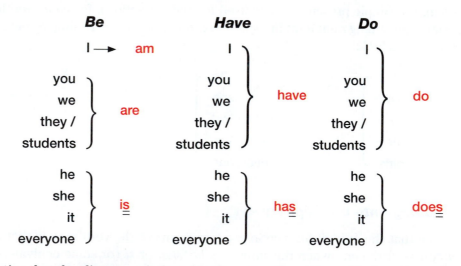

Power Tip
Often, the -s ending moves from the verb to the subject when the subject becomes plural.

Singular Subject: The girl plays.

Plural Subject: The girls play.

You will have to add an -es instead of an -s to the end of some verbs, such as those that end in -ch or -sh: teach → teaches; catch → catches; fish → fishes; wish → wishes.

Notice that the slippery **-s** is found in the same place even with these irregular verbs.

ACTIVITY 2
EASY

For each sentence, do the following:

- In the space provided, write the correct present tense form of the verb in parentheses.
- If the verb ends in -s, circle the s or mark it with a highlighter.

For more practice with present tense verbs, go to **bedfordstmartins.com/ steppingstones.**

EXAMPLE: I _____ *am* _____ (be) excited about going on vacation next month.

1. Margaret _____ (have) a bad headache.
2. He _____ (do) a good job painting.
3. The band members _____ (be) on stage.
4. Marco _____ (be) a flight attendant.
5. Our neighbors _____ (have) a vacation home in Colorado.
6. The students _____ (do) well on tests after class reviews.
7. My boss _____ (be) hard to please sometimes.
8. Randall _____ (have) a new job.
9. Maria _____ (do) dishes twice a day.
10. I _____ (be) confused about the new tax laws.

ACTIVITY 3

MODERATE

For the passage below, do the following:

- In the spaces provided, write the correct present tense forms of the verbs in parentheses.
- If a verb ends in -s, circle the s or mark it with a highlighter.

The first space in the passage has been filled in for you.

(1) Going to a museum _____ *is* _____ (be) an interesting and fun way to spend a day. (2) There _____ (be) museums where you can learn about art, history, science, and music.

(3) There _____ (be) even museums for fashion and technology. (4) Many museums _____ (have) one day per week when admission is free, and some museums are always free.

(5) It _____ (be) a good idea to allow plenty of time for a single visit, as there are always many different exhibits that may interest you. (6) Although it _____ (be) tempting to try to see every single item or work of art, you might want to choose only a few exhibits so that you can take your time. (7) One thing you can _____ (do) to learn more about a particular exhibit is to check to see if the museum offers free guided tours. (8) Many

Power Tip
In everyday speech, we sometimes leave out *be* verbs (*am/is/are/was/were*). Avoid this error in writing.

Incorrect: I sick.
    He happy.

Revised: I <u>am</u> sick.
    He <u>is</u> happy.

Power Tip
If English is not your first language, see Appendix B for special advice on verb usage and other grammar topics.

CONTINUED >

museums _____ (have) a café or restaurant inside if you

get hungry or want to take a break. (9) If you _____ (do)

not work during weekdays, you can avoid larger crowds by visiting the

museum during off-peak hours. (10) No matter how many times you

visit a particular museum, it _____ (be) likely that you will

learn new information each time you visit.

USING THE PAST TENSE

Power Tip
Remember these spelling points:

If a verb already ends in e, you usually add just a d to form the past tense.

If a verb ends in a consonant (b, c, d, f, g, and so on), both the e and the d must be added.

A final y usually must change to i before ed is added, unless a vowel precedes the y — for example, *convey* →
conveyed.

Again, the simple past tense is used for actions completed in the past (*I
walked four miles every day*). All regular past tense verbs follow a simple
rule. Take a look:

Base Form		Past Tense
look		looked
laugh	} + ed	laughed
spell		spelled
love		loved
type	} + d	typed
refuse		refused
cry		cried
try	} – y + ied	tried
marry		married

Keeping an Eye on the Elusive -ed

elusive: difficult to see, find, or grasp

Notice that all of these verbs — regardless of their present tense spelling — end
in *-ed* in the past tense. Most students know this, but they may forget to add
the *-ed*. (Often, they *hear* the *-ed* in their head, but they don't *see* that it's
missing on the page.) For this reason, we call this the "elusive *-ed*." Like the
"slippery *-s*," it is another major cause of verb errors, so remember to keep a
close eye on it in your writing.

ACTIVITY 4
EASY

For each sentence below, write the correct past tense form of the verb in
parentheses.

For more practice with regular past tense verbs, go to **bedfordstmartins.com/ steppingstones**.

EXAMPLE: In 2003, the nation _____*watched*_____ (watch) as authorities ended two famous criminal careers.

1. Craig Pritchert and Nova Guthrie _____ (rob) banks for a living.

2. Authorities _____ (compare) them to the 1930s bank robbers Bonnie Parker and Clyde Barrow.

3. While Pritchert robbed the banks, Nova _____ (wait) in the getaway car.

4. The outlaw couple _____ (live) a luxurious lifestyle.

5. They _____ (rent) a condo in an Oregon ski resort for two months.

6. They also _____ (vacation) in Belize.

7. Naturally, Pritchert and Guthrie's crime spree _____ (end).

8. The police finally _____ (locate) the couple in Cape Town, South Africa.

9. They _____ (arrest) them in 2003 and returned them to the United States to be tried.

10. The judge _____ (sentence) them both to long prison terms.

The Elusive -ed

IRREGULAR PAST TENSE VERBS

Now, it is time to prepare for some memorization work. Many past tense verbs have an "irregular" form that is not spelled with an *-ed* ending. Some of these irregular spellings you already know by heart. The following pre-test will help you identify the forms that you do not know so that you can focus on these in your memorization work.

CHECKING YOUR KNOWLEDGE: Irregular Past Tense Verbs

For each sentence pair, do the following:

- Look at the underlined verb in the first sentence.
- Then, in the second sentence, fill in the blank with the correct past tense form of this verb. Your answer should consist of only one word: the past tense verb. Do not add any words to the sentence or change any words in the sentence.
- When you have finished this pre-test, check your answers by using the chart on page 393.

If you want this test to work for you, do it honestly. Do not look for the answers while you're taking it.

CONTINUED >

EXAMPLE:

My son <u>brings</u> me a flower on my birthday.

My son _____brought_____ me a flower on my birthday.

1. I <u>am</u> happy about the raise.

I _____ happy about the raise.

2. You <u>are</u> a good student.

You _____ a good student.

3. The children <u>become</u> restless.

The children _____ restless.

4. The playoffs <u>begin</u> on Friday.

The playoffs _____ on Friday.

5. Our dog <u>bites</u> letter carriers.

Our dog _____ letter carriers.

6. The wind <u>blows</u>.

The wind _____.

7. The fragile vases <u>break</u>.

The fragile vases _____.

8. The guests <u>bring</u> gifts.

The guests _____ gifts.

9. My cousin <u>builds</u> porches.

My cousin _____ porches.

10. The teenagers <u>buy</u> jeans.

The teenagers _____ jeans.

11. The vacationers <u>catch</u> fish.

The vacationers _____ fish.

12. You <u>choose</u> wisely.

You _____ wisely.

13. They <u>come</u> to our parties.

They _____ to our parties.

14. Shoes <u>cost</u> a lot now.

Even ten years ago, shoes _____ a lot.

15. We <u>dive</u> into the pool.

We _____ into the pool.

16. The kids <u>do</u> the laundry.

The kids _____ the laundry.

17. Bernice <u>draws</u> well.

Bernice _____ well.

18. We <u>drink</u> lots of water.

We _____ lots of water.

19. The truckers <u>drive</u> all night.

The truckers _____ all night.

20. The Changs <u>eat</u> healthfully.

The Changs _____ healthfully.

21. The books <u>fall</u> from the shelf.

The books _____ from the shelf.

22. Shontelle <u>feeds</u> the dog.

Shontelle _____ the dog.

23. The boys <u>feel</u> sick.

The boys _____ sick.

24. The boxers <u>fight</u> aggressively.

The boxers _____ aggressively.

25. I <u>find</u> mushrooms in the woods.

I _____ mushrooms in the woods.

26. We <u>fly</u> to Kentucky.

We _____ to Kentucky.

27. The rain puddles <u>freeze</u>.

The rain puddles _____.

28. My sister <u>gets</u> an employee discount.

My sister _____ an employee discount.

29. We <u>give</u> to charity.

We _____ to charity.

30. My roommates <u>go</u> to the gym.

My roommates _____ to the gym.

31. The vegetables <u>grow</u> quickly.

The vegetables _____ quickly.

32. You <u>have</u> a cold.

You _____ a cold.

33. The babysitter <u>hears</u> strange noises.

The babysitter _____ strange noises.

34. We <u>hide</u> the children's presents.

We _____ the children's presents.

35. The box <u>holds</u> a precious gem.

The box _____ a precious gem.

36. Jason <u>hurts</u> his knees running.

Jason _____ his knees running.

37. The Grimaldis <u>keep</u> their house clean.

The Grimaldis _____ their house clean.

38. The students <u>know</u> the answer.

The students _____ the answer.

39. Chris <u>lays</u> the tablecloth on the table.

Chris _____ the tablecloth on the table.

40. The mountaineer <u>leads</u> our hike.

The mountaineer _____ our hike.

41. I <u>leave</u> my shoes in the hall.

I _____ my shoes in the hall.

42. We <u>let</u> the boys play outside every day.

We _____ the boys play outside yesterday.

43. The sunbathers <u>lie</u> on the beach.

The sunbathers _____ on the beach.

44. Cassie <u>lights</u> the candles before dinner.

Cassie _____ the candles before dinner.

45. We <u>lose</u> every time we play.

We _____ every time we played.

46. James <u>makes</u> the bed.

James _____ the bed.

47. I know what the note <u>means</u>.

I know what the note _____.

48. Our class <u>meets</u> on Tuesdays.

Our class _____ on Tuesdays.

49. My job <u>pays</u> well.

My job _____ well.

50. I always <u>put</u> the glasses on the top shelf.

Yesterday, I _____ the glasses on the top shelf.

51. Dan <u>quits</u> his job every few years.

Yesterday, Dan _____ his fifth job.

52. I <u>read</u> the newspaper every day.

I _____ the newspaper yesterday.

53. We <u>ride</u> the subway.

We _____ the subway.

54. The church bells <u>ring</u> over the city.

The church bells _____ over the city.

55. The dough <u>rises</u> in the warm oven.

The dough _____ in the warm oven.

56. Lisette <u>runs</u> every day.

Lisette _____ every day.

57. My daughter <u>says</u> she's tired.

My daughter _____ she was tired.

58. Jo <u>sees</u> a movie every week.

Jo _____ a movie every week.

59. The lost travelers <u>seek</u> help.

The lost travelers _____ help.

60. Karin <u>sells</u> jewelry.

Karin _____ jewelry.

CONTINUED >

61. I <u>send</u> funny cards to my sister.

I _____ funny cards to my sister.

62. Carrie <u>sets</u> the table every night.

Last summer, Carrie _____ the table every night.

63. The bartender <u>shakes</u> the drinks.

The bartender _____ the drinks.

64. That theater <u>shows</u> old movies.

That theater _____ old movies.

65. The clothes <u>shrink</u> in the wash.

The clothes _____ in the wash.

66. I <u>shut</u> the windows at night.

I _____ the windows last night.

67. Darnell <u>sings</u> beautifully.

Darnell _____ beautifully.

68. My heart <u>sinks</u> when you leave.

My heart _____ when you left.

69. Grandpa <u>sits</u> in that chair.

Grandpa _____ in that chair.

70. My son <u>sleeps</u> late on Saturdays.

My son _____ late on Saturday.

71. The mayor <u>speaks</u> at most town events.

The mayor _____ at most town events.

72. We <u>spend</u> our vacations at the beach.

We _____ our vacations at the beach.

73. Flowers <u>spring</u> from the ground in May.

Flowers _____ from the ground in May.

74. I <u>stand</u> by my decision.

I _____ by my decision.

75. Ian <u>steals</u> candy from his brother.

Ian _____ candy from his brother.

76. Our shoes <u>stick</u> to the dirty floor.

Our shoes _____ to the dirty floor.

77. The bees <u>sting</u> the picnickers.

The bees _____ the picnickers.

78. Lightning <u>strikes</u> the barn often.

Lightning _____ the barn often.

79. I <u>swim</u> at the community pool.

I _____ at the community pool.

80. I <u>take</u> doughnuts to work.

I _____ doughnuts to work.

81. Mr. Vega <u>teaches</u> my daughter.

Mr. Vega _____ my daughter.

82. Betsy <u>tears</u> tickets at the concert hall.

Betsy _____ tickets at the concert hall.

83. Constance <u>tells</u> the truth.

Constance _____ the truth.

84. I <u>think</u> of you often.

I _____ of you often.

85. The quarterback <u>throws</u> the ball.

The quarterback _____ the ball.

86. We <u>understand</u> the directions.

We _____ the directions.

87. Luis <u>wakes</u> the baby.

Luis _____ the baby.

88. We <u>wear</u> casual clothes to work.

We _____ casual clothes to work.

89. Aziza <u>wins</u> every card game.

Aziza _____ every card game.

90. The soldier <u>writes</u> to his family every day.

The soldier _____ to his family every day.

As you check your work on the pre-test against the following chart, circle each irregular verb that you spelled incorrectly in the past tense.

Power Tip

For an expanded list of irregular verbs, you might consult online resources, such as **www.englishpage.com.**

Irregular Past Tense Verbs

BASE FORM	PAST TENSE FORM	BASE FORM	PAST TENSE FORM	BASE FORM	PAST TENSE FORM
be (I *am*; you/we/they *are*; he/she/it *is*)	was/were (I/he/she/it *was*; you/we/they *were*)	give	gave	send	sent
		go	went	set	set
		grow	grew	shake	shook
		have	had	show	showed
become	became	hear	heard	shrink	shrank
begin	began	hide	hid	shut	shut
bite	bit	hold	held	sing	sang
blow	blew	hurt	hurt	sink	sank
break	broke	keep	kept	sit	sat
bring	brought	know	knew	sleep	slept
build	built	lay (*to put down*)	laid	speak	spoke
buy	bought			spend	spent
catch	caught	lead	led	spring	sprang
choose	chose	leave	left	stand	stood
come	came	let	let	steal	stole
cost	cost	lie (*to recline*)	lay	stick	stuck
dive	dived, dove	light	lit	sting	stung
do (I/you/we/they *do*; he/she/it *does*)	did (I/you/we/he/she/it/they *did*)	lose	lost	strike	struck
		make	made	swim	swam
		mean	meant	take	took
		meet	met	teach	taught
draw	drew	pay	paid	tear	tore
drink	drank	put	put	tell	told
drive	drove	quit	quit	think	thought
eat	ate	read	read	throw	threw
fall	fell	ride	rode	understand	understood
feed	fed	ring	rang	wake	woke, waked
feel	felt	rise	rose	wear	wore
fight	fought	run	ran	win	won
find	found	say	said	write	wrote
fly	flew	see	saw		
freeze	froze	seek	sought		
get	got	sell	sold		

For more practice with irregular past tense verbs, go to **bedfordstmartins.com/ steppingstones.**

Memorizing Irregular Past Tense Verbs

Once you have identified the irregular past tense forms that you do not know, it's time to use some memorization strategies to help the correct forms "stick" in your mind. These strategies work best in combination, so plan to use as many of them as possible.

Priority Lists.   Review the chart on page 393 and pick the three to five verbs that you use most frequently but missed on the pre-test. This will be your **priority list**. Practice only these words for two or three days (or more, if necessary) until you know them by heart. To practice, invent sentences using these verbs, say the correct forms out loud, and complete online practices (visit **bedfordstmartins.com/steppingstones**). You can also try some of the other strategies that we'll discuss later in this section.

Next, go back to the chart and pick three to five more verbs that you missed on the pre-test. Add these words to your priority list. Then, practice *all* the words on your priority list until you know them by heart.

Repeat this process until you have incorporated all the verbs that you missed on the pre-test into your practice. Remember not to rush; practice each new group for as many days as you need to until you can say and write the correct past tense form without hesitation.

Visual Aids.   For each new word on your priority list, make a **flash card**. To do this, use small index cards that you can hold comfortably in your hand. On one side of a card, write the present tense verb in large, bold print. (Write only one word per card to increase the visual impact.) On the back of the card, write the past tense form in large, bold print. Keep your cards with you as often as possible throughout the day (in your backpack, in a convenient place at work, or other convenient location) and review them whenever you have a few free minutes: on the bus, eating breakfast, on a break at work, waiting for your class to start. These moments of practice will add up to make a big difference in your mastery of verbs.

You might also buy a pack of medium or large **sticky notes**. On the front of each note, write the past tense form of a different verb from your priority list. Then, stick these notes on surfaces in your daily environment: one on the refrigerator, one on the bathroom mirror, one on your dashboard, one on your boyfriend's or girlfriend's forehead, and so on. Each time you see one of the sticky notes, pause to pronounce the verb and spell it out loud so that your brain records each letter. These few seconds of concentration can really boost your mastery of verbs.

Auditory Aids.   For some of the verbs that you find especially challenging, create a **rhyme** using the past tense form. For example, *I **bit** the **pit** of a perfect peach.* If you have made flash cards for these verbs (see Visual Aids), write the rhyme under the past tense form. Each time you review the flash cards, say the rhymes out loud. Often, rhymes are easier to remember than isolated words.

Also, review the chart of irregular verbs, looking for two or more past tense verbs that rhyme with one another. For example, *fought* and *bought* rhyme. Now, create a rhyming sentence using both of these words: *The couple **fought** about the house they **bought**.* Write this rhyme on the flash cards for both verbs, under the past tense form, and say it out loud each time you review the flash cards.

If you have trouble thinking of rhymes, ask your family or friends to help you: many people love to make up sayings.

Tactile Aids. For this strategy, you will need to make small **letter blocks**. Cut out 1-by-1-inch squares of cardboard and use a marker to write one bold letter on each block. Look at the verbs on your first priority list (see page 394) and make sure that you have all the letter blocks necessary to spell each of these words, one at a time. (If you own the *Scrabble* game, you can use the letter tiles for this strategy.) Put all of these letter blocks into a pile.

Now, it's time to practice. Select one of the words from your first priority list, using flash cards if you made them (see Visual Aids). First, look at the present tense verb. Then, pick the letter blocks necessary to spell the past tense form, placing the letters side by side. Then, check the spelling by flipping over the flash card or referring to the irregular verbs chart. Mix the letter blocks back into the pile and move on to another verb from your priority list. Manipulating these letter blocks will help you remember the verbs more easily.

As you add new verbs to your priority list, create new letter blocks that you will need to spell each additional past tense verb. You can keep the letter blocks in a plastic Baggie and carry them with you.

ACTIVITY 5: Teamwork
MODERATE

Working with two or three classmates, identify five to ten irregular past tense verbs that you all have trouble with. Then, as a group, try one or more of the memorization strategies. For example, you might

- have each person create a flash card for two or three different verbs, with the present tense on one side and the past tense on the other. Then, have someone collect the cards, keeping the cards present-tense-up, and scramble them. Going through one card at a time, see who can call out the past tense form the fastest.

- have each person pick a verb and make up a rhyme with it. Decide whose rhyme is the funniest or most original.

FIX IT: Common Verb Problems

The following sections discuss some errors that often occur with use of the present and past tenses.

SUBJECT-VERB AGREEMENT ERRORS

A verb is said to "agree" with its subject when it is in the correct form for that subject according to the rules of English grammar. As you have already learned, when the subject is *he*, *she*, or *it* (or some equivalent of *he*, *she*, or *it*, such as *Terri* or *the iPod*), the verb must end in **-s** in the present tense (*play***s**).

Making sure that verbs agree with their subjects can be tricky in certain instances, such as with the verbs *be*, *have*, and *do* (see page 386). Here, we'll look at some other situations where agreement problems may occur. As you'll see, these errors are often made in the present tense.

Verbs Separated from the Subject

As you learned in earlier chapters, words or word groups often separate the subject of a sentence from its verb. Let's look at some examples.

> **PREPOSITIONAL PHRASE**
> The workers <u>on the first shift</u> eat lunch early.

For more on prepositional phrases, see Chapter 10.

> **DESCRIPTIVE CLAUSE**
> The veterinarian <u>who cares for my dogs</u> recommends all-natural pet food.

For more on descriptive clauses, see Chapter 13.

> **MODIFYING PHRASE**
> Global climate change, <u>worsening every year</u>, continues to draw concern.

For more on modifying phrases, see Chapter 14.

When words come between the subject and verb, you need to make the verb agree with the subject, not with the word that comes right before the verb. Crossing out prepositional phrases, descriptive clauses, modifying phrases, and other such word groups can help you identify the subject and its verb. Take a look:

Power Tip

On pages 396–400, only subjects (not other nouns) are highlighted in blue.

INCORRECT   The babysitter who watches my children are friendly.

> **HE/SHE EQUIVALENT**   **-S ENDING ON VERB**

REVISED   The babysitter ~~who watches my children~~ is friendly.

The subject of the sentence is *babysitter*, not *children*, as we can see by crossing out the prepositional phrase. The verb *is* agrees with *babysitter*.

📶 **ACTIVITY 6**

MODERATE

For each sentence below, do the following:

- Cross out any prepositional phrases, descriptive clauses, or modifying phrases.
- Underline the subject, and circle the verb.
- If the verb agrees with the subject, write "OK" in the space provided.
- If the verb does not agree with the subject, rewrite the sentence in the space provided, using the correct form of the verb.

EXAMPLE: The <u>clothes</u> <del>at P.J.'s Discount</del> (is) hipper than most expensive brands.

The clothes at P.J.'s Discount are hipper than most expensive

brands.

1. The coffee at work tastes like varnish.

2. The bread that I purchased for my children's lunches look moldy.

3. Identity theft on online shopping sites are increasingly common.

4. The police officer who parks in the CVS lot tickets many speeders each morning.

5. The children, tired after their long days of school and homework, collapses on the couch every night.

Verbs before the Subject

In some sentences, the verb comes before the subject. For example, such reversals happen in questions and in statements that begin with *There is* or *There are*.

Take a look at the following questions:

Where is the entrance?

Who are your favorite athletes?

The subjects are the words in blue, not *Who* or *Where*. If you are confused about how to identify subjects in questions, turn the questions around:

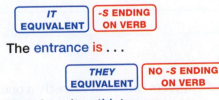

The entrance is . . .

Your favorite athletes are . . .

As we can see, the subjects and verbs in these examples agree. Now, take a look at the following statements:

There is a big bug on the wall.

There are three infants at my daughter's daycare.

For more practice on subject-verb agreement, go to **bedfordstmartins.com/ steppingstones**.

Again, the subjects are blue. If you are confused about how to identify subjects in statements that begin with *There is* or *There are*, turn the statements around:

> **IT EQUIVALENT** **-S ENDING ON VERB**
>
> A big bug is on the wall.

> **THEY EQUIVALENT** **NO -S ENDING ON VERB**
>
> Three infants are at my daughter's daycare.

As we can see, the subjects and verbs in these examples agree.

ACTIVITY 7

MODERATE

For each sentence below, do the following:

- Underline the subject, and circle the verb. If you have trouble identifying the subject, you may want to turn the question or statement around.
- If the verb agrees with the subject, write "OK" in the space provided.
- If the verb does not agree with the subject, rewrite the sentence in the space provided, using the correct form of the verb.

EXAMPLE: There is three plants in this room.

There are three plants in this room.

1. What are your favorite type of music?

_____

2. There is plates in the sink.

_____

3. There is a lot of good restaurants in that neighborhood.

_____

4. Where are those books you borrowed?

_____

5. Who are the nicest person you know?

_____

Verbs with Compound Subjects

As you learned in Chapter 11, **compound subjects** consist of more than one subject. Often, compound subjects are joined with the conjunction *and*. Take a look:

> **COMPOUND SUBJECT**
>
> Emily and Jason laugh.

However, if *or* instead of *and* is used as the conjunction, the verb needs to agree with the subject that is closest to the verb. Consider these examples:

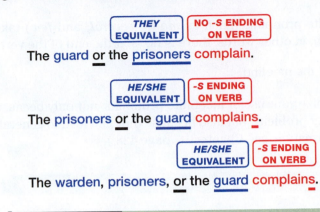

The guard or the prisoners complain.

The prisoners or the guard complains.

The warden, prisoners, or the guard complains.

 ACTIVITY 8

EASY

For each sentence below, do the following:

- In the space provided, write the correct present tense form of the verb in parentheses.
- If the verb ends in -s, circle the s or mark it with a highlighter.

EXAMPLE: Sandro and Ellen _____ *are* _____ (be) worried about their finances.

1. Grandma and the children _____ (watch) movies together.
2. Jonathan and Chanda _____ (be) in love.
3. The Morettis or their son _____ (park) in this space.
4. Roy, Janice, and Tanya _____ (cook) delicious food for every neighborhood picnic.
5. The parents or the child _____ (fill) out the form.

Indefinite Pronoun Subjects

Indefinite pronouns refer to general people or things. Most indefinite pronouns, like those in the following list, take the *he/she/it* form of the verb; in other words, there is an -s at the end of the verb. (See the chart in Chapter 16, page 418 as a reminder.)

anybody	neither
anyone	no one
anything	nobody
each	nothing
either	one
everybody	somebody
everyone	someone
everything	something

Everyone is excited about the game.

Nothing bothers me more than mosquitoes.

However, some indefinite pronouns (such as *many, several,* and *few*) take the *they* form of the verb; in other words, there is no *-s* at the end of the verb.

Few plan to attend the meeting.

It's a good idea to minimize your use of indefinite pronouns, not only because they can cause agreement problems but also because they can lead to generalizations. (For more information, see Chapter 16, page 428.)

ACTIVITY 9

For each sentence, do the following:

- In the space provided, write the correct present tense form of the verb in parentheses.

- If the verb ends in *-s,* circle the *s* or mark it with a highlighter.

EXAMPLE: Everything _____i(s)_____ (be) fine.

1. Everybody _____ (like) pizza.

2. Many _____ (be) called, but few _____ (be) chosen.

3. No one _____ (want) to deliver bad news.

4. Somebody _____ (leave) muddy footprints across our driveway every morning.

5. Most members of my church contribute to charities, and several _____ (volunteer) at local organizations.

ERRORS BASED ON PRONUNCIATION

When we speak, we sometimes run words together in our pronunciation. Then, when we write these words, we try to spell them the way we pronounce them. This is how we end up with nonstandard verbs like **gonna, wanna, gotta, should of, would of,** and **could of.** Study the following examples:

FOUNDATION WORDS

NOUNS
VERBS

DESCRIPTIVE WORDS
ADJECTIVES
ADVERBS

CONNECTING WORDS
PREPOSITIONS
CONJUNCTIONS

NONSTANDARD ENGLISH	STANDARD ENGLISH
Our team is gonna win the game.	Our team is going to win the game.
I wanna lose some weight.	I want to lose some weight.
They gotta find a new apartment.	They have to find a new apartment.
Julio should of studied.	Julio should have studied.
We would of forgotten the date.	We would have forgotten the date.
Sheila could of found a better job.	Sheila could have found a better job.

It is common to see these nonstandard verb forms in personal e-mails. However, you should eliminate them from your academic and professional writing.

ACTIVITY 10

MODERATE

Rewrite each of the following sentences to eliminate nonstandard verbs. There may be more than one nonstandard verb in each sentence.

EXAMPLE: We gotta leave or we're gonna be late.

We have to leave or we're going to be late.

1. Do you wanna try my recipe for lasagna?

2. We gotta finish this report if we're gonna leave early on Friday.

3. Ernest would of won the lottery if he had played his number this week.

4. We could of taken that shortcut, and we should of.

5. Nobody is gonna believe your story; you should of made up a better one.

SHIFT ERRORS

Some errors result from accidental shifts (inconsistencies) in verb tense or in other verb usages. The following sections will examine these shifts and how they happen.

Shifts in Verb Tense

As you have learned, we use verb tenses to show when an action took (or takes) place. Take a look at these examples:

| AN ACTION IN THE PAST | The airplane landed on the wrong runway. |
| A REGULAR ACTION (PRESENT TENSE) | I cash my paycheck on Friday afternoon. |

If we are describing several actions that took (or take) place *together*, we need to be sure that the verb tenses match. Take a look:

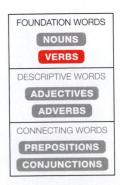

FOUNDATION WORDS

NOUNS

VERBS

DESCRIPTIVE WORDS

ADJECTIVES

ADVERBS

CONNECTING WORDS

PREPOSITIONS

CONJUNCTIONS

For more practice with fixing nonstandard verbs, go to **bedfordstmartins.com/ steppingstones**.

TWO RELATED ACTIONS IN THE PAST	The airplane landed on the wrong runway and narrowly missed another plane.
TWO RELATED, REGULAR ACTIONS (PRESENT TENSE)	I cash my paycheck on Friday afternoon and buy food for the weekend.

In both sentences, the verbs are consistent (the same) in tense. However, if we change one of the verbs to a different tense without a good reason for doing so, the sentence will not make sense:

Incorrect Shift in Verb Tense

> **PAST**   **PRESENT**
>
> The airplane landed on the wrong runway and narrowly misses another plane.

> **PAST**   **PRESENT**
>
> I cashed my paycheck on Friday afternoon and buy food for the weekend.

This unnecessary change in verb tense usually happens when we are not paying close attention to the spelling of our verbs.

Sometimes, a sentence may contain two actions that happen at different times. In this case, a change in verb tense may make sense:

> **AN ACTION IN THE PAST**   **A CURRENT STATE (PRESENT TENSE)**
>
> Rebecca joined the National Guard, but she regrets her decision.

Rebecca joined the National Guard at some point in the past, but she regrets her decision now, in the present. This change in verb tense makes perfect sense.

 ACTIVITY 11

EASY

For each sentence below, do the following:

- Decide whether or not the verb tense is consistent.
- If the tense is consistent, write a **C** in the margin.
- If the tense is inconsistent, cross out one of the verbs and write the correct verb tense above it.

EXAMPLE: Last night I went to a restaurant and ~~have~~ a frustrating experience.   *had*

1. People in line for tables were upset because the wait was more than an hour and a half.

2. After we sat down, our server ignores us for another half an hour.

3. The kitchen sent my friend the wrong dish, so we wait twice as long for our entrées.

For more practice with using consistent verb tense, go to **bedfordstmartins .com/steppingstones**.

4. When our food finally came out, mine resembles dog food and my

friend's tastes like dirt.

5. When we asked the manager for a discount, he refuses.

Shifts When Describing Historical Events

Incorrect shifts in verb tense commonly occur when we are describing historical events or telling stories because these descriptions may involve multiple sentences and multiple verbs. In these instances, it is important to pay close attention to verbs, keeping them consistent.

In describing a historical event, most writers relate the facts in the past tense. Here is a description of the Boston Tea Party:

> On an icy December evening in 1773, Boston's Old South Meeting House <u>was</u> ablaze with the fury of revolution. Samuel Adams <u>led</u> the revolt against the British government's taxation of colonists. He <u>convinced</u> a group of Boston patriots to disguise themselves as Mohawk Indians and attack three British cargo ships carrying tea for which colonists would be taxed. The patriots, known as the Sons of Liberty, <u>stormed</u> out of the meeting house and <u>descended</u> on Boston Harbor. There, they <u>boarded</u> the ships and <u>destroyed</u> 342 crates of tea by throwing them into the water. The hoots and howls of the revolutionaries <u>were</u> heard late into the night.

However, a writer may choose to narrate a historical event in the present tense to give it more dramatic impact. Here is an example:

> On an icy December evening in 1773, the Old South Meeting House <u>is</u> ablaze with the fury of revolution. Samuel Adams <u>leads</u> the revolt against the British government's taxation of colonists. He <u>convinces</u> a group of Boston patriots to disguise themselves as Mohawk Indians and attack three British cargo ships carrying tea for which the colonists would be taxed. The patriots, known as the Sons of Liberty, <u>storm</u> out of the meeting house and <u>descend</u> on Boston Harbor. There, they <u>board</u> the ships and <u>destroy</u> 342 crates of tea by throwing them into the water. The hoots and howls of the revolutionaries <u>are</u> heard late into the night.

Both of these descriptions of the Boston Tea Party are grammatically correct because the verb tense is consistent in each one. Notice that the first sentence of each narrative establishes the tense that the entire story will use. Always be sure that the verbs in the first sentence of any narrative that you write are in the tense you really intend. In most cases, you will want to stay with this tense to avoid confusing shifts like the following:

> On an icy December evening in 1773, the Old South Meeting House <u>was</u> ablaze with the fury of revolution. Samuel Adams <u>led</u> the revolt against the British government's taxation of colonists. He <u>convinces</u> . . .

Boston Tea Party: an act of protest of colonial Americans against Britain's policy of taxing the colonists without giving them government representation. The Boston Tea Party is one of the events that led to the Revolutionary War (1775–1783), which resulted in America's independence from Britain.

Power Tip

If you are writing about past events for a history class, ask your professor what tense he or she prefers. In writing about events in a work of literature, it is conventional to use the present tense. For example, *In The Scarlet Letter, Hester Prynne* **maintains** *her dignity despite being branded with the letter* A, *for* adultery.

Power Tip

For more information on narration, see Chapter 8.

Shifts When Telling a Story

Incorrect shifts in verb tense can also occur when telling stories.

Many writers use the past tense correctly when telling a personal story. Writers can also tell stories in the present tense to heighten the dramatic energy. However, sometimes we may begin a story in the *past* tense but then get so involved in the action or details that we shift to the *present* tense without realizing it, creating an incorrect shift.

My happiest memory <u>was</u> leading my high school basketball team to victory in the regional championship. Imagine this scene: just thirty seconds <u>remained</u> on the clock. The gymnasium <u>was</u> packed with fans. My team, Lincoln Heights, and the rival team, Bonaventure, <u>struggle</u> for control of the ball as Bonaventure <u>fights</u> to hold onto its one-point lead. Sweat <u>drips</u> in my eyes and nearly <u>blinds</u> me. Suddenly, the ball <u>flies</u> in front of me, and I <u>intercept</u> it. I <u>see</u> three seconds on the clock and <u>make</u> a wild, half-blind toss toward the net—SCORE!

At other times, writers get so swept up in the drama of a story that they jump back and forth between tenses. Read this version of the basketball story and notice how the verb tenses start shifting back and forth. For example:

My happiest memory <u>was</u> leading my high school basketball team to victory in the regional championship. Imagine this scene: just thirty seconds <u>remained</u> on the clock. The gymnasium <u>was</u> packed with fans. My team, Lincoln Heights, and the rival team, Bonaventure, <u>struggle</u> for control of the ball as Bonaventure <u>fights</u> to hold onto its one-point lead. Sweat <u>dripped</u> in my eyes and nearly <u>blinded</u> me. Suddenly, the ball <u>flies</u> in front of me, and I <u>intercepted</u> it. I <u>see</u> three seconds on the clock and <u>made</u> a wild, half-blind toss toward the net—SCORE!

This sort of "out of control" shift in verb tense is a common problem for inexperienced writers. If you are ever unsure about your use of verb tense when writing a story, ask your instructor for guidance.

ACTIVITY 12

For the passage below, do the following:

- Read the first sentence and decide whether the story is in the past or present tense.
- Read the rest of the passage, crossing out any verbs that are not in the correct tense.
- In each place where you have crossed out a verb, write the correct verb form above it.

You should find five verb tense errors.

(1) Isabella Baumfree, who later took the name Sojourner Truth, was a former slave who became a passionate spokesperson for

African American and women's rights. (2) Born in 1797 to slave parents in New York, she spent half her life as a slave. (3) She endured savage treatment, and her young son Peter is sold to another family who abused him. (4) Finding refuge in religion, Baumfree becomes an inspiring preacher and abolitionist. (5) In 1843, she changes her name to Sojourner Truth and spread her message everywhere she went. (6) In 1854, at a women's rights convention in Akron, Ohio, she delivers a now famous speech in which she asked, "Ain't I a woman?" (7) In this speech, this genuine, plain-speaking woman drives home the point that women should be regarded as equals to men. (8) In 1883, Sojourner Truth died, leaving a powerful legacy.

> **abolitionist:** someone who fought for the elimination of slavery

Interrupting a Story with Current Information or Facts. Again, most stories are told in the past tense. Sometimes, however, we may want to interrupt the action of a story with current information or facts. This information may make more sense in the present tense. As you read the following story, notice that the action is in the past tense (the verbs highlighted in yellow) and that current information and facts are in the present tense (highlighted in purple):

> When the patrol car flashed its lights behind my brother and me, I sensed that something wasn't right. My brother, who was driving, has a spotless record and drives conservatively. He also keeps his registration tags and his vehicle maintenance up to date, so I knew that the cops hadn't chosen us because of a traffic violation, old tags, or an extinguished taillight. My brother pulled carefully onto the shoulder of the road and turned off the engine. As the cops approached from both sides, they aimed their flashlights in the backseat like they were searching for something. Suddenly, I remembered what my cousin always said about the police in our town: they are often guilty of racial profiling, stopping innocent drivers just because of their race. My brother and I happen to be Latino, so I prepared myself for the worst . . .

The brother's driving record and responsible behavior, the profiling by police, and the race of the writer and his brother are *current* and *factual* details, so it makes sense to keep them in the present tense. Interrupting a story with current information in the present tense can be tricky. Check any story you write carefully to make sure that any shifts to the present tense are justified. If you are uncertain about whether a shift to the present tense is correct, ask your instructor for guidance.

ACTIVITY 13

For the passage below, do the following:

- Read the passage to confirm that it's generally in the past tense.
- Look for any sentences that contain current information or facts.
- In these sentences, cross out any verbs that are in the past tense. Above them, write the correct present tense verbs.

You should find three sentences that contain current information or facts.

NASA: the National Aeronautics and Space Administration, the U.S. government agency responsible for space exploration

(1) Of all NASA's space missions, one of the most familiar to Americans was Apollo 13 even though it never reached its destination. (2) The three-man crew of Apollo 13 lifted off on April 11, 1970, bound for the moon. (3) Official NASA records showed that almost 56 hours into the flight, oxygen tank 2 on the spacecraft blew up. (4) That explosion caused oxygen tank 1 to fail also. (5) As a result, the craft lost oxygen and critical electrical power. (6) The moon landing was canceled, and all attention was turned to bringing the astronauts home safely. (7) The crew deactivated some systems to preserve power needed for re-entry and landing. (8) During the crisis, the crew endured loss of cabin heat and limited water supplies. (9) In the end, a NASA team led the three astronauts safely back to Earth. (10) This true space drama continued to fascinate people. (11) It inspired the 1995 film *Apollo 13,* starring Tom Hanks as astronaut Jack Swigert.

Terminology Tip
Helping verbs "help" other (main) verbs. For more information, see Chapter 10, page 231.

Using *Can/Could* and *Will/Would*. Most students have no trouble using the helping verbs *can* and *will*. *Can* shows an <u>ability</u> to do something, and *will* shows an <u>intention</u> (plan) to do something. Take a look:

AN <u>ABILITY</u> TO BALANCE   I can balance a spoon on my nose.

AN <u>INTENTION</u> TO BUY   I will buy three lottery tickets.

Could and *would* are often used to express an ability or an intention in the past tense:

For more practice with using consistent verb tenses, go to **bedfordstmartins.com/ steppingstones**.

AN ABILITY TO BALANCE	When I was six years old, I could balance a spoon on my nose.
AN INTENTION TO BUY	I told my mother I would buy three lottery tickets.

In the following passage, you can see how the writer keeps the verb tense consistent, using *can* and *will*. Notice that the highlighted verbs in the first sentence establish this story in the present tense:

> I am still a student, so I have to follow my parents' house rules. For example, I can go out only two nights a week, Friday and Saturday. On the other nights, I can invite friends to the house to study. My parents will allow me to have a part-time job, but I can work up to only twenty hours per week. If my grades start to slip, I will have to cut back on hours at work or quit. My parents will also let me participate in one extracurricular activity, like a sports team or student government. However, if I neglect my studies because of this activity, I will have to give it up. These rules may seem strict, but I know they can help me succeed, so I will obey them. When I live on my own, I can make my own house rules, but as long as I live at home, I will respect my parents' wishes.

Now, watch what happens when this story changes to the past tense. The helping verbs change to *could* and *would*, and they stay consistent. Once again, notice how the highlighted verbs in the first sentence establish this story in the past tense:

> When I was a high school student, I had to follow my parents' house rules. For example, I could go out only two nights a week, Friday and Saturday. On the other nights, I could invite friends to the house to study. My parents would allow me to have a part-time job, but I could work up to only twenty hours per week. If my grades started to slip, I would have to cut back on hours at work or quit. My parents would also let me participate in one extracurricular activity, like a sports team or student government. However, if I neglected my studies because of this activity, I would have to give it up. These rules may have seemed strict, but I knew they could help me succeed, so I would obey them. I knew that when I lived on my own, I could make my own house rules, but as long as I lived at home, I would respect my parents' wishes.

Some writers have difficulty staying consistent when using these helping verbs. In conversation, we often jump back and forth between *can/could* and *will/would*, and most people don't notice. In our writing, we sometimes repeat this error without recognizing it. As an example, read the following passage and notice that it *sounds* correct:

> I am still a student, so I have to follow my parents' house rules. For example, I can go out only two nights a week, Friday and Saturday. On the other nights, I can invite friends to the house to study. My parents would allow me to have a part-time job, but I could work up to only twenty hours per week. If my grades start to slip, I will have to cut back on hours at work or quit. My parents would also let me participate in one extracurricular activity, like

Power Tip

Notice that when you use *can, could, will,* and *would*, the verb that appears after these helping verbs does not change form; instead, it is always in the base form (for example, *balance*, not *balanced*).

extracurricular: occurring outside of class

a sports team or student government. However, if I neglect my studies because of this activity, I <u>would</u> have to give it up. These rules may seem strict, but I know they <u>could</u> help me succeed, so I <u>will</u> obey them. When I live on my own, I <u>could</u> make my own house rules, but as long as I live at home, I <u>will</u> respect my parents' wishes.

Although this passage may sound correct, by now you know that it contains inconsistent verb tenses. The writer begins the story in the present tense but then jumps back and forth between *can/could* and *will/would*.

ACTIVITY 14

For the passage below, do the following:

- Read the first sentence and decide whether the writing is in the past or present tense.
- Read the rest of the passage, crossing out any ***can/could/will/would*** helping verbs that are not in the correct tense.
- In each place where you have crossed out a helping verb, write the correct verb form above it.

You should find three errors.

(1) More and more women are entering trades like plumbing, construction, and vehicle repair. (2) There are several reasons for this trend. (3) For one thing, women can earn a good living in these jobs. (4) Experienced plumbers, construction workers, and mechanics could earn $100,000 a year or more. (5) Also, workers can sometimes choose their hours. (6) For example, a plumber with young children might be able to accept jobs only when her children are in school. (7) Also, working in the trades could provide a lot of satisfaction and a sense of accomplishment. (8) If some people think that females can't weld iron or install an engine, women in the trades would prove them wrong again and again. (9) Finally, there will never be a shortage of dripping faucets, leaky roofs, and squealing brakes. (10) Therefore, job security is practically guaranteed for skilled workers.

Could and *would* are also used when we express wishes or possibilities:

    A WISH   I wish I could balance a spoon on my nose.

    A POSSIBILITY   If I had some money, I would buy three lottery tickets.

In college, some writing topics ask you to express your wishes or imagine possibilities. You can recognize these topics by the presence of *could* and *would*:

    If you **could** travel anywhere, which country **would** you like to visit?

    If you **could** spend a day with one famous person, who **would** it be?

    If you **could** change one thing about the world, what **would** it be?

    If you **could** have the career of your dreams, what **would** it be?

When you express a wish or possibility, you should use *could* and *would* consistently; do not jump back and forth unnecessarily between *can/could* and *will/would*. In the following paragraph, the writer has made this mistake:

If I could spend a day with one famous person, it would be Bill Gates, chairman and former CEO of Microsoft. For starters, I would like him to give me an "insider's" tour of the Microsoft headquarters. I would like to start my tour in Bill's executive office. I can sit in his chair and pretend that I am in command of the world's greatest software empire. I can also pick up the phone and surprise my girlfriend with a call from Bill's office. Then, I would like Bill to escort me to the "inner sanctum," where top-secret software design takes place. I will meet with Microsoft's elite designers—some of the highest-paid engineers in the world—and tell them what I don't like about Windows 7, the newest version of Windows. I could give them some tips on how to improve it. I would like to finish my tour by viewing exhibits on Microsoft's products and history at the company's visitor center. Bill can guide me through the exhibits, sharing the details of his many inventions.

When we read this passage quickly, it may *sound* correct because we are used to shifting verb tenses in our casual conversation. However, if you turn in a paper with tense shifts like this, it will likely be marked down. Here is the same passage revised for consistent verb tense:

If I could spend a day with one famous person, it would be Bill Gates, chairman and former CEO of Microsoft. For starters, I would like him to give me an "insider's" tour of the Microsoft headquarters. I would like to start my tour in Bill's executive office. I could sit in his chair and pretend that I am in command of the world's greatest software empire. I could also pick up the phone and surprise my girlfriend with a call from Bill's office. Then, I would like Bill to escort me to the "inner sanctum," where top-secret software design takes place. I would meet with Microsoft's elite designers—some of the highest-paid engineers in the world—and tell them what I don't like about Windows 7, the newest version of Windows. I could give them some tips on how to improve it. I would like to finish my tour by viewing exhibits on Microsoft's products and history at the company's visitor center. Bill could guide me through the exhibits, sharing the details of his many inventions.

◢◢◢ ACTIVITY 15

ADVANCED

For the passage below, do the following:

• Read the passage and determine the general tense of the writing.
• Cross out any **can/could/will/would** helping verbs that are not in the correct tense.
• In each place where you have crossed out a helping verb, write the correct verb form above it.

You should find four errors.

(1) Ashley just graduated from college and is considering moving to a new place. (2) If Ashley could live anywhere in the country, she would choose to live in Chicago. (3) She got her degree in business and she knows that there are many opportunities there. (4) Plus, if she decided to go back to school, she can get a master's degree in business at one of the many schools in the city. (5) She will sell her car and rely on the city's many trains and buses to get around. (6) Her best friend moved there last year and loves it. (7) Ashley could always stay with her friend until she found a place on her own. (8) Or, if her friend decides to move into a new apartment soon, the two of them could find a place together. (9) Although she will miss her friends and family in Detroit, Ashley could easily fly home during the holidays or a long weekend to see them. (10) Plus, she knows they will really enjoy visiting her in Chicago.

FOUNDATION WORDS

NOUNS

VERBS

DESCRIPTIVE WORDS

ADJECTIVES

ADVERBS

CONNECTING WORDS

PREPOSITIONS

CONJUNCTIONS

Shifts in Voice

In most sentences that we write, the subject takes some kind of action. Take a look:

SUBJECT

Judy Hernandez received the employee-of-the-month award.

These sentences are said to be in the **active voice**.

In some cases, however, the subject is <u>acted upon</u>:

SUBJECT

<u>The employee-of-the-month award</u> **was received** by Judy Hernandez.

These sentences are said to be in the **passive voice**. Notice that when we form the passive voice, a *be* helping verb precedes the main verb (*received* in this example).

Generally, it's a good idea to avoid the passive voice because it is less direct than the active voice. However, writers may choose the passive voice when they want to emphasize an object over a human actor or when they do not know who the human actor is:

Some dirty plates **were left** in the sink.

Also, avoid shifting between the active and passive voices. Take a look at these examples:

SHIFT IN VOICE	Judy Hernandez **received** the employee-of-the-month award, and the sales award **was** also **received** by her.
REVISED	Judy Hernandez **received** the employee-of-the-month award, and she also **received** the sales award.

ACTIVITY 16

ADVANCED

Edit the following passage to eliminate four shifts to the passive voice. (In other words, the entire passage should be in the active voice.)

(1) All of the Talanian family members contributed something to make their reunion dinner special. (2) Adam prepared a refreshing salad of cucumbers, lettuce, carrots, and peppers, while a spicy appetizer of beans, garlic, and herbs was made by his sister, Anna. (3) Adam and Anna's parents grilled fish and roasted lamb, and a special yogurt sauce for the lamb was prepared by their Aunt Marie. (4) For dessert, Aunt Marie baked a fruit-and-walnut cake. (5) Many additional desserts were provided by other guests. (6) After the meal, the youngest Talanian, Zakar, played his guitar while romantic tunes were hummed by Anna. (7) Most agreed that the music was their favorite part of the event, and couples danced under the moonlight until late into the evening.

For more practice with avoiding shifts in voice, go to **bedfordstmartins.com/ steppingstones**.

FIXING MIXED VERB ERRORS IN WHOLE PARAGRAPHS

The following activity will give you more practice with recognizing and fixing the verb problems that you have learned about so far in this chapter. You will correct these errors in whole paragraphs—a valuable skill for improving your own writing.

ACTIVITY 17: Mastery Test or Teamwork

Read each of the following paragraphs carefully, looking for verb errors. Then, rewrite each error to fix the problem. The errors will include:

- missing -*s* endings and other subject-verb agreement problems. (See pages 385 and 395–400.)
- missing -*ed* endings on regular past tense verbs. (See page 388.)
- incorrect forms of irregular verbs, both present and past tense. (See pages 389 and 393.)
- some of the verb errors based on pronunciation. (See page 400.)
- inconsistent tense and/or voice. (See page 401.)

The first error in each paragraph has been edited for you.

The following paragraph has thirteen verb errors, including the one that has been edited for you.

1. (1) If I could change one thing about my city, I ~~will~~ *would* make it more bicycle-friendly. (2) This is not an easy task, and not everyone agreed it is necessary. (3) However, I believed that it will address many problems and make the city a better place to live. (4) First, if there was more bicyclists on the road, motorists would get use to sharing it with them. (5) Statistics show that the more cyclists there is, the safer roads are. (6) Second, more people riding bicycles would cut down on the pollution that come from so many cars and taxis. (7) The amount of fossil fuels we use can be reduce drastically, and traffic would be much lighter. (8) Bicycles causes less wear and tear on the roads than cars do, so the city would not half to spend as much money repairing damaged streets. (9) Finally, bicycling was a great way for people to stay in shape. (10) Even if people are too busy to exercise regularly, they

could get a workout on their way to and from work. (11) A big change is required of people, but a bike-friendly city would be better for everyone.

The following paragraph has sixteen verb errors, including the one that has been edited for you.

                             gets

2. (1) It happens every day: someone ~~get~~ a forwarded e-mail from a friend that contains a serious-sounding warning or "news" item.

(2) Often, the e-mail say "This is not a hoax!" or "Forward this to everyone you can!" (3) In many cases, such e-mails are in fact hoaxes. (4) Since e-mail beginned to be used widely, many hoaxes have circulated.

(5) One recent "news flash" claim that using a cell phone while it is charging could lead to electrocution. (6) Another suggest that boycotting major gasoline providers like Mobil and Exxon would bring gas prices down. (7) Investigators finded these items — and many others — to be false. (8) If you wanna avoid being taken in by Internet hoaxes, you does not have to be an expert, but you gotta be a critical consumer. (9) First, if an e-mail shout "This is not a hoax!" it may very well be one. (10) Also, be suspicious if the e-mail report something that you have never heard of before or that has not been confirmed by a trusted news source.

(11) Most important, if an e-mail ask for money, your credit card information, or any other personal information, do not respond, even if the sender claims to be a bank or another trustworthy-sounding organization. (12) Consumers who provide personal information in these cases faces financial losses or even identity theft. (13) Consumer affairs offices in many states says that Internet fraud is mounting, and they recommended that people report potential scams to the authorities. (14) Finally, if you suspects that you have received a hoax e-mail, be courteous and do not forward it to others.

hoax: an attempt to trick others

scams: deceptions, often aimed at making money

📶
MASTERY   **ACTIVITY 18: Mastery Test or Teamwork**

When you have finished correcting one of the paragraphs from Activity 17, get together with two or three classmates. Then, compare the errors that you found and the corrections that you made. If you corrected errors differently, discuss why this might be. If you still have questions about the verbs covered in the activity, ask your instructor.

BRINGING IT ALL TOGETHER:
Using Verbs Correctly

In this chapter, you have learned about using verbs correctly and avoiding common problems caused by incorrect verb usage. Confirm your knowledge by filling in the blank spaces in the following sentences. If you need help, review the pages listed after each sentence.

✔ Nonstandard English tends to be used in _____

_____. Standard English should be used in _____.
(pages 382–83)

✔ The _____ tense is used for regular actions, facts, and actions happening right now. Often, verb errors in this tense happen because of the absence or unnecessary addition of an _____ ending. (page 385)

✔ The _____ tense is used for action completed in the past. Often, verb errors in this tense happen because of the absence or unnecessary addition of an _____ ending. (page 388)

✔ Irregular past tense verbs are not spelled with an _____ ending. (page 389)

✔ Four strategies for learning and memorizing irregular past tense verbs are: 1) _____, 2) _____, 3) _____, and 4) _____. (pages 394–95)

✔ When the ending on a present or past tense verb does not match the subject, this is called an error in _____. (page 395)

✔ Spelling verbs the way you (incorrectly) pronounce them—such as *wanna, gonna, should of, could of*—is called an error based on _____. (page 400)

✔ Jumping back and forth unnecessarily between present and past tense verbs creates incorrect _____ in verb tense. (page 401)

✔ A story told in the past tense may shift into the present tense to include _____. (page 405)

✔ The past tense of *can* is _____. The past tense of *will* is _____. If you are using *will/can* or *would/could* in your writing, you should never _____. (pages 406–7)

CHAPTER 16

Using Pronouns Correctly

Before you read this chapter, it's a good idea to test your understanding of pronouns. You may know more than you think.

OVERVIEW OF THIS CHAPTER

BUILD IT: Pronoun Usage 417

FIX IT: Common Pronoun Problems 422

Bringing It All Together 437

WHAT DO YOU KNOW?

Circle "Yes" if each word group below is a complete, correct sentence. Circle "No" if it is incorrect. Then, explain your choice.

1. **Reggie thinks playing the lotto is a waste of money because you have almost no chance of winning.**

   Yes   No

   Explanation: _____

   _____

2. **Everyone has to take a test to get their driver's license.**

   Yes   No

   Explanation: _____

   _____

3. **Melissa and me decided to pool our money to go to Las Vegas.**

   Yes   No

   Explanation: _____

   _____

4. **Somebody left their cell phone on, and it rang during the movie.**

   Yes   No

   Explanation: _____

   _____

5. **Nobody wants his or her taxes raised.**

   Yes   No

   Explanation: _____

   _____

Pronouns (noun substitutes) take different forms. You'll learn these forms — and how to avoid errors when using them — in this chapter.

SUBJECT   **OBJECT**

I study with him.

POSSESSIVE

His grades are improving.

BUILD IT: Pronoun Usage

A **pronoun** is a word that <u>takes the place</u> of a noun (a person, place, or thing):

NOUN		NOUN
~~Alonzo~~	enjoys	~~espresso~~.
He	enjoys	it.
PRONOUN		PRONOUN

Often, a pronoun <u>refers back to</u> (renames) a specific noun that has already been mentioned:

Alonzo enjoys espresso. It is his favorite drink.

Pronouns can also replace and refer to *noun phrases* (a noun plus descriptive words or a prepositional phrase). Take a look:

NOUN PHRASE		NOUN PHRASE
The whole class	liked	the idea of a take-home exam.
Everybody	liked	that.
PRONOUN		PRONOUN

TYPES OF PRONOUNS

The goal of this chapter is to help you avoid common pronoun errors. To achieve this goal, we will focus on three major groups of pronouns:

1. <u>specific</u> and <u>general</u> pronouns
2. <u>subject</u> and <u>object</u> pronouns
3. <u>possessive</u> pronouns

KEY TO BUILDING BLOCKS

FOUNDATION WORDS
- **NOUNS**
- **VERBS**

DESCRIPTIVE WORDS
- **ADJECTIVES**
- **ADVERBS**

CONNECTING WORDS
- **PREPOSITIONS**
- **CONJUNCTIONS**

Terminology Tip
As you learned in Chapter 10, a pronoun is a type of noun that functions as a noun substitute. In English grammar, the noun that a pronoun refers back to is known as an *antecedent*.

417

Specific versus General Pronouns

Pronouns can be used to identify both <u>specific</u> people and things and <u>general</u> people and things. Look at the examples in the following chart:

SPECIFIC		GENERAL	
People	**Things**	**People**	**Things**
I you he she we they	it this that they these those	anybody anyone everybody everyone no one nobody one somebody someone	anything everything nothing one something

KEY TO CHALLENGE METER

WARMUP

EASY

MODERATE

ADVANCED

MASTERY

Identify the difficulty level of each activity using the key above.

ACTIVITY 1
WARMUP

In each of the following sentences, underline the pronoun(s). Then, label the pronouns as follows:

- Write **SP** above the pronouns that refer to specific people.
- Write **ST** above the pronouns that refer to specific things.
- Write **GP** above the pronouns that refer to general people.
- Write **GT** above the pronouns that refer to general things.

EXAMPLE: Many citizens want to make a difference; <u>this</u> is a natural desire. *(ST above "this")*

1. Malika wanted to do something to help people in need.

2. She wasn't sure what deed would have the most impact.

3. Therefore, she asked for advice from several friends, but the best advice came from a poster on poverty; it read, "Just do something . . . anything."

4. Malika and three friends organized a food drive at school, and they collected many boxes of canned goods and other foods.

5. Everyone at the local homeless shelter was pleased when Malika delivered the donations.

ACTIVITY 2: Teamwork
EASY

Working with two or three classmates, pick a reading from Part Four of this book. Working separately, see how many specific and general pronouns each of you can circle in the reading in three minutes. When time is up, work

For more practice with pronouns, go to **bedfordstmartins.com/ steppingstones**.

together to label the pronouns as identifying specific people, specific things, general people, or general things.

Subject and Object Pronouns

Specific pronouns can take subject or object forms, depending on their role in the sentence. Subject pronouns act as the subject of the sentence: who or what the sentence is about. Look at these examples:

SUBJECT	Marianne fears horses.
SUBJECT PRONOUN (REPLACES *MARIANNE*)	She fears horses.

Objects receive the action of a verb:

OBJECT	A horse kicked Marianne.
OBJECT PRONOUN (REPLACES *MARIANNE*)	A horse kicked her.

In these examples, *Marianne* and *her* receive the action of *kicked*. Notice that the object pronoun has a different form from the subject pronoun: *her* instead of *she*.

Objects can also complete prepositional phrases:

OBJECT PRONOUN

The snoring man was <u>behind me</u>.

PREPOSITIONAL PHRASE (UNDERLINED)

For more on prepositions and prepositional phrases, see Chapter 10, page 240.

Power Tip

In the sentences in this chapter, the blue highlighting is used for pronouns *and* for the words that pronouns replace.

Power Tip

Note that the pronouns *she/her* and *he/him* identify someone as male or female; *she* and *her* can refer only to females, and *he* and *him* can refer only to males.

Subject and Object Pronouns

PEOPLE		THINGS	
Subject	**Object**	**Subject**	**Object**
I →	me	it →	it
we →	us	this →	this
you →	you	that →	that
he/she →	him/her	they →	them
they →	them	these →	them
who →	whom	those →	them

ACTIVITY 3

WARMUP

In each of the following sentences, label the underlined pronouns as **S** for subject pronoun or **O** for object pronoun.

CONTINUED >

o

EXAMPLE: Small children often challenge <u>us</u>.

1. <u>We</u> think that <u>we</u> are in control, but sometimes our children seem to control <u>us</u>.

2. <u>I</u> want my three-year-old, Celia, to learn independence, but <u>she</u> has other ideas.

3. When <u>I</u> leave <u>her</u> at daycare, <u>she</u> cries and says <u>she</u> wants to go to work with <u>me</u>.

4. The daycare providers jiggle toys and try to distract Celia when <u>I</u> leave, and <u>I</u> am grateful to <u>them</u> for helping.

5. <u>I</u> know that Celia will adjust eventually, but her crying still upsets <u>me</u>.

ACTIVITY 4
EASY

In each sentence below, circle the correct subject or object form of the pronoun in parentheses.

EXAMPLE: Recently, (**I** / me) moved to a new town, and (**I** / me) would like to meet more people.

1. It would be nice to meet people to date, but (I / me) would like to make friends, too.

2. My sister tells (I / me) to talk to more people at work and school, but I am shy.

3. I met a nice person, Randi, at school, and (she / her) is going to study with (I / me) on Friday.

4. I would also like to invite (she / her) to the movies since (we / us) both like the same kinds of films.

5. Also, some co-workers have asked (I / me) to go for walks with (they / them) at lunch; (that / them) would be a great way for me to stay in shape and get to know new people.

ACTIVITY 5: Teamwork
EASY

Working with two or three classmates, pick a reading from Part Four of this book. Working separately, see how many subject and object pronouns each of you can circle in the reading in three minutes. When time is up, work together to label the pronouns as subject versus object.

Possessive Pronouns

Possessive pronouns (*my, mine, ours, yours,* and so on) show ownership. Take a look at the following examples (the possessive pronouns are in blue):

> That is my car. That car is mine.
>
> Our house is old and drafty, but yours is warm.
>
> The shark flashed its sharp teeth.

Possessive Forms of Specific Pronouns

SUBJECT PRONOUNS	POSSESSIVE FORMS
I	my, mine
we	our, ours
you	your, yours
he	his
she	her, hers
it	its
they	their, theirs

Power Tip

You do not need to add an apostrophe (') to show possession when you use a possessive pronoun.

Incorrect: This cabin is your's; our's is across the lake.

Revised: This cabin is yours; ours is across the lake.

ACTIVITY 6

EASY

In each of the following sentences, underline the possessive pronoun(s).

EXAMPLE: Last week, <u>our</u> neighborhood had a huge yard sale to benefit a local elementary school.

1. My father brought his old baseball gloves and other sports equipment from our garage.

2. My mother brought some of her old jewelry and a television that we don't use anymore.

3. I contributed some of my old toys, including a clown that laughs when a string is pulled in its back.

4. "You are going to scare someone with that old thing," my mom said, shaking her head.

5. However, one of our neighbors paid five dollars for this treasure.

WHY WE USE PRONOUNS

We use pronouns for convenience, so that we do not have to repeat a noun or a noun phrase over and over. Take a look at the following passage, in which two noun phrases are repeated in every sentence:

My cousin Angel from Puerto Rico bought a classic 1968 Ford Mustang. <u>My cousin Angel from Puerto Rico</u> won the <u>classic 1968 Ford Mustang</u> on eBay. When <u>the classic 1968 Ford Mustang</u> arrived by ship, <u>my cousin Angel from</u>

Puerto Rico inspected the classic 1968 Ford Mustang. My cousin Angel from Puerto Rico discovered that the classic 1968 Ford Mustang was not the classic 1968 Ford Mustang shown on eBay. My cousin Angel from Puerto Rico called the seller about the classic 1968 Ford Mustang and learned that the wrong classic 1968 Ford Mustang had been shipped. My cousin Angel from Puerto Rico returned the classic 1968 Ford Mustang and waited for the right classic 1968 Ford Mustang to be shipped.

Of course, most people would substitute single-word nouns (*Angel, Mustang*) and shorter noun phrases (*my cousin, the car*) for the longer noun phrases:

My cousin Angel from Puerto Rico bought a classic 1968 Ford Mustang. My cousin won the car on eBay. When the Mustang arrived by ship, Angel inspected the car. Angel discovered that the car was not the Mustang shown on eBay. Angel called the seller about the Mustang and learned that the wrong car had been shipped. My cousin returned the car and waited for the right Mustang to be shipped.

This version is more efficient, but it still sounds wordy and repetitive. The most efficient way to communicate this information is to replace some of the nouns and noun phrases with pronouns (*he, it,* and so on):

My cousin Angel from Puerto Rico bought a classic 1968 Ford Mustang. He won it on eBay. When the car arrived by ship, Angel inspected it. He discovered that it was not the Mustang shown on eBay. He called the seller about this and learned that the wrong car had been shipped. Angel returned the Mustang and waited for the right one to be shipped.

In this version, the writer has achieved a nice balance of nouns and pronouns to make the information smoother and easier to digest.

In conversation, we use pronouns as a shortcut to communicate quickly and efficiently. Pronouns are common in academic writing, too; however, in the writing that we do for college, we must use pronouns with extra care, making sure to balance the need for efficiency with the need for *clarity* at all times.

FIX IT: Common Pronoun Problems

The final passage in the previous section shows how an experienced writer uses pronouns to identify <u>specific</u> people and things (Angel, the Mustang, etc.). When used with care, these pronouns can make your academic writing clear and efficient.

Be aware, however, that even specific pronouns, which are friends of the academic writer, can cause problems if used carelessly. The following sections discuss common problems with pronouns.

UNCLEAR REFERENCE

You have learned that a pronoun refers to a noun—a specific person, place, or thing. However, if we use pronouns carelessly, the reference (what the pronoun refers to) may not be 100 percent clear to our reader. In a conversation, we

For more practice with pronouns, go to **bedfordstmartins.com/ steppingstones**.

can always ask for or provide clarification if a pronoun does not make sense. Take a look:

Vince: I had a blind date with a girl named Kirsten on Saturday night. I took her to dinner at a new restaurant. It was a disaster.

Earl: Yeah, I went on a blind date once, and it was a disaster too.

Vince: No, I mean the restaurant was a disaster. The service was slow. It took almost forty minutes to get our food, and it was cold.

Here, the pronoun *it* has an unclear reference: it might refer to *the date* or to *the restaurant*. When Earl gets confused, Vince is able to clarify that the pronoun refers to *the restaurant*. In our conversations, this sort of clarification happens all the time.

However, when we use unclear pronouns in our writing, the reader may not have the opportunity to ask for clarification. Read the following passage and see how difficult it is to follow the writer's ideas:

The hardest thing I ever had to do was put my dog Chester to sleep. To begin with, making the decision to end Chester's life was tough. For a long time, I was in denial about it. They told me to learn more about this. I read a book on it and even saw a documentary on that. It helped me understand our responsibility to them. She explained that allowing it to suffer should not be an option. We decided to make an appointment with him to discuss this. This was the first step in coming to terms with it.

This passage is confusing because most of the pronouns have an unclear reference: we don't know *exactly* what they mean. Take a look:

   . . . in denial about it (In denial about what, exactly?)

   . . . They told me (Who told, exactly?)

   . . . to learn more about this (About what, exactly?)

   . . . I read a book on it (A book on what, exactly?)

   . . . saw a documentary on that (A documentary on what, exactly?)

   . . . It helped me understand (What helped, exactly?)

   . . . our responsibility to them (Our responsibility to whom, exactly?)

   . . . She explained (Who explained, exactly?)

   . . . allowing it to suffer (Allowing what to suffer, exactly?)

   . . . We decided (Who decided, exactly?)

   . . . an appointment with him (An appointment with whom, specifically?)

   . . . to discuss this (To discuss what, exactly?)

   . . . This was the first step (What was the first step, exactly?)

   . . . in coming to terms with it (Coming to terms with what, exactly?)

The reader should not have to pause to guess about what a pronoun means. If you suspect that a pronoun in your writing is unclear, replace it with a noun or noun phrase that clarifies your meaning. Compare the following version of the passage to its original:

euthanasia: humanely ending the life of a very ill creature

The hardest thing I ever had to do was put my dog Chester to sleep. To begin with, making the decision to end Chester's life was tough. For a long time, I was in denial about Chester's terminal condition. My family told me to learn more about cancer in animals. I read a book on cancer in dogs and even saw a documentary on pet euthanasia. The film helped me understand our responsibility to our terminally ill pets. The author of the book explained that allowing a pet to suffer should not be an option. My family and I decided to make an appointment with the vet to discuss Chester's situation. Making this appointment was the first step in coming to terms with my responsibility to Chester.

ACTIVITY 7

MODERATE

For the paragraph below, do the following:

- Underline any pronouns that have an unclear reference.
- Using your imagination, rewrite the paragraph, adding more specific words in place of the unclear pronouns.

(1) When Dean got to the restaurant on Tuesday morning, it was unlocked. (2) He walked in and they were all turned over and misplaced. (3) It was a mess. (4) He looked around frantically for signs of them, but found nothing. (5) He ran over quickly to see if the money was still in it. (6) Finding nothing stolen, Dean was perplexed. (7) Then, he heard it. (8) He turned around and saw them giggling at him from behind one of them. (9) They hopped out from hiding and told him he should have seen the look on his face. (10) This had scared him at first, but then he realized that it was pretty funny. (11) He gave him a playful punch in the arm and vowed to get back at them soon.

OVERUSE OF *YOU*

In conversation, we often use the pronoun *you* to mean "people in general." In academic writing, however, be careful when using *you*. In the following passage, notice that the writer begins by narrating a personal experience, using the pronouns *I*, *me*, and *my* (see the words highlighted in yellow). Then, unexpectedly, she shifts to the pronouns *you* and *your* to refer to people in general (see the words highlighted in blue).

Doing research for my history assignment was easier than I had expected. First, I found all the materials that I needed online. For instance, the librarian showed me how to use a database called LexisNexis, which contains thousands of articles and documents. All you have to do is type in keywords related to your topic, and you get hundreds of professional articles on that topic. Also, my local library now has whole books in digital format. I was able to read a digital version of Women and Slavery by Gwyn Campbell. You can also Google your topic, but you have to be careful about the quality of the Web sites you find with this search engine.

This shift in pronoun usage is considered nonstandard English. Such shifts are so common in conversational English that many students repeat them in their academic writing without even realizing the error. However, if the subject of a sentence or a paragraph is a specific person, place, or thing, the pronouns referring to that subject should be <u>consistent</u> with it. Take a look at this revision of the previous paragraph:

Doing research for my history assignment was easier than I had expected. First, I found all the materials that I needed online. For instance, the librarian showed me how to use a database called LexisNexis, which contains thousands of articles and documents. All I had to do was type in keywords related to my topic, and I got hundreds of professional articles on that topic. Also, my local library now has whole books in digital format. I was able to read a digital version of Women and Slavery by Gwyn Campbell. I also Googled my topic, but I had to be careful about the quality of the Web sites I found with this search engine.

There are really only two situations in which the pronoun *you* is useful in academic writing:

1. In a direct quotation:

   My boss said to me, "**You** are going to be president of this company one day."

   Here, *you* refers to a specific person, not to people in general.

2. In a paragraph or essay in which you are addressing the reader directly to explain a process:

   To prepare for the SAT exam, **you** should first consider enrolling in a special training class.

   Here, *you* refers to a specific person, the reader.

Terminology Tip
The pronoun error described here is called a **shift in person** because the pronoun shifts unexpectedly from a specific person to the generalized *you*. For more on shifts, see Chapter 15, page 401.

Power Tip
For more on standard and nonstandard English, see Chapter 15, pages 382–83.

Power Tip
Some instructors may prefer that students do not use *you* even when explaining a process. If you are in doubt about your instructor's preference, it's always a good idea to ask.

ACTIVITY 8

WARMUP

For each sentence below, do the following:

- Cross out each *you* pronoun that refers to people in general.
- Above this crossed-out word, write in the pronoun that is consistent with the specific subject of the sentence. (See Chapter 10 for more on identifying subjects.)

CONTINUED >

EXAMPLE: My father likes the view from the hills because ~~you~~ can see for miles.
                                                              he

1. We have always loved Artie's Seafood Restaurant because you can get delicious red snapper there.

2. I'm nervous about the final exam because you need to pass the exam in order to pass the course.

3. As we drove over the summit of the mountain, you could see all the lights of Las Vegas glittering in the valley.

4. Students are pleased with the new class schedule options because you can take classes on weekends.

5. Samantha wants to work on a cruise ship because you will be able to meet so many different people there.

ACTIVITY 9

MODERATE

For the paragraph below, do the following:

- Cross out each *you* pronoun that refers to people in general.
- Above each crossed-out word, write in the pronoun that is consistent with the specific subject of the paragraph.

(1) When Anne was interviewed by a local TV station, she was surprised by what went on behind the scenes. (2) Because the interview was short, she didn't think you would have to get made up by the crew. (3) Anne had figured they would just let you talk into the reporter's large handheld microphone instead of also having a small one pinned to your shirt, and a huge microphone held over your head. (4) She was overwhelmed by all the lights and camera equipment surrounding you for what seemed like such a simple interview. (5) She was also unprepared for how many questions were asked of you, especially since most of them didn't end up on TV. (6) While Anne appreciated the final product that aired, she will never look at TV interviews the same way again.

For more practice with pronouns, go to bedfordstmartins.com/ steppingstones.

OVERUSE OF *IT*

The pronoun *it* is sometimes called the "king of the pronouns" because it is used so frequently. However, the careless use or overuse of this pronoun in academic writing can confuse readers. Take a look:

> Dropping out of high school can lead to a number of problems. To begin with, a teenager can experience a sense of isolation and loneliness without the social opportunities that high school provides. For example, <u>it</u> really made my brother crazy when he quit school in the eleventh grade. He watched television all day to try to forget about <u>it</u>. Even though he still saw his old buddies on the weekends, <u>it</u> was painful. Worst of all, the girls stopped calling, and <u>it</u> became unbearable for him. <u>It</u> proves that dropping out of high school can be a risky choice.

In this passage, each use of the pronoun *it* leads to a lack of clarity:

> . . . <u>it</u> really made my brother crazy (What made him crazy, exactly?)
>
> . . . to forget about <u>it</u> (To forget about what, exactly?)
>
> . . . <u>it</u> was painful (What was painful, exactly?)
>
> . . . <u>it</u> became unbearable for him (What became unbearable, exactly?)
>
> . . . <u>It</u> proves (What proves, exactly?)

The answers to these questions might be clear *in the writer's mind*, but the reader will have to guess, which can result in confusion. A more experienced writer avoids the careless use of *it*, replacing this pronoun with more specific nouns and noun phrases. Let's see how the previous paragraph could be revised:

> Dropping out of high school can lead to a number of problems. To begin with, a teenager can experience a sense of isolation and loneliness without the social opportunities that high school provides. For example, <u>the sudden isolation</u> really made my brother crazy when he quit school in the eleventh grade. He watched television all day to try to forget about <u>his growing sense of loneliness</u>. Even though he still saw his old buddies on the weekends, <u>losing daily contact with them</u> was painful. Worst of all, the girls stopped calling, and <u>the loss of dates</u> became unbearable for him. <u>My brother's example</u> proves that dropping out of high school can be a risky choice.

ACTIVITY 10: Teamwork

ADVANCED

For the paragraph below, do the following:

- Underline unclear uses of *it*.
- Using your imagination, replace the unclear pronouns with more specific words. You may need to replace other words, too.

> (1) A job interview can be stressful, but applicants can take certain steps to make the experience better. (2) For example, they can do research

CONTINUED >

on it. (3) Also, applicants can prepare for it by thinking of questions to ask. (4) It will show their interest in the job. (5) Applicants should also think about questions that the interviewer might ask. (6) These questions might include, "Why do you want this job?" "What skills would you bring to this job?" and "Where do you see yourself in two to five years?"

(7) Doing it in front of a mirror will help an applicant respond confidently during the interview. (8) It doesn't have to be scary; applicants just need to be ready. (9) For those who prepare well, it can be a life-changing experience.

OVERUSE OF INDEFINITE PRONOUNS

The following pronouns are used to identify general people or things:

Indefinite Pronouns

GENERAL	
People	**Things**
anybody	anything
anyone	everything
everybody	nothing
everyone	one
no one	something
nobody	
one	
somebody	
someone	

Using indefinite pronouns to identify general people and things can harm your academic writing for two reasons:

1. They can lead to generalizations.
2. They can lead to awkward agreement.

Next, we'll discuss both reasons in more detail.

Indefinite Pronouns and Generalizations

Pronouns that identify people or things in general are called *indefinite* because they do not identify a *definite* (specific) person or thing. Take a look:

Everybody would like to win the lottery. (Who, exactly?)

If we make this statement, we are saying that *most people* or *people in general* would like to win the lottery. However, this statement is weak because it is not universally true: certainly, there are individuals who do not care about the lottery.

Such *generalizations* are common in spoken language; however, in academic writing, specifics are preferable to generalizations. Therefore, whenever possible, it's a good idea to replace indefinite pronouns with nouns or noun phrases that are more specific:

WEAK	Everybody would like to win the lottery.
BETTER	Most people would like to win the lottery.
MORE SPECIFIC	The average working-class person would like to win the lottery.
	Lottery players would like to win the lottery.
	My best friends would like to win the lottery.

Here is another example of an indefinite pronoun that leads to a generalization:

Nothing upsets me.

If I make this a statement, I mean that *not one single thing upsets me*, with "thing" being a nonspecific term. However, it's hard to imagine that this statement is always true: certainly, a tragedy or a catastrophic event is likely to upset *me*.

In your own academic writing, be careful to find specific nouns or noun phrases to express your thoughts:

WEAK	Nothing upsets me.
BETTER	Very few things upset me.
MORE SPECIFIC	Ordinary difficulties do not upset me.
	Day-to-day problems do not upset me.
	Small failures do not upset me.

As you can see from these examples, indefinite pronouns can lead to weak statements that are not universally true or that are hard to prove. For this reason, you should avoid using indefinite pronouns in your academic writing. Whenever possible, replace an indefinite pronoun with a more specific noun or noun phrase.

ACTIVITY 11

MODERATE

For each sentence below, do the following:

- Underline the indefinite pronoun.
- Using your imagination, rewrite the sentence to replace the pronoun with more specific words. You may need to rewrite other parts of the sentence, too.

CONTINUED >

EXAMPLE: With five seconds left on the clock, <u>everyone</u> was anxious.

With five seconds left on the clock, the fans were anxious.

1. In my history class, someone always knows the answer.

2. Everybody will be going to Janeese's party.

3. If we leave the house unlocked, anything could happen.

4. Anybody can quit smoking.

5. No one can beat Barry's home run record.

Indefinite Pronouns and Awkward Agreement

If you decide to use an indefinite pronoun as the subject of a sentence, you may encounter another common problem. Take a look:

Nobody wants to have their taxes raised.

[SUBJECT]   PRONOUN
                             REFERRING
                             BACK TO
                             SUBJECT

Terminology Tip
When singular pronouns refer back to singular nouns/pronouns and plural pronouns refer back to plural nouns/pronouns, these words are said to agree in **number**.

Although the sentence above *sounds* correct, it contains a common pronoun error: the possessive pronoun *their* (plural) does not match with the subject *nobody* (singular). In other words, the pronoun *their* does not *agree* with the subject.

Remember that <u>most indefinite pronouns are singular</u> even though many of them have plural meanings (*everybody, everyone, everything*). There are just three ways to fix agreement errors with indefinite pronouns:

Singular subject + Singular pronoun

1. Nobody wants to have his or her taxes raised.
2. Nobody wants to have her taxes raised.
3. Nobody wants to have his taxes raised.

Each of these sentences is now grammatically correct. However, each one sounds awkward:

1. *His or her* is wordy, and if you use it over and over, your writing can become cluttered.
2. *Her* by itself sounds odd because not all taxpayers are women.
3. *His* by itself also sounds odd because not all taxpayers are men.

The best way to correct the problem may be to change *nobody* to a more specific subject. Take a look:

Plural subject   +   Plural pronoun

Few taxpayers want to have their taxes raised.

This sentence is a better choice for academic writing because it has a more specific subject, it has a plural pronoun to match a plural subject, and it is not awkwardly worded.

ACTIVITY 12: Teamwork

ADVANCED

Each sentence below has a pronoun agreement error. For each one, underline the subject pronoun and the possessive pronoun that refers back to the subject pronoun. Then rewrite the sentence in two ways:

- First, replace the possessive pronoun, but leave the subject pronoun alone.
- Second, replace the subject pronoun, but leave the possessive pronoun alone.

You may need to change other words as well. For example, if you make the subject plural, you may need to change the verb to agree with it. (For more information, see Chapter 15.)

EXAMPLE: <u>Somebody</u> left <u>their</u> shoes on the porch.

Somebody left her shoes on the porch.

The children left their shoes on the porch.

1. Everyone brings their kids to the company picnic.

   _____

   _____

2. No one wants to have their identity stolen.

   _____

   _____

3. Someone dumps their garbage on the street every week.

   _____

   _____

4. With enough time and patience, anyone can paint their own house.

   _____

   _____

5. Everybody wants their children to succeed.

   _____

   _____

Power Tip
Don't think that you can *never* use indefinite pronouns, but be aware of the problems they can cause. Whenever you are tempted to use such a pronoun, ask yourself if you can find a more specific noun or noun phrase. If you still want to use an indefinite pronoun, make sure it agrees with (matches) the noun it refers back to.

For more practice with agreement of indefinite pronouns, go to **bedfordstmartins.com/ steppingstones**.

OTHER PRONOUN PROBLEMS

Finally, we'll look at some other problems that can occur with pronouns. We'll begin with errors in the use of subject versus object pronouns. To remind yourself of the differences between these types of pronouns, see page 419.

Problems with Subject versus Object Forms

In most sentences with a single subject or object, we have no trouble understanding what type of pronoun to use. Take a look:

SINGLE SUBJECT PRONOUN	I shop for groceries every week.
SINGLE OBJECT PRONOUN	Robin gave the books to <u>me</u>.

When there is more than one subject or object, however, it's sometimes harder to "hear" what pronouns are correct. Take a look at the following sentences, in which the pronoun usage is incorrect:

COMPOUND SUBJECT	<u>Bob and me</u> shop for groceries every week.
COMPOUND OBJECT	Robin gave the books to <u>Maura and I</u>.

Remember, if a pronoun is acting as a subject, the subject form must be used, and if a pronoun is acting as an object, the object form must be used. Let's look at corrected versions of the previous sentences:

> **SUBJECT PRONOUN**

<u>Bob and</u> I shop for groceries every week.

> **OBJECT PRONOUN**

Robin gave the books to <u>Maura and me</u>.

 **ACTIVITY 13**

MODERATE

In the following paragraph, circle the correct pronouns from the choices given in parentheses.

(1) Saturday, Dan and (I/me) went to the museum. (2) Because I live close to (he/him), we met at his house and walked there together. (3) We saw a lot of art that neither (he/him) nor (I/me) had ever seen before.

(4) After that, Dan went with two of my friends and (I/me) to lunch.

(5) Dan and (I/me) have a lot in common, so we have great conversations.

(6) This week, I am going to watch a movie with (he/him) and his friends at his house.

When we make comparisons, we may also have trouble deciding between a subject or an object pronoun. What pronoun would you choose to complete the following sentence?

Bill drives faster than (I / me).

The object pronoun *me* might sound right, but it is incorrect. How can we tell? Let's add words to flesh out the second part of the sentence:

Bill drives faster than (I / me) drive.

or

Bill drives faster than (I / me) do.

It may be clearer now that the subject pronoun *I* is the correct choice. It is correct because *I* is the <u>subject</u> that goes with the added-on verbs (*drive, do*).

Whenever you are in doubt about whether to use a subject or an object pronoun in a comparison, flesh out the comparison.

 ACTIVITY 14
MODERATE

In the following sentences, circle the correct pronoun from the choices in parentheses.

EXAMPLE: Rodney is nicer than (I / me).

1. You are more experienced than (I / me).

2. I wish I could be as tall as (he / him).

3. Grace is generous; no one I know has donated more money than (she / her).

4. My son was upset because the other children got more candy than (he / him).

5. Anita's strength is admirable; not many people have faced as many difficulties as (she / her).

A REMINDER ABOUT *WHO* AND *WHOM*

Who and *whom* are often misused in writing. *Who* is the subject form of the pronoun, and *whom* is the object form. *Who* is usually used before verbs, while *whom* is usually used before nouns and pronouns:

> [VERB]
>
> The person who <u>made</u> lunch used too much pepper.

> [PRONOUN]
>
> The woman whom <u>I</u> met at the party knows you.

Problems with Collective Nouns

Collective nouns refer to groups of people or things. Following are some examples:

audience	company
crowd	family
class	jury
committee	team

In everyday conversation, we often use the plural possessive *their* to refer to collective nouns, but this usually is incorrect in academic writing. Take a look:

The company laid off half of their employees.

In most cases like this one, the members of a group described by a collective noun act as one. Therefore, collective nouns usually are treated as singular. This means that pronouns referring to them usually are singular too.
    Let's look at the corrected version of the previous sentence.

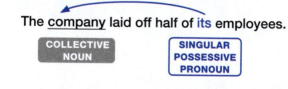

The <u>company</u> laid off half of its employees.

[COLLECTIVE NOUN]   [SINGULAR POSSESSIVE PRONOUN]

And here's another correct example:

The <u>team</u> won its third straight championship.

[COLLECTIVE NOUN]   [SINGULAR POSSESSIVE PRONOUN]

However, collective nouns may be referred to by a plural pronoun if the members of a group are acting as individuals. In the following example, different family members picked up different swimsuits; they acted individually, not as one. Thus, the collective noun has a plural meaning and takes a plural possessive pronoun.

The family picked up their wet swimsuits and hung them on the line.

ACTIVITY 15

MODERATE

For each sentence below, do the following:

- Underline the collective noun. If the members of the collective noun are acting as one, write **O** next to the sentence.
- If they are acting as individuals, write **I** next to the sentence.
- Circle the possessive pronoun (singular or plural) that goes with the collective noun.

EXAMPLE: The jury shared (its / their) decision with the court. o

1. Because of severe weather, the committee decided to delay (its / their) vote.
2. The class turned in (its / their) notebooks to be graded.
3. The audience clapped loudly to show (its / their) appreciation for the performance.
4. The crowd repeated (its / their) angry cheer several times: "Senator Joe must go!"
5. Over the summer, the junior-high team outgrew (its / their) uniforms.

FIXING MIXED PRONOUN ERRORS IN WHOLE PARAGRAPHS

The following activity will give you more practice with recognizing and fixing pronoun errors in whole paragraphs—a valuable skill for improving your own writing.

ACTIVITY 16: Mastery Test or Teamwork

MASTERY

Read the following paragraphs carefully, looking for pronoun errors. Then, rewrite each error to fix the problem. The errors will include:

- unclear pronoun references (see pages 422–24)
- shifts from specific subjects to *you* (see pages 424–25)
- incorrect pronoun agreement (see pages 428–31 and 434–35)
- incorrect use of subject versus object pronouns (see pages 432–34)

CONTINUED >

For more practice with agreement of indefinite pronouns, go to **bedfordstmartins.com/ steppingstones**.

The first error in each paragraph has been edited for you.

The following paragraph has eleven pronoun errors (including the one that has been edited for you).

1. (1) Everyone who meets my mom says that she and ~~me~~ ^I are exactly alike. (2) For starters, I have the same hair and eye color as her, and our faces are the same shape. (3) But the similarities don't stop there. (4) We have the same goofy sense of humor and always make the same types of jokes—sometimes at the exact same time. (5) You will often notice that we make the same facial expressions. (6) Sometimes my similarities with my mom make her feel left out. (7) My mom and me like to cook, but she doesn't. (8) Plus, she likes to go running or play tennis with me, but my sister doesn't usually have the time to go with us. (9) I feel guilty about this, but I don't think it's on purpose. (10) Everybody gets along with one family member better than another. (11) Besides, she likes to go to concerts and go shopping with me, which my mom does not enjoy. (12) When my mom, dad, brother, and I are together, we all enjoy it. (13) I am lucky that my family are so close and that we get along so well.

The following paragraph has thirteen pronoun errors (including the one that has been edited for you).

2. (1) Imagine this situation: a biker hits a pothole and flies from her bike, landing on the sidewalk. (2) Clearly, ~~her~~ ^{she} is injured. (3) Whom would help her, and whom would stand on the sidelines? (4) A research team has investigated these questions, and their answers are quite interesting. (5) First, witnesses who feel positive or fortunate are more likely to help than those experiencing more negative emotions. (6) Also, witnesses who are feeling guilty about something may be more likely to help, perhaps to make up for the act that prompted their guilt. (7) It could stem from anything — from a dishonest act at work to a fight with a friend.

(8) Finally, if you see others who are willing to help, you are more likely to come to a stranger's aid than if you are a lone witness. (9) It might inspire witnesses to act. (10) My personal experience suggests that these observations are true. (11) Once, my husband and me saw a pedestrian get bumped by a car. (12) We had just had a disagreement, and me, personally, was feeling guilty. (13) Also, we saw another person coming to the pedestrian's aid. (14) In seconds, the two of us ran to help. (15) The other person arrived at the scene faster than us, but we were all able to help. (16) Fortunately, the pedestrian had experienced only minor injuries. (17) Based on this experience and the research findings, I conclude that everybody has the ability to help their fellow citizens. (18) Some of us are just more motivated than others, for various reasons.

ACTIVITY 17: Mastery Test or Teamwork

MASTERY

When you have finished correcting one of the paragraphs from Activity 16, get together with two or three classmates. Then, compare the errors that you found and the corrections that you made. If you corrected errors differently, discuss why this might be. If you still have questions about the pronoun problems covered in the activity, ask your instructor.

BRINGING IT ALL TOGETHER:
Using Pronouns Correctly

In this chapter, you have learned about using pronouns correctly. Confirm your knowledge by filling in the blank spaces in the following sentences. If you need help, review the pages listed after each sentence.

✔ A _____ is a word that takes the place of a noun. Often, a pronoun refers back to a specific _____ that has already been mentioned. (page 417)

✔ Three major groups of pronouns are _____,

_____, and _____. (page 417)

CONTINUED >

✔ We use pronouns for _____, so that we do not have to _____. (page 421)

✔ When the pronoun does not refer clearly to a specific noun or noun phrase, this problem is called an _____. (pages 422–23)

✔ One pronoun that means "people in general" and is often overused in student writing is _____. (pages 424–25)

✔ Another pronoun is sometimes called "the king of pronouns" because it is used so frequently. Overusing it can cause confusion. This pronoun is _____. (page 427)

✔ _____ pronouns are used to identify general people or things. These pronouns can lead to two problems: 1) _____ and 2) _____. (page 428)

✔ In academic writing, collective nouns—such as *audience, crowd, class,* and *family*—are usually treated as singular. Consequently, the singular possessive pronoun used to refer to a collective noun is _____ instead of *their*. (page 434)

PART FOUR
A Writer's Reader

CHAPTER 17

School and Learning

READINGS

"The Joy of Reading and Writing: Superman and Me"

"The Sanctuary of School"

As you read the following essays, think about your own educational experiences, both positive and negative. Which of those experiences changed your life, for better or worse? How has your home life supported or worked against your efforts to become educated? Finally, what does it mean to "become educated"? How far can teachers and classroom lessons take us in this effort, and what responsibility must we take on ourselves?

Sherman Alexie

The Joy of Reading and Writing: Superman and Me

Sherman Alexie is a poet, fiction writer, and filmmaker known for his portrayals of contemporary Native American life. He grew up on the Spokane Indian Reservation in Wellpinit, Washington.

I learned to read with a Superman comic book. Simple enough, I suppose. I cannot recall which particular Superman comic book I read, nor can I remember which villain he fought in that issue. I cannot remember the plot, nor the means by which I obtained the comic book. What I can remember is this: I was 3 years old, a Spokane Indian boy living with his family on the Spokane Indian Reservation in eastern Washington state. We were poor by most standards, but one of my parents usually managed to find some minimum-wage job or another, which made us middle-class by reservation standards. I had a brother and three sisters. We lived on a combination of irregular paychecks, hope, fear, and government surplus food.

My father, who is one of the few Indians who went to Catholic school on purpose, was an avid reader of westerns, spy thrillers, murder mysteries, gangster epics, basketball player biographies, and anything else he could find. He bought his books by the pound at Dutch's Pawn Shop, Goodwill, Salvation Army, and Value Village. When he had extra money, he bought new novels at supermarkets, convenience stores, and hospital gift shops. Our house was filled with books. They were stacked in crazy piles in the bathroom, bedrooms, and living room. In a fit of

Power Tip

In the readings in this part of the book, many challenging words are defined. However, you may be unsure of the meanings of other words. Put a check mark by these words and guess their meanings as you read. Then, after you have finished reading, look these words up in a dictionary. Also, consider recording new vocabulary in a special log. (See Chapter 6, page 131, for advice on keeping a vocabulary log.)

1

2

avid: enthusiastic

epics: long, involved tales

441

unemployment-inspired creative energy, my father built a set of book-shelves and soon filled them with a random assortment of books about the Kennedy assassination, Watergate, the Vietnam War, and the entire 23-book series of the Apache westerns. My father loved books, and since I loved my father with an aching devotion, I decided to love books as well.

I can remember picking up my father's books before I could read. **3** The words themselves were mostly foreign, but I still remember the exact moment when I first understood, with a sudden clarity, the purpose of a paragraph. I didn't have the vocabulary to say "paragraph," but I realized that a paragraph was a fence that held words. The words inside a paragraph worked together for a common purpose. They had some specific reason for being inside the same fence. This knowledge delighted me. I began to think of everything in terms of paragraphs. Our reservation was a small paragraph within the United States. My family's house was a paragraph, distinct from the other paragraphs of the LeBrets to the north, the Fords to our south, and the Tribal School to the west. Inside our house, each family member existed as a separate paragraph but still had genetics and common experiences to link us. Now, using this logic, I can see my changed family as an essay of seven paragraphs: mother, father, older brother, the deceased sister, my younger twin sisters, and our adopted little brother.

At the same time I was seeing the world in paragraphs, I also picked **4** up that Superman comic book. Each panel, complete with picture, dialogue, and narrative, was a three-dimensional paragraph. In one panel, Superman breaks through a door. His suit is red, blue, and yellow. The brown door shatters into many pieces. I look at the narrative above the picture. I cannot read the words, but I assume it tells me that "Superman is breaking down the door." Aloud, I pretend to read the words and say, "Superman is breaking down the door." Words, dialogue, also float out of Superman's mouth. Because he is breaking down the door, I assume he says, "I am breaking down the door." Once again, I pretend to read the words and say aloud, "I am breaking down the door." In this way, I learned to read.

This might be an interesting story all by itself. A little Indian boy **5** teaches himself to read at an early age and advances quickly. He reads "Grapes of Wrath" in kindergarten when other children are struggling through "Dick and Jane." If he'd been anything but an Indian boy living on the reservation, he might have been called a prodigy. But he is an Indian boy living on the reservation and is simply an oddity. He grows into a man who often speaks of his childhood in the third person, as if it will somehow dull the pain and make him sound more modest about his talents.

A smart Indian is a dangerous person, widely feared and ridiculed **6** by Indians and non-Indians alike. I fought with my classmates on a daily basis. They wanted me to stay quiet when the non-Indian teacher asked for answers, for volunteers, for help. We were Indian children who were expected to be stupid. Most lived up to those expectations inside the classroom but subverted them on the outside. They struggled with basic reading in school but could remember how to sing a few dozen pow-wow songs. They were monosyllabic in front of their non-Indian teachers but could tell complicated stories and jokes at the dinner table. They

***The Grapes of
Wrath:*** a classic
American novel written
by John Steinbeck
(1902–1968) and
published in 1939

Dick and Jane: main
characters in a series of
children's books aimed
at teaching basic
reading skills

prodigy: a child with
unusual talent

subverted: overturned
or disrupted

powwow: a Native
American ceremony

monosyllabic: consist-
ing of one syllable

submissively ducked their heads when confronted by a non-Indian adult but would slug it out with the Indian bully who was 10 years older. As Indian children, we were expected to fail in the non-Indian world. Those who failed were ceremonially accepted by other Indians and appropriately pitied by non-Indians.

I refused to fail. I was smart. I was arrogant. I was lucky. I read books late into the night, until I could barely keep my eyes open. I read books at recess, then during lunch, and in the few minutes left after I had finished my classroom assignments. I read books in the car when my family traveled to powwows or basketball games. In shopping malls, I ran to the bookstores and read bits and pieces of as many books as I could. I read the books my father brought home from the pawnshops and secondhand. I read the books I borrowed from the library. I read the backs of cereal boxes. I read the newspaper. I read the bulletins posted on the walls of the school, the clinic, the tribal offices, the post office. I read junk mail. I read auto-repair manuals. I read magazines. I read anything that had words and paragraphs. I read with equal parts joy and desperation. I loved those books, but I also knew that love had only one purpose. I was trying to save my life.

Despite all the books I read, I am still surprised I became a writer. I was going to be a pediatrician. These days, I write novels, short stories, and poems. I visit schools and teach creative writing to Indian kids. In all my years in the reservation school system, I was never taught how to write poetry, short stories, or novels. I was certainly never taught that Indians wrote poetry, short stories, and novels. Writing was something beyond Indians. I cannot recall a single time that a guest teacher visited the reservation. There must have been visiting teachers. Who were they? Where are they now? Do they exist? I visit the schools as often as possible. The Indian kids crowd the classroom. Many are writing their own poems, short stories, and novels. They have read my books. They have read many other books. They look at me with bright eyes and arrogant wonder. They are trying to save their lives. Then there are the sullen and already defeated Indian kids who sit in the back rows and ignore me with theatrical precision. The pages of their notebooks are empty. They carry neither pencil nor pen. They stare out the window. They refuse and resist. "Books," I say to them. "Books," I say. I throw my weight against their locked doors. The door holds. I am smart. I am arrogant. I am lucky. I am trying to save our lives.

submissively: meekly; obediently

7   **arrogant:** proud; having an attitude of superiority

8

sullen: silent and resentful

DISCUSS WITH YOUR PEERS

1. In paragraph 3, what metaphor (creative comparison) does the author use to describe "the purpose of a paragraph"? As a college student, how do you think your ability to organize and write coherent paragraphs will help you succeed in other areas of your life?

2. In paragraph 6, underline or highlight examples of how the Indian children hide their intelligence from the non-Indian teachers. Does their behavior make sense to you? Discuss why a child might choose to *play* stupid in an environment where all the adults expect that child to *be* stupid.

CONTINUED >

3. Discuss how the author tries to challenge the failures of the reservation school system when he grows up. Pay close attention to the following sentences: "I throw my weight against their locked doors. . . . I am trying to save our lives." What does the author know about these children that motivates him? If he is already a successful author, why does he say, "save *our* lives"?

IDENTIFY THE PATTERNS

For more on the various writing patterns referenced here, see Chapter 8, Patterns of Development.

1. In paragraphs 2–3 and 6–7, the author uses **exemplification** to develop his writing. First, select one or two of these paragraphs to work with. Next, identify the main idea of each paragraph. Then, underline or highlight some of the examples that the author gives to support each main idea.

2. In paragraph 4, the author uses both **process** and **description**. Because Alexie learned to read by looking at pictures in comic books, he wants to make this process as visual as possible for readers. First, he uses descriptive details to help us visualize the images in the comic book. Next, he specifies each step in the learning process. Underline or highlight some of these details. On a separate sheet of paper, list these steps.

WRITE ABOUT THE READING

1. Discuss the failure of the school system on Alexie's reservation. In what ways does the school fail to educate the children? Use examples from the reading to support your ideas.

2. Discuss how Alexie succeeds in becoming an educated person. Use examples from the reading to support your ideas.

WRITE ABOUT YOUR LIFE

1. Discuss the importance of reading in your life.

2. Discuss your feelings about your own intelligence and how these feelings have affected your school experiences. Are you secure or insecure about your intelligence? Do you hide your intelligence or show it off? Are you more like Alexie when he says, "I refused to fail. I was smart. I was arrogant. I was lucky"? Or are you more like the young Indians who "stare out the window" and "refuse and resist"?

Lynda Barry
The Sanctuary of School

Lynda Barry was born in Wisconsin and raised in Seattle, Washington. Barry has published numerous collections of her comics as well as the novels *The Good Times Are Killing Me* (1988) and *Cruddy* (1999).

I was 7 years old the first time I snuck out of the house in the dark. It **1** was winter and my parents had been fighting all night. They were short on money and long on relatives who kept "temporarily" moving into our house because they had nowhere else to go.

My brother and I were used to giving up our bedroom. We slept on **2** the couch, something we actually liked because it put us that much closer to the light of our lives, our television.

At night when everyone was asleep, we lay on our pillows watch- **3** ing it with the sound off. We watched Steve Allen's mouth moving. We watched Johnny Carson's mouth moving. We watched movies filled with gangsters shooting machine guns into packed rooms, dying soldiers hurling a last grenade and beautiful women crying at windows. Then the sign-off finally came and we tried to sleep.

The morning I snuck out, I woke up filled with a panic about needing **4** to get to school. The sun wasn't quite up yet but my anxiety was so fierce that I just got dressed, walked quietly across the kitchen and let myself out the back door.

It was quiet outside. Stars were still out. Nothing moved and no one **5** was in the street. It was as if someone had turned the sound off on the world.

I walked the alley, breaking thin ice over the puddles with my shoes. **6** I didn't know why I was walking to school in the dark. I didn't think about it. All I knew was a feeling of panic, like the panic that strikes kids when they realize they are lost.

That feeling eased the moment I turned the corner and saw the dark **7** outline of my school at the top of the hill. My school was made up of about 15 nondescript portable classrooms set down on a fenced concrete lot in a rundown Seattle neighborhood, but it had the most beautiful view of the Cascade Mountains. You could see them from anywhere on the playfield and you could see them from the windows of my classroom—Room 2.

I walked over to the monkey bars and hooked my arms around the **8** cold metal. I stood for a long time just looking across Rainier Valley. The sky was beginning to whiten and I could hear a few birds.

In a perfect world my absence at home would not have gone unno- **9** ticed. I would have had two parents in a panic to locate me, instead of two parents in a panic to locate an answer to the hard question of survival during a deep financial and emotional crisis.

But in an overcrowded and unhappy home, it's incredibly easy for **10** any child to slip away. The high levels of frustration, depression and anger in my house made my brother and me invisible. We were children with the sound turned off. And for us, as for the steadily increasing number of

Steve Allen (1921–2000) and **Johnny Carson** (1925–2005): popular comedians and late-night talk-show hosts

nondescript: bland; not distinctive or interesting

neglected children in this country, the only place where we could count on being noticed was at school.

"Hey there, young lady. Did you forget to go home last night?" It was **11** Mr. Gunderson, our janitor, whom we all loved. He was nice and he was funny and he was old with white hair, thick glasses and an unbelievable number of keys. I could hear them jingling as he walked across the playfield. I felt incredibly happy to see him.

He let me push his wheeled garbage can between the different por- **12** tables as he unlocked each room. He let me turn on the lights and raise the window shades and I saw my school slowly come to life. I saw Mrs. Holman, our school secretary, walk into the office without her orange lipstick on yet. She waved.

I saw the fifth-grade teacher, Mr. Cunningham, walking under the **13** breezeway eating a hard roll. He waved.

And I saw my teacher, Mrs. Claire LeSane, walking toward us in a **14** red coat and calling my name in a very happy and surprised way, and suddenly my throat got tight and my eyes stung and I ran toward her crying. It was something that surprised us both.

It's only thinking about it now, 28 years later, that I realize I was cry- **15** ing from relief. I was with my teacher, and in a while I was going to sit at my desk, with my crayons and pencils and books and classmates all around me, and for the next six hours I was going to enjoy a thoroughly secure, warm and stable world. It was a world I absolutely relied on. Without it, I don't know where I would have gone that morning.

Mrs. LeSane asked me what was wrong and when I said "Nothing," **16** she seemingly left it at that. But she asked me if I would carry her purse for her, an honor above all honors, and she asked if I wanted to come into Room 2 early and paint.

She believed in the natural healing power of painting and drawing for **17** troubled children. In the back of her room there was always a drawing table and an easel with plenty of supplies, and sometimes during the day she would come up to you for what seemed like no good reason and quietly ask if you wanted to go to the back table and "make some pictures for Mrs. LeSane." We all had a chance at it—to sit apart from the class for a while to paint, draw and silently work out impossible problems on 11 × 17 sheets of newsprint.

Drawing came to mean everything to me. At the back table in Room **18** 2, I learned to build myself a life preserver that I could carry into my home.

We all know that a good education system saves lives, but the peo- **19** ple of this country are still told that cutting the budget for public schools is necessary, that poor salaries for teachers are all we can manage and that art, music and all creative activities must be the first to go when times are lean.

Before- and after-school programs are cut and we are told that pub- **20** lic schools are not made for baby-sitting children. If parents are neglectful temporarily or permanently, for whatever reason, it's certainly sad, but their unlucky children must fend for themselves. Or slip through the cracks. Or wander in a dark night alone.

We are told in a thousand ways that not only are public schools not **21** important, but that the children who attend them, the children who need them most, are not important either. We leave them to learn from the blind eye of a television, or to the mercy of "a thousand points of light" that can be as far away as stars.

I was lucky. I had Mrs. LeSane. I had Mr. Gunderson. I had an abun- 22 dance of art supplies. And I had a particular brand of neglect in my home that allowed me to slip away and get to them. But what about the rest of the kids who weren't as lucky? What happened to them?

By the time the bell rang that morning I had finished my drawing 23 and Mrs. LeSane pinned it up on the special bulletin board she reserved for drawings from the back table. It was the same picture I always drew—a sun in the corner of a blue sky over a nice house with flowers all around it.

Mrs. LeSane asked us to please stand, face the flag, place our right 24 hands over our hearts and say the Pledge of Allegiance. Children across the country do it faithfully. I wonder now when the country will face its children and say a pledge right back.

a thousand points of light: a term used by the first President George Bush in his 1989 inaugural speech. The "thousand points of light" are community and volunteer organizations.

DISCUSS WITH YOUR PEERS

1. In paragraph 3, the author explains that she and her brother watched television "with the sound off." Then, in paragraph 5, she repeats this idea when she says, "It was as if someone had turned the sound off on the world." Finally, in paragraph 10, she states, "We were children with the sound turned off." Discuss with your peers what the author means by these descriptions. Why do you think the author repeats this idea so many times?

2. Reread paragraph 14 and discuss why the author starts crying. Does this reaction make sense to you? Does Mrs. LeSane do something that causes the author to cry? Discuss why a child might react so dramatically to a teacher.

3. Discuss whether you agree or disagree with the author's views, expressed in paragraphs 19 and 20, that public schools are often neglected in the United States. Do you believe that public schools should be given greater funding and support? If possible, discuss examples from your own school experiences.

IDENTIFY THE PATTERNS

For more on the various writing patterns referenced here, see Chapter 8, Patterns of Development.

1. From the first sentence of paragraph 1, it is clear that the author is using **narration** to develop her writing. In your own words, describe the story that the author tells. What happens? What is the time frame? Who are the main characters?

2. Throughout this essay, the author uses **comparison and contrast** to develop her writing. In particular, she shows how the home environment and the school environment are dramatically different. Discuss

CONTINUED >

some of the key elements that are contrasted, including the people, the places, the activities, and the emotions.

3. In paragraphs 19–22, the author uses **argument** to develop her writing. What general argument does the author make about the attitude toward public schools in the United States? Underline or highlight some of the key points that she makes to support her argument. Then, underline or highlight some of the details that the author uses to help convince the reader that her argument is a valid one.

WRITE ABOUT THE READING

Discuss how the author's school "saves her life." What does the school—its environment, faculty and staff, and activities—offer her that she does not have at home? Use examples from the reading to support your ideas.

WRITE ABOUT YOUR LIFE

1. Discuss your earliest feelings about school, when you were in elementary school. Did you love going to school, or did you dread it? How did people treat you? What sort of activities did you participate in? How satisfying or unsatisfying were these activities?

2. Discuss how your home environment made you feel when you were a child.

CHAPTER 18

Prejudice and Forgiveness

READINGS

"A Duty to Heal"
"Devotion"

What is *prejudice*? One way to think about prejudice is as a pre-judgment—judging a person based on stereotypes (of race, religion, gender, ability, and so on) before you get to know that person as an individual. As you read the following selections, consider your own experience with prejudice. Have you been a victim of prejudice? Have you ever acted out of prejudice yourself? Could you forgive someone who treated you with prejudice—even if that person was not sorry?

Pius Kamau

A Duty to Heal

Pius Kamau was born in Kenya, Africa. He has studied in Spain, England, and Kenya, and he moved to the United States in 1971. He is now a surgeon and lives in Aurora, Colorado.

Growing up in the grinding poverty of colonial Africa, America was my shining hope. Martin Luther King's nonviolent political struggle made freedom and equality sound like achievable goals. America's ideals filled my head. Someday, I promised myself, I would walk on America's streets. **1**

But, as soon as I set foot in America's hospitals, reality—and racism—quickly intruded on the ideals. My color and accent set me apart. But in a hospital I am neither black nor white. I'm a doctor. I believe every patient that I touch deserves the same care and concern from me. **2**

In 1999, I was on-call when a nineteen-year-old patient was brought into the hospital. He was coughing up blood after a car accident. He was a white supremacist, an American Nazi with a swastika tattooed on his chest. **3**

The nurses told me he would not let me touch him. When I came close to him, he spat on me. In that moment, I wanted no part of him, either, but no other physician would take him on. I realized I had to minister to him as best as I could. **4**

I talked to him, but he refused to look at me or acknowledge me. He would only speak through the white nurses. Only they could check his body for injury. Only they could touch his tattooed chest. **5**

As it turned out, he was not badly hurt. We parted strangers. **6**

Martin Luther King Jr. (1929–1968): an African American minister who became a key figure in the American civil rights movement of the 1960s

white supremacist: someone who believes that whites are superior to all other races

Nazi: originally a political party in World War II–era Germany. Nazis hold white-supremacist beliefs and espouse hatred of Jews, African Americans, and other minorities.

swastika: symbol of Nazism

449

I still wonder: Was there more I could have done to make our encounter 7 different or better? Could I have approached him differently? Could I have tried harder to win his trust?

I can only guess his thoughts about me, or the beliefs he lived by. His 8 racism, I think, had little to do with me, personally. And, I want to think it had little to do with America, with the faith of Martin Luther King and other great men whose words I heard back in Africa, and who made me believe in this nation's ideals of equality and freedom.

My hands—my black hands—have saved many lives. I believe in my 9 duty to heal. I believe all patients, all human beings, are equal, and that I must try to care for everyone, even those who would rather die than consider me their equal.

DISCUSS WITH YOUR PEERS

1. Look at paragraphs 4 and 5. Try to imagine what the patient might actually be thinking and feeling when he sees the author. What might the author have done differently to improve the situation for the patient?

2. Even after the incident, the author continues to search his soul: "Could I have tried harder to win his trust?" (para. 7). First, discuss with your peers how you would react if someone spat on you for racist reasons. Would you fight back or be forgiving? In your opinion, are there many people in America like this doctor, or is he more like a saint than a real person?

3. In paragraph 8, the author says that he "want[s] to think" that the patient's racism "had little to do with America . . ." Discuss whether you agree or disagree with the author's optimism. In your opinion, has racism always been — and will it always be — woven into the fabric of American society? Or is it reasonable to believe that it has been, or will be, overcome?

IDENTIFY THE PATTERNS

For more on the various writing patterns referenced here, see Chapter 8, Patterns of Development.

1. The author uses **narration** to develop his writing. Notice how his story is organized into three parts: background, the incident, and reflections on the incident. Identify which paragraphs belong to each part.

2. In paragraph 5, the author uses **exemplification** to show how the patient refuses the doctor's help. Identify the four examples that he gives. Then, discuss how these four examples are effective in re-creating the scene and its emotional impact.

3. In paragraph 9, the author uses **definition** to clarify what he has learned from the incident and to define his beliefs. Reread this paragraph and identify the main parts of his definition.

WRITE ABOUT THE READING

If the doctor were a personal friend of yours, what advice would you give him about this experience, the way he reacted, and his reflections after the event? Use examples from the reading to support your ideas.

WRITE ABOUT YOUR LIFE

Describe a situation in which you (1) behaved in a prejudiced manner, (2) were a victim of prejudiced behavior, or (3) observed a prejudiced exchange between other people. Explain what happened, how the participants behaved, and what might be learned from the event.

Sarah Lin

Devotion

Sarah Lin is a fiction MFA candidate and composition instructor at Colorado State University. *Devotion* is her first publication.

W here I grew up in Queens, New York City, there was a boy living in the 1 house across the street. His name was Sherman. Somewhere, there is a photo of the two of us from the day I turned seven: I am in a yellow dress and a yellow birthday hat, running down the driveway with friends; he is standing in the background, watching. He is tall, lurching, awkward; his small, sloped eyes are magnified behind the thick lenses of his brown glasses. On his face is a gummy and lopsided smile.

lurching: swaying, rolling to one side

All through my childhood and adolescence, Sherman called my 2 family's house two or three times a day, hoping to engage whomever picked up the receiver in conversation. He never wanted to hang up. He invited my family to his birthday party every year, came heaving up our driveway whenever he saw one of us outside, and once a week he asked my older brother and me to come over for microwaved White Castle cheeseburgers and to hang out in his bedroom. Sometimes we went, and sometimes we didn't.

When I was twelve years old, a boy named Sherman decided he 3 loved me. Sherman was nine years older than me and had been born with Down syndrome, an unfortunate effect of his father's exposure to the chemical Agent Orange during the Vietnam War. For nearly all of his life, Sherman wore a hearing aid and depended on crutches and a wheelchair for mobility.

Down syndrome: a genetic disorder characterized by mental retardation

Puberty had thickened his body and turned his belly into a potbelly; 4 his skin had inflamed with red pustules of acne and then scarred. Sherman's laugh was guttural and so was his speech. He repulsed me, but my feelings did not sway his devotion. Whenever he saw me he gripped me in a number of uncomfortable, humiliating embraces, and no matter what I told

pustule: a pimple-like bump

guttural: from the throat

indignant: to feel
insulted or offended

him, he stubbornly insisted that I was his girlfriend. The very idea made me
indignant. But Sherman thought I was his; he believed this for years.

I was twenty-eight years old when my neighbor Sherman passed away.   5
His body had weakened from strokes and organ failure until, on a sunny
morning in early October, his heart gave out for good. He was thirty-seven.

groping: grabbing,
searching

I had last seen Sherman a year earlier, as he lay in a metal bed resem-   6
bling a crib, his body wasted, his eyes blind. His skin was soft and swollen
from medications and lack of exercise; his fingers were pale and groping.
Since I moved out of my parents' house, I had not gone to see him, so
I had not understood or witnessed his deterioration. But now I entered
his bedroom, moving gingerly around the stacks of adult diapers and pill
bottles. I breathed through my mouth to avoid the smell of disinfectant
that permeated the room.

permeated: covered,
filled

defecation: to pass
feces

I stayed for an hour, and during that time a live-in nurse assisted him   7
with defecation. I waited in the living room, pretending I couldn't hear him.
When I went to say good-bye, his hand reached up from the crib, seeking
contact with mine. "I love you," he said. He wanted me to stay. Would I?

"It was nice to see you," I said. I ignored his words. I took my hand   8
away from his and went up the stairs and out of his house.

absolved: forgiven

I've narrated exactly what happened and still I am not absolved.   9

This is what I wish were true: I treated his affection for me with   10
grace and humility. I did not embarrass him; I was not embarrassed. I
made him feel respected and whole. During an afternoon in his bedroom,
I ignored the smells and my discomfort, came close enough to the bed so
that Sherman could reach me. I held his hand until he fell asleep. I was not
a monster, no.

DISCUSS WITH YOUR PEERS

1. In paragraphs 1–6, the narrator shows the progression of Sherman's
   condition. Describe how his body and mind change over the course of
   his short lifetime.

2. Reread paragraphs 6 and 7. Explain why the narrator walks out of
   Sherman's house. What do you believe she is feeling at this moment?

3. In the last paragraph, the narrator says that she "was not a monster."
   Why does she compare herself to a monster? Do you agree that she
   behaved like a monster? Does she deserve forgiveness for her
   behavior? Explain your answer.

IDENTIFY THE PATTERNS

For more on the various writing patterns referenced here, see Chapter 8,
Patterns of Development.

1. In paragraphs 1, 4, and 6, the author uses **description** to show
   Sherman's physical condition. Underline some of the key descriptive
   details and explain how they help you visualize Sherman's condition.

2. The author uses **narration** as the main pattern of development. In your own words, retell the main events of the story, locating the beginning, middle, and end of it. Does the story hold your attention? Why or why not? Do you think the ending of the story is effective? Explain your answer.

WRITE ABOUT THE READING

Do you believe that the narrator's behavior toward Sherman is that of a "monster" (lacking in compassion, even cruel) or that she is simply trying to protect herself and Sherman by not misleading him? Use examples from the story to support your opinion.

WRITE ABOUT YOUR LIFE

1. Write about a time when you were insensitive, selfish, or even cruel to another person. Describe your behavior, the effect of your behavior on the other person, and how you felt about your behavior afterward.

2. Write about a time when you showed special compassion or kindness to someone who was disadvantaged in some way. Describe your behavior, the effect of your behavior on the other person, and how you felt about your behavior afterward.

As you read the following selections, consider the sources of conflict between parents and children. What causes children to be resentful of or embarrassed by their parents? When are these emotions justified, and when might they be immature reactions? When is conflict between children and their parents not only unavoidable but necessary? And what about the inner conflicts that nearly every parent experiences? Can they ever be resolved?

Enrique Hank Lopez
Why Couldn't My Father Read?

Enrique Hank Lopez grew up in Denver, Colorado, and was the first Hispanic American to graduate from Harvard Law School. He taught at Yale University, Harvard University, and the University of California–Berkeley and published several books.

articulate: clear and effective in expressing one's thoughts

proficient: skilled

Bachimba Chihuahua: a village in northern Mexico

barrio: neighborhood inhabited mostly by Spanish-speaking people

Pancho Villa (1878–1923): a hero of the Mexican Revolution (1910–1920).

Recent articles on immigration and education remind me of my father, who was an articulate, fascinating storyteller but totally illiterate. By the time I entered fourth grade in Denver, I was a proud, proficient reader — and painfully aware of my father's inability to read a single word in either Spanish or English. Although I'd been told there were no schools in his native village of Bachimba Chihuahua, I found it hard to accept the fact that he didn't even know the alphabet.   **1**

Consequently, every night as I watched my mother read to him, I would feel a surge of resentment and shame. Together they bent over *La Prensa* from San Antonio — the only available Spanish language newspaper. "How can he be so dumb?" I would ask myself. "Even a little kid can read a damned newspaper." Of course many adults in our barrio couldn't read or write, but that was no comfort to me. Nor did it console me that my hero Pancho Villa was also illiterate. After all, this was my own father, the man I considered to be smarter than anyone else, who could answer questions not even my mother could answer, who would take me around the ice factory where he worked and show me how all the machinery ran, who could make huge cakes of ice without any air bubbles, who could fix any machine or electrical appliance, who could tell me all those wonderful stories about Pancho Villa.   **2**

454

But he couldn't read. Not one damned word!   **3**

Whenever I saw my mother reading to him—his head thrust forward   **4**
like a dog waiting for a bone—I would walk out of the kitchen and sit on
the back porch, my stomach churning with a swelling anger that could
easily have turned to hatred. So bitter was my disappointment, so deep
was my embarrassment, that I never invited my friends into the house
during that after-dinner hour when my mother habitually read to him. And
if one of my friends had supped with us, I would hastily herd them out of
the kitchen when my mother reached for *La Prensa*.

Once, during a period of deepening frustration, I told my mother that   **5**
we ought to teach him how to read and write. And when she said it was
probably too late to teach him—that it might hurt his pride—I stomped
out of the house and ran furiously down the back alley, finally staggering
behind a trash can to vomit everything I'd eaten for supper.

supped: shared a meal

Standing there in the dark, my hand still clutching the rim of the can,   **6**
I simply couldn't believe that anyone as smart as my dad couldn't learn to
read, couldn't learn to write "cat" or "dog" or even "it." Even I, who could
barely understand the big words he used when he talked about Pancho
Villa (revolucion, libertad), even I, at the mere age of ten, could write big
words in both English and Spanish. So why couldn't he?

revolucion
[Spanish]: revolution

Eventually, he did learn to write two words—his name and surname.   **7**
Believing that he would feel less humble if he could sign his full name rather
than a mere "X" on his weekly paycheck, my mother wrote "José Lopez"
on his Social Security card and taught him to copy it letter by letter. It was
a slow, painstaking process that usually required two or three minutes
as he drew each separate letter with solemn tight-lipped determination,
pausing now and then as if to make sure they were in the proper sequence.
Then he would carefully connect the letters with short hyphen-like lines,
sometimes failing to close the gaps or overlapping letters.

libertad
[Spanish]: liberty

I was with him one Friday evening when he tried to cash his paycheck   **8**
at a furniture store owned by Frank Fenner, a red-faced German with a bulbous nose and squinty eyes. My father usually cashed his check at Alfredo
Pacheco's corner grocery store, but that night Pacheco had closed the store to
attend a cousin's funeral, so we had crossed the street to Fenner's place.

bulbous: bulging

"You cambiar this?" asked my father, showing him the check.   **9**

"He wants you to cash it," I added, annoyed by my father's use of the   **10**
word *cambiar*.

cambiar [Spanish]: to
change; in this case, to
cash

"Sure, Joe," said Fenner. "Just write your signature on the back of it."   **11**

"Firme su nombre atrás," I told my father, indicating that Fenner   **12**
wanted him to sign it.

"Okay, I put my name," said my father, placing his Social Security   **13**
card on the counter so he could copy the "José Lopez" my mother had
written for him.

With Fenner looking on, a smirk building on his face, my father   **14**
began the ever-so-slow copying of each letter as I literally squirmed with
shame and hot resentment. Halfway through "Lopez," my father paused,
nervously licked his lips, and glanced sheepishly at Fenner's leering face.
"No write too good," he said. "My wife teach me."

smirk: a mean smile

sheepishly: with
embarrassment or
shyness

Then, concentrating harder than before, he wrote the final "e" and   **15**
"z" and slowly connected the nine letters with his jabby little scribbles.

leering: having a cruel
or malicious expression

But Fenner was not satisfied. Glancing from the Social Security card to the check, he said, "I'm sorry, Joe, that ain't the same signature. I can't cash it."

"You bastard!" I yelled. "You know who he is! And you just saw him signing it." **16**

Then suddenly grabbing a can of furniture polish, I threw it at Fenner's head but missed by at least six inches. As my father tried to restrain me, I twisted away and screamed at him, "Why don't you learn to write, goddamn it! Learn to write!" **17**

humiliation: shame

He was trying to say something, his face blurred by my angry tears, but I couldn't hear him, for I was now backing and stumbling out of the store, my temples throbbing with the most awful humiliation I had ever felt. My throat dry and sour, I kept running and running down Larimer Street and then north on 30th Street toward Curtis Park, where I finally flung myself on the recently watered lawn and wept myself into a state of complete exhaustion. **18**

Hours later, now guilt-ridden by what I had yelled at my dad, I came home and found him and my mother sitting at the kitchen table, writing tablet between them, with the alphabet neatly penciled at the top of the page. **19**

wistful: sad or longing

"Your mother's teaching me how to write," he said in Spanish, his voice so wistful that I could hardly bear to listen to him. "Then maybe you won't be ashamed of me." **20**

But for reasons too complex for me to understand at that time, he never learned to read or write. Somehow, the multisyllabic words he had always known and accurately used seemed confusing and totally beyond this grasp when they appeared in print or in my mother's handwriting. So after a while, he quit trying. **21**

DISCUSS WITH YOUR PEERS

1. Look at paragraphs 5 and 21. Discuss why the father never learned to read. What might have been the main obstacles to his success? Do you agree with the author that his father was still an exceptionally smart person? Explain your opinions.

2. Look at paragraphs 2, 14, 18, and 19, and underline or highlight descriptions of the son's emotions in response to his father's illiteracy. Discuss whether these emotions seem reasonable and fair. Or is the son being childish and selfish?

3. Reread paragraphs 8–17, describing what happens when the son and father go to the furniture store to cash a check. Is the son right to yell at the owner? How might he have handled the situation more effectively?

IDENTIFY THE PATTERNS

For more on the various writing patterns referenced here, see Chapter 8, Patterns of Development.

1. In paragraph 2, the author uses **exemplification** to show that his father is "smarter than anyone else." Underline or highlight the examples of his father's intelligence. How do these examples illustrate how the son sees his father?

2. In paragraph 7, the author uses **process** to develop his writing. Underline or highlight some of the details that show the father's process of learning to write his name. How does the author show the parts of this process and bring it to life?

3. The author also uses powerful **description** to develop his writing. For example, take a close look at paragraphs 14 and 18. Underline or highlight some of the action verbs, vivid adjectives, and concrete nouns that give readers a strong mental image of the events.

WRITE ABOUT THE READING

In this story, do you feel that the son has failed his father, or has the father failed his son? Or, do you think that they have equally failed one another? Use examples from the story to support your opinion.

WRITE ABOUT YOUR LIFE

1. Discuss some limitations of your own parents that were difficult for you to accept. Explain how you handled their limitations.

2. Discuss whether you supported or failed your parents in their times of difficulty. If you could relive those difficult times with your parents, would you do anything differently?

Amy Tan

Four Directions

Amy Tan was born in Oakland, California, in 1952. She has written several best-selling novels, including *The Joy Luck Club* (1989), which also became a successful film.

I was ten years old. Even though I was young, I knew my ability to play   1
chess was a gift. It was effortless, so easy. I could see things on the chess-board that other people could not. I could create barriers to protect myself that were invisible to my opponents. And this gift gave me supreme confidence. I knew at exactly what point their faces would fall when my seemingly

irrevocable: impossible to stop or reverse

simple and childlike strategy would reveal itself as a devastating and irrevocable course. I loved to win.

And my mother loved to show me off, like one of many trophies she polished. She used to discuss my games as if she had devised the strategies.

"I told my daughter, 'Use your horses to run over the enemy,'" she informed one shopkeeper. "She won very quickly this way." And of course, she had said this before the game—that and a hundred other useless things that had nothing to do with my winning.

To our family friends who visited she would confide, "You don't have to be so smart to win chess. It is just tricks. You blow from North, South, East, and West. The other person becomes confused. They don't know which way to run."

I hated the way she tried to take all of the credit. And one day I told her so, shouting at her on Stockton Street, in the middle of a crowd of people. I told her she didn't know anything, so she shouldn't show off. She should shut up. Words to that effect.

That evening and the next day she wouldn't speak to me. She would say stiff words to my father and brothers, as if I had become invisible and she was talking about a rotten fish she had thrown away but which had left behind its bad smell.

to pounce: jump forcefully

I knew this strategy, the sneaky way to get someone to pounce back in anger and fall into a trap. So I ignored her. I refused to speak and waited for her to come to me.

After many days had gone by in silence, I sat in my room, staring at the sixty-four squares of my chessboard, trying to think of another way. And that's when I decided to quit playing chess.

Of course I didn't mean to quit forever. At most, just for a few days. And I made a show of it. Instead of practicing in my room every night, as I always did, I marched into the living room and sat down in front of the television with my brothers, who stared at me, an unwelcome intruder. I used my brothers to further my plan; I cracked my knuckles to annoy them.

"Ma!" they shouted. "Make her stop. Make her go away."

But my mother did not say anything.

Still I was not worried. But I could see I would have to make a stronger move. I decided to sacrifice a tournament that was coming up in one week. I would refuse to play in it. And my mother would certainly have to speak to me about this. Because the sponsors and the benevolent associations would start calling her, asking, shouting, pleading to make me play again.

benevolent: charitable, kind

And then the tournament came and went. And she did not come to me, crying, "Why are you not playing chess?" But I was crying inside, because I learned that a boy whom I had easily defeated on two other occasions had won.

I realized my mother knew more tricks than I had thought. But now I was tired of her game. I wanted to start practicing for the next tournament. So I decided to pretend to let her win. I would be the one to speak first.

"I am ready to play chess again," I announced to her. I had imagined she would smile and then ask me what special thing I wanted to eat.

2

3

4

5

6

7

8

9

10

11

12

13

14

15

But instead, she gathered her face into a frown and stared into my   16
eyes, as if she could force some kind of truth out of me.

"Why do you tell me this?" she finally said in sharp tones. "You think   17
it is so easy. One day quit, next day play. Everything for you is this way. So
smart, so easy, so fast."

"I said I'll play," I whined.   18

"No!" she shouted, and I almost jumped out of my scalp. "It is not so   19
easy anymore."

I was quivering, stunned by what she said, in not knowing what she   20
meant. And then I went back to my room. I stared at my chessboard, its
sixty-four squares, to figure out how to undo this terrible mess. And after
staring like this for many hours, I actually believed that I had made the
white squares black and the black squares white, and everything would
be all right.

And sure enough, I won her back. That night I developed a high   21
fever, and she sat next to my bed, scolding me for going to school without my sweater. In the morning she was there as well, feeding me rice
porridge flavored with chicken broth she had strained herself. She said
she was feeding me this because I had the chicken pox and one chicken
knew how to fight another. And in the afternoon, she sat in a chair in my
room, knitting me a pink sweater while telling me about a sweater that
Auntie Suyuan had knit for her daughter June, and how it was most unat-
tractive and of the worst yarn. I was so happy that she had become her
usual self.

But after I got well, I discovered that, really, my mother had changed.   22
She no longer hovered over me as I practiced different chess games. She
did not polish my trophies every day. She did not cut out the small newspaper item that mentioned my name. It was as if she had erected an invisible wall and I was secretly groping each day to see how high and how
wide it was.

hovered: hung around

At my next tournament, while I had done well overall, in the end   23
the points were not enough. I lost. And what was worse, my mother said
nothing. She seemed to walk around with this satisfied look, as if it had
happened because she had devised this strategy.

I was horrified. I spent many hours every day going over in my mind   24
what I had lost. I knew it was not just the last tournament. I examined
every move, every piece, every square. And I could no longer see the
secret weapons of each piece, the magic within the intersection of each
square. I could only see mistakes, my weaknesses. It was as though I had
lost my magic armor. And everybody could see this, where it was easy to
attack me.

Over the next few weeks and later months and years, I continued   25
to play, but never with that same feeling of supreme confidence. I fought
hard, with fear and desperation. When I won, I was grateful, relieved. And
when I lost, I was filled with growing dread, and then terror that I was no
longer a prodigy, that I had lost the gift and had turned into someone quite
ordinary.

prodigy: a gifted
person

When I lost twice to the boy whom I had defeated so easily a few   26
years before, I stopped playing chess altogether. And nobody protested. I
was fourteen.

DISCUSS WITH YOUR PEERS

1. Reread the first paragraph. In your own words, describe the personality of the narrator.

2. Reread paragraph 5. Do you blame the narrator for her behavior toward her mother? Why or why not?

3. How is the relationship between the mother and daughter like a game of chess? In your opinion, how is this relationship either healthy or unhealthy?

4. What does the mother mean when she says, "It is not so easy anymore"? What, specifically, is not so easy? Do you agree with the mother's approach to handling this situation? Why is her approach appropriate or inappropriate?

IDENTIFY THE PATTERNS

For more on the various writing patterns referenced here, see Chapter 8, Patterns of Development.

1. The author uses **narration** as the main pattern of development. Identify the background information, the key events, and the outcome of the story.

2. In paragraphs 7–14, the author uses **exemplification** to show how she tries to "beat" her mother in their standoff. Identify the examples that the author gives of strategies she used to beat her mother.

3. In paragraphs 22–26, the author uses **cause and effect** to show how her mother's behavior caused her (the author's) personality to change. Underline some examples of the mother's behavior (the cause), and some of the changes in the author's personality (the effect).

WRITE ABOUT THE READING

Would you want the mother in this story for your own mother? Explain your reasons and use examples from the story to support your ideas.

WRITE ABOUT YOUR LIFE

Did you have a competitive or difficult relationship with one of your parents? In what ways did that parent's behavior motivate or discourage you?

Work and Career

Most Americans work hard at their job or career, and many take pride in their work-related accomplishments. Some people even feel that their professional success defines who they are. As you read these selections, consider your own attitudes about work. Should your career define you? Should your career choices be determined by other people's opinion of that career? Would you rather have a job that you love or a job that other people consider important and prestigious? Finally, how will you balance your own career interests with the expectations of other people in your life?

Yolanda O'Bannon

Living What You Do Every Day

Yolanda O'Bannon was born in Phoenix, Arizona, and grew up on Air Force bases all around the world. She now lives with her husband in Richmond, California, where she works as an executive assistant.

I believe in being what I am instead of what sounds good to the rest of the world. **1**

Last year, I left a job I hated as a programmer for a job I love as an executive assistant, which is just a fancy word for secretary. I still feel a little embarrassed when people ask me about my new job. Not because of what I do, but because of what some people, including myself, have thought of secretaries. **2**

I had always thought that secretaries were nice and maybe competent, but not smart or strong or original. I have a master's degree in English literature, have interviewed the Dalai Lama, and co-founded a nonprofit organization. People who know me wondered why I would go for what seemed to be such a dull and low status job. Even my new boss asked if I would be bored. **3**

Why would I want to be a secretary? Because it fits me like a glove. I get to do what I love best all day, which is organize things. I like the challenge of holding the focus on the top priorities in my boss' wildly busy schedule. I can function with a high degree of chaos. Untangling finances feels like playing detective to me. I find filing restful. **4**

Dalai Lama: a religious leader and Tibetan Buddhist monk

The only hard part is dealing with my own and other people's ste- **5**
reotypes, and learning to focus on internal rewards rather than humble
appearances. I admit that I feel vaguely embarrassed bringing the faculty
lunch or serving coffee to my boss' visitors. But deep down I don't believe
that serving food is humiliating. Really, I think of it as a practice in humility. My husband is Tibetan. In Tibetan communities, you serve each other
tea as a form of respect. When I'm serving coffee at work, I imagine that
I'm serving a monk.

The West Wing: a
television show about
the White House staff

savvy: keenly intelligent

articulate: able to
express oneself
precisely

Whenever I get down or defensive about being a secretary, I think of **6**
those sharp, fast-talking assistants on *The West Wing*, and how they speak
in paragraphs and remember everything, and I feel pretty cool. Sometimes
I just look around at my fellow secretaries—savvy and articulate women
who are masters at multitasking. I know I'm in good company.

I've done a lot of solo travel in my life—in New Zealand, Japan, **7**
Africa, and India. Taking this job was harder than any of that. When I said
I was going to spend a year in northern India, I'd get points. When I said I
was going to be a secretary, people wondered what happened to me.

It would be easier if I were someone whose skills were more **8**
respected and better compensated—a doctor, an architect, a scientist. I
would feel cool when I meet someone at a party. But a friend reminded me
that you only have to talk about what you do for five minutes at parties,
but you have to live what you do every day of your life, so better to do
what you love and forget about how it looks. And this, I believe.

DISCUSS WITH YOUR PEERS

1. Name several stereotypes that many people have about secretaries.
   What truth does O'Bannon discover about secretaries? Find the paragraph in which she expresses her discovery.

2. Why does O'Bannon think serving coffee to her boss is useful? Do
   you agree with her, or do you think she is exaggerating to make herself feel better? What does she mean by "internal rewards"?

3. According to O'Bannon, why is it important to love what you do, even
   if other people don't respect your choice?

IDENTIFY THE PATTERNS

For more on the various writing patterns referenced here, see Chapter 8,
Patterns of Development.

1. The author uses **exemplification** to show why she likes her job. Identify four or five examples of why O'Bannon likes her job.

2. The author uses **argument** to persuade her readers to do something.
   What is it that she wants her readers to do? What reason (or reasons)
   does she provide to persuade her readers? Do you think O'Bannon
   provides enough evidence to make her case persuasive?

WRITE ABOUT THE READING

In your opinion, has O'Bannon made a smart career choice? Think about the sacrifices and rewards connected with her choice. Consider whether she gives enough evidence to make her choice seem like a smart one. Provide specific examples from the essay to support your opinion.

WRITE ABOUT YOUR LIFE

Discuss the job or career you would like to have for the pleasure and satisfaction of the work—regardless of the pay or prestige. Why specifically would you like this work? Who would agree or disagree with your choice and why? Would these opinions matter to you?

Daniel Meier

About Men; One Man's Kids

Daniel Meier is a professor of elementary education at San Francisco State University. In addition to teaching early childhood education and memoir writing, Meier has written several books on learning and literacy in children.

1   I teach first graders. I live in a world of skinned knees, double-knotted shoelaces, riddles that I've heard a dozen times, stale birthday cakes, hurt feelings, wandering stories, and one lost shoe ("and if you don't find it my mother'll kill me"). My work is dominated by 6-year-olds.

2   It's 10:45, the middle of snack, and I'm helping Emily open her milk carton. She has already tried the other end without success, and now there's so much paint and ink on the carton from her fingers that I'm not sure she should drink it at all. But I open it. Then I turn to help Scott clean up some milk he has just spilled onto Rebecca's whale crossword puzzle.

3   While I wipe my milk-and-paint-covered hands, Jenny wants to know if I've seen that funny book about penguins that I read in class. As I hunt for it in a messy pile of books, Jason wants to know if there is a new seating arrangement for lunch tables. I find the book, turn to answer Jason, then face Maya, who is fast approaching with a new knock-knock joke. After what seems like the tenth "Who's there?" I laugh and Maya is pleased.

4   Then Andrew wants to know how to spell "flukes" for his crossword. As I get to "u," I give a hand signal for Sarah to take away the snack. But just as Sarah is almost out the door, two children complain that "we haven't even had ours yet." I stop the snack mid-flight, complying with their request for graham crackers. I then return to Andrew, noticing that he has put "flu" for 9 Down, rather than 9 Across. It's now 10:50.

5   My work is not traditional male work. It's not a singular pursuit. There is not a large pile of paper to get through or one deal to transact. I don't have one area of expertise or knowledge. I don't have the singular

singular: having only one purpose

power over language of a lawyer, the physical force of a construction worker, the command over fellow workers of a surgeon, the wheeling and dealing transactions of a businessman. My energy is not spent in pursuing, climbing, achieving, conquering, or cornering some goal or object.

My energy is spent in encouraging, supporting, consoling, and prais-   6
ing my children. In teaching, the inner rewards come from without. On any given day, quite apart from teaching reading and spelling, I bandage a cut, dry a tear, erase a frown, tape a torn doll, and locate a long-lost boot. The day is really won through matters of the heart. As my students groan, laugh, shudder, cry, exult, and wonder, I do too. I have to be soft around the edges.

exult: rejoice

A few years ago, when I was interviewing for an elementary-school   7
teaching position, every principal told me with confidence that, as a male, I had an advantage over female applicants because of the lack of male teachers. But in the next breath, they asked with a hint of suspicion why I chose to work with young children. I told them that I wanted to observe and contribute to the intellectual growth of a maturing mind. What I really felt like saying, but didn't, was that I loved helping a child learn to write his name for the first time, finding someone a new friend, or sharing in the hilarity of reading about Winnie the Pooh getting so stuck in a hole that only his head and rear show.

I gave that answer to those principals, who were mostly male, because   8
I thought they wanted a "male" response. This meant talking about intellectual matters. If I had taken a different course and talked about my interest in helping children in their emotional development, it would have been seen as closer to a "female" answer. I even altered my language, not once mentioning the word "love" to describe what I do indeed love about teaching. My answer worked; every principal nodded approvingly.

Some of the principals also asked what I saw myself doing later in   9
my career. They wanted to know if I eventually wanted to go into educational administration. Becoming a dean of students or a principal has never been one of my goals, but they seemed to expect me, as a male, to want to climb higher on the career stepladder. So I mentioned that, at some point, I would be interested in working with teachers as a curriculum coordinator. Again, they nodded approvingly.

curriculum: courses or subjects of study

If those principals had been female instead of male, I wonder whether   10
their questions, and my answers, would have been different. My guess is that they would have been.

At other times, when I'm at a party or a dinner and tell someone   11
that I teach young children, I've found that men and women respond differently. Most men ask about the subjects I teach and the courses I took in my training. Then, unless they bring up an issue such as merit pay, the conversation stops. Most women, on the other hand, begin the conversation on a more immediate and personal level. They say things like "those kids must love having a male teacher" or "that age is just wonderful, you must love it." Then, more often than not, they'll talk about their own kids or ask me specific questions about what I do. We're then off and talking shop.

Possibly, men would have more to say to me, and I to them, if my job **12**
had more of the trappings and benefits of more traditional male jobs. But
my job has no bonuses or promotions. No complimentary box seats at the
ballpark. No cab fare home. No drinking buddies after work. No briefcase.
No suit. (Ties get stuck in paint jars.) No power lunches. (I eat peanut butter and jelly, chips, milk and cookies with the kids.) No taking clients out
for cocktails. The only place I take my kids is to the playground.

Although I could have pursued a career in law or business, as several **13**
of my friends did, I chose teaching instead. My job has benefits all its own.
I'm able to bake cookies without getting them stuck together as they cool,
buy cheap sewing materials, take out splinters, and search just the right
trash cans for useful odds and ends. I'm sometimes called "Daddy" and
even "Mommy" by my students, and if there's ever a lull in the conversa-   **lull:** a slow moment
tion at a dinner party, I can always ask those assembled if they've heard
the latest riddle about why the turkey crossed the road. (He thought he
was a chicken.)

DISCUSS WITH YOUR PEERS

1. Reread paragraphs 5, 9, and 12. According to the author, what is "traditional male work"? In your own words, explain what men typically
   do in their job. Do you agree or disagree with this description of men's
   work?

2. In paragraph 7, why does Meier have to lie about his desire to be an
   elementary school teacher? What is the "hint of suspicion" that his
   interviewers have? Do you think this suspicion is fair? Explain your
   answer.

3. Reread paragraphs 8 and 11. How do men and women respond differently to Meier's job choice? Would the men and women you know be
   likely to respond in these ways? Why or why not?

IDENTIFY THE PATTERNS

For more on the various writing patterns referenced here, see Chapter 8,
Patterns of Development.

1. The author uses abundant **exemplification** throughout the essay. In
   paragraphs 1–4, 6, 7, 12, and 13, identify your favorite examples of
   what the author does at his job.

2. The author uses **contrast** to show how his job is different from traditional men's work. Reread paragraphs 5 and 6 and pick out a few key
   ideas that show these important differences. Aside from the specific
   tasks he mentions, how is the author's job generally different from
   traditional men's work?

WRITE ABOUT THE READING

1. In your opinion, has Meier made a smart career choice? Think about both the sacrifices and rewards connected with his choice. Consider whether he gives enough evidence to make his choice seem like a smart one. Provide specific examples from the essay to support your opinion.

2. If you were a parent of a young child, would you want Meier to be your child's elementary school teacher? Explain your reasons and give examples from Meier's essay to support your ideas.

WRITE ABOUT YOUR LIFE

Discuss a job you've had that you especially liked or disliked. Describe the work that you did and explain why it was satisfying or unsatisfying. Discuss what you learned about yourself from this experience, if anything, and how it might influence *your future* job choices.

If you've never had a job, discuss someone you know well who loves or hates his or her job. To the best of your ability, describe the work that this person does and explain why he or she is happy or unhappy with the work.

People and Pets

Some statistics say that people with pets tend to live longer than those without. With the vast number of resources and amount of time people devote to their pets, they must feel they are receiving valuable companionship in return. As you read the following selections, examine your own feelings about pets. Do you relate to the authors' feelings about pets? Have you had similar experiences with your own pets? Is there something unique that pets offer people that other human beings cannot?

Troy Chapman

Caring Makes Us Human

Troy Chapman was convicted of second-degree murder in 1985 and is currently incarcerated at Kinross Correctional Facility in Kincheloe, Michigan. He helps teach ESL and literacy classes, and is a music leader for church services in the prison.

1   When the scruffy orange cat showed up in the prison yard, I was one of the first to go out there and pet it. I hadn't touched a cat or a dog in over 20 years. I spent at least 20 minutes crouched down by the Dumpster behind the kitchen as the cat rolled around and luxuriated beneath my attention. What he was expressing outwardly I was feeling inwardly.

2   It was an amazing bit of grace to feel him under my hand and know that I was enriching the life of another creature with something as simple as my care. I believe that caring for something or someone in need is what makes us human.

3   Over the next few days, I watched other prisoners responding to the cat. Every yard period, a group of prisoners gathered there. They stood around talking and taking turns petting the cat. These were guys you wouldn't usually find talking to each other. Several times I saw an officer in the group—not chasing people away, but just watching and seeming to enjoy it along with the prisoners.

4   Bowls of milk and water appeared, along with bread, wisely placed under the edge of the Dumpster to keep the seagulls from getting it. The cat was obviously a stray and in pretty bad shape. One prisoner brought

crouched: bent down low

luxuriated: enjoyed himself fully

out his small, blunt-tipped scissors, and trimmed burrs and matted fur from his coat.

People said, "That cat came to the right place. He's getting treated like a king." This was true. But as I watched, I was also thinking about what the cat was doing for us.   5

There's a lot of talk about what's wrong with prisons in America. We need more programs; we need more psychologists or treatment of various kinds. Some even talk about making prisons more kind, but I think what we really need is a chance to practice kindness ourselves. Not receive it, but give it.   6

After more than two decades here, I know that kindness is not a value that's encouraged. It's often seen as weakness. Instead the culture encourages keeping your head down, minding your own business, and never letting yourself be vulnerable.   7

For a few days a raggedy cat disrupted this code of prison culture. They've taken him away now, hopefully to a decent home—but it did my heart good to see the effect he had on me and the men here. He didn't have a PhD, he wasn't a criminologist or a psychologist, but by simply saying, "I need some help here," he did something important for us. He needed us—and we need to be needed. I believe we all do.   8

DISCUSS WITH YOUR PEERS

1. In the first paragraph, the author observes, "What he was expressing outwardly, I was feeling inwardly." In your own words, explain what it is that *both* the cat and the author are feeling.

2. Reread paragraphs 7 and 8. Explain the "code of prison culture." Do you think this code is unavoidable in a prison environment or can it be changed?

3. Reread the last paragraph. Why is the cat more effective at helping the prisoners than a criminologist or a psychologist would be? Do you agree with the author on this point, or do you think he is being unrealistic?

IDENTIFY THE PATTERNS

For more on the various writing patterns referenced here, see Chapter 8, Patterns of Development.

1. The author uses **cause and effect** to show how the cat (the cause) changes the behavior of the prisoners and guards (the effect). Identify how the behavior of the prisoners and guards changes when the cat appears.

2. The author uses **definition** to clarify what it means (in his opinion) to be human. In paragraph 2, how does the author define *human*? Do you agree with his definition? Why or why not?

3. The author uses **argument** to persuade his readers about what's wrong with prisons in America. Reread paragraphs 6–8 and identify his main argument. Then, decide whether the author's story is strong enough evidence for you to agree with his position.

WRITE ABOUT THE READING

Based on the evidence in this reading, would you argue in favor of introducing real pets into America's prisons? Would this be a worthwhile way to reform criminals? Give reason and examples to support your position.

WRITE ABOUT YOUR LIFE

Discuss something (an animal, etc.) that gave you hope at a tough time. Explain what happened and the effect this something had on you.

Abigail Thomas

Comfort

Abigail Thomas teaches fiction at the New School. "Comfort" is an excerpt from her memoir, *A Three Dog Life*, which was chosen by the *Washington Post* and the *LA Times* as one of the best books of 2006. She lives in Woodstock, New York, with her three dogs.

Every October the Cathedral of Saint John the Divine celebrates the Feast of Saint Francis and is host to a ceremony known as the Blessing of the Animals. Thousands of people come with their pets; the enormous church is crowded to overflowing. A farm provides some of the bigger beasts, the humble cows and horses and sheep who make a procession to the altar, their necks garlanded with flowers. There are snakes and giant parrots and eagles and hawks. Once there was even an elephant. Outside in the parking lot there are small petting zoos; a litter of piglets was especially popular. The peacocks who live on the grounds of the cathedral strut their stuff. The year I went, 2001, the brave dogs who searched the burning graveyard that had been the World Trade Center were honored along with their human companions. A lot of us couldn't stop crying.

procession: moving in a line

garlanded: decorated or draped with

I spotted Rosie from half a block away; she was sitting under a table in the parking lot with two other dogs up for adoption. It really was love at first sight, although she looked like a handful—high-strung, and nervous. Half dachshund, half whippet (a union that must have come with an instruction sheet), she was simply the most beautiful creature I'd ever seen. She looked like a miniature deer, a gazelle, or a dachshund's dream come true, as someone remarked, looking at Rosie's long legs. Is she housebroken? Spayed? I asked a few unnecessary questions. I knew I wanted her no matter what. I knelt down and stroked her silky brown coat, and looked into a very nervous pair of brown eyes. Her slender body quivered. I had been thinking about a second dog, and here she was.

My beagle, Harry, didn't exactly jump for joy when Rosie arrived. In fact he growled. He was occupying his half of the sofa (which he takes in the middle) and Rosie's approach was unwelcome, to say the least. But he looked a little more alive, I was happy to see. Harry and I had both been leading a reclusive life for a long time, neither of us inclined to leave the house unless we had to. Since the accident* Harry had refused to go out. I had to carry him trembling into the elevator, through the lobby, across the street into Riverside Park, and once I put him down he lunged toward home. I had taken his photograph with me to church that day; he would not have liked being there.

reclusive: solitary, isolated

Harry had been with us only four months when the accident happened. We had gotten him through a friend who'd found him starving in the woods. The day he arrived we were worried: we gave him food but he wouldn't eat; we put down water but he wouldn't drink; we took him for walks and he skulked close to the ground, his tail between his legs. If we approached him, he tried to make himself as small as possible in a corner of the sofa. Finally, despairing, we went to bed. Ten minutes later we heard the click of toenails across the bare floor and then there was Harry, in bed with us. It was going to be all right. It was going to be better than all right.

skulked: moved in a cautious manner

"How do you feel about your dog now?" I recall someone asking soon after the disaster. "I love my dog," I said. It seemed a peculiar question. "I couldn't get through this without Harry." In the first weeks of Rich's hospitalization I would often wake in the night to reach for him only to find that the warmth I felt at my side was Harry's small body. In those moments grief and gratitude combined in a way I have since gotten accustomed to.

After some initial squabbling over property rights, Harry and Rosie reached a détente. The only real fight they had was over a glazed doughnut I had foolishly left within reach, but it was an Entenmann's doughnut, well worth fighting for. Within days of Rosie's arrival Harry was out and about, his tail held high. Now we head off for the dog run every morning. Walking Rosie is like having a kite on the end of a leash while Harry stumps along maturely, a small solid anchor. In the dog run Harry and I sit on the bench watching as Rosie runs, leaps, bounds, races any dog who will follow her, and outruns all of them except two—a saluki named Sophie and an Afghan named Chelsea. They are the only dogs faster than Rosie but most days they are too elegant to run at all.

squabbling: arguing

détente: a peaceful pause

Entenmann's: a brand of baked goods

Rosie got us out of our slump, but she sleeps with one eye open; if I so much as sigh she is alert. If I look up from my book, or take off my reading glasses, she is tensed to follow. I found out that her owner died in the World Trade Center, and she had been brought to the shelter by a weeping relative. Whoever the man was, he must have loved her as I do; he trained her, and when I tell her to sit and she sits, I swear I can feel his

* "The accident" refers to a car accident that left Thomas's husband with severe brain injuries.

ghost hovering nearby. I want to tell the people who loved him that his dog is part of a family now, that she is doing fine.

I visit my husband once a week. Now he is cared for in a facility   8
upstate that specializes in traumatic brain injury. The accident was more than two years ago, and I still can't get my mind around it. He is there and not there, he is my husband and not my husband. His thoughts seem to break apart and collide with each other, and I try not to think at all. On good days we sit outside. We don't talk; we just sit very close together and hold hands. It feels like the old days; it feels like being married again. When I get home at night my dogs greet me, Rosie bounding as if on springs, Harry wiggling at my feet. Sometimes I sit right down on the floor before taking off my coat.

If you were to look into our apartment in the late morning, or early   9
afternoon, or toward suppertime, you might find us together sleeping. Of course a good rainy day is preferable, but even on sunny summer days, the dogs and I get into bed. Rosie dives under the quilt on my right, Harry on my left, and we jam ourselves together. After a little bit Harry starts to snore, Rosie rests her chin on my ankle, the blanket rises and falls with our breathing, and I feel only gratitude. We are doing something as neces-   **steeping:** saturating
sary to our well-being as food or air or water. We are steeping ourselves, reassuring ourselves, renewing ourselves, three creatures of two species, finding comfort in the simple exchange of body warmth.

DISCUSS WITH YOUR PEERS

1. Explain where Harry and Rosie came from. Describe their personalities.

2. Reread paragraph 8. Describe what happens when the author visits her husband in the facility for traumatic brain injury. What seems satisfying and unsatisfying about their relationship?

3. Explain the special connection that the author has with her two dogs. Although the author claims that it is a "simple exchange of body warmth," do you think it is more than this? What special ability do these dogs have to keep the author going?

IDENTIFY THE PATTERNS

For more on the various writing patterns referenced here, see Chapter 8, Patterns of Development.

1. The author uses **description** to help her readers visualize her dogs. Reread paragraphs 2 and 4 and pick out several strong descriptive details that help you visualize Rosie and Harry.

2. The author uses **cause and effect** to show how Rosie's arrival (the cause) gets the author and Harry out of their slump (the effect). Reread paragraph 6 and explain in your own words the effect that Rosie has on Harry and the author.

WRITE ABOUT THE READING

Do you think the author depends too much on the companionship and affection of her dogs? Would you recommend that she "get out and get a life" or continue living the way she does? Give specific examples from the text to explain and support your opinion.

WRITE ABOUT YOUR LIFE

Write about a pet in your life, now or in the past. You may discuss where the animal came from, its personality, what it did for you, what its presence meant in your life, and, if applicable, what finally happened to it. If you have never had a pet, write about a pet that you would love to have or discuss why you are not interested in having a pet.

CHAPTER 22

Deprivation and Privilege

READINGS

"The Jacket"
"Passing Through"

Did you ever feel deprived of the "better things" in life? When you look around you, does it seem like a few lucky people have all the privilege and opportunities—nicer clothes, better education, higher-paying jobs? Have you ever felt embarrassed or limited by your (or your family's) economic hardship? As you read the following selections, think about what it means to be deprived *and* privileged. Sometimes our sense of deprivation could be someone else's idea of privilege. In truth, we may be more privileged than we think.

Gary Soto

The Jacket

Gary Soto was born to working-class Mexican American parents and spent many years working in factories and in fields to help support his family. He is now an author and a poet and lives in Northern California.

My clothes have failed me. I remember the green coat that I wore in fifth and sixth grades when you either danced like a champ or pressed yourself against a greasy wall, bitter as a penny toward the happy couples. 1

When I needed a new jacket and my mother asked what kind I wanted, I described something like bikers wear: black leather and silver studs with enough belts to hold down a small town. We were in the kitchen, steam on the windows from her cooking. She listened so long while stirring dinner that I thought she understood for sure the kind I wanted. The next day when I got home from school, I discovered draped on my bedpost a jacket the color of day-old guacamole. I threw my books on the bed and approached the jacket slowly, as if it were a stranger whose hand I had to shake. I touched the vinyl sleeve, the collar, and peeked at the mustard-colored lining. 2

From the kitchen mother yelled that my jacket was in the closet. I closed the door to her voice and pulled at the rack of clothes in the closet, hoping the jacket on the bedpost wasn't for me but my mean brother. No luck. I gave up. From my bed, I stared at the jacket. I wanted to cry because it was so ugly and so big that I knew I'd have to wear it a long time. I was a 3 small kid, thin as a young tree, and it would be years before I'd have a new one. I stared at the jacket, like an enemy, thinking bad things before I took off my old jacket whose sleeves climbed halfway to my elbow.

I put the big jacket on. I zipped it up and down several times, and rolled the cuffs up so they didn't cover my hands. I put my hands in the pockets and flapped the jacket like a bird's wings. I stood in front of the mirror, full face, then profile, and then looked over my shoulder as if someone had called me. I sat on the bed, stood against the bed, and combed my hair to see what I would look like doing something natural. I looked ugly. I threw it on my brother's bed and looked at it for a long time before I slipped it on and went out to the backyard, smiling a "thank you" to my mom as I passed her in the kitchen. With my hands in my pockets I kicked a ball against the fence, and then climbed it to sit looking into the alley. I hurled orange peels at the mouth of an open garbage can and when the peels were gone I watched the white puffs of my breath thin to nothing. **4**

I jumped down, hands in my pockets, and in the backyard on my knees I teased my dog, Brownie, by swooping my arms while making birdcalls. He jumped at me and missed. He jumped again and again, until a tooth sunk deep, ripping an L-shaped tear on my left sleeve. I pushed Brownie away to study the tear as I would a cut on my arm. There was no blood, only a few loose pieces of fuzz. Damn dog, I thought, and pushed him away hard when he tried to bite again. I got up from my knees and went to my bedroom to sit with my jacket on my lap, with the lights out. **5**

That was the first afternoon with my new jacket. The next day I wore it to sixth grade and got a D on a math quiz. During the morning recess Frankie T., the playground terrorist, pushed me to the ground and told me to stay there until recess was over. My best friend, Steve Negrete, ate an apple while looking at me, and the girls turned away to whisper on the monkey bars. The teachers were no help: they looked my way and talked about how foolish I looked in my new jacket. I saw their heads bob with laughter, their hands half-covering their mouths. **6**

Braille: a system of writing used by the blind with raised dots on the page

Even though it was cold, I took off the jacket during lunch and played kickball in a thin shirt, my arms feeling like Braille from the goose bumps. But when I returned to class I slipped the jacket on and shivered until I was warm. I sat on my hands, heating them up, while my teeth chattered like a cup of crooked dice. Finally warm, I slid out of the jacket but a few minutes later put it back on when the fire bell rang. We paraded out into the yard where we, the sixth graders, walked past all the other grades to stand against the back fence. Everybody saw me. Although they didn't say out loud, "Man, that's ugly," I heard the buzz-buzz of gossip and even laughter that I knew was meant for me. **7**

And so I went, in my guacamole-colored jacket. So embarrassed, so hurt, I couldn't even do my homework. I received Cs on quizzes, and forgot the state capitals and rivers of South America, our friendly neighbor. Even the girls who had been friendly blew away like loose flowers to follow the boys in neat jackets. **8**

I wore that thing for three years until the sleeves grew short and my forearms stuck out like the necks of turtles. All during that time no love came to me—no little dark girl in a Sunday dress she wore on Monday. At lunchtime I stayed with the ugly boys who leaned against the chain-link **9** fence and looked around with propellers of grass spinning in our mouths. We saw girls walk by alone, saw couples, hand in hand, their heads like bookends pressing air together. We saw them and spun our propellers so fast our faces were blurs.

I blame that jacket for those bad years. I blame my mother for her **10** bad taste and her cheap ways. It was a sad time for the heart. With a friend I spent my sixth-grade year in a tree in the alley, waiting for something good to happen to me in that jacket, which had become the ugly brother who tagged along wherever I went. And it was about that time that I began to grow. My chest puffed up with muscle and, strangely, a few more ribs. Even my hands, those fleshy hammers, showed bravely through the cuffs, the fingers already hardening for the coming fights. But that L-shaped rip on the left sleeve got bigger, bits of stuffing coughed out from its wound after a hard day of play. I finally Scotch-taped it closed, but in rain or cold weather the tape peeled off like a scab and more stuffing fell out until that sleeve shriveled into a palsied arm. That winter the elbows began to crack and whole chunks of green began to fall off. I showed the cracks to my mother, who always seemed to be at the stove with steamed-up glasses, and she said that there were children in Mexico who would love that jacket. I told her that this was America and yelled that Debbie, my sister, didn't have a jacket like mine. I ran outside, ready to cry, and climbed the tree by the alley to think bad thoughts and watch my breath puff white and disappear.

palsied: paralyzed, shrunken

But whole pieces still casually flew off my jacket when I played hard, **11** read quietly, or took vicious spelling tests at school. When it became so spotted that my brother began to call me "camouflage," I flung it over the fence into the alley. Later, however, I swiped the jacket off the ground and went inside to drape it across my lap and mope.

I was called to dinner: steam silvered my mother's glasses as she **12** said grace; my brother and sister with their heads bowed made ugly faces at their glasses of powdered milk. I gagged too, but eagerly ate big rips of buttered tortilla that held scooped-up beans. Finished, I went outside with my jacket across my arm. It was a cold sky. The faces of clouds were piled up, hurting. I climbed the fence, jumping down with a grunt. I started up the alley and soon slipped into my jacket, that green ugly brother who breathed over my shoulder that day and ever since.

DISCUSS WITH YOUR PEERS

1. Why do you think the mother buys a green vinyl jacket even though her son has requested a black leather jacket?

2. Although the narrator dislikes the jacket, he smiles a "thank you" to his mother. Why does he do this instead of complaining?

3. Why doesn't the mother replace the jacket when it is clearly falling to pieces? Why does she say that there are "children in Mexico who would love that jacket"? Do you think she is being sarcastic or sincere? Do you support her attitude and actions? Why or why not?

For more on the various writing patterns referenced here, see Chapter 8, Patterns of Development.

IDENTIFY THE PATTERNS

1. The author uses **cause and effect** to show how the jacket (the cause) ruined his young life (the effect). Reread paragraphs 6–9 and identify the important effects that the jacket had on his life.

2. The author uses **description** to help his readers visualize the jacket and its gradual deterioration. Reread paragraphs 2 and 10 and identify the descriptive details that help you visualize the jacket. In your opinion, are these descriptive details successful? Why or why not?

3. The author uses **narration** to tell the story of the jacket (how he received it, how it changed his childhood, how it determined his future). If you had to retell this story to a friend, what major parts or events would you include to make the story clear and complete? Also, read the last paragraph of the story. Is this a satisfactory ending? Why or why not?

WRITE ABOUT THE READING

The author blames the jacket for many of his failures and much of his unhappiness as a child. Is he blaming the jacket unfairly and unrealistically, or do you believe that the jacket is actually responsible for his troubles? Give specific examples from the story to support your ideas.

WRITE ABOUT YOUR LIFE

The narrator of "The Jacket" portrays himself as a victim of his situation. As a child or adolescent, were you a victim of your situation (disadvantage, poverty, insensitive parents, etc.), or did you challenge and defy your situation? Give specific examples to support your ideas.

Yiyun Li

Passing Through

Yiyun Li grew up in Beijing and moved to the United States in 1996. She was named by *The New Yorker* as one of the top 20 writers under 40, and in 2010 she received a prestigious MacArthur Fellowship. She lives in Oakland, California, with her husband and two sons.

hotbed: a very active environment

After the Tiananmen Square massacre in 1989, the Chinese Ministry of   1
Education began sending future students of Beijing University, a hotbed of pro-democratic protest, into the military for a year, So in 1991, at the age of 18, instead of beginning studies, I entered the army. There along

with 1,500 other students, I spent hours in formation training and even more time being lectured on the inevitable demise of capitalism and the victory of Communism.

The next spring, the army sent us on a march through Mount Dabie to get to know our "revolutionary heritage"; the mountain area served, between the 1920s and 1930s, as a base for the Communist Party. Hard as the marching was, with no bath for weeks and blisters on our feet, the mountain air and spring fields made the trip into a kind of sightseeing adventure. That was why we entered a village one particular evening smiling and holding our hands up to the sky.

We were the only girls' company, and we marched behind a battalion of boys; the road across the village was shrouded by dust. A water buffalo, used to the tramping, grazed undisturbed. A villager saw us and called out, "Girl-soldiers this time." The villagers appeared in every door, bowls of rice in their hands, pointing at us with their chopsticks. "Girl-soldiers," young children echoed, running along beside us. We smiled, waved, and kept walking. An old woman was pounding dried peppers in a huge stone mortar. The breeze spread the fine powders, and many of us sneezed; the villagers laughed.

Outside the village, we were ordered to take a break. The dust settled, and hundreds of green-uniformed figures sat single-file by the winding road. The scene was soon disrupted by the village children, all holding out their hands, begging for candies and refusing to leave when they got their share. Even the most charitable soldiers among us started to shoo away the children like flies. When yet another girl stood in front of me, I said, "How many do you have to have before you go home?"

"Can I just have a candy wrapper?" she asked. I looked at the girl, too small for her passed-down blouse. "Do you collect candy wrappers?" I said. She nodded and showed me a dog-eared book. Between the pages were mostly cheap wrappers, red and green with plain characters, *tang guo* (candy) printed on them diagonally.

"How old are you?" I asked. "Eight," she said. "Are you in school?" She shrugged. Not many girls in the mountains would receive much education. They worked hard for their parents until they were old enough to work for their husbands. Today, I suppose, if girls from this region manage to leave their villages, they might try to participate in the Chinese economic boom by becoming laborers in a factory.

I handed her a candy. She unfolded the wrapper and returned the chocolate to me. I watched her flatten it between her palms. It had snowy mountains and blue sky in the background, with a small white flower blooming in the center.

At her age, I collected candy wrappers, too, and I understood the joy of having a prize wrapper in your collection. I had one that was given to me by a Westerner in the late 1970s, when foreign faces were still rare in Beijing. It was made of cellophane with transparent gold and silver stripes, and if you looked through it, you would see a gilded world, much fancier than our everyday, dull life.

By the time I turned 10, I was working at the goal set by my parents: to excel in schoolwork so that one day I could go to the United States. I attended a high school in Beijing that admitted only the students with

---

formation training: education in a particular form of government

2 **inevitable:** unavoidable

demise: downfall, collapse

3 **shrouded:** covered, hidden

4

5 **dog-eared:** with the page corners folded

6

7

8

gilded: made of gold

9

the best scores in the entrance exam. Financed by Unesco, it had an indoor swimming pool, color TVs, and a science building.

I did not change my life because of a candy wrapper, but it was the   10
seed of a dream that came true: I left China for an American graduate
school in 1996 and have lived here since.

The girl studied the wrapper before putting it in her book. I won-   11
dered if it would nourish thoughts about other worlds. But I did not tell
her about my collection. I did not tell her that the candy had come all the
way from Switzerland. I could not explain that the flower on the wrapper
was edelweiss or that it was featured in a song in the American movie *The
Sound of Music*—I had watched it many times at my school so that we
could perform the songs when Western delegates visited.

Even at 18, despite my forced reeducation in the army, I knew I was   12
luckier than she was, a passer-by on this mountain and bound for a better
destination. I knew that she would never see a blooming edelweiss anywhere but on a wrapper.

DISCUSS WITH YOUR PEERS

1. Reread paragraphs 5, 7, and 8. Why do you think the Chinese children collect candy wrappers? What special value did the Western candy wrapper have for the narrator?

2. Why does the village girl return the chocolate candy to the narrator? Why doesn't she keep the wrapper *and* the candy?

3. Why does the narrator believe she cannot explain to the village girl where the candy wrapper came from and what it represents? In your opinion, would it have been worth her effort to try to explain this to the girl?

IDENTIFY THE PATTERNS

For more on the various writing patterns referenced here, see Chapter 8, Patterns of Development.

1. The author uses **description** to help her readers visualize the mountain village and the Western-style candy wrapper. Reread paragraphs 3 and 8 and identify some of the descriptive details that help you visualize the village and the wrapper. In your opinion, are these descriptive details successful? Why or why not?

2. The author uses **narration** to tell her story about her military service and her encounter with a village girl. How does the author tell her story effectively? How does the story capture your imagination, hold your interest, and leave you thinking after you have finished reading? Explain your answers.

WRITE ABOUT THE READING

Compare and contrast the life of the village girl and the life of the narrator. How are their lives similar and how are they different? What are the advantages and disadvantages of each girl's life?

WRITE ABOUT YOUR LIFE

In your own life, what path seemed to lie ahead of you when you were a child? What were the opportunities and limitations set by your parents and other factors out of your control? Did you follow this path, or did you take actions to determine your own path? Give specific examples to support your ideas.

CHAPTER 23

Addiction and Risks

Addictions come in many forms—from "harmless" addictions such as chocolate and television to "serious" addictions such as drugs and alcohol. In fact, addiction is so widespread today that almost everyone has been touched by it in some way. As you read the following selections, think about what it means to be an addict or the loved one of an addict. What are the risks to self and others, and how can we protect ourselves from the significant damages that often accompany addiction?

Laura Rowley

As They Say, Drugs Kill

Laura Rowley is a print and television journalist originally from Chicago, Illinois. She has worked for CNN and *Self* magazine and has published two books, *On Target: How the World's Hottest Retailer Hit a Bull's-Eye* (2003) and *Money and Happiness: A Guide to Living the Good Life* (2005).

The fastest way to end a party is to have someone die in the middle of it. 1

At a party last fall I watched a 22-year-old die of cardiac arrest after 2 he had used drugs. It was a painful, undignified way to die. And I would like to think that anyone who shared the experience would feel his or her ambivalence about substance abuse dissolving.

ambivalence:
uncertainty; conflicting feelings

Len Bias (b. 1963): college basketball star who died of a cocaine overdose in 1986

This victim won't be singled out like Len Bias as a bitter example 3 for "troubled youth." He was just another ordinary guy celebrating with friends at a private house party, the kind where they roll in the keg first thing in the morning and get stupefied while watching the football games on cable all afternoon. The living room was littered with beer cans from last night's party—along with dirty socks and the stuffing from the secondhand couch.

And there were drugs, as at so many other college parties. The drug 4 of choice this evening was psilocybin, hallucinogenic mushrooms. If you're cool you call them "'shrooms."

This wasn't a crowd huddled in the corner of a darkened room with 5 a single red bulb, shooting needles in their arms. People played darts, made jokes, passed around a joint and listened to the Grateful Dead on the stereo.

Suddenly, a thin, tall, brown-haired young man began to gasp. His eyes **6** rolled back in his head, and he hit the floor face first with a crash. Someone laughed, not appreciating the violence of his fall, thinking the afternoon's festivities had finally caught up with another guest. The laugh lasted only a second, as the brown-haired guest began to convulse and choke. The sound of the stereo and laughter evaporated. Bystanders shouted frantic suggestions:

"It's an epileptic fit, put something in his mouth!"   **7**

"Roll him over on his stomach!"   **8**

"Call an ambulance; God, somebody breathe into his mouth."   **9**

A girl kneeling next to him began to sob his name, and he seemed **10** to moan.

"Wait, he's semicoherent." Four people grabbed for the telephone, **11** to find no dial tone, and ran to use a neighbor's. One slammed the dead phone against the wall in frustration—and miraculously produced a dial tone.

But the body was now motionless on the kitchen floor. "He has a **12** pulse, he has a pulse."

"But he's not breathing!"   **13**

"Well, get away—give him some f—ing air!" The three or four guests **14** gathered around his body unbuttoned his shirt.

"Wait—is he OK? Should I call the damn ambulance?"   **15**

A chorus of frightened voices shouted, "Yes, yes!"   **16**

"Come on, come on, breathe again. Breathe!"   **17**

Over muffled sobs came a sudden grating, desperate breath that **18** passed through bloody lips and echoed through the kitchen and living room.

"He's had this reaction before—when he did acid at a concert last **19** spring. But he recovered in 15 seconds . . . ," one friend confided.

The rest of the guests looked uncomfortably at the floor or paced **20** purposelessly around the room. One or two whispered, "Oh, my God," over and over, like a prayer. A friend stood next to me, eyes fixed on the kitchen floor. He mumbled, just audibly, "I've seen this before. My dad died of a heart attack. He had the same look. . . ." I touched his shoulder and leaned against a wall, repeating reassurances to myself. People don't die at parties. People don't die at parties.

Eventually, no more horrible, gnashing sounds tore their way from **21** the victim's lungs. I pushed my hands deep in my jeans pockets wondering how much it costs to pump a stomach and how someone could be so careless if he had had this reaction with another drug. What would he tell his parents about the hospital bill?

Two uniformed paramedics finally arrived, lifted him onto a stretcher **22** and quickly rolled him out. His face was grayish blue, his mouth hung open, rimmed with blood, and his eyes were rolled back with a yellowish color on the rims.

The paramedics could be seen moving rhythmically forward and **23** back through the small windows of the ambulance, whose lights threw a red wash over the stunned watchers on the porch. The paramedics' hands

semicoherent: somewhat capable of thought and speech

were massaging his chest when someone said, "Did you tell them he took psilocybin? Did you tell them?"

"No, I . . ."   24

"My God, so tell them—do you want him to die?" Two people ran to   25
tell the paramedics the student had eaten mushrooms five minutes before the attack.

irreverent:
disrespectful

It seemed irreverent to talk as the ambulance pulled away. My friend,   26
who still saw his father's image, muttered, "That guy's dead." I put my arms around him half to comfort him, half to stop him from saying things I couldn't believe.

The next day, when I called someone who lived in the house, I found   27
that my friend was right.

My hands began to shake and my eyes filled with tears for someone   28
I didn't know. Weeks later the pain has dulled, but I still can't unravel the knot of emotion that has moved from my stomach to my head. When I told one friend what happened, she shook her head and spoke of the stupidity of filling your body with chemical substances. People who would do drugs after seeing that didn't value their lives too highly, she said.

But others refused to read any universal lessons from the incident.   29
Many of those I spoke to about the event considered him the victim of a freak accident, randomly struck down by drugs as a pedestrian might be hit by a speeding taxi. They speculated that the student must have had special physical problems; what happened to him could not happen to them.

Couldn't it? Now when I hear people discussing drugs I'm haunted by   30
the image of him lying on the floor, his body straining to rid itself of substances he chose to take. Painful, undignified, unnecessary—like a wartime casualty. But in war, at least, lessons are supposed to be learned, so that old mistakes are not repeated. If this death cannot make people think and change, that will be an even greater tragedy.

DISCUSS WITH YOUR PEERS

1. Look at the author's opening sentence: "The fastest way to end a party is to have someone die in the middle of it." Do you think this is an appropriate and effective way to begin the story? Why or why not?

2. In paragraph 21, the author wonders how "someone could be so careless if he had had this reaction with another drug." Discuss what may have motivated the young man to use drugs again. Do you believe that this sort of careless behavior is fairly common among teenagers and young adults, or is this a truly exceptional case? Explain your opinions.

3. Look at paragraphs 28 and 29. Discuss whether the party guests are likely to change their habits after witnessing this scene. In your opinion, would *reading* about this event be likely to change the thinking or behavior of a recreational drug user? Might this story actually save lives? Why or why not?

IDENTIFY THE PATTERNS

For more on the various writing patterns referenced here, see Chapter 8, Patterns of Development.

1. The author uses **narration** as the main pattern of development. In your own words, retell the main events of the story. In your opinion, what makes this a powerful story? (If you don't think the story is powerful, explain why.)

2. The author also uses **description** to develop her writing. Reread paragraphs 6, 22, and 23. Underline or highlight some of the powerful descriptive details that bring this story to life.

3. Additionally, the author uses **argument** to develop her writing. Both the second paragraph and the last sentence of the essay argue that people should change their attitude and behavior after learning about such a tragic event. For the author, the details of the young man's death are powerful *evidence* that using drugs is dangerous. Is the author's argument successful?

WRITE ABOUT THE READING

Based on the details in this story, do you think that recreational drug users are adequately informed about and prepared for the dangers of substance abuse? Give specific examples from the story to support your ideas.

WRITE ABOUT YOUR LIFE

1. Tell the story of a tragic event involving drugs or other substance abuse. What lessons can be learned from this story?

2. Discuss whether you are against recreational drug use or whether you believe it should be allowed in certain circumstances. Give examples to support your ideas.

Scott Russell Sanders
Under the Influence

Scott Russell Sanders is currently Distinguished Professor of English at Indiana University. He has written more than 20 books, including *A Private History of Awe* (2006), which was nominated for the Pulitzer Prize. He was born in Memphis, Tennessee.

Soon after my parents moved back to Father's treacherous stomping ground, my wife and I visited them in Mississippi with our five-year-old daughter. Mother had been too distraught to warn me about the return of   1

stomping ground: the place where a person grows up

distraught: upset

lurched: swayed or staggered

Papaw: Grandpa

stupor: a state of numbness or reduced sensibility

the demons. So when I climbed out of the car that bright July morning and saw my father napping in the hammock, I felt uneasy, for in all his sober years I had never known him to sleep in daylight. Then he lurched upright, blinked his bloodshot eyes, and greeted us in a syrupy voice. I was hurled back helpless into childhood.

"What's the matter with Papaw?" our daughter asked. 2

"Nothing," I said. "Nothing!" 3

Like a child again, I pretended not to see him in his stupor, and behind 4 my phony smile I grieved. On that visit and on the few that remained before his death, once again I found bottles in the workbench, bottles in the woods. Again his hands shook too much for him to run a saw, to make his precious miniature furniture, to drive straight down back roads. Again he wound up in the ditch, in the hospital, in jail, in treatment centers. Again he shouted and wept. Again he lied. "I never touched a drop," he swore. "Your mother's making it up."

I no longer fancied I could reason with the men whose names I found 5 on the bottles—Jim Beam, Jack Daniels—nor did I hope to save my father by burning down a store. I was able now to press the cold statistics about alcoholism against the ache of memory: ten million victims, fifteen million, twenty. And yet, in spite of my age, I reacted in the same blind way as I had in childhood, ignoring biology, forgetting numbers, vainly seeking to erase through my efforts whatever drove him to drink. I worked on their place twelve and sixteen hours a day, in the swelter of Mississippi summers, digging ditches, running electrical wires, planting trees, mowing grass, building sheds, as though what nagged at him was some list of chores, as though by taking his worries on my shoulders I could redeem him. I was flung back into boyhood, acting as though my father would not drink himself to death if only I were perfect.

redeem: to save someone or make up for his or her shortcomings

I failed of perfection; he succeeded in dying. To the end, he consid- 6 ered himself not sick but sinful. "Do you want to kill yourself?" I asked him. "Why not?" he answered. "Why the hell not? What's there to save?" To the end, he would not speak about his feelings, would not or could not give a name to the beast that was devouring him.

biblical swine: a reference to a Bible story in which Jesus commands a group of demons to enter a herd of swine (hogs) and depart. The swine then jump off a cliff.

stalwart: strong and brave

squandered: wasted

flounder: to struggle

banish: to send away

In silence, he went rushing off the cliff. Unlike the biblical swine, 7 however, he left behind a few of the demons to haunt his children. Life with him and the loss of him twisted us into shapes that will be familiar to other sons and daughters of alcoholics. My brother became a rebel, my sister retreated into shyness, I played the stalwart and dutiful son who would hold the family together. If my father was unstable, I would be a rock. If he squandered money on drink, I would pinch every penny. If he wept when drunk—and only when drunk—I would not let myself weep at all. If he roared at the Little League umpire for calling my pitches balls, I would throw nothing but strikes. Watching him flounder and rage, I came to dread the loss of control. I would go through life without making anyone mad. I vowed never to put in my mouth or veins any chemical that would banish my everyday self. I would never make a scene, never lash out at the ones I loved, never hurt a soul. Through hard work, relentless work, I would achieve something dazzling—in the classroom, on the basketball floor, in the science lab, in the pages of books—and my achievement would distract the world's eyes from his humiliation. I would become a worthy sacrifice, and the smoke of my burning would please God.

humiliation: shame

It is far easier to recognize these twists in my character than to undo them. Work has become an addiction for me, as drink was an addiction for my father. Knowing this, my daughter gave me a placard for the wall: WORKAHOLIC. The labor is endless and futile, for I can no more redeem myself through work than I could redeem my father. I still panic in the face of other people's anger, because his drunken temper was so terrible. I shrink from causing sadness or disappointment even to strangers, as though I were still concealing the family shame. I still notice every twitch of emotion in the faces around me, having learned as a child to read the weather in faces, and I blame myself for their least pang of unhappiness or anger. In certain moods I blame myself for everything. Guilt burns like acid in my veins.

8

futile: useless

I am moved to write these pages now because my own son, at the age of ten, is taking on himself the griefs of the world, and in particular the griefs of his father. He tells me that when I am gripped by sadness he feels responsible; he feels there must be something he can do to spring me from depression, to fix my life. And that crushing sense of responsibility is exactly what I felt at the age of ten in the face of my father's drinking. My son wonders if I, too, am possessed. I write, therefore, to drag into the light what eats at me—the fear, the guilt, the shame—so that my own children may be spared.

9

I still shy away from nightclubs, from bars, from parties where the solvent is alcohol. My friends puzzle over this, but it is no more peculiar than for a man to shy away from the lions' den after seeing his father torn apart. I took my own first drink at the age of twenty-one, half a glass of burgundy. I knew the odds of my becoming an alcoholic were four times higher than for the sons of nonalcoholic fathers. So I sipped warily.

10

solvent: liquid

warily: cautiously

I still do—once a week, perhaps, a glass of wine, a can of beer, nothing stronger, nothing more. I listen for the turning of a key in my brain.

11

DISCUSS WITH YOUR PEERS

1. When the author returns to Mississippi to visit his father, why does he say that he was "hurled back helpless into childhood" and that he was "like a child again"? What power does his father's alcoholism have over him to make him feel this way?

2. Reread paragraph 9. What does the author hope to achieve from the act of writing? Discuss whether writing has ever helped you or someone you know survive a difficult situation. Can you imagine that writing might someday serve this purpose in your life? Why or why not?

3. What does the author mean by the metaphor in the last sentence: "I listen for the turning of a key in my brain"? Do you think this is an effective metaphor for his life?

IDENTIFY THE PATTERNS

For more on the various writing patterns referenced here, see Chapter 8, Patterns of Development.

1. In paragraph 5, the author uses **exemplification** to explain how he tries to save his father from alcoholism. Underline or highlight some of the examples he uses. Do you think these examples show the son's desperation in a vivid way? Why or why not?

2. In paragraph 7, the author uses **cause and effect** to show the powerful influence of the father's alcoholism on the child. First, underline details about the father's behavior (the cause); then, underline details about the son's behavior (the effects). Does this paragraph adequately show the strong cause-and-effect relationship between a parent's alcoholism and the consequences for a child?

3. In paragraph 7, the author uses **contrast** to show how he will be different from his father. Underline each contrast that he makes.

WRITE ABOUT THE READING

Based on the details in this story, do you believe that the narrator will ever fully escape from the effects of his father's alcohol addiction? Give specific examples to support your ideas.

WRITE ABOUT YOUR LIFE

Discuss how a family member with an addiction (alcohol, drugs, gambling, shopping, or something else) can affect other members of the family. Or, discuss how a close friend, boyfriend, or girlfriend with an addiction can affect his or her friend or partner.

Punctuation and Capitalization

Using Correct Punctuation

Punctuation marks are like little traffic signals for your readers, telling them when to pause, stop, notice where your own words stop and another's start, and so on. The following sections briefly review some punctuation uses covered in earlier chapters and introduce a few new ones.

COMMAS (,)

Let's begin by reviewing some comma uses that may be familiar to you.

Commas after Introductory Words

Usually, commas come after beginning words that set up, describe, or otherwise introduce the main ideas in a sentence. Here are five types of expressions that are typically followed by commas.

1. Transitional expressions. Look at these examples:

> <u>In the first place</u>, athletes need to be team players.
>
> <u>More important</u>, the building failed to meet safety codes.
>
> <u>Last</u>, you should find a good financial adviser.
>
> <u>Nevertheless</u>, she will apply for the scholarship.

Sometimes, a transitional expression will appear after a semicolon (;). It should be followed by a comma in this case, too:

> I woke up late for my first day of work; <u>furthermore</u>, I forgot to iron my dress shirt.

For more information on transitional expressions, see Chapter 6, page 117, and Chapter 11, page 292.

2. Simple adverbs. Look at these examples:

<u>Sadly</u>, our hamster escaped from its cage.

<u>Suddenly</u>, the lights went out in the stadium.

<u>Reluctantly</u>, James signed the new contract.

For more information on adverbs, see Chapter 10, page 234.

3. Prepositional phrases. Look at these examples:

<u>In the morning</u>, light fills my bedroom.

<u>After the party</u>, we will go dancing.

<u>Under her pillow</u>, Joanne found a diamond necklace.

For more information on prepositional phrases, see Chapter 10, page 240.

4. Word groups beginning with subordinating conjunctions. Look at these examples:

<u>Unless we shout</u>, they won't hear us.

<u>Because you are my friend</u>, I told you the truth.

<u>Although I am tired</u>, I will go to the party.

For more information on subordination, see Chapter 12.

5. Modifying phrases. Look at these examples:

<u>Backing down the driveway</u>, the car ran over a tricycle.

<u>To escape from the handcuffs</u>, the magician picked the lock.

<u>Disappointed with his salary</u>, Jaime looked for a new job.

For more information on modifying phrases, see Chapter 14.

Commas in Compound Sentences

As you learned in Chapter 11, a **compound sentence** is two or more related simple sentences joined together. When simple sentences are joined with a coordinating conjunction (such as *and*, *but*, *or*, or *so*), a comma must precede this conjunction. Take a look:

However, remember that no comma is used when forming a compound subject or a compound verb:

Liz **and** Ryan collect antiques **and** restore furniture.

For more information, see Chapter 11.

Commas Setting Off Descriptive/Modifying Word Groups

You already know that when a modifying phrase begins a sentence, it must be followed by a comma. Let's review some other rules for descriptive word groups.

Remember from Chapter 13 that if you add a descriptive clause that is *not essential* to the meaning of a sentence, you usually must set it off with commas. If the clause is in the middle of a sentence, commas come before and after the clause:

Monopoly, <u>which I hate</u>, is my in-laws' favorite game.

If the clause is at the end of a sentence, use one comma, immediately before the clause:

DESCRIPTIVE CLAUSE
AT THE END

My in-laws like to play Monopoly, <u>which I hate</u>.

Do not use commas to set off *essential* information:

The old Monopoly game <u>that we purchased</u> is missing three pieces.

Also, note these rules for modifying phrases that begin with *-ing*, *to*, or *-ed*:

- When the phrase is in the middle of a sentence, commas are used before and after it.
- When a modifying phrase comes at the end, commas generally are not used.

A modifying phrase in the middle:

Deirdre, <u>listening to classical music</u>, fell into a deep sleep.
The judge, <u>annoyed by the attorney</u>, called a recess.

A modifying phrase at the end:

Deirdre fell into a deep sleep <u>listening to classical music</u>.
My cousin visited his local recruiting office <u>to enlist in the army</u>.

For additional information on punctuating modifying phrases, see Chapter 14, page 357.

Other Uses of Commas

Here, we will introduce four additional uses of commas.

1. To separate items in a series.   When you list three or more items, separate them with commas. Take a look:

You can select whole, skim, or 2 percent milk.

Shirley bought apples, peaches, cherries, and grapes.

For more practice with commas, go to **bedfordstmartins.com/ steppingstones**.

Note that for clarity, most instructors and other writing experts recommend putting a comma before the conjunctions *and* and *or*.

Terminology Tip
Words that rename a noun are known as *appositives*.

2. To set off information that renames another item.   Sometimes, we follow a noun with a word group that renames that noun. Take a look at the underlined word group in this sentence:

Andre Gomez, <u>my new boss</u>, goes to your gym.

My new boss renames *Andre Gomez*. Here's another example:

We no longer go to Murphy's, <u>the restaurant that received three health violations</u>.

The underlined word group renames *Murphy's*.

3. To separate parts of an address.   Look at this example:

Danielle lives at 5 Foster Lane, Boston, MA 02130.

Notice that no comma appears before the zip code.

When the name of a city and state appear in the middle of a sentence, a comma should follow the state name:

The brothers stayed in Dayton, Ohio, before driving on to Nebraska.

4. To separate parts of dates.   When a date includes the month, day, and year, a comma must come between the day and the year:

My daughter was born on September 15, 1998.

If a date with the month, day, and year appears in the middle of a sentence, a comma should follow the year:

September 15, 1998, was a big day for our family.

When only a month and year are specified, no comma is needed between them:

You must submit your application by the end of December 2012.

ACTIVITY 1: Mastery Test

Edit the following paragraph, adding necessary commas and deleting unnecessary ones. There are twenty-six missing commas and four unnecessary commas.

(1) On June 2 2007 my husband and I got married, and started a big adventure: our honeymoon. (2) My husband Dan had always wanted

to visit New England, so he rented a cabin for us in Barton Vermont.

(3) On the day after our wedding we drove to Barton which is in a beautiful area of Vermont known as the Northeast Kingdom. (4) As we traveled country roads, we admired the green fields dotted with cows the misty lakes and the rolling hills. (5) Unfortunately that was as good as the honeymoon got. (6) Our cabin was down a muddy, rutted lane and it looked nothing like the photo of it, that we'd seen on the Internet.

(7) Although Dan and I were somewhat shocked we decided to make the best of things. (8) We figured that we would be spending most of our time outdoors anyway. (9) We didn't realize how true that prediction would be until that first night, when a rainstorm caused part of the roof to cave in. (10) Disturbed by this incident we decided to camp outdoors; fortunately we'd brought a tent. (11) The next morning Dan called the cabin owner about getting a refund. (12) Then he and I set off for a hike up Jay Peak. (13) As we walked up the trail at the base of the mountain, we looked forward to the dramatic views from the summit.

(14) However just one mile into the hike, Dan tripped on some rocks and sprained his ankle. (15) Luckily some very kind hikers came to the rescue, and helped us back to the trailhead. (16) After Dan got his ankle bandaged at a local hospital we spent the next few days in a motel, and watched the pouring rain from our window. (17) Finally we headed home.

(18) Now that some time has passed, we can laugh at our honeymoon. (19) We plan to return to Vermont sometime soon and we're hoping that we'll have better luck.

COLONS (:)

Sometimes, we follow a complete sentence with examples or explanations related to the complete sentence. In such cases, a colon may be used before the examples or explanations. Take a look:

COMPLETE SENTENCE   COLON   EXAMPLES

I am allergic to three things: shrimp, peanuts, and housework.

COMPLETE SENTENCE   COLON   EXPLANATION

Milo didn't get the job for one reason: He lied on his application.

Notice that in the second example, the word group after the colon begins with a capital *H* because it is a complete sentence.

Colons are also used in the following situations:

- Between the main titles and subtitles of books, reports, and other publications. Look at these examples:

  I read a fascinating book titled *Sellout: The Politics of Racial Betrayal*.

  The report that we were assigned, *Great Transitions: Preparing Adolescents for a New Century*, came to many surprising conclusions.

- After greetings or *to/from* directives in letters or memos. Take a look:

  Dear Ms. Landiss:

  To: The IT staff

  From: Jan Rogers

ACTIVITY 2: Mastery Test

Write five sentences that include colons.

SEMICOLONS (;)

As you learned in Chapter 11, a semicolon can be used instead of a conjunction to connect two closely related simple sentences. Here are two simple sentences joined with a comma and a coordinating conjunction:

SENTENCE 1   COMMA AND COORDINATING CONJUNCTION   SENTENCE 2

Watching basketball is fun   , but   playing it is better.

Here are the same sentences joined with a semicolon:

For more practice with colons and semicolons, go to **bedfordstmartins.com/ steppingstones**.

SENTENCE 1   SENTENCE 2

Watching basketball is fun; playing it is better.

Remember that semicolons must always *follow* a complete sentence. Also, semicolons (and often periods) must also *be followed* by another complete sentence.

For more on joining sentences with a semicolon, see Chapter 11.

Now we'll introduce a new use of the semicolon: *to separate items in a series that already contains commas.*

As you learned on pages 489–90, in lists of three or more items, the items are separated with commas. Now, look at these examples:

> **The interview candidates will meet with Vera Canseco, director of marketing; Dennis Liu, vice president of operations; and Chris Snow, vice president of sales.**

> **The choir traveled to Detroit, Michigan; Gary, Indiana; and Madison, Wisconsin.**

Without the semicolons, the groupings of items might not be immediately clear to readers. The semicolons clarify the groupings.

ACTIVITY 3: Mastery Test

Add missing semicolons to each of the following sentences, replacing commas if necessary. (You should use semicolons instead of periods to separate sentences.)

EXAMPLE: I want only to become class president ; you wish to lead the nation.

1. Chocolate alone is a treat chocolate and red wine together are divine.

2. You know that I'm older than Lisette you will discover that I'm also

   wiser than Lisette.

3. My European travel plans will take me to Barcelona, Spain, Lisbon,

   Portugal, and Paris, France.

4. Hiking up the mountain took three hours coming down took just two.

5. Robin's healthy dinner menu included spinach, which is loaded with

   B vitamins, lean chicken, a good source of protein, and brown rice,

   which is rich in fiber.

APOSTROPHES (')

Here, we will introduce three common uses of apostrophes.

1. To show ownership.   When you want to show that a singular noun (*girl, boy, teacher*) owns something, add *-'s*:

> The girl's horse threw her.
>
> The teacher's lessons were easy to follow.
>
> Chris's dogs are cute and friendly.

When you want to show that a plural noun ending in *-s* (*girls, boys, teachers*) owns something, add only an apostrophe:

> The girls' horses slept in the barn.
>
> The teachers' offices were locked.

If a plural noun does not end in *-s* (*men, women, children*), you need to add *-'s* to form the possessive:

> The women's restroom is closed.
>
> Our library has a children's story hour.

When time expressions show ownership, apostrophes should also be used:

> Last year's holiday party was more crowded than this year's.
>
> When I resigned from my job, I gave two weeks' notice.

2. To shorten words.   Sometimes, especially in speech, we shorten words by omitting letters. When writing these shortened forms, known as *contractions*, we use an apostrophe to show where letters have been left out:

LONG FORM	CONTRACTION
are not	aren't
cannot	can't
did not	didn't
do not	don't
I will	I'll
I am	I'm
is not	isn't
it is, it has	it's
was not	wasn't

Be careful not to misplace apostrophes when you are writing contractions:

> **INCORRECT** are'nt; is'nt   **REVISED** aren't; isn't

Some instructors prefer that students avoid contractions in papers. If you are unsure of your instructors' preferences, be sure to ask.

Power Tip

You do not need to add an apostrophe to show possession when you use a possessive pronoun.

Incorrect: This cabin is your's; our's is across the lake.

Revised: This cabin is yours; ours is across the lake.

For more on possessive pronouns, see Chapter 16, page 421.

3. To make numbers and letters plural. Occasionally, you will write plural forms of numbers and letters. Use apostrophes in these cases:

Bill writes his 2's like 7's.   I got three A's and two B's last semester.

ⅷⅷ ACTIVITY 4: Mastery Test
MASTERY

Edit the following paragraph, adding apostrophes where necessary and fixing any incorrectly placed apostrophes. There are nine missing apostrophes and two incorrectly placed apostrophes.

(1) During his first year of college, Mark got mostly Cs and Ds.

(2) Holding down two jobs, going to school full-time, and helping take care of his girlfriends children made it difficult for him to do well.

(3) Not long into Marks second year, it was clear that what he had done his first year wasnt going to work. (4) With his supervisors permission, Mark cut his hours at one job, and he also cut back slightly on his course load. (5) He did'nt miss any classes, and he went to all of his teachers office hours as often as he could. (6) At night and during the childrens' nap times, he studied hard. (7) So far, Marks grades have improved, and he has started receiving his first As.

QUOTATION MARKS (" ")

When we use someone's exact words in writing, these *direct quotations* need to be enclosed in quotation marks. Take a look:

The comedian Steven Wright once asked, "If a word in the dictionary were misspelled, how would we know?"
As the suspect fled, the officer yelled, "Halt! Police!"

If we report what someone said without using his or her exact words, quotation marks are not used. Such reported speech is known as an *indirect quotation*.

The officer told the fleeing suspect to stop.

For more practice with apostrophes and quotation marks, go to **bedfordstmartins.com/ steppingstones**.

Following are some basic guidelines for using direct quotations.

- Put quotation marks at the beginning and end of the quotation.
- If the quotation is a complete sentence, capitalize the first word of it. For example: *Bill's father said, "Don't forget to take your lunch."*
- If the quotation is not a complete sentence, you do not need to capitalize it. For example: *All of us were told about the "mysterious green glow" that shone in Petrie Forest at night.*
- Use a comma to separate the quotation from the identification of the speaker. For example: *Tom said, "Go away." OR "Go away," Tom said.* Notice that in both examples, the closing quotation mark is *after the period or comma.*
- If a question mark is part of a quoted speaker's words, put it inside the quotation marks. For example: *During the fire, Rona yelled, "Where are the exits?"*
- If a question is being posed by you, the writer, not the quoted speaker, put the question mark outside of the quotation marks. For example: *Did you know what Paul meant by "dire situation"?*

ACTIVITY 5: Mastery Test

Edit the following paragraph, adding quotation marks where necessary and fixing any incorrectly used quotation marks. You may need to fix other punctuation and some capitalization as well.

You should add three pairs of missing quotation marks, remove three pairs of unnecessary quotation marks (for indirect quotations), fix four other punctuation errors, and correct two capitalization errors.

(1) My best friend told me that "she has had one bad experience" with Internet dating. (2) She said my first mistake was to go out with a guy based only on his picture; if I had read his profile, I would have realized that he was a stuck-up jerk. (3) "Her second mistake," she said, was that "she let the date go on too long." (4) The guy talked and talked about himself and wouldn't let me get a word in she painfully recalled. (5) In response to this complaint, I asked my friend "Would you go on an Internet date again"? (6) She replied, in fact, I'm going on one this Friday, but this time I read the profile.

Using Correct Capitalization

Capital letters are large letters, like the *C* at the beginning of this sentence. Aside from capitalizing the first word of every sentence, you should also capitalize

- proper nouns
- major words in titles

As you learned in Chapter 10, proper nouns name *specific* people, places, and things. Let's take a closer look at different types of proper nouns.

- **People.** Capitalize the names of specific people, including titles preceding those names.

Aunt Lucia	Ms. Hernandez
Father	Professor Grant
Maria Hernandez	Vice President Hayes

Do not capitalize titles like *president*, *vice president*, or *aunt* if they are used without a name.

- **Places/geographic features.** Capitalize the names of specific locations, monuments, and geographic features.

Empire State Building	Lincoln Memorial
Homer, Alaska	Amazon River
Park Street	Mount Rainier
Rome	the North / the South
Yellowstone National Park	

Do not capitalize locations like *street*, *park*, or *river* if you are not naming a specific street, park, river, or other location:

> Our street is next to a park.
>   ↑   ↑

Capitalize *north*, *south*, *east*, and *west* when they name specific regions, but do not capitalize them in directions:

> The South had an agricultural economy at the time of the Civil War.
>   ↑

> Drive west for three miles, and then go south on I-71.
>   ↑   ↑

- **Racial and ethnic groups, nationalities, and languages**

African American	French
Asian	Guatemalan
Hispanic	Spanish
Latino/Latina	

Power Tip

Father, mother, and other family titles are capitalized when they are used in place of the person's specific name: *Yes, Father is retired.* Otherwise, such titles should not be capitalized: *My father is retired.*

For more practice with capitalization, go to **bedfordstmartins.com/ steppingstones**.

- **Organizations, teams, and other specific groups or establishments.** Capitalize the names of specific groups.

  American Civil Liberties Union   Curry College
  Red Sox   Fraternal Order of Police
  Sonic Youth   Sony

Do not capitalize groups or establishments if you are not naming them specifically:

Ken dropped out of his rock band and went to college.
                           ↑   ↑

- **Religions**

  Catholic   Jewish   Protestant
  Hindu   Muslim   Sikh

- **Months, days, and holidays**

  August   Monday   Hanukkah
  November   Wednesday   Thanksgiving

Note that *winter, spring, summer,* and *fall* are not capitalized.

- **Brand names.** Capitalize the names of specific brands.

  Johnson & Johnson   Puma
  The North Face   Toyota

Do not capitalize products when you are not naming a specific brand:

Jonelle put on her coat and sneakers and left the house.
                      ↑   ↑

- **Academic courses.** Capitalize the names of specific academic courses.

  Calculus 1
  Economics 100
  English 090
  German 101

Unless you are naming a specific course, do not capitalize a course name unless it is a specific language, nationality, or other term that you would normally capitalize:

Last semester, I took three difficult courses: math, chemistry, and
German.
↑

In addition to capitalizing proper nouns, you should also capitalize major words in the titles of publications, films, television shows, songs, and other media. You should not capitalize *a, an,* and *the,* prepositions (like *at, in, on, to,* and *with*), or conjunctions (*and, but, or,* and so on) unless they begin or end the title.

Have you read John Irving's novel *The World According to Garp*?

Today, the *Leeville Gazette* published a troubling story: "The Problem with Plastics."

Jess's favorite movie is *Romy and Michele's High School Reunion*.

Dancing with the Stars is one of the most popular television shows.

Power Tip
Notice that the titles of books, newspapers, movies, and television shows are italicized (or underlined). Titles of articles, essays, and short stories appear in quotation marks.

ACTIVITY 6: Mastery Test

Correct the capitalization errors in each of the following sentences.

              A   L W
EXAMPLE: In august, our family will vacation at lake winnipesaukee.

1. At our College, african American students have formed a scholarship fund.

2. Next Fall, professor Sara Paradis will teach western civilization 101 and history 102.

3. In the summer, aunt Barb and uncle Pete like to take boat trips along the mississippi river.

4. During the christmas holiday, I read a hilarious book: *a confederacy of dunces*.

5. Drive South for three miles, and then turn left at the kentucky fried chicken onto Delancey street.

Guidelines for ESL Writers

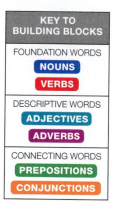

If English is not your first language, or if you grew up in a home where standard English was not spoken, every chapter in Part Three of this book will improve your grammar skills. Additionally, you may benefit from reviewing this appendix and completing the activities in it, as well as getting additional practice online at this book's companion Web site, **bedfordstmartins.com/steppingstones**.

Remember, too, that the more you hear and read standard English, the faster your language skills will improve. Try to listen to news broadcasts or podcasts while driving, exercising, or preparing meals. Also, read magazine or newspaper articles as often as you can.

Note: This appendix color codes the building blocks of language according to the system used in Part Three. See the nearby box for a reminder.

Count and Noncount Nouns

As you learned in Chapter 10, a **noun** is a word that identifies a person, place, or thing (for instance, *girl, Beatrice, city, Chicago, ball*).

Count nouns refer to people, places, or things that can be counted (for example, three *girls*, two *boys*, two *towns*, six *shoes*, seven *apples*). **Noncount nouns** refer to items, qualities, or concepts that can't be counted (for example, *flour, granite, honesty*). Here are some more examples:

COUNT NOUNS	NONCOUNT NOUNS
ball/balls	advice
boat/boats	beauty
car/cars	gold
computer/computers	health
letter/letters	information
plate/plates	jewelry
shirt/shirts	knowledge

CONTINUED >

COUNT NOUNS	NONCOUNT NOUNS
street/streets tree/trees window/windows	money sadness sand sugar wheat

Note that noncount nouns usually do not have plural forms; in other words, do not add *-s* or *-es* to the end of them.

INCORRECT   golds, healths, sadnesses, wheats

CORRECT   gold, health, sadness, wheat

ACTIVITY 1: Mastery Test

Identify each of the following nouns as *count* or *noncount* by writing "C" or "N" in the space provided.

EXAMPLE: airplane _____C_____

1. road _____

2. book _____

3. pollution _____

4. steel _____

5. peach _____

6. bead _____

7. information _____

8. toe _____

9. salt _____

10. stick _____

Articles

The **articles** *a*, *an*, and *the* are small but important words that signal that a noun is coming up. Look at the following examples, in which the articles are underlined.

The judge entered the courtroom.

A bird perched on the railing.

An apple fell from the tree.

Use *a* or *an* to signal nonspecific nouns, and *the* to signal specific nouns:

A police officer arrived on the scene. (the officer's identity is not specified)

An eyewitness testified. (the eyewitness's identify is not specified)

The police officer who interviewed us filed a report. (the officer is the one who interviewed us)

The sand on our local beach washed away. (the sand is on our beach)

As you use articles, keep the following rules in mind:

1. Do not use *a* or *an* with noncount nouns.   In standard English, the following sentence would be incorrect:

INCORRECT   Eduardo borrowed a̲ sugar from his neighbor.

You do not need the article *a* before the noncount noun *sugar*. However, if you specify a quantity of a noncount noun, you may use the article:

CORRECT   Eduardo borrowed a̲ cup of sugar from his neighbor.

2. Do not use *the* before noncount or plural nouns that mean "in general."   Take a look at the following sentences:

INCORRECT   The̲ money is all Bill thinks about.

INCORRECT   I buy the̲ carrots whenever I go grocery shopping.

In the first example, the intended meaning is that Bill constantly thinks about money in general, not a specific kind of money. Therefore, the article should be dropped:

CORRECT   Money is all Bill thinks about.

In the second example, the intended meaning is that I buy carrots in general whenever I shop; I do not buy a specific kind of carrot. Therefore, the article should be dropped:

CORRECT   I buy carrots whenever I go grocery shopping.

3. In article + adjective + noun combinations, use the article that fits the sound of the adjective, not the sound of the noun.

INCORRECT   An tasty apple is a good snack.

CORRECT   A tasty apple is a good snack.

4. Use *a* before consonant sounds, and *an* before vowel sounds.

- Consonant sounds include: *b, c, d, f, g, j, k, l, m, n, p, q, r, s, t, v, w, x, z*, usually *h* (as in words like *hand* and *harbor*), sometimes *u* (as in words like *university* and *universe*), and usually *y*.
- Vowel sounds include: *a, e, i, o*, sometimes *h* (as in words like *herb* and *hour*), and sometimes *u* (as in words like *understanding* and *unlikely*).

For more practice with nouns and articles, go to **bedfordstmartins .com/steppingstones**.

ACTIVITY 2: Mastery Test

For each blank in the following paragraph, fill in the correct article. If no article is needed, write "N.A." in the blank.

(1) While she was in bed one night, Rosario heard _____ mysterious sound at her window. (2) It sounded as if _____ sand was being tossed at the glass. (3) She went to _____ window and saw that _____ violent storm was whipping sleet against her house. (4) To Rosario, _____ storms of all kinds are interesting, so she stood there and watched the scene for several long moments. (5) She watched _____ trees in her yard bend from side to side. (6) The remaining leaves from last fall spun in little circles along the street. (7) On the sidewalk, _____ hunched-over neighbor hurried home against the wind. (8) This sight intensified _____ warmth and comfort of Rosario's room.

Verbs

As you learned in Chapter 15, mastering English verbs doesn't have to be difficult; you just need patience and practice. Also, as noted earlier, it's a good idea to read and listen to as much standard English as possible so that standard verb usage begins to sound more natural to you.

If you haven't already worked through Chapter 15, it's a good idea to do so now. Try to do as many of the activities in the chapter as you can. Also, you may want to review the coverage of helping verbs in Chapter 10 (page 231).

This section expands on the advice contained in earlier chapters, covering issues that are most challenging for English-as-a-second-language (ESL) students.

VERBS WITH GERUNDS AND INFINITIVES

Gerunds are verbs that have *-ing* endings and that function as nouns. Look at these examples:

GERUND   GERUND

I like running.   Jordan enjoys sewing.

Infinitives combine *to* and a base verb (for example, *to run, to sew*). Look at these examples:

INFINITIVE   INFINITIVE

I like <u>to run</u>.   Jordan wants <u>to sew</u> a quilt.

In standard English, some verbs may be followed by a gerund or an infinitive:

GERUND   INFINITIVE

I like <u>running</u>.   I like <u>to run</u>.

Other verbs may be followed by a gerund but not by an infinitive:

GERUND

CORRECT   Jordan enjoys <u>sewing</u>.

INFINITIVE

INCORRECT   Jordan enjoys <u>to sew</u>.

Yet other verbs may be followed by an infinitive but not a gerund:

INFINITIVE

CORRECT   Jordan wants <u>to sew</u> a quilt.

GERUND

INCORRECT   Jordan wants <u>sewing</u> a quilt.

The following chart shows some of the verbs that are used with gerunds and/or infinitives.

VERBS THAT CAN BE FOLLOWED BY A GERUND OR AN INFINITIVE			
begin	hate	remember	try
continue	like	start	
forget	love	stop	
VERBS THAT CAN BE FOLLOWED BY A GERUND BUT NOT BY AN INFINITIVE			
admit	enjoy	practice	suggest
avoid	finish	quit	
deny	imagine	recall	
discuss	miss	risk	
VERBS THAT CAN BE FOLLOWED BY AN INFINITIVE BUT NOT BY A GERUND			
agree	decide	need	promise
ask	expect	offer	refuse
beg	hope	plan	wait
claim	manage	pretend	want

For more practice with using verbs correctly, go to **bedfordstmartins.com/ steppingstones**.

iiii
MASTERY
ACTIVITY 3: Mastery Test

For each blank in the following paragraph, fill in the gerund or infinitive form of the verb in parentheses.

(1) I try _____ (do) my best as a parent, but I'm not perfect. (2) When I decided _____ (have) children, I knew parenting would be difficult, but I figured I would know what to do most of the time. (3) When my son was born, I promised _____ (avoid) preaching to him. (4) I knew I wouldn't have all the answers, but I expected _____ (be) knowledgeable about most things he might ask me. (5) However, when he turned fifteen, he asked if he could get a tattoo. (6) I said, "No, not until you're older," and I preached to him about how the skull symbol he liked now might not look as good to him when he was thirty. (7) He agreed _____ (accept) my decision, but then he asked a tough question: "Are you tired of the shooting star on your ankle?" (8) The star was a tattoo that I got during my senior year of high school; I hid it from my own mother for years. (9) I thought for a minute. (10) Then, I managed _____ (tell) my son the truth: I didn't like the tattoo as much now as I did when I got it, but it is a reminder of who I was at seventeen. (11) For that reason, I still enjoy _____ (look) at it. (12) If it were gone, I would miss _____ (see) it. (13) Finally, I said, "Ben, you get that tattoo if you really want to." (14) For now, he has decided _____ (wait).

NEGATIVE STATEMENTS AND QUESTIONS

The rules for forming negative statements and questions vary, depending on whether the original (positive) statement has a helping verb. Look at these positive statements:

Dontell **likes** cars.

> **HELPING VERB**
> **(FOLLOWED BY MAIN VERB)**

Dontell **has purchased** a car.

As you can see, the second example has a helping verb, while the first example does not. Let's look at how to form negative statements first.

Negative Statements

To turn a sentence with a helping verb into a negative statement, put the word *not* right after the helping verb:

Dontell **has** not **purchased** a car.

Now, let's look back at the example without the helping verb:

Dontell **likes** cars.

To turn this type of sentence into a negative statement, put the helping verb *do* + *not* before the base form of the main verb. (The base form of *likes* is *like*.) The helping verb *do* must change to *does* to agree with *Dontell*. (For more on subject-verb agreement, see Chapter 15, pages 395–99.)

Dontell **does** not **like** cars.

If the verb in the original positive statement is a form of *be* (*am, is, are, was,* or *were*), you do not need to add the helping verb *do* before *not* when forming a negative statement.

Positive	→	**Negative**
Rita **is** happy.		Rita **is** not happy.

ACTIVITY 4: Mastery Test

Rewrite the following positive statements as negative statements.

EXAMPLE: You have burned the toast.

<u>You have not burned the toast.</u>

1. Marco is happy about the game's outcome.

_____

2. They have written angry e-mails to the congresswoman.

_____

3. The travelers are staying in an expensive hotel.

_____

4. Althea vacations at the beach.

_____

5. Eduardo has postponed the party at his new house.

_____

Questions

Let's look back at the positive statements presented earlier:

Dontell **likes** cars.

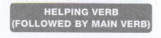

Dontell **has purchased** a car.

To turn a sentence with a helping verb into a question, put the helping verb before the subject (*Dontell*) and change the period at the end of the sentence to a question mark:

> **Has** Dontell **purchased** a car?

Now, let's look back at the example without the helping verb:

> Dontell **likes** cars.

To turn this type of sentence into a question, put the helping verb *do* before the subject. (Note that *do* must change to *does* to agree with *Dontell*.) Then, after the subject, provide the base form of the original verb (*likes* → *like*). Finally, change the period at the end of the sentence to a question mark:

> **Does** Dontell **like** cars?

If the verb in the original positive statement is a form of *be* (*am, is, are, was,* or *were*), you do not need to add the helping verb *do* when forming a question. Simply move the verb to precede the subject.

Positive	→	**Question**
Rita **is** happy.		**Is** Rita happy?

ACTIVITY 5: Mastery Test

Rewrite the following positive statements as questions.

EXAMPLE: You have burned the toast.

> *Have you burned the toast?*

1. Marco is happy about the game's outcome.

   _____

2. They have written angry e-mails to the congresswoman.

   _____

3. The travelers are staying in an expensive hotel.

   _____

4. Althea vacations at the beach.

   _____

5. Eduardo has postponed the party at his new house.

   _____

For more practice with forming questions and negative statements, go to **bedfordstmartins.com/ steppingstones**.

Prepositions

As you learned in Chapter 10, a **preposition** connects a word to more information about the word. Take a look:

> The book fell in the water.

The preposition *in* connects the verb *fell* to more information: Where did the book fall? In the water. (*In the water* is known as a prepositional phrase.)

MEANINGS OF COMMON PREPOSITIONS

Some of the most common English prepositions are *at*, *in*, and *on*. These prepositions may show either time or location, and you have to memorize the proper uses.

Whenever you are confused about how to use one of these prepositions, refer to the following chart.

PREPOSITION	USAGE TO SHOW TIME	USAGE TO SHOW LOCATION
at	Indicates a specific time: *The meeting began at 6:30.*	Indicates a specific place: *We arrived at the hotel early.* *Turn right at the light.* *I sat at my desk.*
in	Indicates a specific time or date: *In a week, we will leave.* *We got married in 2008.* Indicates a duration of time: *The movie will start in 15 minutes.*	Indicates someone or something being inside something else: *I stayed in my room.* *The papers were in the folder.* Indicates being in a geographic location: *I live in Boston.*
on	Indicates a specific day or date: *We were married on May 24, 2008.*	Indicates that something rests on or hangs from a surface: *Please put the book on the shelf.* *We hung the mirror on the wall.*

For a full list of prepositions, see Chapter 10, page 240.

ACTIVITY 6: Mastery Test

For each of the following sentences, fill in the blank with the correct preposition: *at, in,* or *on.*

EXAMPLE: We arrived _____*at*_____ the party early.

1. You will find Antonio _____ his office.

2. Josie graduated _____ June 6, 2009.

3. Every weekday morning, I get up _____ 5:30.

4. The little yellow bird sat _____ the fence and groomed its feathers.

5. _____ a moment, we will leave for the airport.

PREPOSITIONS AFTER ADJECTIVES

As you learned in Chapter 10, **adjectives** are words that describe nouns. Some English adjectives are often followed by specific prepositions. Again, you have to memorize the correct combinations, some of which are shown in the following chart.

ADJECTIVE + PREPOSITION COMBINATION	EXAMPLE
addicted to	Charlotte is <u>addicted to</u> chocolate.
afraid of	Timmy is <u>afraid of</u> the dark.
angry about/at	I am <u>angry about</u> this offensive e-mail.
angry with (used for people)	I am <u>angry with</u> Joe for sending this offensive e-mail.
confused by	The taxpayers were <u>confused by</u> the new rules.
excited about	We were <u>excited about</u> the concert.
grateful for	They were <u>grateful for</u> the assistance.
happy about	The students were <u>happy about</u> the exam postponement.
interested in	The teacher is <u>interested in</u> our progress.
pleased with	The Wongs are <u>pleased with</u> their new landscaping.
proud of	We are <u>proud of</u> our children.
responsible for	Workers are <u>responsible for</u> setting up their own retirement accounts.
sorry about	Betsy is <u>sorry about</u> the mistake.
tired of	The children are <u>tired of</u> spaghetti.

ACTIVITY 7: Mastery Test

For each of the following sentences, fill in the blank with the correct preposition.

EXAMPLE: All of us are responsible _____*for*_____ our own success.

1. I am interested _____ all movies about aliens and outer space.

2. The students were proud _____ their high scores on the math test.

3. The children were excited _____ the new game station, but they were confused _____ its instructions.

4. The tourists were tired _____ looking for parking, so they were happy _____ the free parking garage by their hotel.

5. Milo is angry _____ the dent in his car, but he is angrier _____ himself for driving recklessly.

PREPOSITIONS AFTER VERBS

Some English verbs are followed by specific prepositions. Here's just one example:

The students **handed** in the homework.

With some verb + preposition combinations, words can come between the verb and the preposition. Take a look:

The students **handed** the homework **in**.

With other combinations, however, the verb and preposition cannot be separated.

CORRECT   The soldiers **fought** for independence.

INCORRECT   The soldiers **fought** independence **for**.

Again, you have to memorize the correct combinations and which ones can and cannot be separated. The following chart shows just some of the possible combinations.

VERB + PREPOSITION COMBINATIONS THAT CAN BE SEPARATED	
Combination	**Example**
bring up (raise an issue)	Don't <u>bring up</u> that sensitive topic. / Don't <u>bring</u> it <u>up</u>.
call off (cancel)	The couple <u>called off</u> the wedding. / They <u>called</u> it <u>off</u>.
drop off (leave at a location)	The letter carrier <u>dropped off</u> a package. / She <u>dropped</u> it <u>off</u>.
fill in (add a substance until something is full / complete)	The workers <u>filled in</u> the old swimming pool. / They <u>filled</u> it <u>in</u>.
fill out (complete)	We must <u>fill out</u> these tax forms by April 15. / We must <u>fill</u> them <u>out</u>.
hand in (submit)	The customers <u>handed in</u> their loan applications. / The customers <u>handed</u> them <u>in</u>.
look up (find or check)	Janeece <u>looked up</u> the information on Google. / She <u>looked</u> it <u>up</u> on Google.
pick up (collect)	Josh <u>picked up</u> the children after school. / He <u>picked</u> them <u>up</u> after school.
put away (place something somewhere / remove from sight)	I <u>put away</u> the clean laundry. / I <u>put</u> it <u>away</u>.
put off (delay)	Don <u>put off</u> his dental appointment. / He <u>put</u> it <u>off</u>.
take off (remove)	Please <u>take off</u> your shoes before entering the house. / Please <u>take</u> them <u>off</u>.
throw away / throw out (discard)	I <u>threw away</u> my credit card. / I <u>threw</u> it <u>away</u>. I <u>threw out</u> my credit card. / I <u>threw</u> it <u>out</u>.
turn down (lower the volume of)	The party hosts <u>turned down</u> the stereo. / They <u>turned</u> it <u>down</u>.
turn off (shut off)	Remember to <u>turn off</u> the lights when you leave the room. / Remember to <u>turn</u> them <u>off</u>.
wake up (interrupt the sleep of / rise from sleep)	The barking dog <u>woke up</u> the baby. / He <u>woke</u> her <u>up</u>.
VERB + PREPOSITION COMBINATIONS THAT CANNOT BE SEPARATED	
Combination	**Example**
drop in (pay a visit)	I will <u>drop in</u> to see you.
fight against (combat)	The researchers will <u>fight against</u> the deadly disease.
fight for (work on behalf of / defend)	Senator Rose will <u>fight for</u> the legislation.
go over (review)	Let's <u>go over</u> the math problems.
grow up (mature)	Some children <u>grow up</u> too quickly.
show up (make an appearance)	Dan <u>showed up</u> at the party.
stand by (stand next to)	<u>Stand by</u> me so that I can talk to you.

ılıl
MASTERY   **ACTIVITY 8: Mastery Test**

Read each sentence pair below and do the following:

- Determine which sentence has the correct word order and circle it.
- If *both* sentences are in the correct order, write "C" next to them.

EXAMPLE: a. Let's go the plans for our trip over.

b. Let's go over the plans for our trip.

1. **a.** I accidentally threw away my credit card.
   b. I accidentally threw my credit card away.

2. **a.** My ex showed up at Danica's party.
   b. My ex showed at Danica's party up.

3. **a.** The car alarm woke up everyone.
   b. The car alarm woke everyone up.

4. **a.** The neighbors in will drop over the holidays.
   b. The neighbors will drop in over the holidays.

5. **a.** The neighborhood group fought for the speed bumps.
   b. The neighborhood group fought the speed bumps for.

Order of Adjectives

Again, **adjectives** are words that describe nouns. In the following example, the adjective *ugly* describes the noun *mushrooms*:

the ugly mushrooms

If you use more than one adjective to describe a noun, the adjectives must come in a certain order, or the sentence will sound funny in standard English. To a native speaker, the first example below would sound odd, while the second one would sound "right":

AWKWARD   the ear-shaped ugly little mushrooms

STANDARD   the ugly little ear-shaped mushrooms

Again, as you listen to and read more standard English, you too will develop a sense of what sounds right. Until then, be aware that descriptions of more than one adjective generally follow this order:

1. Article or other word indicating number or ownership: *a, an, the, three, some, Roberto's*

2. Judgment or opinion: *pretty, ugly, honest, delicate, generous*

3. Size: *big, little, large, small*

For more practice with using prepositions and adjectives, go to **bedfordstmartins.com/ steppingstones**.

4. Shape or length: *short, long, round, ___-shaped* (as in *ear-shaped*)

5. Age: *new, young, old*

6. Color: *red, blue, green, orange*

7. Nationality/region: *Mexican, Korean, Egyptian, western*

8. Material: *metal, glass, wooden*

9. Noun used as adjective: *gas* (as in *gas station*), *wedding* (as in *wedding cake*)

10. Noun being described: *child, shoe, mushroom, car*

ACTIVITY 9: Mastery Test

In each of the following sentences, the adjectives are scrambled. Rewrite each sentence in the space provided, putting the words in the correct order.

EXAMPLE: Bret bought a yellow cute car.

> Bret bought a cute yellow car.

1. The oval Japanese fragile platter was a wedding gift.

    _____

2. Flavio collects new unusual metal sculptures.

    _____

3. We baked a train-shaped delicious birthday cake for Jordan.

    _____

4. The little pretty green parrot repeated the sailors' nasty swearwords.

    _____

5. The generous Italian old gentleman gave us some red delicious tomatoes.

    _____

Other Guidelines

This section briefly reviews some other points to be aware of if you are an ESL student or if you generally want to build your skills in standard English. Because most of these issues have been covered in more depth in earlier chapters, we provide references to those chapters.

- Remember to include subjects in all sentences:

    INCORRECT   Likes movies.

    REVISED   Dan likes movies.

    For more details on including subjects in sentences, see Chapter 10.

Power Tip
A prepositional phrase cannot be the subject of a sentence.
Incorrect: In the trees have many leaves.
Revised: The trees have many leaves.

- Many English sentences begin with *There is/There are* or *It is*. Do not leave out *There* or *It* in these sentences:

INCORRECT	Are three reasons to stay in this job.
	Is raining today.
REVISED	<u>There</u> are three reasons to stay in this job.
	<u>It</u> is raining today.

- Remember to use verbs in all sentences:

INCORRECT	Rick happy about his promotion.
REVISED	Rick **is** happy about his promotion.

  For more details on including verbs in sentences, see Chapter 10.

- Do not use pronouns to repeat subjects within a simple sentence.

  As you learned in Chapter 10, **pronouns** are noun substitutes. In the following compound sentence (joining two simple sentences), the pronoun *she* substitutes for *Tara* so that you don't have to repeat Tara's name.

  SENTENCE 1   SENTENCE 2
  Tara speeds, and she gets a lot of tickets.
  NOUN   PRONOUN

  Within a simple sentence, however, do not use pronouns to repeat subjects:

INCORRECT	Tara, she gets a lot of tickets.
REVISED	Tara gets a lot of tickets.

  For more on simple sentences, see Chapter 10. For more on compound sentences, see Chapter 11.

Acknowledgments

Sherman Alexie. "The Joy of Reading and Writing: Superman and Me." Copyright © 1998 by Sherman Alexie. All rights reserved. Reproduced by permission of Nancy Stauffer Associates.

Lynda Barry. "The Sanctuary of School." *New York Times*, January 5, 1992. Used by permission of Darhansoff & Verrill Literary Agents.

Troy Chapman. "Caring Makes Us Human." Used by permission of the author.

Maria Cheng. "More Than 600,000 People Killed by Secondhand Smoke." The Associated Press, November 26, 2010. Reprinted by permission of the YGS Group.

Pius Kamau. "A Duty to Heal." © 2006 by Dr. Pius Kamau. From the book *This I Believe: The Personal Philosophies of Remarkable Men and Women*, edited by Jay Allison and Dan Gediman. Copyright © 2006 by This I Believe, Inc. Reprinted by permission of Henry Holt and Company, LLC.

Yiyun Li. "Passing Through." *New York Times*, September 25, 2005. Used by permission of the author.

Sarah Lin. "Devotion." Used by permission of the author.

Enrique Hank Lopez. "Why Couldn't My Father Read?" Used by permission of Drusilla Lopez.

Daniel Meier. "About Men; One Man's Kids." *New York Times*, November 1, 1987. Used by permission of the author.

Yolanda O'Bannon. "Living What You Do Every Day." Used by permission of the author.

Laura Rowley. "As They Say, Drugs Kill." Originally published in the February 1987 issue of *Newsweek on Campus*. Reprinted by permission of Laura Rowley, business journalist and author of several books, including *Money and Happiness* and *On Target*.

Scott Russell Sanders. "Under the Influence." Copyright © 1989 Scott Russell Sanders; first published in *Harper's*; from the author's *Secrets of the Universe* (Beacon, 1991); reprinted by permission of the author.

Gary Soto. "The Jacket." From *The Effects of Knut Hamsun on a Fresno Boy: Recollections and Short Essays*, by Gary Soto. Copyright © 1983, 2000 by Gary Soto. Reprinted by permission of Persea Books, Inc., New York.

Amy Tan. "Four Directions." From *The Joy Luck Club* by Amy Tan, copyright © 1989 by Amy Tan. Used by permission of G.P. Putnam's Sons, a division of Penguin Group (USA) Inc.

Abigail Thomas. "Comfort." From *A Three Dog Life*, compilation copyright © 2006 Abigail Thomas, reproduced by permission of Houghton Mifflin Harcourt Publishing Company. This material may not be reproduced in any form or by any means without prior written permission of the publisher.

Laura D'Andrea Tyson. "Needed: Affirmative Action for the Poor." *Bloomberg Businessweek.com*, July 7, 2003. Reprinted by permission of the YGS Group.

Photograph and Illustration Credits

Page 32: © Alamy
Page 118: © Nordic Photos/Getty Images
Page 123: © PM Images/Getty Images
Page 130: © Jupiter Images/Poka Dot/Alamy
Page 148 (top): © Thomas Dobner/Alamy
Page 148 (bottom): © Alamy
Page 151: © Stuart Dee/Getty Images
Page 154: © Chang W. Lee/New York Times/Redux
Page 158: © Alloy Photography/Veer
Page 162: © Photodisc
Page 165: © Morgue File
Page 169: © Veer/Corbis
Page 173: © Grant Faint/Getty Images
Page 175 (top): © Ted Aljibe/Getty Images
Page 175 (middle): © Jefferson Bernandes/Getty Images
Page 175 (bottom): © Elloy Alonso/Landov
Page 176: © Brooke Fassani/Corbis
Page 180 (top): © Luiz Vasconcelos/Landov
Page 180 (middle): © Lenny Ignelzi/AP Photo
Page 180 (bottom): © AFP/Getty Images
Page 190: © Gene Herrick/AP Photo
Page 192: © Eon Images
Page 194 (middle): © Shamil Zhumatov/Landov
Page 194 (bottom): © Finbarr O'Reilly/Landov
Page 195 (top): © Lucas Jackson/Landov
Page 195 (middle): © Ben Margot/AP Photo
Page 195 (bottom): © Gabriel Bouys/Getty Images

Index

Reference Material

The material in this section gives you a quick review of common issues in the writing classroom. Refer to it when you need help remembering major grammatical errors, or when you need to look up a correction symbol that your instructor has marked on your assignment. This section also lists where to find helpful lists, charts, and visuals of important subjects in the book. Finally, the last page provides a handy reference to the major parts of speech.

 # Comma Usage

Follow Four Comma Rules:

Comma Rule 1:
Use a comma after any introductory expressions that begin a sentence. (pages 487–88)

In June, the team won the championship.

However, the team won the championship.

Luckily, the team won the championship.

Scoring 32 points, the team won the championship.

Comma Rule 2:
Use a comma in a compound sentence. (pages 256–57)

The team won the championship, and the captain won most valuable player.

Comma Rule 3:
Use a comma in a complex sentence. (pages 303–12)

Since they practiced hard, the team won the championship.

Comma Rule 4:
Use a comma after all but the last item in a list of three or more items. (pages 489–90)

The team won the game, the championship, and the division title.

For more on comma usage, see Chapter 11, pages 256–57; Chapter 12, pages 303–12; and Appendix A, pages 487–91.

QUICK GUIDE TO Fragments

There Are Three Types of Fragments:

**Missing subject,
missing verb,
incomplete verb**
(pages 246–49)

Looking for a new apartment.

The runner .

The kids **lost** in the mall.

**Incomplete thought,
subordinate clause**
(pages 320–24)

Since his car broke down.

Although I studied for three hours.

Before the store opened at nine.

**Incomplete thought,
relative clause**
(pages 343–50)

The door **that** slammed.

An old friend **who** contacted me.

The park **where** we played.

Fix It!

Add the missing information OR connect the fragment to another sentence:

Fragment →	Fix It
Looking for a new apartment.	**Lizzy** looks for a new apartment.
Since his car broke down. Sal was late.	Since his car broke down, Sal was late.
The door **that** slammed. It woke me.	The door that slammed woke me.

For more on fragments, see Chapter 10, pages 246–53; Chapter 12, pages 320–24; and Chapter 13, pages 343–50.

Run-Ons and Comma Splices

Four Groups of Words Cause Run-Ons (RO) and Comma Splices (CS):

I, you, she/he, it, they, we (page 286)

Class was cancelled we left. (RO)

Class was cancelled, we left. (CS)

this, that, these, those (page 288)

My friend lied that upset me. (RO)

My friend lied, that upset me. (CS)

then, next, also, plus, for example, for instance (page 290)

We ordered then we ate. (RO)

We ordered, then we ate. (CS)

therefore, as a result, consequently, however, furthermore, in addition, instead, nevertheless (page 292)

Jim studied therefore, he passed. (RO)

Jim studied, therefore, he passed. (CS)

Fix It!

Add a period OR a semicolon OR a comma with a joining word (*and, or, but, so, nor, for, yet*).

Run-On or Comma Splice →	Fix It
Class was cancelled we left.	Class was cancelled. We left.
Class was cancelled, we left.	Class was cancelled; we left.
	Class was cancelled, so we left.

For more on run-ons and comma splices, see Chapter 11, pages 283–300.

QUICK GUIDE TO Sentence Combining

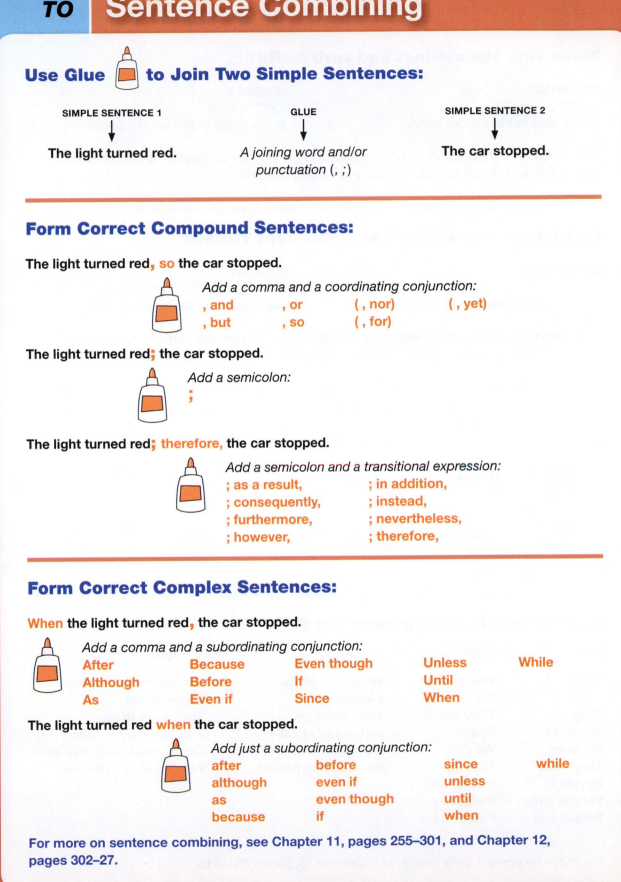

Use Glue to Join Two Simple Sentences:

SIMPLE SENTENCE 1   GLUE   SIMPLE SENTENCE 2

The light turned red.   *A joining word and/or punctuation (, ;)*   The car stopped.

Form Correct Compound Sentences:

The light turned red**, so** the car stopped.

Add a comma and a coordinating conjunction:

| , and | , or | (, nor) | (, yet) |
| , but | , so | (, for) | |

The light turned red**;** the car stopped.

Add a semicolon:

;

The light turned red**; therefore,** the car stopped.

Add a semicolon and a transitional expression:

; as a result,	; in addition,
; consequently,	; instead,
; furthermore,	; nevertheless,
; however,	; therefore,

Form Correct Complex Sentences:

When the light turned red**,** the car stopped.

Add a comma and a subordinating conjunction:

After	Because	Even though	Unless	While
Although	Before	If	Until	
As	Even if	Since	When	

The light turned red **when** the car stopped.

Add just a subordinating conjunction:

after	before	since	while
although	even if	unless	
as	even though	until	
because	if	when	

For more on sentence combining, see Chapter 11, pages 255–301, and Chapter 12, pages 302–27.

Correct Verb Usage

Make sure the subject and verb AGREE:

INCORRECT

Jenny **play** in the school band.

CORRECT

Jenny **plays** in the school band.

If you add an unnecessary -s or forget to add an -s, your subject and verb may not agree. So, watch out for the "slippery **-s**" (see page 385).

Make sure your verbs have consistent TENSE:

INCORRECT

Joe **tripped** on the rug and **falls**.

CORRECT

Joe **tripped** on the rug and **fell**.

If you add an unnecessary -ed ending, or forget to add an -ed ending, your verbs may not have consistent tense. Here are the rules for regular past tense verbs:

Base Form		Past Tense
look **laugh**	} + ed	**looked** **laughed**
love **refuse**	} + d	**loved** **refused**
cry **marry**	} – y + ied	**cried** **married**

Avoid errors based on incorrect PRONUNCIATION:

INCORRECT	CORRECT	INCORRECT	CORRECT
You is	You **are**	We gonna study.	We **are going** to study.
We is	We **are**	I wanna eat.	I **want** to eat.
They is	They **are**	They gotta go.	They **have** to go.
You does	You **do**	Jan would of called.	Jan **would have** called.
We does	We **do**	Our team should of won.	Our team **should have** won.
They does	They **do**	Ben could of helped.	Ben **could have** helped.
People is	People **are**		
People does	People **do**		
People has	People **have**		

For more on correct verb usage, see Chapter 15, pages 381–415.

Correction Symbols

Your instructor may use certain symbols to mark writing and grammar problems in your papers. Following are some common symbols and their meanings. (If your instructor uses different symbols than those shown here, write those in the spaces provided.) On the right, we've shown (in bold) chapters or sections of *Stepping Stones* that you can refer to for more help.

YOUR INSTRUCTOR'S SYMBOL	STANDARD SYMBOL	MEANING	CHAPTER OR SECTION IN THIS BOOK
	adj	Problem with adjective use	**10, Appendix B**
	adv	Problem with adverb use	**10**
	agr	Agreement problem between subject and verb	**15**
		Agreement problem between pronoun and what it refers back to (antecedent)	**16**
	awk	Awkward wording	**6**
		Awkward sentence structure	**10–14**
	cap	Capitalization error	**Appendix A**
	case	Pronoun case error	**16**
	cliché	Clichéd language	**7**
	coh	Lack of coherence/unity in writing	**6**
	combine	Combine sentences	**11–14**
	coord	Coordinate sentences/coordination problem	**11**
	cs	Comma splice	**11**
	dev	Strengthen development of writing	**2, 5, 7**
	dm	Dangling modifier	**14**
	frag	Fragment	**10, 12–13**
	mm	Misplaced modifier	**13–14**
	prep	Problem with prepositions/prepositional phrases	**10, Appendix B**
	ref	Unclear pronoun reference	**16**
	ro	Run-on	**11**
	shift	Shift in tense or voice	**15**
	sp	Spelling error	**6**
	sub	Subordinate sentences/subordination problem	**12**
	tense	Verb tense problem	**15**
	trans	Transition needed	**4–5**
	unity	Lack of unity/coherence in writing	**6**
	vb/verb	Verb problem	**15, Appendix B**
	wc	Problem with word choice	**6**
	¶	Start a new paragraph	**9**
	, ; : ' " " . - ( ) !	Problem with punctuation	**Appendix A**
	∧	Insert	
	℮	Delete	
	⌣	Close space	
	⌐⌐	Reverse order of letters/words	

Helpful Lists, Charts, and Visuals